100
Eastern Oregon
William L. Sullivan
Navillus Press

Juniper Hills Preserve (Hike #18).

Published by the Navillus Press
1958 Onyx Street
Eugene, Oregon 97403

oregonhiking.com
ISBN 9781939312235
Printed in USA

Cover: Jewett Lake in the Wallowa Mountains (Hike #54). Back cover: Alvord Desert near Big Sand Gap (Hike #94). Frontispiece: Gunsight Butte from Anthony Lake (Hike #40). This page: Deschutes River from the Criterion Tract (Hike #5).

SAFETY CONSIDERATIONS: Many of the trails in this book pass through Wilderness and remote country where hikers are exposed to unavoidable risks. On any hike, the weather may change suddenly. The fact that a hike is included in this book, or that it may be rated as easy, does not necessarily mean it will be safe or easy for you. Prepare yourself with proper equipment and outdoor skills, and you will be able to enjoy these hikes with confidence.

Every effort has been made to assure the accuracy of the information in this book. The author has hiked all 100 of the featured trails, and the trails' administrative agencies have reviewed the maps and text. Nonetheless, construction, logging, and storm damage may cause changes. Corrections and updates are welcome, and often rewarded. They may be sent to the publisher or to *sullivan@efn.org*.

Contents

- Horses OK - Bicycles OK - Dogs on leash - No pets
- Wildflowers (count petals for peak month) *NW Forest Pass site **Other parking fee
C - Crowded or restricted backpacking area - Rough access road

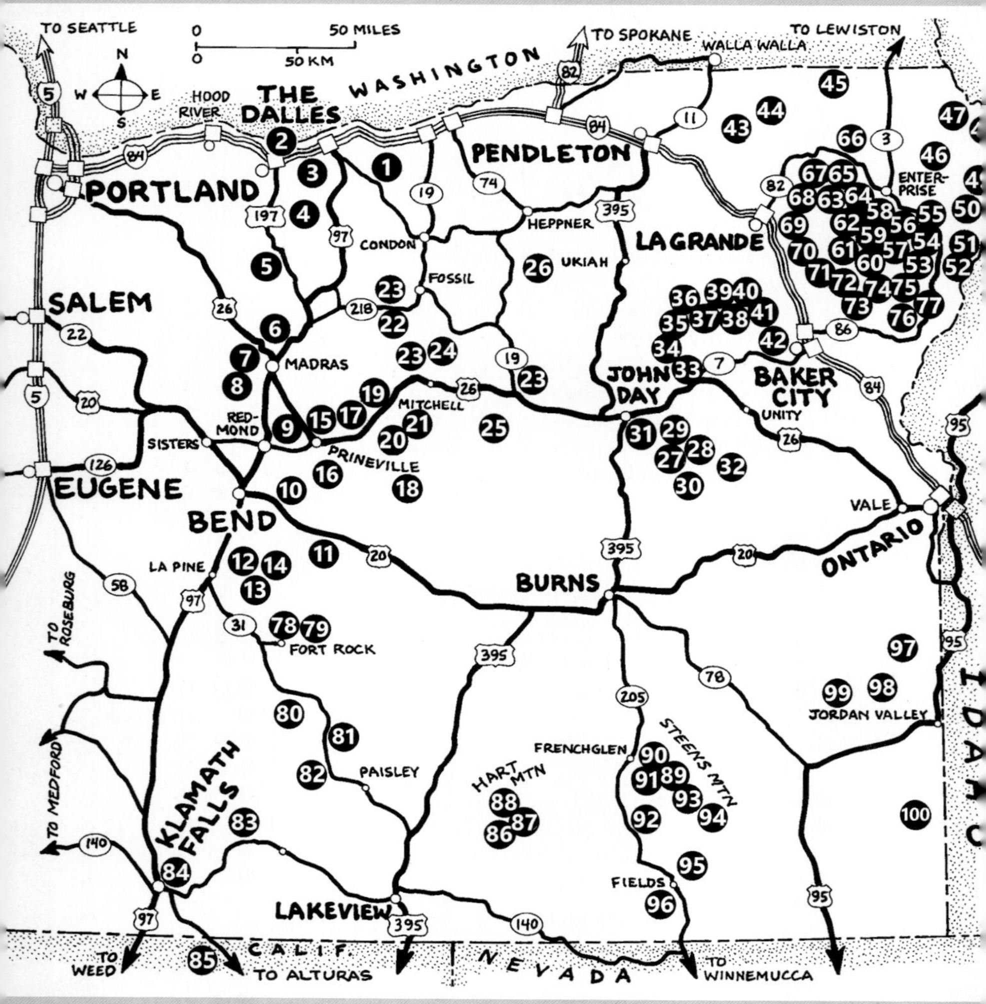

TO SEATTLE
0 50 MILES
0 50 KM
N S W E
TO SPOKANE
WALLA WALLA
TO LEWISTON
WASHINGTON
HOOD RIVER
THE DALLES
PORTLAND
PENDLETON
CONDON
HEPPNER
FOSSIL
UKIAH
LA GRANDE
ENTERPRISE
SALEM
MADRAS
MITCHELL
JOHN DAY
BAKER CITY
UNITY
REDMOND
SISTERS
PRINEVILLE
EUGENE
BEND
VALE
ONTARIO
LA PINE
BURNS
TO ROSEBURG
FORT ROCK
JORDAN VALLEY
IDAHO
TO MEDFORD
KLAMATH FALLS
PAISLEY
FRENCHGLEN
STEENS MTN
HART MTN
FIELDS
LAKEVIEW
TO WEED
CALIF.
TO ALTURAS
NEVADA
TO WINNEMUCCA

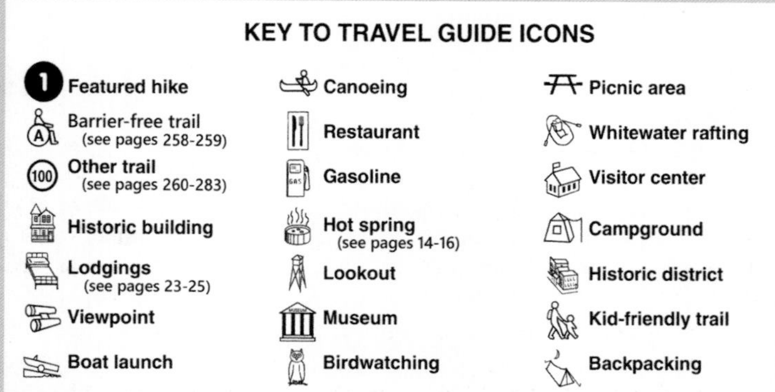

[Horse icon] - Horses OK [Bicycle icon] - Bicycles OK [Dog icon] - Dogs on leash [Crossed dog icon] - No pets
[Flower icon] - Wildflowers (count petals for peak month) *NW Forest Pass site **Other parking fee
C - Crowded or restricted backpacking area [Truck icon] - Rough access road

(horse) - Horses OK (bicycle) - Bicycles OK (dog) - Dogs on leash (crossed dog) - No pets

(flower) - Wildflowers (count petals for peak month) *NW Forest Pass site **Other parking fee

C - Crowded or restricted backpacking area (truck) - Rough access road

(horse icon) - Horses OK (bicycle icon) - Bicycles OK (dog icon) - Dogs on leash (no-dog icon) - No pets
(flower icon) - Wildflowers (count petals for peak month) *NW Forest Pass site **Other parking fee
C - Crowded or restricted backpacking area (truck icon) - Rough access road

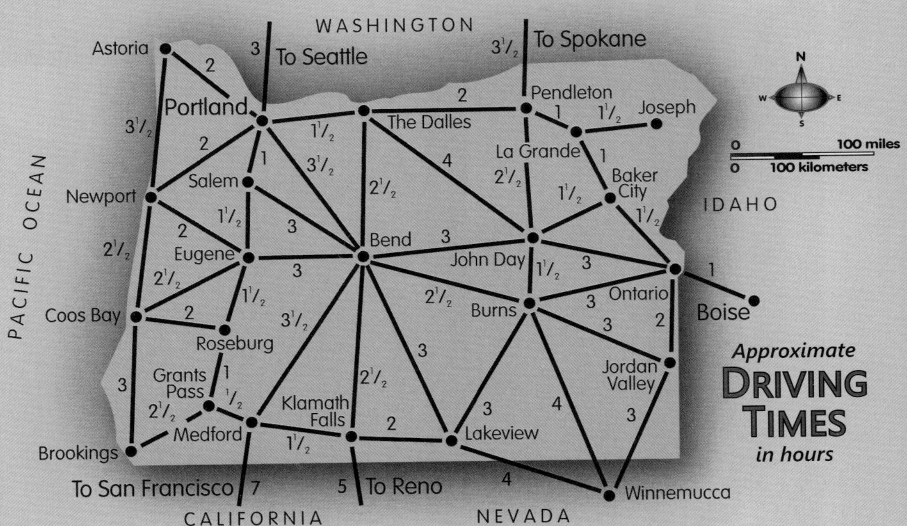

The Wallowas

America's "Little Switzerland," this range has 18 of Oregon's 31 tallest peaks. The Wild West town of Joseph, where the bank was in fact robbed by bandits on horseback in 1896, serves as a gateway to Wallowa Lake and trails on the northern edge of the range's Eagle Cap Wilderness. A scenic, paved road circles the Wallowa Mountains past Hells Canyon and tiny Halfway.

JOSEPH *has mountain views, bronze sculptures, and an 1888 bank building with a museum, open daily 10am-4pm from late May to mid-September.*

MOUNT HOWARD'S *panorama of the range is accessed by an aerial tramway (see Hike #56).*

EAGLE CAP *(Hike #62), at the center of the Wallowa Mountains, reflects in a pond above Mirror Lake.*

THE PINE LAKES *(Hike #77) fill an alpine basin in the Southern Wallowas above the ghost town of Cornucopia.*

TOMBSTONE LAKE *(Hike #72) fills a granite alpine valley in the southern Wallowa Mountains.*

Chief Joseph and the Nez Perce

Among the most peaceable of Northwest tribes, the Nez Perce caught salmon at the outlet of Wallowa Lake and bred prized Appaloosa ponies on the plains below. When the US Army ordered the 400-member Wallowa band to move to an Idaho reservation in May 1877, Chief Joseph led his people across Hells Canyon, crossing the Snake River at flood stage. A shootout just short of the reservation, however, sent the tribe on a 4-month tactical retreat, ending with defeat just 30 miles short of political sanctuary in Canada.

NEZ PERCE (NEE-ME-POO) TRAIL
NATIONAL HISTORIC TRAIL

The tribe was exiled to distant reservations where Joseph died of what his doctor called "a broken heart." In 1997 the federal government granted the tribe 10,000 acres of Wallowa County land as compensation for broken treaties. Since then the tribe has opened a visitor center with displays and photos at 209 E. Second Street in the city of Wallowa (see *wallowanezperce.org* for a virtual tour). Two blocks away, a footbridge across the Wallowa River accesses The Homeland, a powwow ground with trails open to the public (see Hike #66).

Above: A monument beside Wallowa Lake, on Highway 82 just south of Joseph, contains the bones of Chief Joseph's father. North 0.1 mile, the Iwetemlaykin State Heritage Site has a 1-mile trail to one of the tribe's historic fishing sites.

Below: The Homeland in Wallowa.

STEENS MOUNTAIN *looms snowy and sudden a mile above Oregon's driest point, the stark Alvord Desert.*

Steens Mountain

Landmark for all of southeast Oregon, this 50-mile-long mountain rises slowly from the bird-filled marshlands of the Malheur Wildlife Refuge in the west, but crashes to the east in a mile-high cliff down to the Alvord Desert's alkali flats and hot springs (see pages 229-231). The spectacular 56-mile gravel Steens Mountain Loop Road climbs almost to the mountain's 9733-foot summit.

KIGER GORGE *is one of seven giant canyons carved into Steens Mountain by Ice Age glaciers that have since vanished.*

LITTLE BLITZEN GORGE *(Hike #90) is a hiking goal from South Steens Campground. Right: Quaking aspen in the snow at Fish Lake.*

FRENCHGLEN'S remote *1916 hotel (page 25), a base for exploration.*

THE ALVORD DESERT'S *playa is visited by wild horses (see Hike # 94).*

Pete French built this 100-foot-diameter Round Barn about 1880 to train horses.

Peter French was sent to Oregon in 1872 by California ranching mogul James Glenn to buy land. French ruthlessly amassed holdings, including much of the present Malheur National Wildlife Refuge. In 1897 he was shot dead by a homesteader in front of witnesses. French had alienated so many locals that a jury acquitted his murderer.

By 1901, Basque and Irish shepherds were grazing more than 140,000 sheep on Steens Mountain, obliterating grasslands. Domestic sheep were banned from public land on the mountain in 1972. Cattle were excluded from the mountain's fragile summit and canyons in 1982. Ironically, cattle still graze the wildlife refuge, French's old domain.

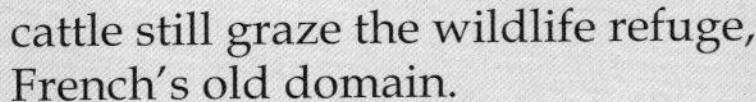

The town of Frenchglen (see page 230) was named for its two original owners, French and Glenn. Also visit Pete French's impressive Round Barn (page 230), built to train horses for ranch work, and French's old headquarters, the P Ranch, along the Donner und Blitzen River.

French's P Ranch is 1.5 miles east of Frenchglen on the Steens Mountain loop.

EAST RIM, *where the tilted plateau of Steens Mountain ends with a 5700-foot cliff.*

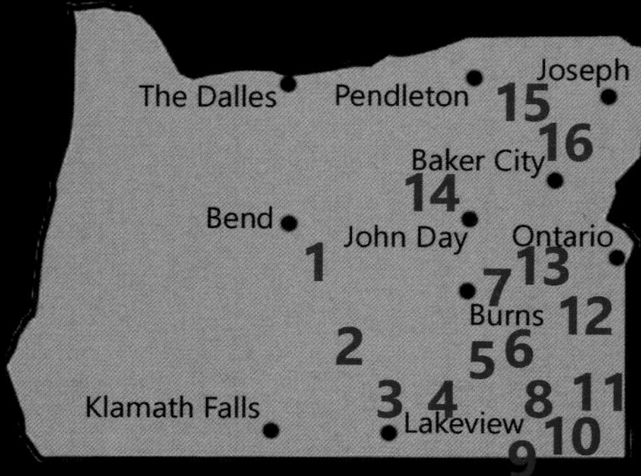

Hot Springs of Eastern Oregon

1. PAULINA LAKE WARM SPRINGS. *Hike 1.2 miles around a lake in the Newberry Volcanic National Monument (see page 70) to a beach with a small pool warmed by hot CO² bubbles.* ▼

2. SUMMER LAKE HOT SPRINGS. *A funky resort by an alkali desert lakebed uses natural hot springs to fill rock-lined outdoor pools for use by overnight guests, but its public indoor pool (below) was drained in 2020. See page 207* ▼

Summer Lake Hot Springs' bathhouse dates to 1928.

3. HUNTER'S HOT SPRINGS. *The Old Perpetual geyser erupts from a well drilled here in 1923. View it free, or pay to soak in the adjacent motel's hot pool, 1.5 miles north of Lakeview on the west side of Highway 395.*

4. HART MOUNTAIN HOT SPRINGS. *A free campground at the Hart Mountain National Antelope Refuge has two free, natural hot springs pools, one screened by rock walls. See page 224.* ▲

5. ALVORD HOT SPRINGS *(see page 231) charges a fee for a soak in small concrete pools with views of Steens Mountain and the Alvord Desert.* ▼

6. MICKEY HOT SPRINGS *(see page 231) has free but dangerous boiling pools, weird scalding mudpots, and one small pool just cool enough for a soak.* ▲

7. CRYSTAL CRANE HOT SPRINGS *(see page 230) is a desert resort with rustic cabins, tepees, and a natural hot spring pool.* ◀

10. WILLOW CREEK HOT SPRINGS *(see map, page 228) has a free primitive campground and natural pool on a remote dirt road. From Fields drive south 8.1 miles and turn left on gravel Whitehorse Ranch Lane for 24.2 miles. (If you reach the ranch entrance you've gone 2.6 miles too far.) Then turn sharply right on an unmarked road 2.3 miles and turn right 0.1 mile to road's end (GPS location 42.2757 -118.2653).* ▼

8. BORAX HOT SPRINGS *(see Hike #95) and Borax Lake are closed to swimming to protect rare fish that survive in the alkaline water full of arsenic.* ▼

9. BOG HOT SPRINGS. *Just over the border in Nevada (see map, page 228), a 10-foot-wide 108° F creek flows through a natural, sandy-bottomed pool, with parking and free primitive camping nearby. From Denio Junction (26 miles south of Fields), take Hwy 140 west toward Lakeview 9 miles, turn right on gravel Bog Hot Road for 4 miles, and turn left 0.2 mile.* ▼

11. OWYHEE HOT SPRINGS *in the remote Three Forks area (see page 257) has a 96° F pool between hot waterfalls overlooking the Owyhee River, but requires a long drive and a hike.* ▶

12 SNIVELY HOT SPRINGS *has a free, natural pool by a cottonwood grove along the lower Owyhee River. From Lake Owyhee State Park, drive the paved road back toward Ontario for 15 miles to a sign for Snively Hot Springs (see page 249).*

13. JUNTURA HOT SPRINGS *(see map, page 248). This large, free, natural pool on the Malheur River can be 110° F. From Juntura (58 miles east of Burns), drive Highway 20 east 3 miles. Turn sharply left on a dirt road for half a mile. Just before a river crossing, turn right on a rough dirt track 0.6 mile to the tip of the river's Horseshoe Bend. Park here, wade a shallow river arm, and head left across an island 300 feet .*

14. RITTER HOT SPRINGS *is a strange, decrepit resort in a remote desert river canyon where upkeep and price changes seem to have stopped when the hotel was built in 1893. Open from Memorial Day weekend through Labor Day weekend, the resort offers hotel rooms for $30-36 and tent sites for $11, including use of the hot swimming pool or 109° F concrete tubs at the springs' source. Drive Highway 395 north of John Day 52 miles (or south of Pendleton 75 miles) to a bridge across the Middle Fork John Day River and turn west on paved Ritter Road 7 miles. Reservations: 541-421-3846.* ▲

15. FOREST COVE WARM SPRINGS *has an old-timey bathhouse and 9-foot-deep concrete pool built over a natural, bubbling 86° F spring in the Wallowa Mountain foothills town of Cove. Open in summer. Expect to pay $6 for adults. See page 160.*

16. HOT LAKE SPRINGS. *This lake with a natural hot springs has a vast spa hotel, restored from the early 20th century. Soak in the mineral hot springs ($20 for all day), or rent one of 16 upscale rooms for the night See page 135. Take Interstate 84 east of La Grande for 4 miles to exit 265 and follow a side road east 5.2 miles.* ▼

Left: Hot Lake Springs in about 1908. Below: The hot springs is between the lake and the hotel.

THE OWYHEE COUNTRY

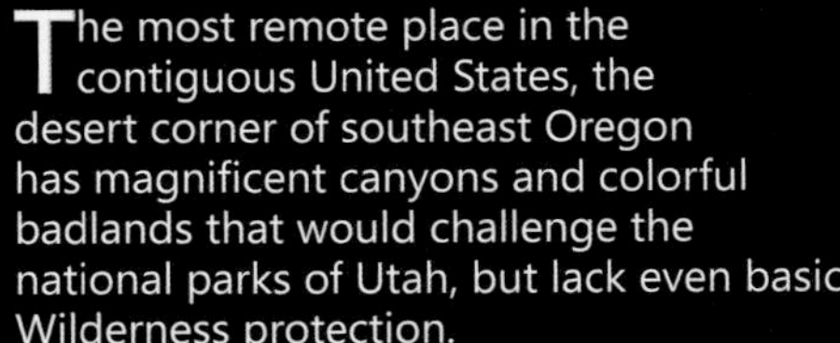

The most remote place in the contiguous United States, the desert corner of southeast Oregon has magnificent canyons and colorful badlands that would challenge the national parks of Utah, but lack even basic Wilderness protection.

THE OWYHEE RIVER *can be floated by drift boats from March to June (page 249).*

THREE FORKS. *Three Owyhee River branches join in this colossal, amazingly remote canyon (see Hike #100).*

LESLIE GULCH. *The "honeycomb" canyons of this Owyhee tributary invite exploration (see Hike #97).*

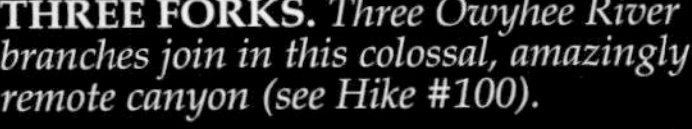

CHALK BASIN'S *colored badlands can be visited only after a long drive (Hike #99).*

History of Eastern Oregon

Excavations at the Paisley Caves south of Fort Rock reveal that people arrived in Oregon from Siberia at least 14,300 years ago, and that their descendants are still here as native tribes today.

Sagebrush sandals from Fort Rock Cave date to 7050 BC.

Lewis and Clark canoed past Eastern Oregon in 1804. After 1840, Oregon Trail pioneers began crossing the region in covered wagons, but the first white settlers stayed only after gold was discovered near Baker City in 1862 and John Day in 1863. Later, the US Army forced the Nez Perce tribe to leave in 1877, sparking a tragic war.

Rock art at Petroglyph Lake (Hike #88).

A covered wagon marks the route of the Oregon Trail near Baker City (page 111 and Hike #134).

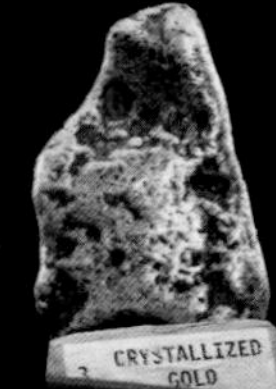

The Armstrong gold nugget is displayed at a Baker City bank (see p. 111).

The Kam Wah Chung Museum in John Day features an 1869 Chinese gold miners' store (see page 98). The armored building includes an opium den, apothecary, and shrine to Chinese gods (below).

When the gold rush faded, other booms focused on sheep (1890-24), the logging of ponderosa pine (1890-1940), and dry land wheat farming (1910-25). Each rush left interesting ghost towns in its wake.

A drier climate and a trend toward urban life have left Eastern Oregon struggling with a loss of population and jobs. But for tourists the area is a treasure, packed with historic Old West charm, inexpensive places to stay, colossal scenery, and the feel of a foreign land.

Gold rush hotel in Baker City (pages 24 and 111).

A gold dredge dug its own lake at the ghost town of Sumpter (see page 113 and Hike #33).

THE RIDDLE RANCH *at Steens Mountain (page 234) is a museum of early 20th century cowboy life.*

A PIONEER RANCH *museum is open at the John Day Fossil Beds Nat'l. Monument (page 90).*

Ghost Towns

The population of Eastern Oregon was larger a century ago than it is today, so ghost towns dot the map. Granite and Cornucopia were founded on gold mining, Whitney and Bates on logging, and the many towns around Fort Rock on dry land farming.

GRANITE'S *City Hall is back in use now that the town has several dozen inhabitants (see page 113).*

WHITNEY *was a logging town (for location, see map on p. 114).*

CORNUCOPIA'S *gold mines have closed, but some private buildings remain. The site is now a Wallowa Mountain trailhead (see page 204).*

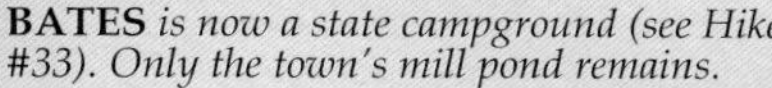

BATES *is now a state campground (see Hike #33). Only the town's mill pond remains.*

FORT ROCK'S *Homestead Museum preserves buildings from a dozen ghost towns (see page 207).*

Fossils and Rocks

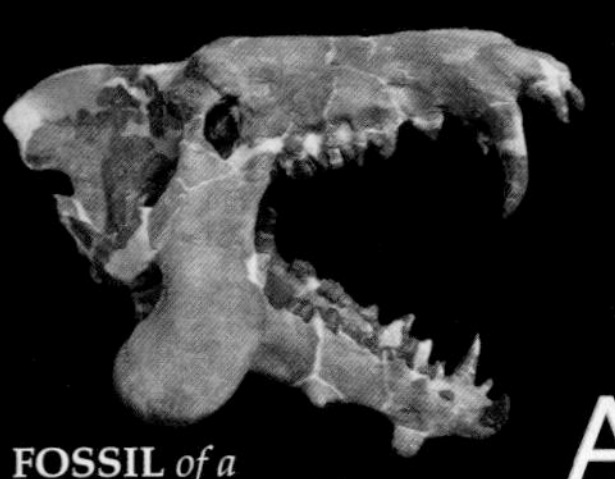

FOSSIL *of a 26-million-year-old entolodont at the visitor center.*

An arid climate has left the rocks of Eastern Oregon exposed, making geologic exploration easy and fun. Start at the John Day Fossil Beds National Monument (see page 90), where a visitor center and hiking trails explain the landscape. It's OK to dig for fossils in the town of Fossil, and to collect glassy obsidian at Glass Buttes, but digging most other places requires a permit, and collecting arrowheads or artifacts is a federal crime.

COLORED VOLCANIC ASH on *a trail at the John Day Fossil Beds National Monument (Hike #23).*

SHEEP ROCK *is the view from the national monument's free paleontology museum (Hike #23).*

DIGGING FOR FOSSILS *is allowed only outside the national monument, on a hill behind Wheeler High School's baseball diamond at B and Main Streets in the town of Fossil.*

Glass Buttes Obsidian

A mountain of obsidian—shiny black volcanic glass—is open to collectors in the desert between Bend and Burns. You can take 250 pounds per person per year. All you need is a high-clearance vehicle.

From Bend, drive Highway 20 east toward Burns 77 miles. Just before milepost 77, turn right across a cattle guard on a gravel road marked by a fire sign. After 2.9 miles, at a junction just beyond a cattle pond, go straight on a smaller, bumpier road. Continue straight 1.9 miles to a T-shaped junction. Then turn left along a fenceline for 0.9 mile up to a big parking area on the left.

Collecting obsidian at Glass Buttes.

The shiny rock can be black, red, or marbled.

HELLS CANYON

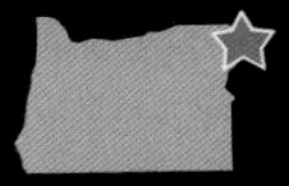

The deepest river gorge in the United States, this chasm gapes like the ragged edge of a broken planet. From the brawling whitewater of the Snake River, treeless terraces stack up a vertical mile to a rim of wildflower meadows, with the snow-capped Wallowas to the west and Idaho's Seven Devils to the east. Unlike the Grand Canyon, this gorge has no hotels or crowds. And the few viewpoints overlooking Hells Canyon are at the end of long gravel roads.

Hat Point.

FREEZEOUT SADDLE *(Hike #50) offers a view west across the Imnaha River Canyon to the snowy Wallowa Mountains.*

THE HELLS CANYON DAM *(Hike #51) has the only paved road access to the Snake's gorge.*

A SIGN AT DUG BAR *(Hike #163) warns of the remoteness of the Hells Canyon Wilderness, where most trails are long, steep, and faint.*

THE SNAKE RIVER *is 7.7 trail miles from the Hat Point Lookout, but with 5600 feet of elevation loss it may be Oregon's toughest day trip (Hike #49).*

HELLS CANYON *gapes below the Buckhorn Lookout (Hike #47).*

Winter in Eastern Oregon

Icy winds rake the high desert and snow fills the mountains of Eastern Oregon in winter, but adventurers who are prepared can discover great skiing, solitude, and stunning scenery.

STEENS MOUNTAIN'S *scenic summit loop road is gated from November through June, but trekkers can get a key from the Burns BLM.*

◄ **ANTHONY LAKES** *has Eastern Oregon's largest ski area, with a triple chairlift, groomed Nordic trails, and powder snow.* *See page 113.*

▲ **SNOW TENT CAMPS** *in the Wallowas allow trekkers to access pristine powder. Check wallowahuts.com or 541-398-1980.*

THE WALLOWA MOUNTAINS *are beautiful but dangerous in winter. Venture out only with avalanche gear and knowledge.*

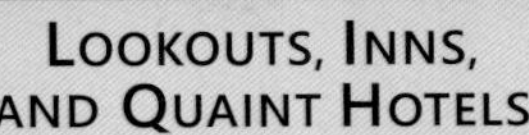

Lookouts, Inns, and Quaint Hotels

Hager Mountain Lookout.

#	Description	Rental units	Private bath	Breakfast	Open (mos.)	Rate range
CENTRAL OREGON						
1	**COVE PALISADES.** Rent 3 log cabins that sleep 5 for $199-209 (Res: 800-420-2915 *or covepalisadesresort.com*), or 9 luxury houseboats for $1100-4400 a weekend. Res: 541-546-9999 or *covepalisadesresort.com*. See Hike #8.	12	●		●	$199-4400
2	**THE MILL INN.** This friendly bed & breakfast is just a walk from downtown Bend at 642 NW Colorado. Reservations: 541-389-9198 or *millinn.com*.	10	5	●	●	$100-170
3	**OLD ST. FRANCIS SCHOOL.** McMenamins converted this Catholic school at 700 NW Bond in downtown Bend to 3 pubs, a theater, a hotel, and a Turkish soaking pool. Res: 877-661-4228 or *mcmenamins.com*.	60	●		●	$215-360
4	**PAULINA LAKE LODGE.** Log cabins at a mountain lake in the Newberry National Volcanic Mon. sleep 2-10. In winter, access by skiing 2.5 miles. See Hike #13. Res: 541-536-2240 or *paulinalakelodge.com*.	13	●		XII-III, V-IX	$145-400
5	**EAST LAKE RESORT.** Lakefront cabins in the Newberry Nat'l. Volcanic Mon. sleep 4-8 and include kitchenettes. Pets welcome. See Hike #104. Res: 541-536-2230 or *eastlakeresort.com*.	17	●		V-IX	$99-299
OCHOCOS						
6	**OCHOCO RANGER HOUSE.** A converted ranger station in the Ochoco Mountains (see Hike #20) sleeps 8. Reservations: *recreation.gov*.	1	●		●	$90
7	**COLD SPRINGS GUARD STATION.** In the Ochocos east of Big Summit Prairie, this 3-bedroom cabin has flush toilets and a propane kitchen. Res: 877-444-6777 or *recreation.gov*.	1	●		V-X	$90
8	**OREGON HOTEL.** In downtown Mitchell (pop. 180), this 1938 hotel retains its Old West ambiance. For reservations call 541-462-3027 or check *theoregonhotel.net*.	14	3	●	●	$60-150
JOHN DAY						
9	**FISH HOUSE INN.** On Highway 26 in Dayville, this quaint motel also has an RV park. Reservations: 541-987-2124 or *fishhouseinn.com*.	6	1		III-XII	$85-150
10	**FALL MOUNTAIN LOOKOUT.** Atop an 18-foot tower in the Aldrich Mtns (6 miles west of the Hwy 395 summit, south of John Day), this cabin has electricity but no water. Reservations: 877-444-6777 or *recreation.gov*.	1			V-X	$40
11	**HOTEL PRAIRIE.** This elegant 1910 hotel in the Old West town of Prairie City at 112 Front Street has restored period rooms. Reservations: *hotelprairie.com* or 541-820-4800.	9	●		●	$112-172

Lookouts, Inns, and Quaint Hotels

BLUE MOUNTAINS

WALLOWAS

#	Description	Rental units	Private bath	Breakfast	Open (mos.)	Rate range
12	**RIVERSIDE SCHOOLHOUSE B&B.** A few miles southeast of Prairie City on Road 61, you can rent a century-old schoolhouse on a working cattle ranch. Res: 541-820-4731 or *riversideschoolhouse.com.*	2	●	●	●	$150
13	**ANTLERS GUARD STATION.** Just 2 miles from the ghost town of Whitney (see Hike #30), this 2-room cabin has a propane kitchen and water from a hand pump. Res: 877-444-6777 or *recreation.gov.*	1			V-X	$78
14	**SUMPTER B&B.** A hospital in the early 1900s, this one building survived Sumpter's 1917 fire, so yes, it may be haunted. Res: 541-894-0048 or *sumpterbnb.com.*	7		●	●	$95-135
15	**THE GRANITE LODGE.** In a mountain ghost town (see page 101), this modern log-style lodge includes a continental breakfast. Res: 541-755-5200 or *thegranitelodgellc.com.*	9	●	●	●	$80-175
16	**FREMONT CABINS.** Three fully-equipped white clapboard houses by the historic Fremont Powerhouse (see page 113) sleep 6, 10, or 12 people. Reservations: 877-444-6777 or *recreation.gov.*	3	●		●	$65-80
17	**ANTHONY LAKE GUARD STATION.** A 1930s ranger cabin by the lake sleeps 8 and includes a kitchen, bathroom with shower, and three bedrooms. Reservations: 877-444-6777 or *recreation.gov.*	1	●		V-VII	$157
18	**PEAVY CABIN.** This 1934 cabin in the Elkhorn Range sleeps 4, with a kitchen, fireplace, and horse corral, but no water. See Hike #137. Reservations: 877-444-6777 or *recreation.gov.*	1	●		VI-X	$78
19	**GEISER GRAND HOTEL.** This turreted 1889 hotel at 1996 Main in Baker City has an elegant restaurant, a library, and rooms with 15-foot ceilings. See page 111. Reservations: 888-434-7374 or *geisergrand.com.*	30	●		●	$109-339
20	**ISON HOUSE.** This turreted 1887 mansion, kitty-corner from downtown Baker City's Geiser Grand at 1790 Washington Avenue, has a downstairs pub with live music. Res: 503-894-4075 or *theisonhouse.com.*	4			●	$110-130
21	**PENDLETON HOUSE.** This elegant 1917 Italian Renaissance mansion in downtown Pendleton (311 N. Main) has original Chinese silk wallpaper. Res: 541-612-8311 or *pendletonhousebnb.com.*	6	4	●	●	$230-399
22	**UNION HOTEL.** In the Old West hamlet of Union (see page 150), this surprisingly grand 1921 hotel is a destination unto itself. Pets OK. Res: 541-562-1200 or *thehistoricunionhotel.com.*	15	●		●	$118-175
23	**ENTERPRISE HOUSE B&B.** This 1910 mansion, now a bed & breakfast, is across from the Wallowa County courthouse at 508 East First South Street. Res: 541-398-1194 or *enterprisehousebnb.com.*	5	●	●	●	$129-239
24	**WALLOWA LAKE LODGE.** Near the state park entrance, this elegant lodge in the grand National Park tradition offers 22 rooms, 8 cabins, and affordable dining (541-432-9821 or *wallowalakelodge.com*).	30	●		●	$166-279
25	 **JENNINGS HOTEL.** A hip modern hotel with a sauna and library/kitchen fills the second floor of a downtown Joseph brick building at 100 N. Main Street. Reservations: *jenningshotel.com.*	12	4		●	$102-187

LOOKOUTS, INNS, AND QUAINT HOTELS

WALLOWAS · FREMONT · LAKEVIEW · STEENS

#	Description	Rental units	Private bath	Breakfast	Open (mos.)	Rate range
26 	**KOKANEE INN.** Rustic yet modern, this large bed & breakfast in Joseph (700 S. Main) offers sumptuous breakfasts. Reservations: 541-432-9765 or *kokaneeinn.com.*  	9	●	●	●	$125-242
27 	 **PINE VALLEY LODGE.** In rustic Halfway (see Hike #77), three houses and an 1891 church have been converted into a lodge, spa, and restaurant. Reservations: 541-742-2027 or *pvlodge.com.*	14	12		●	$40-180
28	**TWO COLOR GUARD STATION.** This huge, rustic 1959 cabin 2 miles before the Main Eagle Trailhead (Hike #73) sleeps 12. Res: *recreation.gov.* 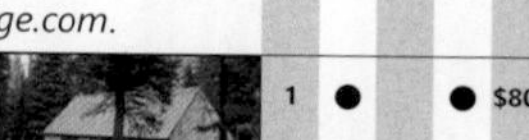 	1	●		●	$80
29	 **HAGER MOUNTAIN LOOKOUT.** From November 15 to May 15, snowshoers or skiers willing to trek 4 miles uphill (see Hike # 80) can rent this lookout 9 miles south of Silver Lake. Res: 877-444-6777 or *recreation.gov.*	1			XI-V	$40
30	**LODGE AT SUMMER LAKE**. Across from the Summer Lake wildlife refuge headquarters (near milepost 70 of Highway 31) this lodge has 5 cabins and prides itself on a dinner menu of 12-oz steaks. Res: 541-943-3993 or *lodgeatsummerlake.com.* 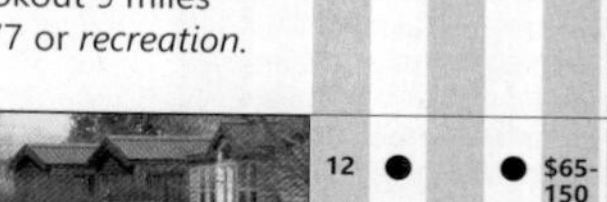	12	●		●	$65-150
31	 **CURRIER GUARD STATION.** Built in 1933, this 2-room cabin amid pines and aspens 7 miles west of Winter Ridge Hike #82 has propane but no water. Res: 877-444-6777 or *recreation.gov.* 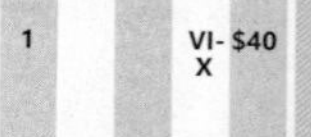	1			VI-X	$40
32	 **ASPEN RIDGE RESORT.** In the Fishhole Valley 20 miles west of Lakeview, this working 14,000-acre cattle ranch has lodge rooms, and log cabins that sleep 6. Res: 541-884-8685 or *aspenrr.com.* 	4	●		●	$90-180
33	**DRAKE PEAK LOOKOUT.** The historic lookout cabin (see Hike #191) sleeps 4 but has no water. Res: 877-444-6777 or *recreation.gov.*	1			VI-X	$40
34 	 **ASPEN CABIN.** This small log cabin in the mountains northeast of Lakeview (see Hike #191) has a woodstove but no other facilities. Res: 877-444-6777 or *recreation.gov.* 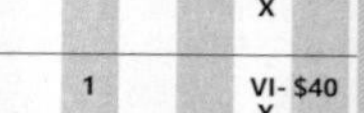	1			VI-X	$40
35	**HORSESHOE INN**. Unlike most motels, this one is on 8 acres of high desert with birds and deer, a mile from Burns at 30836 E. Hwy 20. Reservations: 541-573-2034 or *horseshoeinn.net.* 	32	●		●	$69-79
36 	**MALHEUR FIELD STATION.** Oregon's best birdwatching is at your door in the Malheur National Wildlife Refuge (see page 223). The headquarters offers 9 rental trailers and 150 dormitory beds ($24-33, only for groups). Info: 541-493-2629 or *malheurfieldstation.org.* 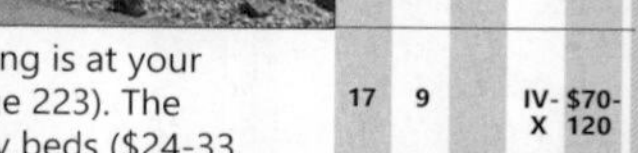	17	9		IV-X	$70-120
37 	**FRENCHGLEN HOTEL.** This charming, remote 1916 hotel still has no public telephone or television. For meals, guests pack family-style around the table. See page 224. Res: 541-493-2825 or *frenchglenhotel.com.* 	8			III-X	$92-100
38 	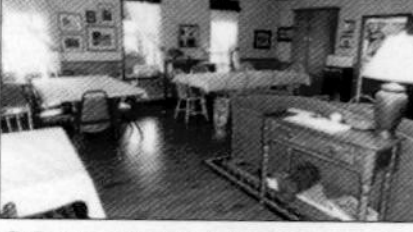 **HOTEL DIAMOND.** Less well known than Frenchglen, the village of Diamond is dominated by a rambling 1898 hotel (see page 224). Reservations: 541-493-1898 or *historichoteldiamond.com.*	9	4	●	IV-X	$81-105
39 	**GOODRICH HOTEL.** This historic brick hotel in downtown Vale has rooms with kitchens above the Happy Horse Apparel store at 229 A Street. Reservations: 541-216-1675. 	7	●		●	$95-150

Wildlife of Eastern Oregon

Bighorn sheep, in herds of a dozen or more, graze cliffy slopes and alpine meadows at Strawberry Mountain, Hells Canyon, and Steens Mountain. Males butt heads at up to 20 miles per hour.

Bull elk can weigh 1000 pounds, collecting "harems" of up to 60 females and bugling to declare their territory. They're not seen a lot because they graze at night and bed in thickets by day.

Mountain goats are rare in the Wallowas but common in the Elkhorn Range, where they sometimes descend from their cliff ledges to nibble an unwatched backpack for salt.

Wolves, once hunted to extinction in Oregon, have reestablished packs in Northeast Oregon and the Cascade Range.

Coyotes are much smaller than wolves, and mostly eat rodents.

Oregon's black bears are smaller and less aggressive than grizzlies, but they do scavenge unsecured food.

Cougars (mountain lions) are shy and nocturnal, so they are rarely seen.

Bobcats are nocturnal, so people rarely see them in Oregon.

American martens hunt chipmunks and squirrels, but are rarely seen because they are nocturnal. Look for their tracks in winter snow.

Raccoons are nocturnal omnivores that adapt easily to the presence of people and are willing to raid garbage, if available.

Mule deer are much smaller than elk, and have large ears.

Porcupines are slow and unaggressive, but often hurt dogs that attack them.

Badgers burrow for rodents, particularly in southeast Oregon.

ed-tailed hawks hunt rodents, and are articularly common at Zumwalt Prairie ear Joseph.

Bald eagles gather by the hundreds in the Klamath Lake area to hunt waterfowl.

The water ouzel (American dipper) swims underwater fo insects in mountain streams.

ack-billed magpies, lated to crows, are sy to spot in Eastern regon.

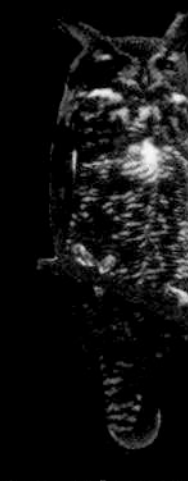

Great-horned owls roost on tree limbs by day and hunt by night.

The hummingbird moth (sphinx moth) looks and acts like a hummingbird, but feeds at twilight.

The mountain bluebird is the state bird of both Idaho and Nevada, but it loves Oregon's high desert too.

The gray jay or "camp robbe boldly swoops to picnic tabl for food scraps. Don't feed them! Human food can hur wild animals.

he great egret (at left) is slightly smaller and more common than he sandhill crane (at right). See both at the Malheur National Vildlife Refuge south of Burns, particularly from March to May.

Two-tailed swallowtail.

The Clark's nutcracker uses its bill to open whitebark pine nu near timberline.

olden-mantled ground quirrels are larger than hipmunks and don't have n eye stripe.

Cottontail rabbits are as common as jackrabbits, but smaller, with a white puffball tail.

he Townsend's hipmunk is smaller han a ground squirrel

Pikas live in alpine rockslides and cry out with a *meep!* when alarmed by passing hik

Jackrabbits have huge ears, eyes, and legs to escape their predators in the high desert

Prairie Wildflowers

SAGEBRUSH *(Artemisia* spp.*).* Dominant shrub of the high desert steppe, sagebrush has lobed leaves.

GRASS OF PARNASSUS *(Parnassia fimbriata*). Look for this saxifrage on grassy streambanks.

YELLOW BELL *(Fritillaria pudica).* Just 6 inches tall, this lily blooms in sagebrush grasslands in spring.

SCARLET GILIA or SKYROCKET *(Gilia aggregata)* blooms on dry, open slopes all summer.

BALSAMROOT *(Balsamorhiza spp.).* In spring this bloom turns entire hillsides yellow.

LARKSPUR *(Delphinium* spp.*).* Stalks of larkspur stand 3 feet tall in wet meadows, 3 inches in dry.

BACHELOR BUTTON *(Centaurea cyanus).* One of many showy blue composite flowers with this name.

RABBIT BRUSH *(Chrysothamnus spp.).* Fall's brightest wildflower turns the high desert yellow.

PRAIRIE STAR *(Lithophragma parviflora)* blooms in May amid sagebrush and pine.

SALSIFY *(Tragopogon dubius).* This dry June roadside flower turns to a giant dandelion-like seed puffball.

WILD ONION *(Allium* spp.*).* This pungent bloom hugs the ground in dry, rocky areas.

BLANKETFLOWER *(Gaillardia aristata),* alias brown-eyed Susan, blooms in grassy foothills all summer.

Canyon Wildflowers

HONEYSUCKLE *(Lonicera ciliosa)*. This fragrant, viney shrub blooms in canyons early in summer.

PRINCE'S PINE *(Chimaphila umbellata)*. Also known as pipsissewa, this blooms in shade.

COLUMBINE *(Aquilegia formosa)*. In wet woodlands, this bloom has nectar lobes for hummingbirds.

TWINFLOWER *(Linnaea borealis)*. This double bloom grows in the far North around the globe.

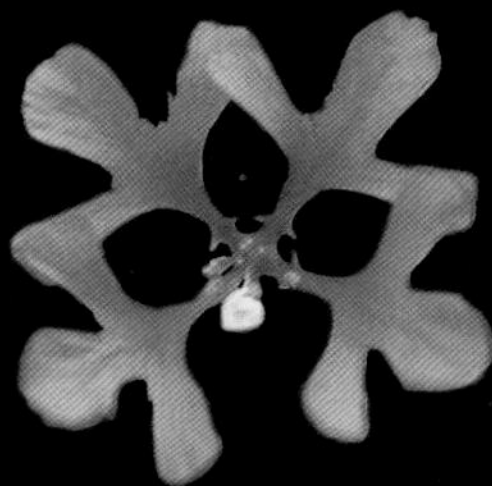

CLARKIA *(Clarkia pulchella)*. Named for Lewis and Clark, this bloom covers canyonsides in June.

STONECROP *(Sedum oreganum)*. This plant survives in bare, rocky ground by storing water in fat leaves.

BLEEDING HEART *(Dicentra formosa)*. Look near woodland creeks for these pink hearts.

OREGON GRAPE *(Berberis aquifolium)*. Oregon's state flower has holly-like leaves and blue berries.

FOXGLOVE *(Digitalis purpurea)*. Showy 5-foot foxglove stalks spangle sunny summer hillsides.

SOURGRASS *(Oxalis oregana)*. The shamrock-shaped leaves carpet forests and taste tart when chewed.

SHOOTING STAR *(Dodecatheon jeffreyi)*. Early in summer, shooting stars carpet wet fields and slopes.

CANDYFLOWER *(Claytonia sibirica)*. Common by woodland creeks and trails, candyflower is edible.

Alpine Wildflowers

GENTIAN *(Gentiana calycosa)*. These thumb-sized blooms near alpine lakes open only in full sun.

PHLOX *(Phlox diffusa)*. Like a colorful cushion, phlox hugs arid rock outcrops with a mat of blooms.

BEARGRASS *(Xerophyllum tenax)* resembles a giant bunchgrass until it blooms with a tall, lilied plume.

ELEPHANTS HEAD *(Pedicularis groenlandica)*. You'll see pink elephants like this in alpine bogs.

MARSH MARIGOLD *(Caltha biflora)*. This early bloomer likes high marshes full of snowmelt.

LUPINE *(Lupinus* spp.*)* has fragrant blooms in early summer and pea-pod-shaped fruit in fall.

GLACIER LILY *(Erythronium grandiflorum)*. These blooms erupt a week after the snow melts.

BROAD-LEAVED FIREWEED *(Epilobium latifolium)*, just inches tall, likes sandy alpine creekbanks.

PENSTEMON *(Penstemon* spp.*)*. Look for these red, purple, or blue trumpets in high, rocky areas.

ASTER *(Aster* spp.*)*. This purple daisy-like flower blooms late in summer, from July to September.

PAINTBRUSH *(Castilleja* spp.*)* has showy red-orange sepals, but the actual flowers are green tubes.

MOUNTAIN BLUEBELL *(Mertensia* spp.*)*. A favorite browse for elk, these plants fill subalpine meadows.

High Desert Wildflowers

DESERT BUCKWHEAT ***(Eriogonum spp.).*** **White, pink, and yellow varieties of this plant like dry areas.**

OREGON SUNSHINE ***(Eriophyllum lanatum).*** **The woolly stalks of this common bloom conserve water.**

BITTERROOT ***(Lewisia rediviva).*** **Noted by Lewis and Clark, these 3-inch blooms have edible roots.**

PRICKLY PEAR ***(Opuntia polyacantha).*** **Most cacti find Oregon's desert too cold. This one's rare too.**

PENSTEMON ***(Penstemon*** **spp.). The desert varieties of this showy flower often grow two feet tall.**

DEATH CAMAS ***(Zigadenus*** **spp.). This poisonous lily can be fatal if you mistake it for edible camas.**

MARIPOSA LILY ***(Calochortus*** **spp.) These showy lilies vary by area. Clockwise from upper left are blooms from Steens Mountain, the Wenaha River, the Wallowa Mountains, and Hells Canyon.**

EVENING PRIMROSE ***(Oenothera tanacetifolia)*** **forms a golden carpet on a Hart Mountain lakeshore.**

STRAWBERRY LAKE *(Hike #29) lies between 9038-foot Strawberry Mountain and the snowy crags of Rabbit Ears.*

Introduction

Welcome to the spectacular trails and byways of Eastern Oregon! This comprehensive guide has everything you need to plan a day hike, a weekend tour, or a weeks-long vacation, with tips on where to stay and what to see.

HOW TO USE THIS BOOK

The Travel Guide

The book divides Eastern Oregon into 11 regions, each identified by a geographic title (for example, *Strawberry Mountain*) and by the name of the nearest city (for example, *John Day*). For each region you'll find travel notes and an overview map featuring campgrounds, historic districts, interpretive centers, hot springs, birdwatching sites, and other attractions.

The Trail Guide

When you're ready to hit the trail, look through the book's 100 featured hikes. To quickly find an outing to match your tastes, look for the following special symbols to the right of the hikes' headings:

 Children's favorites – walks popular with the 4- to 12-year-old crowd, but fun for hikers of all ages.

 All-year trails, hikable most or all of winter.

 Hikes suitable for backpackers as well as day hikers. Crowds unlikely.

Crowded or restricted backpacking areas.

 Dogs on leash. 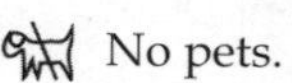 No pets. Rough access road.

The Information Blocks

Each hike is rated by difficulty. **Easy** hikes are between 1 and 7 miles round trip and gain less than 1000 feet in elevation. Never very steep, they make good warm-up trips for experienced hikers or first-time trips for novices.

Trips rated as **Moderate** range from 4 to 10 miles round trip. These routes may gain up to 2000 feet of elevation or may require some pathfinding skills. Hikers must be in good condition and will need to take several rest stops.

Difficult trails demand top physical condition, with a strong heart and strong knees. These challenging hikes are 6 to 20 miles round trip and may gain 3000 feet or more. Backpacking can break difficult hikes into manageable segments.

Distances are given in round-trip mileage, except for those trails where a car or bicycle shuttle is suggested and the mileage is specifically listed as one-way.

The **elevation gains** show the *cumulative* amount of climbing required, including

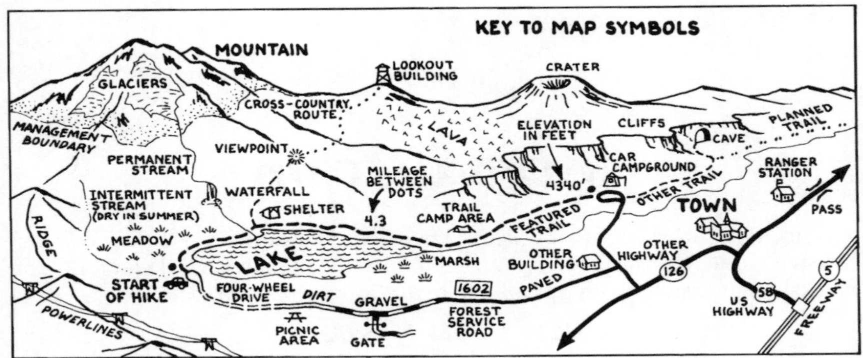

uphill sections on the return trip. Those who puff climbing a few flights of stairs may consider even 500 feet of elevation a strenuous climb, and should watch this listing carefully.

The **hiking season** of any trail varies with the weather. In a cold year, a trail described as "Open May through October" may not yet be clear of snow by May 1, and may be socked in by a blizzard before October 31. Similarly, a trail that is "Open all year" may close due to storms or may be inaccessible when wet weather makes dirt roads undrivable.

The **allowed use** of a trail may be limited to hikers, or may include bicyclists, equestrians, and motorcyclists. For a quick overview of paths recommended for horses and mountain bikes, look for the list of horse and bicycle symbols in the table of contents.

Dogs are allowed on 97 of the 100 featured hikes, and leashes are required on 7 trails. Restrictions are noted both in the text and in the table of contents.

TOPOGRAPHIC MAPS

All hikers in wilderness and other remote areas should carry a **topographic map,** with contour lines to show elevation. Topographic maps can be downloaded at *mytopo.com* and many other Internet sites. Maps of Wilderness Areas can be purchased at outdoor stores. It's also handy to have a visitor map of the local National Forest or Bureau of Land Management District, available at ranger stations and information centers for about $10.

TRAILHEAD PARKING FEES

No fees are charged to use the majority of trails described in this book, but the Forest Service does require a **Northwest Forest Pass** for cars parking within a quarter mile of a few trailheads, primarily in the Wallowa Mountains. A few state parks have their own trailhead parking fees. Affected hikes are marked with asterisks in the table of contents. Usually you can pay at the trailhead. You can also pick up a Northwest Forest Pass at a ranger station or outdoor store. The permit costs $5 per car per day, or $30 per year, but this may change.

WILDERNESS RESTRICTIONS

Fifty of the featured hikes enter designated Wilderness Areas—beautiful, isolated places protected by special restrictions. Advance permits are not required to enter Wilderness Areas in Eastern Oregon, although you may have to fill out a permit at the trailhead. Some rules vary, but in general you can expect certain limits in Wilderness Areas:

- Groups must be no larger than 12.
- Campfires are discouraged, and are banned within 100 feet of any water source or maintained trail.
- Bicycles and other vehicles (except wheelchairs) are banned.
- Horses and pack stock cannot be tethered within 200 feet of any water source or shelter.
- Motorized equipment, drones, hang gliders, and fireworks are banned.
- Live trees and shrubs must not be cut or damaged.

In addition, some rules apply to all federal lands:

- Collecting arrowheads or other cultural artifacts is a federal crime.
- Permits are required to dig up plants.

SAFETY ON THE TRAIL

Wild Animals

Part of the fun of hiking is watching for wildlife. Lovers of wildness rue the demise of our most impressive species. Grizzly bears were hunted to extinction in Oregon by 1891. Wolves, once also extinct in the area, were reintroduced to Idaho in 1990 and have since established packs in Eastern Oregon. They do not interact with people. The black bears and cougars in Oregon are so profoundly shy you probably won't see one in years of hiking. No one has ever been killed by a bear or wolf in the history of Oregon.

Rattlesnakes, too, have become extremely rare. The State Health Division reports that only one Oregonian died from a rattlesnake in the most recent decade. Statistically, this makes rattlesnakes less of a threat than horses, bees, dogs, or even cows. Nonetheless, if you hear a rattle or recognize the snake's diamondback pattern, it's your cue to give this reclusive animal some space.

Ticks have received some publicity as carriers of Lyme disease, which begins with flu-like symptoms and an often circular rash. Very few cases have been reported in Oregon. Nonetheless, ticks can be a nuisance, particularly in dry grass or open woods during May and June. Brush off your clothes after a hike, and check the skin at your collar and pant cuffs. If a tick has attached itself, do not break it loose. Instead untwist its body like a screw for several complete rotations and it will let go.

Mosquitoes can be a problem for a few weeks each year. To avoid them, remember that these insects hatch about ten days after the snow melts from the trails and that they remain in force about two weeks. Thus, if a given trail is listed as "Open mid-June," you might expect mosquitoes there in early July.

Drinking Water

Day hikers should bring all the water they will need—at least a quart per person. A microscopic parasite, *Giardia,* has forever changed the old custom of dipping a drink from every brook. The symptoms of "beaver fever," debilitating nausea and diarrhea, commence a week or two after ingesting *Giardia.*

Many hikers and most backpackers now carry a water filter that has been certified to remove *Giardia*. The filters are generally attached to a small pump or a bottle lid, making it easy to draw water directly from lakes and streams. Alternative methods of removing *Giardia* include adding approved water purification tablets or boiling the water for five minutes.

Proper Equipment

Even on the tamest hike a surprise storm or a wrong turn can suddenly make the gear you carry very important. Always bring a pack with the ten essentials: extra insulation (a warm coat, extra clothing), navigation aids (a map, topographic if possible, and a compass), extra drinking water, extra food, repair tools (knife, tape), a fire starter (butane lighter, waterproof matches), first aid supplies, a flashlight, sun protection (sunglasses, sunscreen), and shelter (a waterproof jacket, large garbage bag, or space blanket). Before leaving on a hike, tell someone where you are going so they can alert the county sheriff to begin a search if you do not return on time. If you're lost, stay put and keep warm. The number one killer in the woods is *hypothermia* – being cold and wet too long.

GLOBAL POSITIONING SYSTEMS (GPS)

Do not trust car navigation systems in Eastern Oregon. People have died following "shortcut" routes recommended by their cars in remote areas with bad roads. Nonetheless, GPS devices can be helpful. Some of the hikes in this book include notations such as *44.3994, -121.0982*. This information can be used to pinpoint your location using satellite signals. If you have a smart phone, an app can turn it into a handy GPS device. The Gaia app is perhaps best, but costs $40. Google Maps works, but has poor quality topos. Other "free" apps generally have hidden fees. For any app, remember to download topo maps *before* your hike. Once the maps are stored on your phone it can track your location even if you have no cell phone coverage. None of these systems is a substitute for a map and compass because batteries can fail and signals can be blocked.

COURTESY ON THE TRAIL

As our trails become more heavily used, rules of trail etiquette become stricter:

- Pick no flowers.
- Leave no litter. Eggshells and orange peels can last for decades.
- Avoid bringing pets into wilderness areas. Dogs can frighten wildlife and disturb other hikers.
- Step off the trail on the downhill side to let horses pass. Speak to them quietly to help keep them from spooking.
- Do not shortcut switchbacks.

For overnight trail trips, low-impact camping is essential to protect the landscape and to preserve a sense of solitude for others. The most important rules:

- Build no campfire. Cook on a backpacking stove.
- Wash 100 feet from any lake or stream.
- Camp on duff, rock, or sand—never on meadow vegetation.
- Pack out garbage—don't burn or bury it.

FOR MORE INFORMATION

Visitor Bureaus

The Travel Guide portion of this book features a selection of the most interesting things to do and see in Eastern Oregon. Local visitor bureaus are glad to provide information about additional restaurants, motels, and commercial attractions:

Baker City, 541-523-5855, *visitbaker.com*
Bend, 877-245-8484, *visitbend.com*
Boardman, 541-481-3014, *boardmanchamber.org*
Burns, 541-573-2636, *harneycounty.com*

Elgin, 541-786-1770, *visitelginoregon.com*
Enterprise, 541-426-4622, *wallowacountychamber.com*
Hermiston, 541-567-6151, *hermistonchamber.com*
John Day, 541-575-0547, *gcoregonlive.com*
Klamath Falls, 800-445-6728, *meetmeinklamath.com*
La Grande, 541-963-8588, *visitunioncounty.org*
La Pine, 541-536-9771, *lapine.org*
Lakeview, 541-947-6040, *lakecountychamber.org*
Madras, 541-475-2350, *madraschamber.com*
Maupin, 541-993-1708, *maupinoregon.com*
Nyssa, 541-372-2264, *nyssacity.org*
Ontario, 541-889-8012, *ontariochamber.com*
Pendleton, 541-276-7411, *pendletonchamber.com*
Prineville, 541-447-5627, *cityofprineville.com*
Redmond, 541-923-5191, *visitredmondoregon.com*
Sisters, 541-549-0251, *sisterscountry.com*
Sunriver, 541-593-8149, *sunriverchamber.com*
The Dalles, 541-296-2231, *thedalleschamber.com*
Umatilla, 541-276-7111, *co.umatilla.or.us*

Trail Management Agencies

If you'd like to check trail conditions or restrictions, call directly to the trail's administrative agencies, listed below with the trails they manage. Ranger districts also post trail reports, fire closures, and road conditions at *fs.fed.us/r6*.

Hike	Managing Agency
11-14	Bend - Fort Rock Ranger District—541-383-5300
27, 31	Blue Mountain Ranger District—541-575-3000
89-94, 96	Burns District BLM—541-573-4400
2	Columbia Hills State Park—509-773-3145
9	Crooked River National Grassland—541-416-6500
53-65, 67-77	Eagle Cap Ranger District—541-426-4978
23	John Day Fossil Beds Nat'l Mon—541-987-2333
86-88	Hart Mountain Antelope Refuge—541-947-2731
47-52	Hells Canyon Nat'l Recreation Area—541-523-6391
26	Heppner Ranger District—541-676-9187
84	Klamath County Dept of Tourism—541-884-0666
79	Lakeview District BLM—541-947-2177
85	Lava Beds National Monument—530-667-8100
18-21	Lookout Mountain Ranger District—541-416-6500
7	Madras Public Works—541-475-2622
18, 46, 95	Nature Conservancy—541-426-3458
66	Nez Perce Wallowa Homeland—541-886-3101
34-36	North Fork John Day Ranger District—541-427-3231
1, 3, 8, 33, 78, 83	Oregon State Parks—800-551-6949
25	Paulina Ranger District—541-416-6500
82	Paisley Ranger District—541-943-3114
45	Pomeroy Ranger District—509-843-1891
28-30, 32	Prairie City Ranger District—541-820-3800
4-6, 10, 16, 22, 24	Prineville District BLM—541-416-6700
15	Prineville Public Works—541-447-7844
80	Silver Lake Ranger District—541-576-2107
81	Summer Lake Wildlife Area—541-943-3152
43-44	Walla Walla Ranger District—509-522-6290
37-42, 75-77	Whitman Ranger District—541-523-4476
97-100	Vale District BLM—541-473-3144

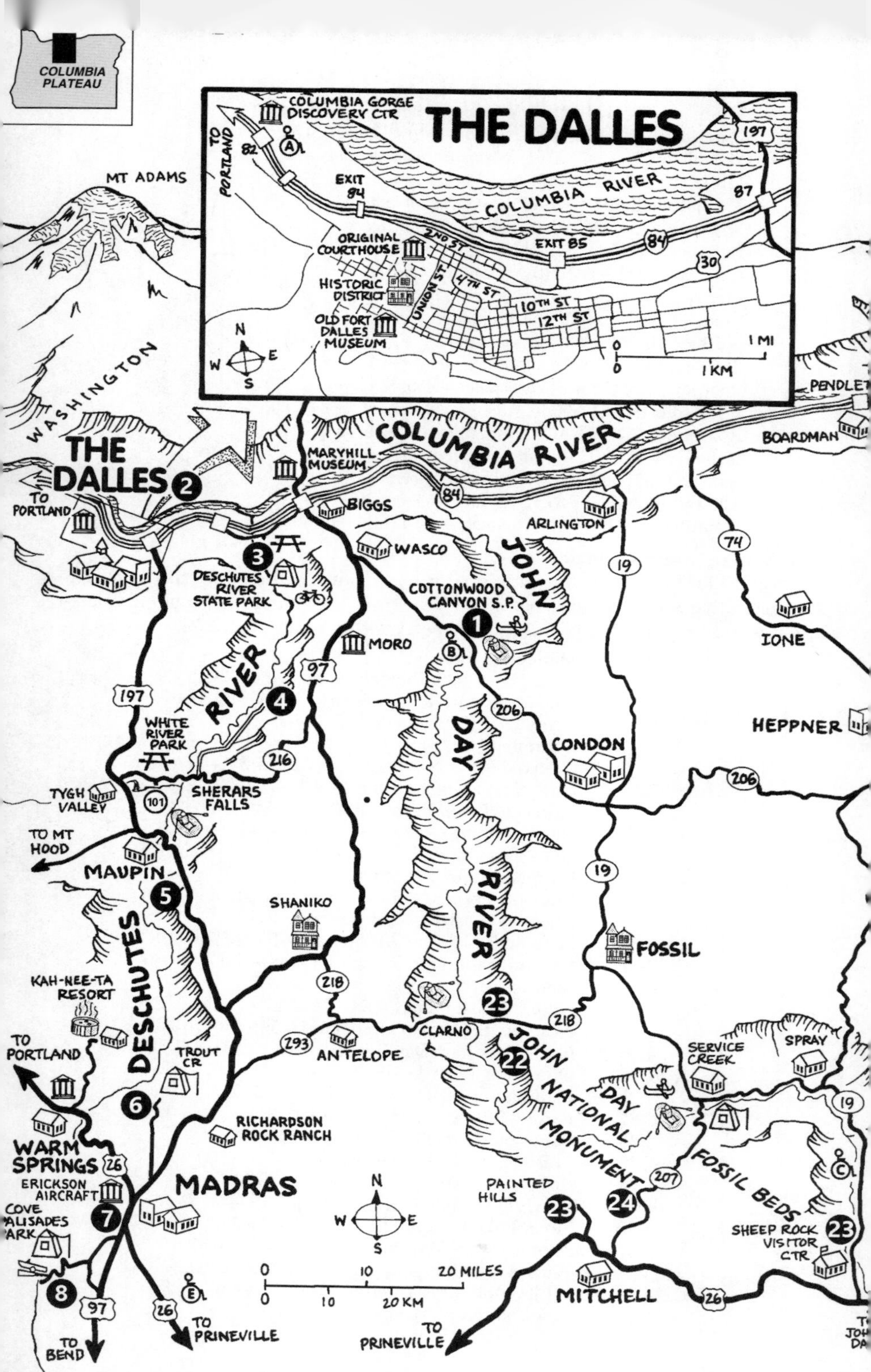

COLUMBIA PLATEAU
THE DALLES
COLUMBIA GORGE DISCOVERY CTR
TO PORTLAND
82
EXIT 84
COLUMBIA RIVER
197
87
84
EXIT 85
30
ORIGINAL COURTHOUSE
2ND ST
HISTORIC DISTRICT
UNION ST
4TH ST
10TH ST
12TH ST
OLD FORT DALLES MUSEUM
1 MI
1 KM
MT ADAMS
WASHINGTON
THE DALLES
TO PORTLAND
MARYHILL MUSEUM
COLUMBIA RIVER
BIGGS
ARLINGTON
BOARDMAN
PENDLET
WASCO
JOHN
DESCHUTES RIVER STATE PARK
COTTONWOOD CANYON S.P.
MORO
RIVER
74
19
IONE
97
197
206
DAY
WHITE RIVER PARK
216
CONDON
HEPPNER
TYGH VALLEY
101
SHERARS FALLS
206
TO MT HOOD
MAUPIN
RIVER
19
SHANIKO
DESCHUTES
FOSSIL
KAH-NEE-TA RESORT
218
218
CLARNO
JOHN
293
ANTELOPE
TROUT CR
SERVICE CREEK
SPRAY
TO PORTLAND
DAY
NATIONAL
19
RICHARDSON ROCK RANCH
MONUMENT
FOSSIL BEDS
WARM SPRINGS
26
MADRAS
PAINTED HILLS
207
ERICKSON AIRCRAFT
COVE PALISADES PARK
SHEEP ROCK VISITOR CTR
20 MILES
20 KM
MITCHELL
97
26
26
TO PRINEVILLE
TO PRINEVILLE
TO BEND

Former mural in The Dalles of Celilo Falls, a Columbia River cataract now submerged.

The Dalles

The Columbia River's narrows at The Dalles has always squeezed traffic at the east end of the Columbia Gorge—first the salmon that leapt upstream past Indian spearfishers, then the wagons of Oregon Trail pioneers, and now travelers exploring east from Portland in search of Eastern Oregon's wide open spaces. Museums and interpretive centers cluster about The Dalles.

Columbia Gorge Discovery Center

This first-class interpretive center in The Dalles features an outdoor collection of pioneer log cabins and Indian dwellings, as well as the displays of the Wasco County Historical Museum. Take I-84 exit 82 at the west end of The Dalles and follow signs. Admission is about $9 for adults, $7 for seniors, and $5 for kids age 6-16. Open 9-5 daily except major holidays *(gorgediscovery.org)*.

Fort Dalles Museum

Tour an officer's quarters from The Dalles' 1856 Army garrison, see two buildings full of antique vehicles, and visit a Swedish pioneer homestead at 15th and Garrison in The Dalles. Open 10am-5pm daily March-Nov. Adults pay $8, kids $1.

Original Wasco County Courthouse

Once The Dalles was the seat of the largest county in the US, stretching to Montana. Today Wasco County is smaller, but artifacts and displays of the pioneer era are preserved in the original wooden courthouse at 410 W. Second Place. The free museum is open Wed-Sat 11-4pm from Memorial Day through Labor Day.

The Dalles Historic Walking Tours

An online map at *historicthedalles.org* describes walking tours through downtown (47 historic buildings and many murals) and the Trevitt Historical Area (54 homes). Nearby is a bed & breakfast inn, the **Columbia House** at 525 East 7th Street (541-298-4686).

Maryhill Museum

Maryhill's replica of Stonehenge is free, but visitors to the museum's marvelously eclectic collection of Rodin sculptures, chess sets, Indian artifacts, and Romanian royal fashions pay $12 per adult, $10 for seniors, and $5 for children ages 7-18. Open daily 11-5 from March 15 to November 15. From Biggs exit 104 of I-84, take Highway 97 north across the Columbia River and turn left on Highway 14 for 2 miles.

Museum at Warm Springs

The beautifully designed **Museum at Warm Springs** features the artifacts, songs, and culture of the five tribes on the Warm Springs Reservation. On Highway 26 in Warm Springs, the museum is open 9-5 daily May through October. Adults are $7, seniors $6, and children 5-12 are $3.50. Closed Sundays and Mondays in winter. Next door is the tribe's **Indian Head Casino**, open 24 hours a day.

Erickson Aircraft Collection

Moved from Tillamook in 2014, this museum of two dozen World War II planes includes a B-17 bomber and a Messerschmidt fighter. Most planes are still able to fly. From Madras, drive Highway 26 north 2 miles to the airport. Open 10-5 daily except Mondays for a $9 admission, less for vets and kids (*ericksoncollection.com*).

Deschutes River

Each year thousands of rubber rafts and whitewater dories drift a popular 51-mile stretch of the rimrock-lined Deschutes River from Maupin to the Columbia River. The 2- or 3-day run includes four thrilling and dangerous rapids, countless lesser riffles, and one mandatory portage, at Sherar Falls. Boaters must bring a Deschutes River pass, available at local sporting goods stores. Fishing is banned from boats or floating devices. Campfires are banned, except in enclosed pans in winter.

John Day River

A lazier river than the turbulent Deschutes, the John Day River wends through a deeper, wilder canyon of desert rimrock. Rubber rafts, drift boats, and even canoes float the John Day River from April to July. Water levels are too low in late summer. Permits from *recreation.gov* are required year round. It's usually a 2- to 3-day trip from the bridge at Service Creek to the bridge at Clarno, and another four days downstream to the Cottonwood Bridge of Highway 206 at Cottonwood Canyon State Park. Clarno Rapids, the most dangerous whitewater, lurks 4.4 miles below the Clarno Bridge.

The John Day River wends through Cottonwood Canyon State Park.

Cottonwood Canyon State Park

On the former Murtha Ranch where Highway 206 crosses the John Day River, this 8000-acre park opened in 2013. The free day use area has an interpretive center, a restored barn, water, restrooms, and free showers. The 21-site campground has fences to block wind and small trees to provide some shade. See Hike #1

Richardson's Rock Ranch

Buy freshly dug geodes and thundereggs on this private ranch 9am-5pm daily May-September (only open Friday-Tuesday in winter). Drive Highway 97 north of Madras 11 miles to milepost 81 and follow signs 3 miles.

Shaniko

This "ghost town" 30 miles north of Madras on Highway 97 counts 26 live residents, several spooks, and a historic hotel. Founded by August *Scherneckau* in the 1870s, the town became an important wool-shipping railhead in 1904, with 600 residents and five saloons, but faded when a competing railroad opened in 1911.

Hike 1 Cottonwood Canyon

In a desert canyon along the John Day River, this sprawling park is a windy place to camp, but a lovely place for a riverside hike, especially when cool afternoon shadows lengthen.

Easy (Hard Stone Trail)
3 miles round trip
200 feet elevation gain
Open all year
Use: hikers

Easy (Pinnacles Trail to Walnut Loop)
3.8-mile loop
100 feet elevation gain
Use: hikers, bicycles

Difficult (to end of Pinnacles Trail)
8.6 miles round trip
100 feet elevation gain

The Pinnacles.

The park opened in 2013 on the old Murtha Ranch. When you drive into the park, stop at the picnic area to see the ranch's restored barn, windmill, and corral, now decorated with art carved into the weathered boards.

The Murthas were Irish immigrants who prospered in the sheepraising boom from 1900-1920. During World War I, millions of sheep were shipped out from the rail terminus in Shaniko to supply armies with wool uniforms and blankets. After 1929, the Depression and synthetic fabrics killed the market for wool. The counties in this part of Eastern Oregon, where people had been building opera houses, fancy hotels, and churches, became a land of ghost towns. Today wheat, cattle, and electricity-generating windmills are the main industries.

The park is open year-round, but avoid the icy winds of winter and the blazing midday sun of summer. In April and May, yellow balsamroot sunflowers splash

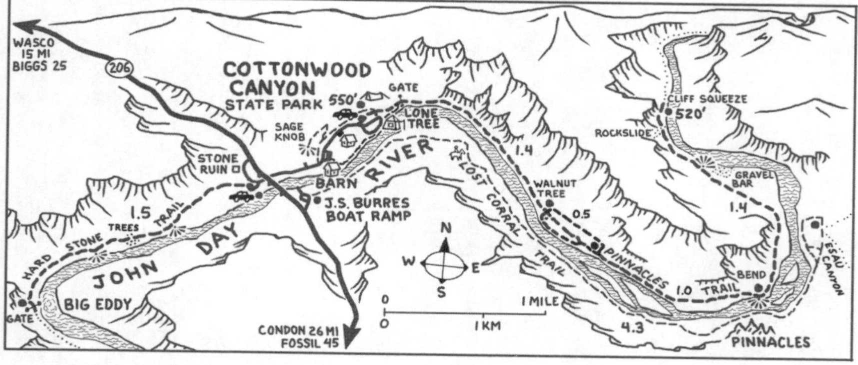

Trails in the park are mostly on abandoned ranch roads.

the slopes with yellow. Mornings and late afternoons are magical, when the shadows lengthen and the dozen layers of rimrock are stair-stepped with colored light. These hours also bring out mule deer, lizards, and mountain bluebirds.

Getting There— Drive Highway 97 north of Madras 86 miles (or south of Interstate 84 exit #104 for Biggs 10 miles), take the turnoff for Wasco, and continue east on Highway 206 for 15 miles.

If you have time for just one hike, take the Hard Stone Trail upriver 1.5 miles to a lazy river whirlpool called Big Eddy. Start at a gravel lot on the park's entrance road beside the John Day River bridge. As soon as you set out on the trail—an abandoned ranch road—look back over your right shoulder. You'll see the ruin of a century-old stone house. Burrowed into the hillside, this shelter dates to the days when Irish shepherds had the time to pile rocks while watching their flocks.

For the first half mile the road/trail skirts an old hay field that has regrown with six-foot-tall sagebrush. Grasshoppers jump out of your way as you walk. You will see a few snakes—and quite possibly a rattler—but they are busy hunting mice, and are eager to get out of your way.

For the final mile the trail clings to the riverbank. Three-foot-long fish idle in backwaters. At Big Eddy, where a giant cliff crowds the trail against the river, a gate marks the end of the official path. The old roadbed continues upriver another 1.5 miles before petering out, but the riverside boulders here make a good turnaround point.

The longer Pinnacles Trail, also on an old ranch road, follows the river downstream to even quieter viewpoints. Park at a restroom beside the park's Lone Tree Campground. The path passes hiker/biker campsites for 0.2 mile to a gate where the Willow Trail joins from the campground. Ahead, the path skirts beneath a rock cliff. At the 1.4-mile mark there's a 4-way junction beside a big walnut tree and a cobble beach. Sometimes bighorn sheep browse the cliffs above. For a loop, either go left (uphill) for views along the Upper Walnut Trail for 0.5 mile, or go right along the river on the Lower Walnut Trail. Both paths return to the Pinnacles Trail.

If you're not tired, continue on the Pinnacles Trail another mile to a riverbend viewpoint of the Pinnacles, a cluster of ragged rock outcrops across the river. It's worth continuing yet another 1.4 miles to the trail's official end, where a rockslide stops park tractors from mowing the path. Just beyond, the narrowed path squeezes between a river rapids and a cliff—another satisfying turnaround point.

Hike 2 Columbia Hills

The Dalles Dam silenced the thunder of Celilo Falls in 1957, but the magic of that Columbia River spiritual center still echoes.

Easy (2 short walks)
1.5 miles total
200 feet elevation gain
Open all year
Use: hikers

Moderate (to the ranch)
6.8-mile loop
900 feet elevation gain
Use: hikers, horses, bicycles

Petroglyphs at Temani Pesh-wa.

At Columbia Hills you'll find petroglyphs, trails, rock climbing, and a historic ranch. Because this is a Washington park, you'll need a Discover Pass for your car. The pass is $10 a day or $30 a year, and can be purchased at trailheads.

Getting There— Start your voyage in The Dalles. Before crossing the Columbia River, pause at the Oregon end of The Dalles Bridge. Water roars from the spillways of the dam that drowned Celilo Falls. A few rickety fishing platforms and unpainted shacks recall the Indian salmon-fishing metropolis that once was the Northwest's economic hub. Petroglyph Canyon lies two miles upstream—and a hundred feet underwater. Just before the dam's waters rose, the Army Corps of Engineers chiseled out a few dozen of the thousands of petroglyphs. In 2003 the art returned to a site with dignity—the Temani Pesh-wa ("Written on Rock") Trail, near its original location.

To see the rock art, drive 3 miles north of The Dalles Bridge, turn right on Washington Highway 14 for 1.6 miles, and then turn right into Columbia Hills State Park for 1.2 miles to a big gravel parking area on the left. From November through March, when a gate closes the end of this road, you'll have to walk the last half mile. A 100-yard paved walkway tours the petroglyphs. The most impressive one, a table-sized spirit face called "She Who Watches," is out of sight around a corner, visitable only on 90-minute tours guided by rangers. Call 509-439-9032 for reservations.

For a 1.4-mile hike to see the petroglpyhs' original home, drive back to Highway 14 and turn east for 1.3 miles to the Horsethief Butte Trailhead. Horsethief Butte is a wind-swept mesa of columnar basalt that's popular with beginning rock climbers. Keep right on the hiking trail to take a tour around the butte's base. Big yellow balsamroot flowers bloom among the sagebrush here in April. The path ends after 0.7 mile at a cliff overlooking the Columbia River. The final 50 feet of the trail are crowded with poison oak, so long pants are best.

After taking in the view, turn back for 0.3 mile to a trail junction. If you don't mind a little scrambling, turn uphill to the right on an alternate return route that climbs to a miniature version of Petroglyph Canyon. The original basalt gorge is downhill to the south, now drowned by the reservoir. You'll need to use your hands to scramble

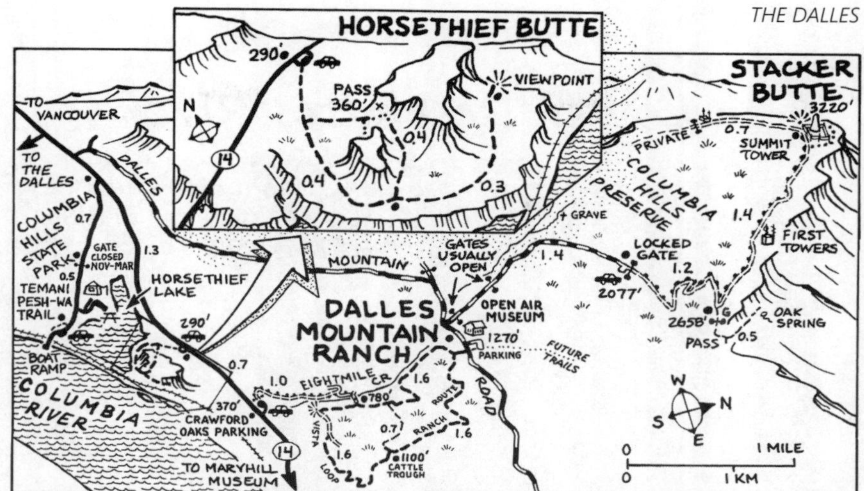

over a rocky pass to return to your car.

It's possible to drive to the historic Dalles Mountain Ranch, but it's actually more fun to hike there. A 6.8-mile loop climbs through panoramic meadows to a picnic site by the old ranch house. Start at the Crawford Oaks Trailhead, on Highway 14 east of Horsethief Butte 0.7 mile, near milepost 87.

The trail begins as a gated old road. Keep right at junctions for a mile and cross Eightmile Creek to a field with a brown post marking the start of the Vista Loop. For the quickest route to the ranch, turn left and keep left for 1.6 miles up Eightmile Creek. When you reach a big gravel road, turn left to explore the ranch buildings. The farm house is locked, and the exhibit of farm machinery is in the field above the barn. To return on a loop (longer by 1.6 miles, but with better views), head back down the trail and keep left at junctions.

***Other Options*—** For the area's best viewpoint, atop 3220-foot Stacker Butte, hike a service road that's closed to cars. The route gains 1140 feet in 2.6 miles. To start, drive Highway 14 west of the main park entrance. Between mileposts 84 and 85, turn north on Dalles Mountain Road and keep right 3.5 miles to a fork at the ranch. Turn uphill to the left 1.4 miles to small parking area beside a locked gate. This final stretch of road is rough and passes two gates that can be closed, lengthening the hike.

The Dalles Mountain Ranch has a collection of old machinery outdoors.

Hike 3 Lower Deschutes River

The charms of a desert river are many: bright blue skies, the pungent smell of sage, birdsong across glassy water, and the cool grass of an oasis-like riverbank.

Easy (to Ferry Springs)
4.2-mile loop
600 feet elevation gain
Open all year
Use: hikers, bicycles

Moderate (to Gordon Canyon)
7.5-mile loop
800 feet elevation gain

Trail on old railroad grade.

You'll find all these charms on a loop hike from the state park at the mouth of the Deschutes River. Part of the loop follows the abandoned grade of the 1909 DesChutes Railroad, now a hiker/biker trail. The trip's prettiest if it's timed to see the wildflowers of spring or the colors of fall. Just avoid the heat of July and August.

Getting There— From The Dalles, take Interstate 84 east 10 miles to Deschutes Park exit 97. Follow park signs 3 miles. On the far side of the Deschutes River turn right and drive straight through the park to the far end of the last parking area. Dogs are allowed on leash only.

Start by walking upriver through a picnic lawn 0.1 mile to a trail sign. Bicyclists must turn left here to the railroad grade, but hikers can keep right along the riverbank. As you hike amid the tall sagebrush and head-high grass of the riverside path, listen for the melodious call of the western meadowlark, Oregon's state bird. The birds you are most likely to see are vultures circling the canyon, Canada geese paddling in river shallows, and flocks of seagulls hovering above rapids for fish.

After 1.2 miles along the river, the path passes a small beach with a bench—a possible turnaround point for hikers with kids. Beyond the beach 0.2 mile the trail forks. Here you face another decision: Do you want to go left for the 4.2-mile loop,

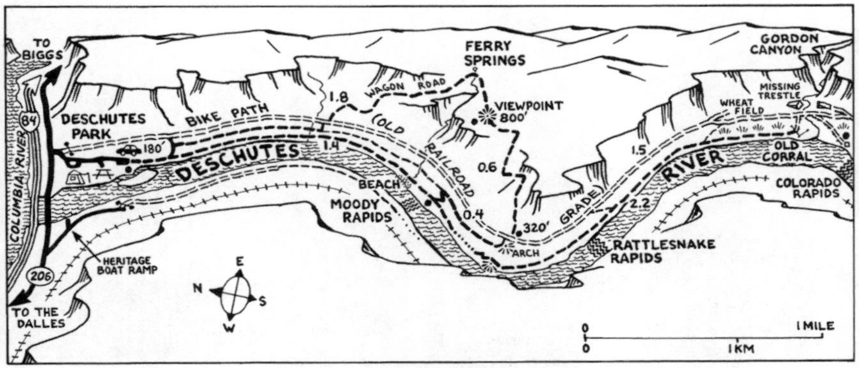

or stay right for the 7.5-mile loop?

If you choose the shorter loop to Ferry Springs, take the left fork up through rocky outcrops 300 feet and turn right on an upper trail 0.3 mile to the old railroad grade. Walk right on this gravel bike path a few feet to a large messageboard. Pause here to notice a natural rock arch 40 feet behind the sign. Then continue along the bike path another 50 feet and turn uphill to the left on a trail marked only by a "No Bicycles" sign.

This surprisingly spectacular footpath climbs through wildflower meadows with ever grander views. In April and May expect orange Indian blanket, yellow balsamroot, and blue lupine. After climbing 0.8 mile, hop across the creek at Ferry Springs, and descend on a section of the Oregon Trail, a wagon road with a rock-work bank. When you reach the gravel bike path, turn right 300 feet to a brown post that marks a hiker trail back down to the park's picnic lawn and your car.

If you'd prefer the longer, 7.5-mile loop to Gordon Canyon, stick to the Deschutes riverbank. After the 1.4-mile mark, where you take the right-hand fork, the trail along the river is rough and bouldery for a quarter mile. The path improves by Rattlesnake Rapids, where the river foams up in 6-foot standing waves. At the 3-mile mark you'll cross a 10-acre wheatfield that's farmed for historic purposes, although the abandoned homestead was transfered to the state in 1983. At the far end of the field follow a gravel road right across Gordon Creek and fork right again to a primitive camp area with an outhouse and a beach that's nice for wading.

Make this your lunchtime turnaround. Then walk back on the gravel road, which becomes the old railroad grade. After 1.5 miles you'll have seen enough of this bike path, so turn right to return on the scenic Ferry Springs loop described above.

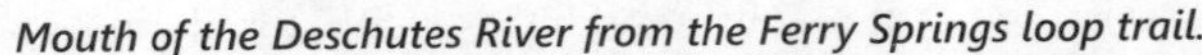

Mouth of the Deschutes River from the Ferry Springs loop trail.

Hike 4 Macks Canyon

The starkly beautiful rimrock canyon of the lower Deschutes River is so remote that it's seen mostly by whitewater rafters and railroad engineers.

Easy (to Sixteen Canyon)
4.2 miles round trip
210 feet elevation gain
Open all year
Use: hikers, bicycles

Missing trestle on the trail.

Hikers can see this canyon too, by following an abandoned railroad grade past canyons once spanned by trestles. The trail starts at the end of an unusual 17-mile riverside road from Sherars Falls, so the drive here is as spectacular as the hike.

Getting There— If you're coming from Interstate 84, take exit 87 at the east end of The Dalles south on Highway 197 for 30 miles to Tygh Valley and turn left on Highway 216 for 8 miles to Sherars Falls, a raging cataract where Indians use their treaty rights to scoop leaping salmon from rickety platforms. If you're coming from Bend, take Highway 97 north 61 miles and turn left on Highway 197 for 31 miles. Beyond Maupin 9 miles at Tygh Valley, turn right on Highway 216 to Sherars Falls.

Drive past the bridge at Sherars Falls 0.8 mile and turn left on Deschutes River Access Road at a sign, "Deadend 17." This gravel road has a strictly marked 20-mile-per-hour speed limit, so it will take you an hour. Along the way you'll pass half a dozen boat launches and campgrounds.

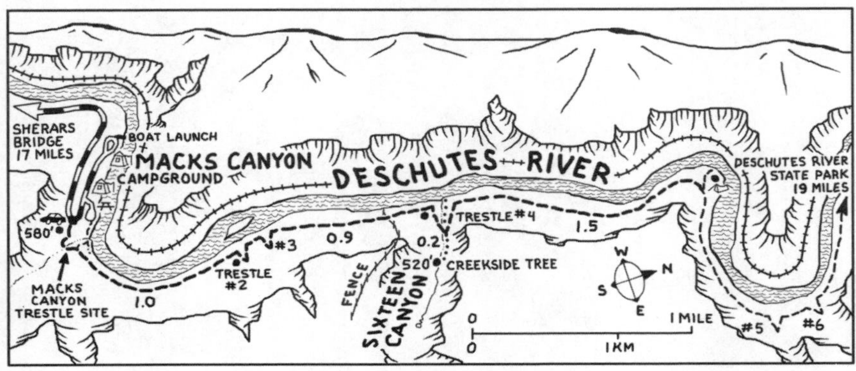

Railroad ties were left behind when the canyon's rails were removed.

When the road finally switchbacks left toward Macks Canyon Campground, park in a wide spot at the curve. A path leads 50 feet up to the old railroad grade amid sagebrush, bunchgrass, aster, thistles, mulleins, and lupines. After just 0.2 mile you'll reach Macks Canyon's missing trestle, which had been 100 feet high and 400 feet long. The bypass trail is steep and scrambly to the other embankment.

On the far side, the railroad grade cuts through a lava slope filled with a rockslide. Then the path skirts a thicket of poison oak—beware of three-leaved shrubs!

After another 0.8 mile along the level railroad grade you'll reach a couple more missing trestles, with easy detours into small canyons. Another 0.9 mile on the railroad grade brings you to the bigger gap of Sixteen Canyon, a nice turnaround goal. Take a cattle trail down to the right into the canyon, and bushwhack 0.2 mile up the dry gulch to find a shady hackberry tree where the creek actually flows. You might also explore downstream to the Deschutes River bank before heading back.

Other Options— If you want to continue farther on the railroad grade, it's 1.5 miles to a corner cut, where a side trail to the left descends to some riverside campsites, often taken early by boaters. Beyond, the railroad grade is very rough, with rocks and sagebrush, for 19 miles to the maintained trails at Deschutes River State Park (Hike #3).

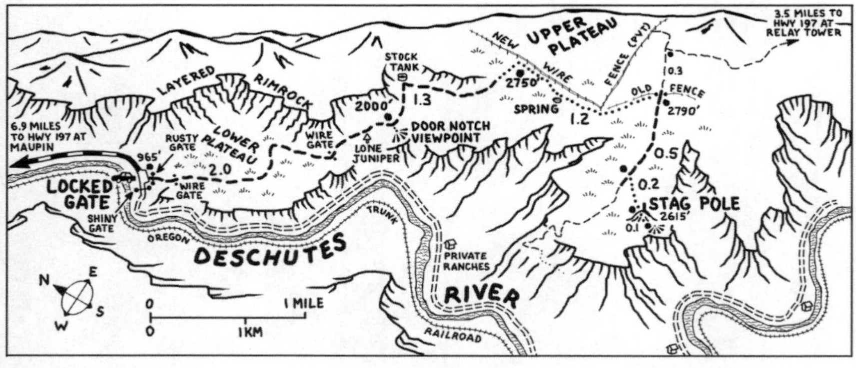

Hike 5 Criterion Tract

Central Oregon's desert can be a delirious retreat, especially in spring when the Deschutes River runs high and the sunny sagebrush hills revel in wildflowers.

Moderate (to notch viewpoint)
4 miles round trip
1035 feet elevation gain
Open all year
Use: hikers, horses, bicycles

Difficult (to Stag pole viewpoint)
10.6 miles round trip
2700 feet elevation gain

Trail on the lower plateau.

A century ago the Deschutes Canyon's charm lured homesteaders. As early as 1906 the federal government offered free land east of the Cascades to anyone willing to risk dry land farming. Today you can hike through scenic badlands to river viewpoints, crossing a collection of ghost ranches known as the Criterion Tract.

Promoters hyped the "free land" scheme heavily in the early 1910s. Hopeful families cleared sagebrush, planted rye, and prayed for rain. But precipitation here can be as low as 12 inches a year.Winter winds howl. Summer bakes in heat. Desperate homesteaders switched to cattle ranching. The boomtown of Criterion had a post office from 1913 to 1926. And yet, even cattle found the land so spare that the Bureau of Land Management wound up owning the ghost town's corral and about 20 square miles of backcountry. Since then the BLM has left the faint ranch roads as trails, closed to motor vehicles.

Getting There— If you're coming from Central Oregon, drive Highway 97 north of Madras 25 miles and fork left onto Highway 197, following signs for The Dalles. After 8 miles you'll drive through the ghost town of Criterion. At a yellow mailbox on the left, 0.3 mile beyond milepost 58, stop to tour the weathered pens of the Criterion Corral. Then drive onward another 12 miles to Maupin. Near the

A cliff near a pole named "Stag" overlooks the Deschutes River.

start of town, 0.2 mile before the Deschutes River bridge, turn left onto a narrow paved road at a large brown sign marked "Deschutes River Rec. Area."

If you're coming from Portland, drive Highway 26 past Mt. Hood for 15 miles to Warm Springs Junction, fork left onto Highway 216 toward Maupin for 26 miles, turn right on Highway 197 for 3.2 miles to the Deschutes River bridge on the far side of Maupin, and continue 0.2 mile to the "Deschutes River Rec. Area" sign.

The narrow paved road beyond this sign follows the riverbank upstream past three campgrounds. Campsites are only $8, but they don't take reservations and car camping is not permitted elsewhere. For the hike, drive 3.6 miles of pavement and another 3.3 miles of good gravel to the end of the road, where there's a parking lot with two locked gates. Landowners with cabins upriver have a key to the shiny gate straight ahead. For the hike, however, walk past the rusty gate to the left, behind the outhouse.

The old ranch road here, now mostly narrowed to a trail, climbs to a prairie plateau ringed with rimrock cliffs. At the 2-mile mark, after climbing to a switchback 0.2 mile beyond a lone juniper tree, walk 80 feet to the right to a door-sized notch in a rock outcrop. This "doorway" is actually a gap atop a cliff, 1000 feet above the Deschutes River. This makes a good turnaround point for a moderate hike.

If you're still going strong, and you have some routefinding skills, continue past the first viewpoint 1.3 miles, climbing on the road/trail until it peters out at a modern barbed wire fence atop a higher plateau. If you have a GPS app for your phone, which is a really good idea, the location here is *45.0702 -121.0843*.

Now comes the hard part. There is no trail for the next 1.2 miles. Turn right, following the shiny wire fence steeply down and up for 0.8 mile to a fence corner. Continue straight, following a rusty abandoned fence up and down for another 0.4 mile to a gap with an old road. Turn right on this track for half a mile across a sagebrush plateau. Now look to the left for a little pointy green knoll with a strange pole on top.

Bushwhack 0.2 mile to the pole, a landmark named "Stag" *(GPS location 45.0518 -121.0933)*. Before turning back, continue straight 0.1 mile to an even better view at the edge of a colossal canyon cliff.

Hike 6 Trout Creek

The Deschutes River winds like a great blue-green snake through a dry rimrock canyon bordering the Warm Springs Indian Reservation.

Easy (to footbridge)
4.8 miles round trip
50 feet elevation gain
Open all year
Use: hikers, bicycles

Moderate (entire trail)
7.6 miles one way
100 feet elevation gain

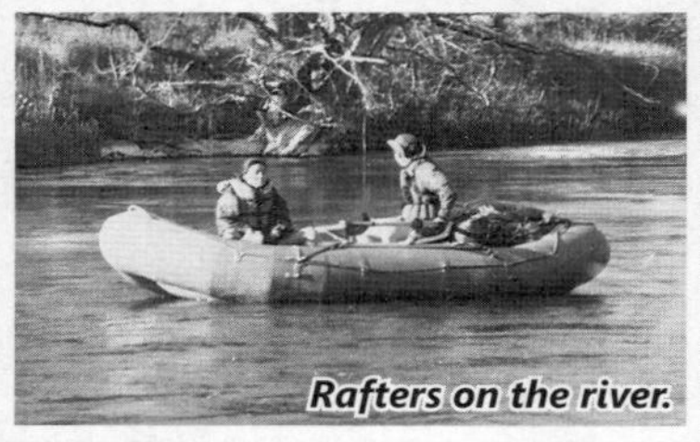
Rafters on the river.

In 1910, when two rival railroad tycoons were racing to build competing lines from The Dalles to Bend, locomotives steamed along the riverbank. Now this portion of the old train route has been converted to a path where you can watch the glassy river glide past.

Both ends of the 7.6-mile river trail are at campgrounds that serve as popular launch sites for whitewater boaters. If you have a shuttle car, you can walk the entire trail one way. If you don't have a shuttle, start downstream at the Trout Creek Recreation Area, in a scenic, twisty part of the canyon full of birdsong.

Getting There— From Madras (43 miles north of Bend), drive Highway 97 north toward The Dalles 3.5 miles. Between mileposts 89 and 90, turn left on Cora Drive for 8.3 miles to the hamlet of Gateway. Along the way this paved road changes names to Clark Drive and then Bulkley Lane. Cross the train tracks in Gateway, turn right onto Clemens Drive, and stick to this gravel road for 5 miles to the campground, following "Trout Creek" pointers. In the campground itself, drive left past two large parking lots to a day-use parking area at the far left end of the campground loop.

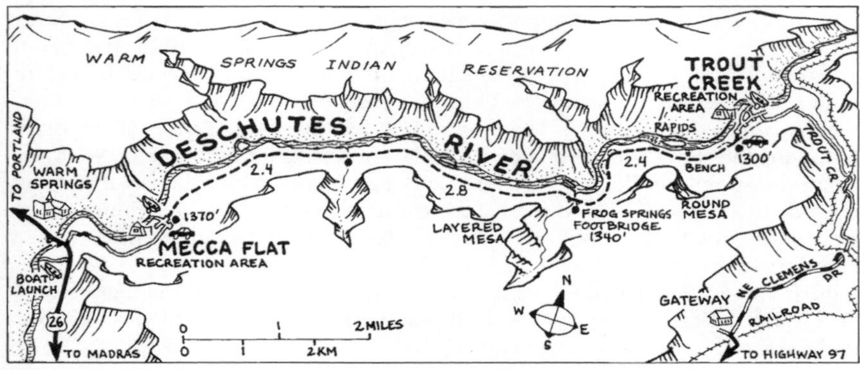

At a signboard, set out on the broad railroad grade, a route lined with tall sagebrush, some juniper trees, bitterbrush, rabbitbrush, mulleins, and teasels. Ignore small side paths where fly fishermen have made their way down to the river's grassy bank. Listen for the squawk of ring-necked pheasants, the melodious warble of meadowlarks, and the chatter of long-tailed, black-and-white magpies. You may even hear a rattle, as rattlesnakes are not uncommon here.

For an easy hike, make your goal the 80-foot Frog Springs bridge at the 2.4-mile mark. Avoid stinging nettles along the side creek here, but do explore a spur trail that leads to a lunch spot by the river with shade trees and a small sandy beach.

If you want to hike the entire trail one-way, you'll need to leave a shuttle car at the far end, at Mecca Flat. To find that trailhead, drive back to Madras and turn right onto Highway 26 toward Mt. Hood for 12.5 miles. Near milepost 105—and just 100 feet before the Deschutes River bridge—turn right at an abandoned gas station on an unmarked gravel road, following the largest track. After 1.6 bumpy miles you'll enter the Mecca Flat Recreation Area, a shadeless campground with a boat ramp. Park in the trailhead day-use lot.

The nearly level trail follows a railroad grade along the Deschutes River.

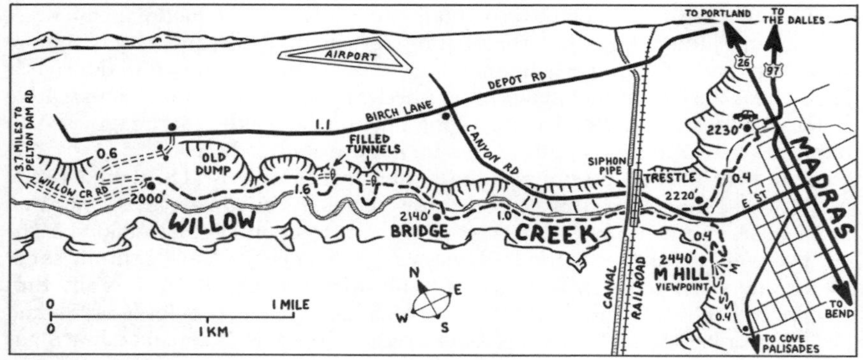

Hike

7 Willow Creek at Madras

From downtown Madras, a trail network climbs to a city viewpoint and descends an old railroad's rimrock canyon.

Easy (to the "M" Hill)
1.6 miles round trip
250 feet elevation gain
Open all year
Use: hikers, bicycles

Easy (to Willow Creek Road)
6 miles round trip
250 feet elevation gain

A trestle and a siphon pipe cross the trail.

When rival railroad moguls laid track through Central Oregon in 1910, one company built up the Willow Creek canyon to Madras, while the other bridged the canyon and bypassed the town. Today trains only run on the bypass line. The abandoned railroad grade below the trestle, however, has become a scenic part of Madras' network of bike paths.

Getting There—Start at the north edge of downtown Madras where Highways 97 and 26 join. At a traffic light for this X-shaped junction, turn west into a large trailhead parking area. Park by a footbridge over Willow Creek *(GPS location 44.6386 -121.1317).*

Cross the bridge and follow a wide paved path 0.4 mile to a trail junction. If you only have time for the short hike, turn left, cross Canyon Creek Road, and follow a paved path up "M" Hill, a slope that displays the city's giant initial letter in white rocks. Lizards bask on cement benches along the way. The circular patio at the summit can be a very windy place. To the east, Madras spreads out like a map. A sighting pedestal identifies Cascade snowpeaks to the west—including Mt. Hood, visible above the train trestle that bypassed the town.

For a less urban hike, you might skip the side trip up "M" Hill and instead continue straight on the bike path down Willow Creek. This trail also crosses

Canyon Road, but then it turns to gravel and leaves the city behind. Sagebrush grows 5 feet tall in this canyon amid junipers and rabbitbrush. Expect to see deer, ground squirrels, and magpies. Overhead is not only the 200-foot-tall trestle, but also a 10-foot-diameter pipe that siphons the entire Main Canal across the canyon. Antique airplanes from the Erickson Aircraft Collection occasionally cross the sky, taking off from the nearby airport.

At the 1.4-mile mark you'll cross a footbridge over Willow Creek, which is usually dry. In another 0.3 mile the path skirts the base of a rimrock cliff that's popular with rock climbers and cliff swallows. This is also where the rail line once entered the first of two tunnels. Look for the concrete header above the filled-in entrance. The modern trail has to detour around this knoll and the next.

After 3 miles you'll pass the rusty cars and tires of a 1940s dump, just before joining gravel Willow Creek Road. This rough track is closed to cars, but it's still a road, so it's a good place to declare victory and return the way you came.

Other Options — For a longer hike, or for a one-way hike with a shuttle, continue down gravel Willow Creek Road 3.7 miles to a lower trailhead at Pelton Dam Road, near Lake Simtustus Resort at the Deschutes River's reservoir. To drive to that trailhead from downtown Madras, turn west off Highway 97 onto D Street at a pointer reading, "To Cove Palisades." After 0.8 mile turn right on SW Elk Drive. At a sign for "Lake Simtustus" turn right on SW Belmont Lane for 5 paved miles. At a crest half a mile past the resort, park in a gravel pullout on the right that's incorrectly marked "No Trespassing." The gravel side road to the right is Willow Creek Road, but there's no parking or turnaround ahead, so this is the trailhead.

The filled-in entrance to the first railroad tunnel overlooks Willow Creek canyon.

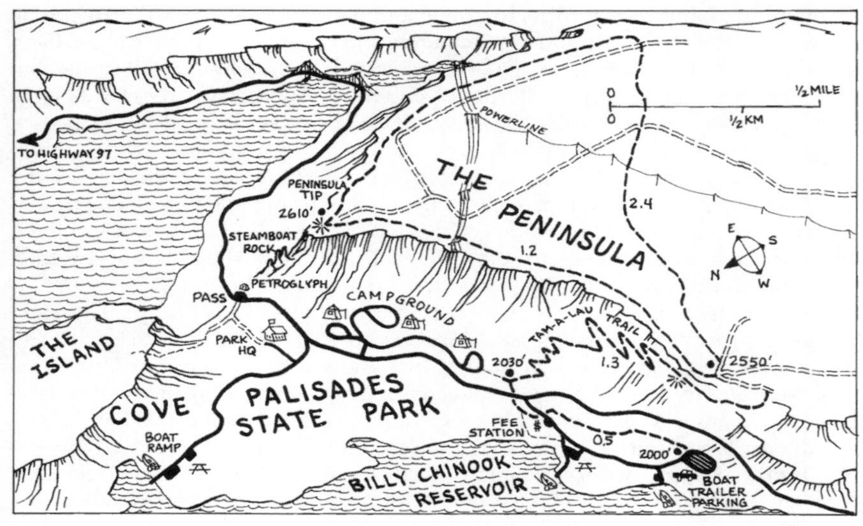

Hike

8 Cove Palisades

The Peninsula, an eerie desert plateau, resembles a gigantic aircraft carrier moored in the midst of the vast Billy Chinook reservoir.

Easy (to The Peninsula)
3.6 miles round trip
550 feet elevation gain
Open all year
Use: hikers only

Moderate (to Peninsula tip)
7.2-mile loop
640 feet elevation gain

View of the bridge from the trail.

From the Tam-a-lau Trail atop the mesa's rim you can watch tiny ski boats from the Cove Palisades State Park cutting white V-shaped wakes into the sunny green waters far below. *Tam-a-lau,* a Sahaptin word meaning "place of big rocks on the ground," hints at the unusual geologic formations along the path. Summer can bring intense heat to this canyonland, so you might start your hike in the morning.

Getting There— Turn off Highway 97 at a sign for Cove Palisades (either 15 miles north of Redmond or in the town of Madras) and follow similar signs on a zigzagging route west to the park's breathtaking canyon. Follow the main road down into the canyon, past a boat launch, across a suspension bridge, and up to a pass with a pullout for the Crooked River Petroglyph, a stone moved here when

From The Peninsula, The Island stands out as a mesa in the reservoir.

the reservoir drowned its original site. Drive 0.1 mile beyond the pass, keep left at a fork in the road, drive straight past the campground half a mile, and turn right at a sign for "Upper Deschutes River Day Use." Here you'll have to pay a $5 parking fee at an automat. Then drive on, keeping left to a large, paved boat trailer parking lot at road's end.

The Tam-a-lau Trail starts by a sign at the left edge of the parking lot and winds through a juniper steppe with sagebrush, bunchgrass, and sunflower-like balsamroot blooms. Grasshoppers leap out of the trail before you. Western fence lizards do push-ups on trailside rocks.

In the first half mile you'll cross a road, turn right on a paved path, and cross another road before reaching a large signboard with trail brochures. Campers at the park's campground can start the hike here simply by walking to the end of the rightmost campground loop.

Beyond the signboard the Tam-a-lau Trail begins switchbacking up through the basalt lava layers of the canyon wall. Most of these terraces are part of the Deschutes Formation, 5- to 25-million-year-old lava flows from the Cascade Range. Halfway up the wall, however, you'll pass remnants of Intracanyon Basalt, a more recent flow that began 60 miles away at the Newberry Volcanic National Monument. That flow surged down the river canyon, puddled up here, and created The Island, a lonely plateau to the north surrounded by cliffs on all sides. If you look between the lava flows you'll see light-colored layers of ash, sand, and cobbles—riverbed deposits that built up during the long intervals between eruptions.

After climbing 1.3 miles you'll follow an old road up to a junction atop The Peninsula. Here the view opens up to the Cascade's snowpeaks. Mt. Jefferson dominates the view, but ghostly Mt. Hood haunts the horizon to its right. If you're tired, or if sun's too hot, plan to turn back here.

For the 3.6-mile loop along The Peninsula's rim, however, keep left on a dirt path. Notice how the surface of this plateau has accumulated tan volcanic ash and cinder rocks, the fallout from millennia of Cascade eruptions. A fragile crust of dark lichens and moss holds the dusty soil in place. Because cattle grazing has been allowed on The Peninsula, hoofprints have largely destroyed the ground cover here. Scientists studying the area's native plants focus instead on The Island across the canyon, inaccessible to cattle.

Follow the path 1.2 miles to the tip of The Peninsula, where you can peer down at the colored pinnacles of Steamboat Rock, a weathered formation of volcanic ash. Then the trail continues along the rim another mile before looping back across The Peninsula's flat top to the junction with the path down to your car.

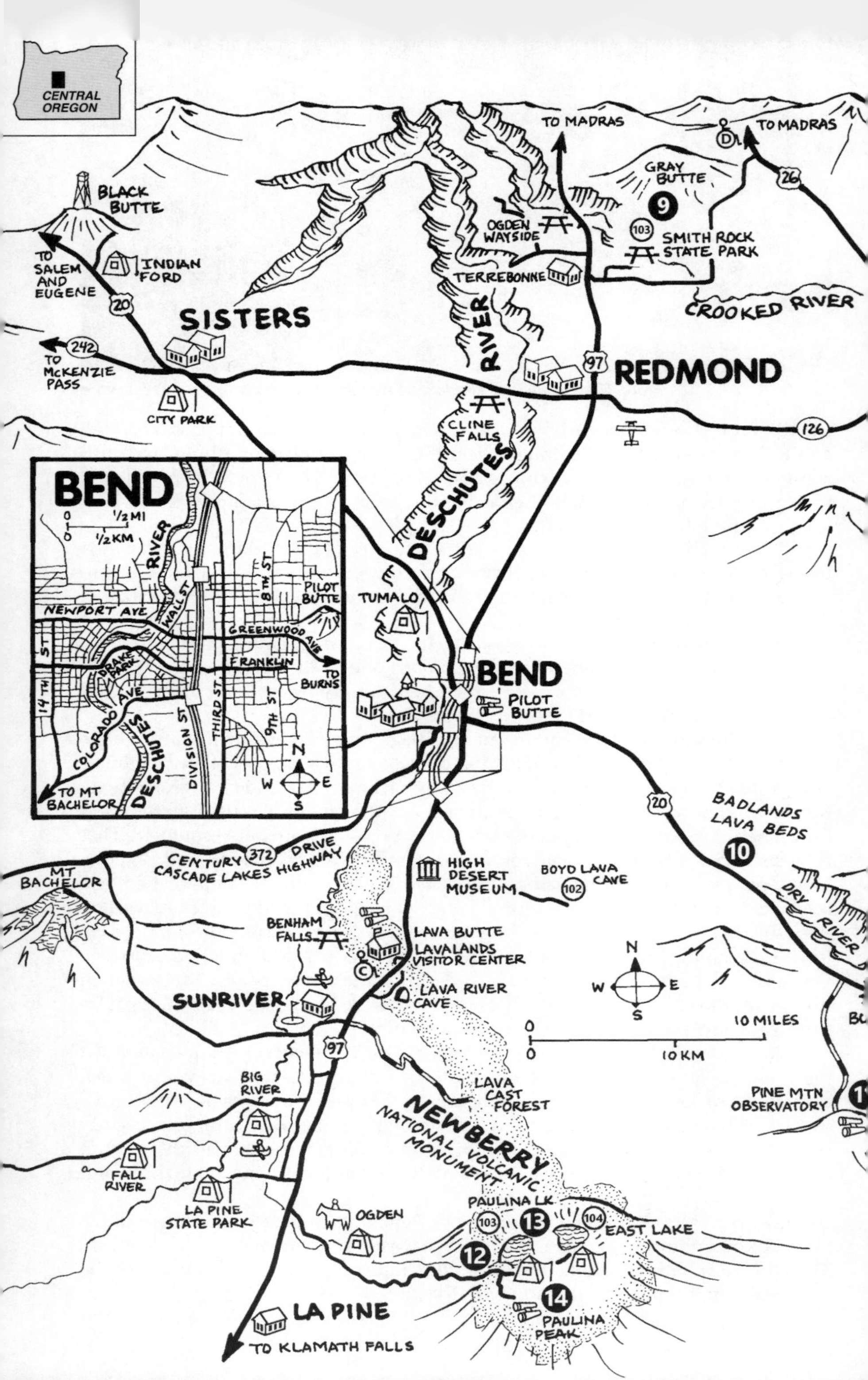
CENTRAL OREGON
TO MADRAS
TO MADRAS
26
GRAY BUTTE
9
BLACK BUTTE
OGDEN WAYSIDE
103
SMITH ROCK STATE PARK
TO SALEM AND EUGENE
INDIAN FORD
TERREBONNE
20
CROOKED RIVER
SISTERS
RIVER
242
TO McKENZIE PASS
97
REDMOND
CITY PARK
CLINE FALLS
126
DESCHUTES
BEND
0
1/2 MI
1/2 KM
RIVER
8TH ST
PILOT BUTTE
NEWPORT AVE
WALL ST
GREENWOOD AVE
14TH ST
DRAKE PARK
FRANKLIN
TO BURNS
COLORADO AVE
DESCHUTES
DIVISION ST
THIRD ST
9TH ST
N
W
E
S
TO MT BACHELOR
TUMALO
BEND
PILOT BUTTE
20
BADLANDS LAVA BEDS
10
CENTURY 372 DRIVE
CASCADE LAKES HIGHWAY
MT BACHELOR
HIGH DESERT MUSEUM
BOYD LAVA CAVE
102
DRY RIVER
BENHAM FALLS
LAVA BUTTE
LAVALANDS VISITOR CENTER
N
W
E
S
SUNRIVER
LAVA RIVER CAVE
0
10 MILES
0
10 KM
97
BIG RIVER
LAVA CAST FOREST
PINE MTN OBSERVATORY
NEWBERRY
NATIONAL VOLCANIC MONUMENT
FALL RIVER
PAULINA LK
LA PINE STATE PARK
OGDEN
103
13
104
EAST LAKE
12
14
LA PINE
PAULINA PEAK
TO KLAMATH FALLS

A footbridge crosses the Deschutes River from Bend's Old Mill District.

BEND

Bend has boomed as the recreation mecca of sunny Central Oregon, but it's also the gateway to the less crowded recreation lands of Eastern Oregon beyond.

Start your visit to Bend at the pine-shaded lawns of **Drake Park**, where Mirror Pond reflects Cascade peaks. At the south end of the park is the 1936 **Pine Tavern** (967 NW Brooks Street), a historic restaurant with a riverside garden. Then stroll to the upscale shops and galleries of **Wall and Bond Streets,** the next two streets up from the river. The centerpiece of this urban scene is the 466-seat **Tower Theatre** (835 NW Wall Street). Built in 1940, it has been restored as a nonprofit venue for concerts, shows, and lectures.

Next head a mile south of downtown to the three silver smokestacks of the **Old Mill District,** a center for shops and restaurants along the Deschutes riverbend where the city began. Stroll a paved riverside trail half a mile downstream to see kayaks surfing in a **whitewater park** created in the river below a footbridge.

High Desert Museum

Burrowing owl.

Plan to spend half a day here touring world-class exhibits of Native American culture, river otters, porcupines, a working sawmill, birds of prey, and more. Admission is $17 for adults ($14 in winter), $14 for seniors, and $10 for children age 5-12. Open 9am-5pm daily except major holidays (10am-4pm in winter), the museum is located 3.5 miles south of Bend on Highway 97 (*highdesertmuseum.org*).

Lava formations in Newberry National Volcanic Monument include Lava River Cave (at left) and the Lava Cast Forest (at right).

Newberry National Volcanic Monument

South of Bend, the giant Newberry volcano has sputtered, collapsed, and leaked lava for half a million years, leaving a vast outdoor museum of geologic oddities. Start at the **Lava Lands Visitor Center** (open Thurs-Mon 9-5, May-Sept), 8 miles south of Bend on Highway 97 near milepost 150. A $5-per-car NW Forest Pass buys entrance to the interpretive center. From there, ride a $3 shuttle bus (departs every 20 minutes 10am-4pm in summer) to the view atop **Lava Butte**, a cinder cone. Then drive one mile south to **Lava River Cave**, a tube-shaped tunnel that's hikable for 1.1 mile underground. Cave admission is $5 if you don't have a Northwest Forest Pass, and lantern rentals run $5.

Next drive another 2 miles south on Highway 97 to milepost 153 and turn left for 9 gravel miles to the **Lava Cast Forest**, where a paved 1-mile loop trail explores a lava flow that inundated a forest, leaving trunk-shaped molds in the rock. Finally drive another 9 miles south on Highway 97 (between mileposts 161 and 162) and turn left on a paved 13-mile road into the heart of the old volcano, where two large mountain lakes fill a 6-mile-wide caldera. Winter snows close the five popular campgrounds at **Paulina and East Lakes** until July. See Hikes #12-14.

Sisters

A charming Western-theme town packed with upscale shops and art galleries, Sisters slows traffic on Highway 20 to a crawl. Crowds are big for the **Sisters Outdoor Quilt Show**, which displays more than 1000 quilts on the second Saturday in July. The **1912 Hotel Sisters** in the middle of town was once a cowboy flophouse. Now the Sisters Saloon & Ranch Grill, it retains its stamped tin ceilings and ornate bar overseen by stuffed animal heads. Explore the streets on either side of Highway 20 to find the pastries at **Angeline's Bakery** (121 W. Main) and the vaulted knotty pine lounge of the **Sisters Coffee Company** (273 W. Hood), across the street from **Paulina Springs Books**, one of Oregon's best independent bookstores..

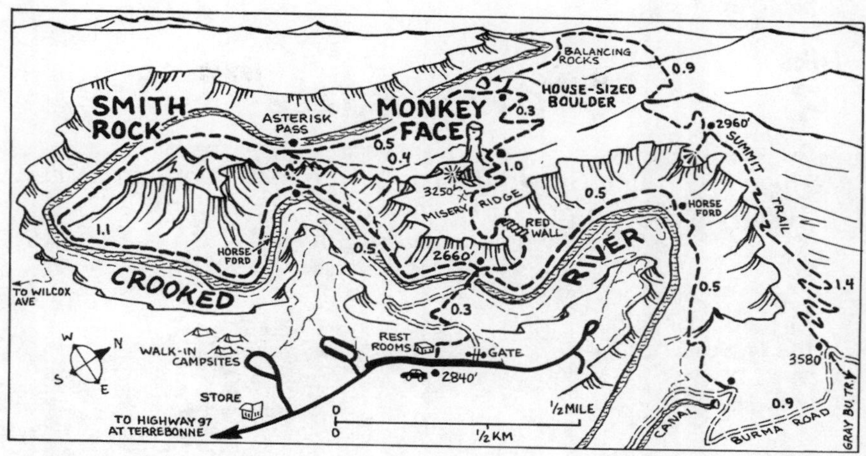

Smith Rock State Park

Smith Rock juts from the Central Oregon lava plains like an orange-sailed ship in the desert. Oregon's most popular rock-climbing area, this park has 3 miles of rhyolite cliffs and Monkey Face, a 300-foot-tall pillar. A 4-mile hiking loop follows the Crooked River downstream past Monkey Face. Drive Highway 97 to Terrebonne (6 miles north of Redmond) and follow park signs east 3.3 zigzagging miles. Expect a $5 parking fee. Walk-in campsites are $8 per person. For a backdoor route to the state park's scenery, start your hike at Gray Butte (Hike #9).

The Crooked River at Smith Rock.

Pine Mountain Observatory

Atop a 6300-foot desert peak where the stars shine bright, this University of Oregon observatory uses its 32-inch telescope for research, but lets visitors peek through 24-inch and 15-inch telescopes for a $5 donation on Friday and Saturday summer nights, starting at sunset. See Hike #11. Check out the observatory's interesting website at *pmo.uoregon.edu*.

The Cove Palisades State Park

Where the Billy Chinook reservoir backs up three rivers into a dramatic cliff-edged desert canyonland, this popular park packs a sunny peninsula with 271 campsites, three ramps for launching powerboats, and a marina. The park even rents log cabins and houseboats that sleep 10. See Hike #8 and page 23.

Hike 9 Gray Butte

The path around Gray Butte is a secret back-door entrance to Smith Rock State Park—avoiding the popular park's crowds and parking fees.

Easy (to Burma Road Pass)
4.8 miles round trip
160 feet elevation gain
Open all year
Use: hikers, horses, bicycles

Easy (to Creson Viewpoint)
3.8 miles round trip
280 feet elevation gain

Gray Butte.

The road to the trailhead at Gray Butte Saddle is rough, but from there an easy hike leads to Smith Rock, traversing sagebrush slopes with views of the Cascades. Another easy segment of the Gray Butte Trail does not lead to Smith Rock, but it's just as nice, spiraling around the peak to a viewpoint bluff. Ambitious hikers can connect the two routes for a longer hike. The area is at its prettiest in spring when wildflowers bloom. Avoid the heat of July and August.

Getting There— Drive Highway 97 north of Redmond 6 miles (or south of Madras 20 miles). At a "Smith Rock State Park" sign in Terrebonne turn east on paved Smith Rock Way. Continue straight on Smith Rock Way for a total of 4.8 miles, ignoring later park signs that tell you to turn left. When the road finally

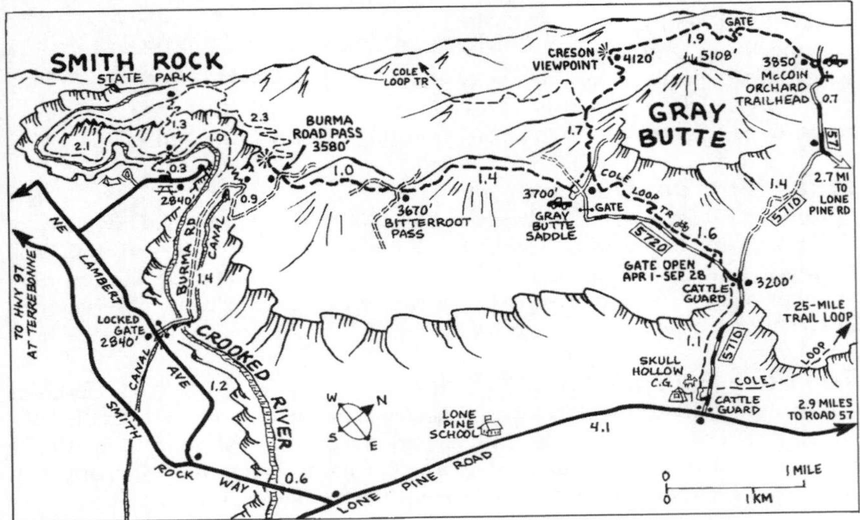

The Three Sisters from the Gray Butte Trail.

ends at a T-shaped junction, turn left on paved Lone Pine Road. After 4.1 miles, follow a "Gray Butte Trailhead" pointer left across a cattle guard onto gravel Road 5710, passing the primitive Skull Hollow Campground.

If you are hauling a horse trailer, park here and take the Cole Loop Trail 2.7 miles to the upper trailhead. If you're planning to hike, drive past the campground 1.1 mile and turn left across another cattle guard onto (unsigned) Road 5720. In winter this road is gated after 0.1 mile. If it's locked, park and hike up the Cole Loop Trail. When the gate is unlocked (from April 1 to September 28), drive up 1.4 rough miles, open a wire gate, and continue up 300 feet to a saddle with a 4-way junction. The main road turns right, but go left 100 feet and park by the trailhead signpost (missing its sign) on the right *(GPS location 44.3994, -121.0982).*

The path begins in a juniper forest but soon emerges onto a hillside of sagebrush. From April to June look among the bushes for lavender cushions of phlox, blue stalks of lupine, white tubes of locoweed, and the big yellow flowers of balsamroot and Oregon sunshine. After 1.4 miles you'll cross a dirt road in a saddle with the pink 2-inch-wide blooms of bitterroot—named *Lewisia rediviva* for Meriwether Lewis, who discovered it on his 1804-06 expedition.

Beyond the bitterroot pass keep straight on the trail another mile to a pass at the crest of Burma Road. On the far side of the road, Smith Rock State Park's Summit Trail switchbacks down to orange cliffs overlooking the Crooked River. Continue as far as you like, but remember that you'll have to climb back up.

The other recommended hike on the Gray Butte Trail begins on the opposite side of the peak beside an ancient orchard. To find this trailhead from Terrebonne, drive Smith Rock Way east 4.8 miles and turn left on Lone Pine Road for 7 miles to Road 57 on the left.

Because the turnoff to this faint road is unmarked, it's easy to miss. In fact, it's safest to drive 0.2 mile farther on Lone Pine Road to the big, well-marked junction with Highway 26. (This intersection is 14 miles south of Madras and 13 miles north of Prineville.) Now turn around, drive back exactly 0.2 mile on Lone Pine Road, and turn right across a cattle guard onto rough, gravel Road 57, passing an old corral. After 1.8 miles veer left to stay on the main road. In another 0.9 mile fork uphill to the right. After another 0.7 mile keep left along the fenced, pioneer McCoin orchard, and then pull into the marked trailhead parking lot on the left *(GPS location 44.4287, -121.0904).*

The trail begins as an abandoned road, but after 0.4 mile becomes a trail through increasingly open sagebrush meadows with flowers and views. The best of all is Creson Viewpoint, a rocky trailside knoll at the 1.9-mile mark. If you're not ready to turn back here, the path continues through dry woods for 1.7 miles to a fork. Left is the Cole Loop Trail down to the Skull Hollow Campground, and right is the trail to Smith Rock described above.

Hike 10 Oregon Badlands

The badlands just east of Bend are a lonely desert labyrinth of jumbled rock and sandy openings.

Easy (Ancient Juniper Trail)
3.3-mile loop
200 feet elevation gain
Open all year
Use: hikers, horses

Moderate (to Flatiron Rock)
6.5 miles round trip
160 feet elevation gain

Easy (to Dry River channel)
3 miles round trip
60 feet elevation gain

Dry River Channel.

Among the surprises in this maze are passageways atop fortress-shaped Flatiron Rock and a cave in the dry channel of a prehistoric river.

The fresh-looking lava here erupted 10,000 years ago, puddled up in a prairie, and then buckled into thousands of ten-foot-tall pressure ridges—in much the same way that paint can wrinkle when it dries. The low spots filled with volcanic sand after Mt. Mazama's cataclysmic eruption powdered the area 7700 years ago.

Bring lots of water, avoid midday heat, wear a big sun hat, and choose loose, long-sleeved clothing. If you stray from the old roads that serve as trails in this area, it's easy to be disoriented, so pack a compass or GPS device. Because this is a designated Wilderness, group size is limited to 12.

Getting There— Drive 16 miles east of Bend on Highway 20 toward Burns. At milepost 16 turn left to the signed Flatiron Rock Trailhead, a rough dirt parking turnaround *(GPS location 43.9576, -121.0514)*.

From the right-hand edge of the parking area, walk past some boulders 50 feet to a mapboard at a T-shaped trail junction. To the left is the return route of the optional loop. So turn right on an ancient sandy roadbed that veers near the highway before heading north.

The desert here is dominated by sagebrush and gnarled, 20-foot juniper trees that can be thousands of years old. Spring brings clumps of yellow, daisy-like Oregon sunshine and the tiny purple blooms of miniature monkeyflower.

After 1.3 miles, veer left at the start of a large triangle where trails meet. A hundred steps farther you'll reach another junction, and you'll face a decision *(GPS location 43.9701, -121.04)*. If you're ready to head back, turn sharply left on the Ancient Juniper Trail, an old roadbed that winds 2 miles back to your car.

If you're headed for Flatiron Rock, however, go straight. Beyond the triangle 1.6 miles you'll reach the 30-foot outcrop of Flatiron Rock *(GPS location 43.9894,*

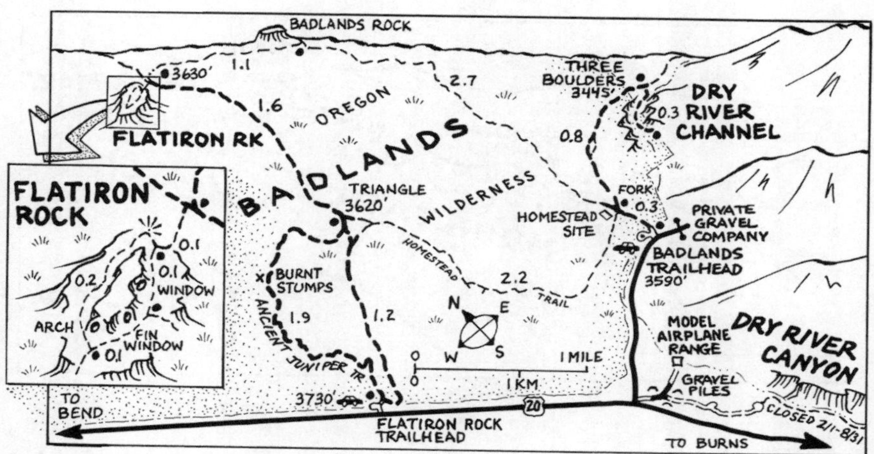

-121.0458). Turn left on a steep sandy path that climbs to the rock castle's parapet, where 10-foot walls line a maze of paths. For a loop, keep right to a viewpoint of distant Mt. Jefferson. Then continue 0.2 mile to a natural arch in a 20-foot pillar. Just beyond, where two slots join, keep left for 0.2 mile to return to Flatiron Rock's entrance. Then turn right to hike back to your car.

The next recommended hike visits a channel of the vanished Dry River. During the Ice Age a tributary of the Deschutes River drained a vast lake on the present site of Millican. Petroglyphs in caves remain from the people who fished here thousands of years ago.

Drive Highway 20 east of the Flatiron Rock Trailhead 1.4 miles (or east of Bend 18 miles). At an "Oregon Badlands Wilderness" sign at the bottom of a hill, turn left on a paved road for one mile. Then turn left into the fenced gravel Badlands Rock Trailhead *(GPS location 43.9536, -121.0147).*

The trail starts as a gated dirt road that's closed to motor vehicles. Walk 0.3 mile to a 3-way fork. You'll want to go right here, but first explore the sagebrush area to the left, a homestead from the early 1900s. A wire fence protects an old cistern. All artifacts are federally protected.

The Dry River channel.

Then take the right-hand fork at the homestead and continue 0.8 mile. Leave the road when you reach *three* large boulders on the right *(GPS location 43.9631, -121.0048).* Take a downhill track sharply to the right and keep to the right for 0.1 mile to a pole fence at the mouth of the Dry River's channel. Beyond is a narrow canyon with 40-foot rock walls. An overhang to the right served as a cave campsite when the river ran with fish, perhaps 6000 years ago. The faint red ochre petroglyphs here can be damaged even by the oil of fingerprints, so don't touch! The canyon peters out after 0.1 mile, where circular pits in the rocks recall the vanished river's swirling waters.

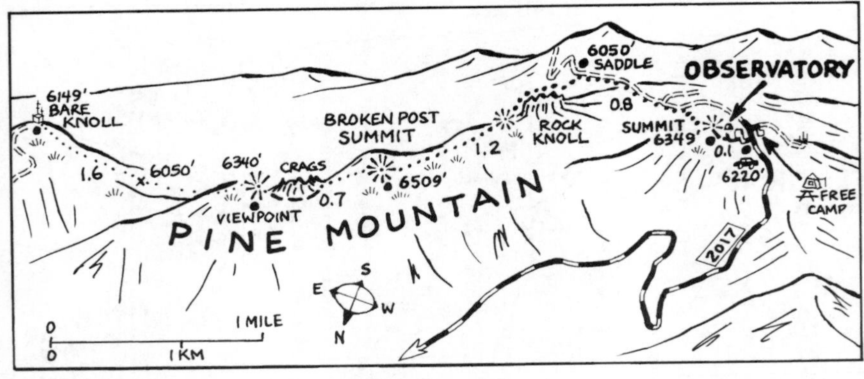

Hike

11 Pine Mountain

This desert summit has a visitable University of Oregon observatory, but the mountain itself is also a star attraction.

Moderate (to crags viewpoint)
5.6 miles round trip
1060 feet elevation gain
Open May to mid-November

The Observatory.

With a bit of easy bushwhacking you can hike from the observatory for 2.8 miles along the open crest of a rolling ridgeline, discovering rock formations, ponderosa pine groves, wildflowers, and views across Eastern Oregon.

Getting There— Drive Highway 20 east of Bend towards Burns for 26 miles. At milepost 26 you'll pass Millican's closed store. Continue another quarter mile to a big green sign for the Pine Mountain Observatory and turn right on a wide red cinder road. After crossing a cattle guard in another 3.3 miles, veer to the right on one-lane gravel Road 2017, climb 4.7 miles to a saddle, and pull into the observatory parking area on the left *(GPS location 43.7917, -120.9412)*. On weekends, volunteers are usually on hand to give observatory tours.

Across the road is a free, primitive campground with picnic tables and an outhouse, but no water. The camp comes in handy if you're planning to stay for nighttime stargazing, but plan to pack out your trash. The public is allowed to use 24-inch and 15-inch reflector telescopes to view the moons of Jupiter, the ring nebula of Lyra, and other wonders every Friday and Saturday night at sunset from the Memorial Day weekend in May through the last weekend of September. Be sure to dress warmly,

After a mile the route along the ridgecrest passes a rock knoll.

show up about an hour before sunset, and bring $5 per person. Flashlights must be small and have red filters. Red filter material can be obtained from staff. Large groups should call 541-382-8331 to confirm a visit.

From the parking area, walk up past a locked green gate marked "Quiet Zone." A ten-foot dome to the right houses the 15-inch telescope, with a surrounding deck of rough-cut juniper lumber. Continue up the road to a larger silver dome on a white concrete block base. This houses the 24-inch scope. Behind is another large dome with a 32-inch research telescope and a smaller dome with a robotic scope manipulated via the Internet. All the telescopes have been placed a little below Pine Mountain's summit to avoid high winds.

For the hike, start beside the white concrete-block observatory and climb a 200-yard trail to the mountaintop. A low stone shelter here serves as a windscreen. Views extend to the Three Sisters and Mt. Jefferson. Twelve-petaled, cream-colored bitterroot flowers bloom among the sagebrush in June.

Long pants, boots, and a sense of adventure are required to bushwhack beyond this point. If you're game, continue straight past a smaller stone circle (due east), descend a steepish sagebrush slope 0.3 mile to a road, and keep left along the road half a mile. Leave the road at a broad forested saddle where the road turns sharply to the right *(GPS location 43.7920, -120.9256)*. Go straight and level on a faint cattle trail amid ponderosa pines. After 0.1 mile, scramble up to the right around a big rock outcrop. Regain the ridgecrest beyond the rock outcrop, and continue along the crest a mile to a summit that is actually the highest point of Pine Mountain, marked only with a broken wooden post.

This is a possible turnaround point, but there's a better view in another 0.7 mile. Continue along the ridgecrest, bushwhacking northeast down through a forest. Cross a semi-open saddle and follow an old cat track left around some rock crags to a viewpoint summit with a post marked "H 530". Although the ridge continues another 1.6 miles to a cluster of radio towers, the route loses a lot of elevation, so this is the place to declare victory and turn back.

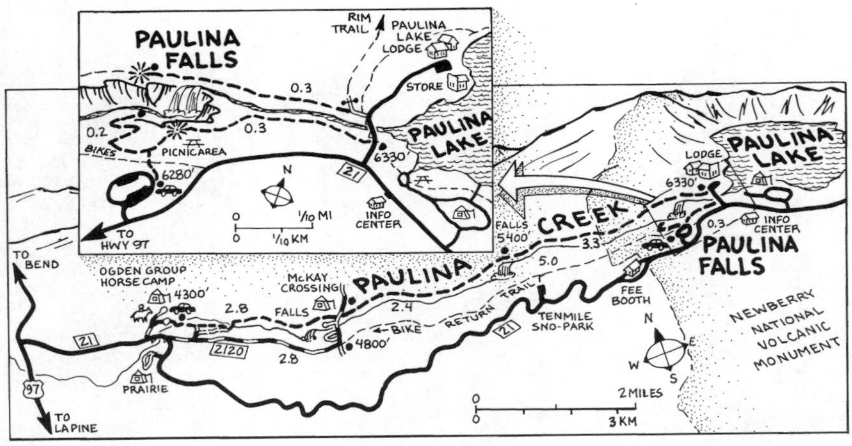

Hike

12 Paulina Falls

Paulina Creek spills from a caldera lake high in the Newberry National Volcanic Monument, tumbles down the volcano's slopes in a series of waterfalls, and meanders across the high desert.

Easy (to falls viewpoints)
1.6 miles round trip
300 feet elevation gain
Open late June to late October

Easy (to McKay Crossing)
5.6 miles round trip
500 feet elevation gain
Open except after winter storms
Use: hikers, horses, bicycles

Difficult (entire trail)
16.6-mile loop
2050 feet elevation gain

McKay Crossing falls.

The 8.5-mile trail tracing the stream is a bit long for a day hike, so most hikers focus on shorter segments—either exploring the spectacular summer viewpoints up at Paulina Falls, or strolling along the lower creek where trails are usually snow-free even in winter.

Getting There— Drive south of Bend 22 miles on Highway 97 (or drive north of La Pine 7 miles). At a "Newberry Caldera" sign between mileposts 161 and 162, turn east on a paved road for 11.3 uphill miles to a fee booth where rangers will check that your car has a Northwest Forest Pass. Then continue 1 mile up this paved road and turn left into the Paulina Falls picnic area.

The trail begins beside a restroom. Walk straight for 300 feet to a railed clifftop viewpoint of two massive, side-by-side 60-foot waterfalls. Most tourists turn back here, but paths lead to two other excellent viewpoints nearby. To find the first, head upstream past the picnic area. You'll discover a lovely trail that follows the creek 0.2 mile up to Paulina Lake's outlet. Horses and bicycles are banned on this path. Turn left across a road bridge, immediately turn left on a spur road, and 50 feet later veer left on a creekside trail that descends 0.3 mile to a railed viewpoint on the far side of Paulina Falls.

To find the third viewpoint, head back to your car, but turn right 50 feet before the parking lot. This trail switchbacks down through the woods 0.2 mile to its end at a decked platform wedged between creek boulders below the falls.

If you'd prefer a longer hike (or if the trail at Paulina Falls is closed by winter snow) try the lower end of the creek's trail instead. To find this route, turn off Highway 97 at the Newberry Caldera exit, drive 2.8 paved miles, turn left at Ogden Group Camp, and follow "Trailhead" pointers to a large gravel parking area for the Peter Skene Ogden Trail.

This path crosses glassy, swift Paulina Creek on a bridge and heads upstream. The creek's meadowed banks form a narrow oasis here, with the dry flora of the high desert on either hand. The sagebrush-like brush is bitterbrush (*Purshia tridentata*)—a member of the rose family, as its tiny blooms reveal. The prominent trailside bunchgrass is known as "needles and thread" because of its needle-like, seed-bearing stalks and curly, thread-like basal leaves.

After a footbridge, half a mile of the path follows the level bed of an abandoned railroad grade, used for logging in the early 1900s. Since then, lodgepole pines have returned in force and ponderosa pines are already a proud 100 feet tall, but occasional 3-foot-thick stumps recall the earlier Central Oregon woods.

At the 2.8-mile mark you'll reach a twisting rock gorge and a 15-foot waterfall just before McKay Crossing Campground. This makes a good turnaround point for an easy hike. If you're out for a challenge, however, continue 5.7 miles upstream to Paulina Lake. Horses and mountain bikes share this route, but bicyclists aren't allowed to zoom back down the same way. Instead they have to ride back on paved Road 21 for 0.2 mile and then veer to the right on a well-marked return trail that follows a powerline 5 miles down to McKay Crossing.

Other Options— Perhaps the best shuttle option for this hike is to drive to Paulina Lake, lock a bicycle at the top of the trail, drive back to the bottom, hike 8.5 miles up to your bike, and then zoom down the paved road to your car.

Viewpoint trails overlook Paulina Falls from both sides.

Hike 13 Paulina Lake

Paulina Lake has the feel of an exotic sea. Deep, azure waters lap against rocky shores. Seagulls cry. Hidden beaches beckon.

Easy (to Warm Springs)
2.4 miles round trip
No elevation gain
Open mid-July through October

Moderate (around lake)
7.5-mile loop
300 feet elevation gain

Paulina Lake in winter.

Despite the oceanic feel, this remarkable lake is actually well over a mile above sea level, and the forested rim that walls it from the outside world is in fact the collapsed caldera of the enormous Newberry Volcano. If all this fails to pique your curiosity, how about a lakeshore hot springs, a gigantic flow of obsidian glass, and a miniature cinder cone crater?

Getting There— Drive south of Bend 22 miles on Highway 97 (or drive north of La Pine 7 miles). At a "Newberry Caldera" sign between mileposts 161 and 162, turn east on a paved road for 11.1 uphill miles to a fee booth where rangers will check that your car has a Northwest Forest Pass. Then continue 1.5 miles to a small information center on the right. If you plan on hiking the entire 7.5-mile loop around the lake, it's best to start here, at the Paulina Day Use Area and boat ramp opposite the information center. Walk to the right on a lakeshore trail that skirts the green edge of the 250-foot-deep lake. The sparse forest here is an odd mix of lowland ponderosa pine and highland firs. Note that the older trees are flocked with glowing green letharia lichen, a sure sign of clean mountain air.

After 2.4 miles you'll reach a paved road. Turn left on the road for 0.8 mile to a trailhead parking area at the far end of Little Crater Campground.

If you're hiking with kids, this is where you should have started in the first place.

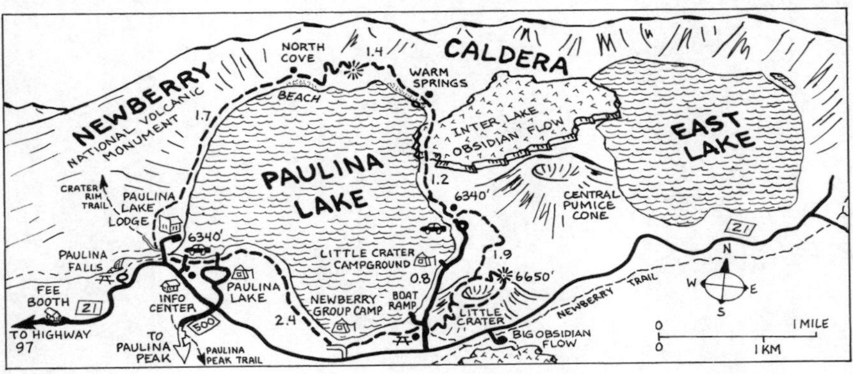

Paulina Lake and Warm Springs beach from the lakeshore trail.

To find this trailhead by car, drive 1.5 miles on the main road past the information center, turn left into the Little Crater Campground entrance, and keep right for 0.9 mile.

From this trailhead, the path continues along a dramatic, rocky part of the lakeshore. The jagged face of Paulina Peak looms across the lake. After 0.7 mile the trail skirts the Inter Lake Flow, passing glassy boulders of banded volcanic obsidian. Then you'll reach Warm Springs' long, meadowed beach, a good turnaround point. Watch for mallards, mule deer, gray jays, and Steller's jays. A 50-foot spur trail leads left to a hot springs on the beach. The hot carbon dioxide gas of this spring bubbles too far out in the lake to be usable until mid-July, but as the lake's level drops it exposes a 6-foot driftwood-and-rock-framed pool in the sand that's just barely large enough for two *(GPS location 43.7295, -121.2467)*. Tents and campfires are not permitted here.

If you're continuing on the loop, you'll climb to a viewpoint with a glimpse of distant, spire-topped Mt. Thielsen and cone-shaped Mt. Scott. Then hike onward to North Cove a day use area with picnic tables and a fine pebble beach suitable for (chilly!) swimming.

Another 1.7 miles brings you to the lake's outlet and the conclusion of the lakeshore loop. Here you can detour left, if you like, to visit Paulina Lake Lodge's boat rental dock and rustic general store.

Other Options— If you add 1.1 mile to the hike you can avoid walking Little Crater Campground's paved road and instead see the cinder cone for which it was named. When you first reach the campground entrance road, turn right a few feet to find a sign for the Little Crater Trail on the far side. The path circles the tiny volcano's crater to a viewpoint overlooking both Paulina and East Lakes.

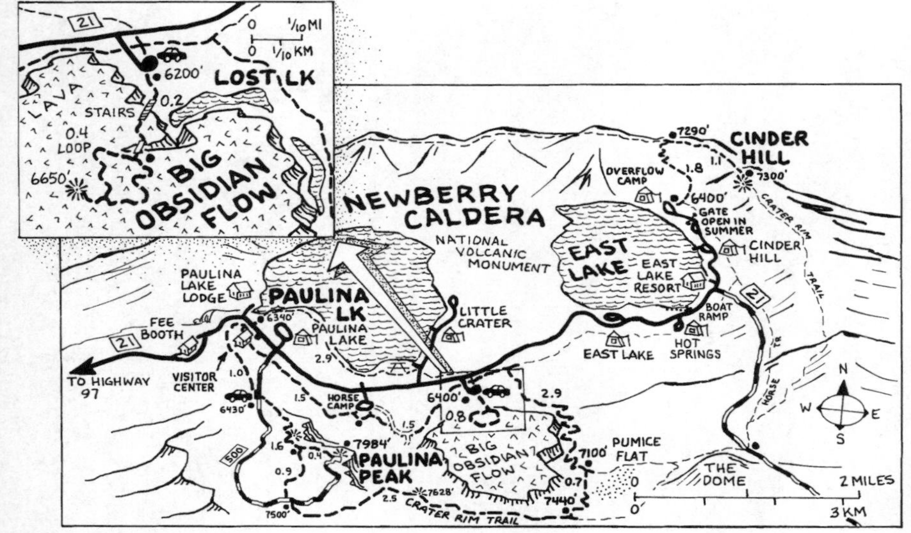

Hike

14 Obsidian Flow

In the ruined shell of Mt. Newberry, an easy nature trail tours the freshest lava flow in Central Oregon, a hill of shiny black obsidian glass.

Easy (Big Obsidian Trail)
0.8-mile loop
450 feet elevation gain
Open late June through October

Moderate (to Paulina Peak)
4 miles round trip
1554 feet elevation gain
Open mid-July through October

Paulina Peak's view in winter.

The Newberry Volcano is the latest protrusion of a geologic "hot spot" that's been moving westward from Idaho for 10 million years, leaving a string of lava flows and volcanic buttes in its wake. Geologists theorize that North America's shearing collision with the Pacific plate has been stretching Oregon diagonally, and lava has been leaking through the cracks.

All that lava has made Newberry the state's most massive volcano, measured by volume. Countless thin basalt lava flows have built up its 25-mile-wide shield-shaped bulk over the past half million years. Like many aging volcanoes, Mt. Newberry's eruptions gradually contained more silica, making the lava thicker, glassier, and more explosive. The entire mountaintop has blown up in Crater Lake fashion at least twice, leaving a gaping, 6-mile-wide caldera. The giant lake that once filled that caldera has since been split in two by lava flows. The largest of these flows, the Big Obsidian Flow, poured more than a square mile of black glass into the caldera just 1300 years ago.

Getting There— Drive south of Bend 22 miles on Highway 97 (or north of La Pine 7 miles). At a "Newberry Caldera" sign between mileposts 161 and 162, turn east on a paved road for 11.3 uphill miles to a fee booth. Rangers here will check that your car has a Northwest Forest Pass, and sell you one if need be. Then continue 3.5 miles on paved Road 21 and turn right into the Big Obsidian Trail's huge parking area. Do not feed the cute, golden-mantled ground squirrels that beg for handouts here, because human food is dangerously unhealthy for them.

Hike a paved path through a picnic area 0.1 mile and then climb metal stairs up the glinting face of the lava flow. The trail skirts a jagged pressure crack in the lava. Much of the rock surface is gray pumice—the flow's frothy scum. Underneath, the silica-rich lava cooled without bubbles to leave shiny obsidian, colored black by a trace of iron oxide. Hike a final 0.4-mile loop to a viewpoint overlooking Paulina Peak (and the distant tips of snowy Mt. Bachelor and South Sister) before returning to your car.

Want to see the better panorama atop Paulina Peak? It's possible to drive there, but the 2-mile trail to the top is spectacular, switchbacking up past colossal cliffs. To find the trailhead, drive the national monument's main road back from the Big Obsidian Trailhead 1.9 miles (or east of the visitor center 0.1 mile), and turn south toward Paulina Peak on Road 500 for 0.7 mile to a big parking pullout on the right. Cross the road to find the segment of the Crater Rim Trail that climbs 2 miles to Paulina Peak. If you have a shuttle car, you could drive up Road 500 another 3.5 miles to the summit and hike back on this trail, all downhill.

Other Options— A quieter 7.4-mile route to Paulina Peak begins at the Big Obsidian Trailhead by a sign for the Silica Trail. Follow this path 0.1 mile to an X-shaped junction, turn right on the Newberry Crater Trail half a mile, and then turn right at a sign for the Lost Lake Trail. After half a mile this path passes near Lost Lake, where you can smell volcanic sulfur. Then the trail switchbacks up through hemlock woods beside the Big Obsidian Flow. Bear right at a fork at the 2.9-mile mark, climb 0.7 mile to the caldera's forested rim, and turn right on the Crater Rim Trail. After another 2.5 scenic miles, cross gravel Road 500 (the path jogs 100 feet to the left), continue 0.9 mile up to a T-shaped junction, and turn right for 0.4 mile to Paulina Peak's summit.

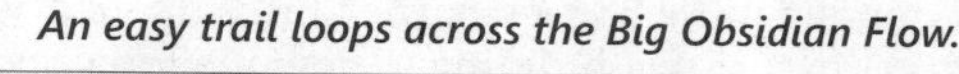

An easy trail loops across the Big Obsidian Flow.

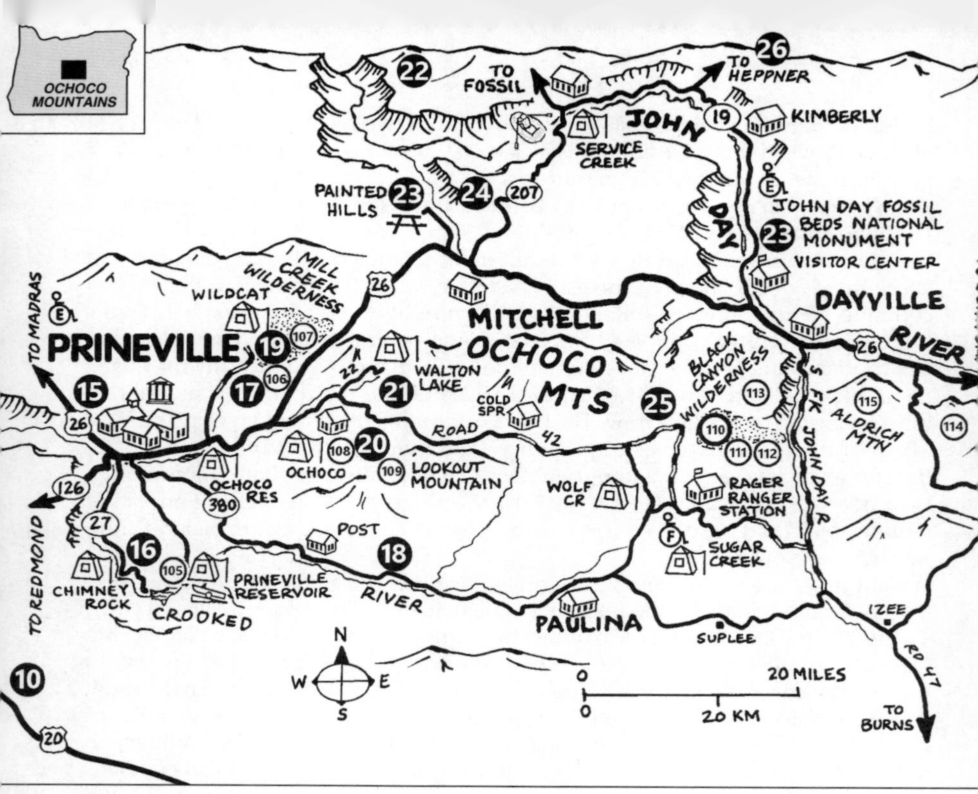

PRINEVILLE

Smack in the geographic center of Oregon, the forested Ochoco Mountains remain so surprisingly undiscovered that many Oregonians can't even pronounce their name (*OH-chuh-co*). The range's high, rounded crest is perhaps prettiest in June, after the snow melts and the wildflowers bloom. To the south, the Crooked River twists through a narrow desert canyon. In the west, Prineville marks the edge of Central Oregon, with its booming cities, pleasure ranches, and increasing sprawl. Founded in 1868 when Barney Prine opened a blacksmith shop, store, saloon, and hotel in a single building, Prineville today boasts a historic county courthouse, three gigantic data centers (Google, Apple, and Facebook), a city-owned railroad line, and the headquarters of the Les Schwab tire store empire.

Bowman Museum

In a stone 1910 bank building, this downtown Prineville museum of local history preserves the original bank's vault room and marble countertops. Exhibits include artifacts from local Indians and pioneers, but the best displays are upstairs, where curators have reconstructed a tack room (complete with old saddles) and a small general store from the early 1900s. Located at the corner of Main and Highway 26, the museum is free, but donations are welcomed. Hours are 10-5 Mon-Fri and 11-4 Sat-Sun from June through August, otherwise Tue-Fri 10-5 and Sat 11-4. Closed January and major holidays *(crookcountyhistorycenter.org)*.

The Crook County Courthouse in downtown Prineville on Highway 26.

Ochoco Reservoir

Conveniently located along Highway 26 east of Prineville 10 miles, this smallish reservoir has a 22-site county park campground (open April-October; 4 teepees rent for $40) and private cafes and lodges. In dry years, expect low water levels.

Walton Lake

Set in the Ochoco Mountains' pine forests, 25-acre Walton Lake has a 29-site campground ($15 fee) with a small swimming beach and a 1-mile shoreline loop trail (see Hike #17). The dam creating the lake was funded by the Prineville chapter of the Izaak Walton League. The campground closes in October and snow blocks the area from December to April. Each spring the lake is stocked with legal rainbow trout that can be caught with flies, lures, or bait. Only rowboats or boats with electric motors are allowed. From Prineville drive Highway 26 east toward John Day 17 miles. Near milepost 35, fork to the right at a sign for Ochoco Creek for 8.3 miles, and then veer left onto paved Road 22 at a sign for Walton Lake 7 miles.

Prineville Reservoir State Park

A dam has backed the Crooked River up into a desert canyonland, creating a lake popular with powerboaters. At the boat ramp, a 67-site state campground, complete with hot showers, charges $21-31 a site. Five rental cabins are available for $89-99. Take Highway 26 east of Prineville 2 miles and turn right, following "Prineville Reservoir" signs 15 paved miles.

Hike 15 Crooked River Wetlands

Prineville's sewage treatment plant beside the Crooked River was a source of embarrassment until city officials realized the ponds had become a huge draw for migrating birds.

Easy
2.9-mile loop
No elevation gain
Open all year
Use: hikers

Tree swallow box.

Prineville has since cleaned up its act, built a network of trails, and opened the area to hikers. A visit here is mostly about birds, so bring binoculars.

Getting There — Drive Highway 126 east of Redmond 19 miles. Immediately before you cross a bridge into the city of Prineville, turn left onto the O'Neil Highway. After 2.1 miles, at the second turnoff for "NW Rimrock Acres Loop," turn right for 0.1 mile to the Crooked River Wetlands Complex on the left. There's a big parking area with a welcome kiosk, picnic shelter, and restroom.

Walk through the picnic shelter and turn right on a paved path behind the restrooms. Curve left at a fork to Kiosk E. A kiosk here describes the Prineville Caldera, formed 29.5 million years ago when a volcanic blast tore a huge hole out of Central Oregon. The same volcanic "hot spot" created the Owyhee canyonlands, the Snake River valley, and Yellowstone National Park as it rampaged east across the continent.

For the recommended 3-mile loop, curve right at "E" around a pond full of birds, scum, and goose poop. Turn left at junctions marked "F" and "G" to follow a wide gravel trail paralleling the mostly unseen Crooked River. Continue straight a mile to the far end of the gravel loop. This is where you'll have the best view of the Crooked River and Gray Butte.

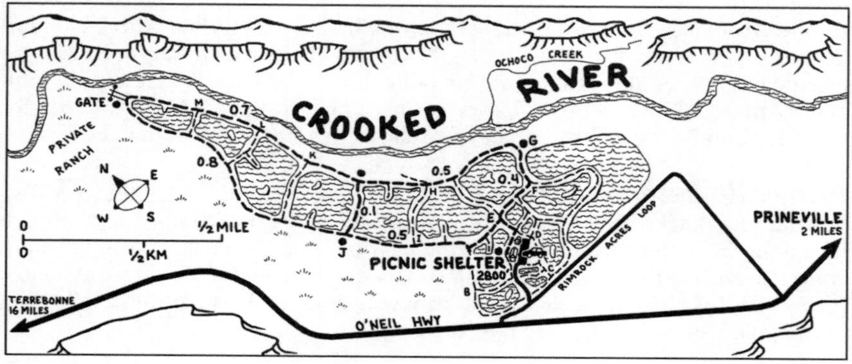

Kiosks beside the ponds describe the area's birds, history, and geology.

Continuing on the loop, note the nesting boxes posted on the fence line every fifty feet. Built and painted by Prineville school kids, these boxes have been claimed by tree swallows that dart in and out of their nests.

Near the end of the loop, when the paved trail turns right, veer left to the "E" kiosk for the shortest route back to the picnic shelter.

Hike 16 Chimney Rock

In one of the crookedest parts of the Crooked River's cliff-rimmed canyon, an easy trail climbs a dry side gulch to a viewpoint beside the thumb-shaped knob of Chimney Rock.

Easy
2.8 miles round trip
500 feet elevation gain
Open all year
Use: hikers, horses

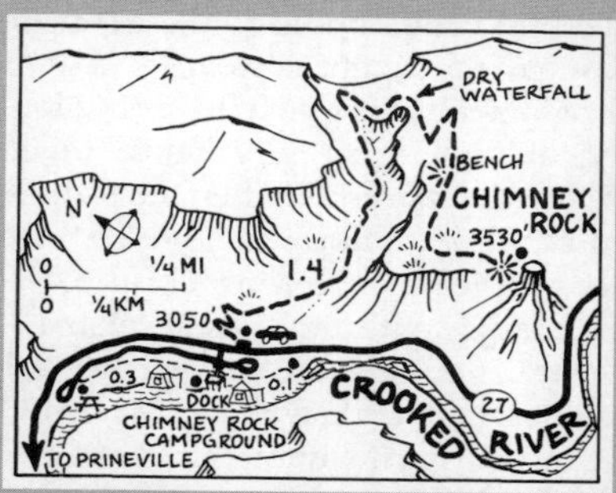

Although this trail is open all year, the nearly shadeless hike can be hot in July and August. After the hike, cross the road to a lovely riverside picnic area and campground, where a short path ambles along the glassy river's cool, grassy bank.

Getting There— Take Highway 26 to the center of downtown Prineville. At a "Fairgrounds" pointer, turn south on Main Street, which soon passes the fairgrounds and becomes Highway 27. After 16.5 miles on this quiet, paved, two-lane road you'll pass a sign for the Chimney Rock Campground on the right.

A campground fishing deck has a view up the the Crooked River to Chimney Rock.

Immediately after the sign, park on the *left* side of the road in a grassy gravel flat with a sign, "Chimney Rock Trailhead."

The trail heads uphill to the left from the parking area, but soon switchbacks across a rocky sagebrush slope to a dry wash. Gnarled old junipers and scurrying lizards inhabit this gulch. In spring look for tiny, bright blue penstemon, purple aster, and white yarrow. After 0.7 mile the path switchbacks up to the rock lip of a 50-foot dry waterfall. Then the trail climbs to a canyon viewpoint with a bench. If you're here in June you'll notice the minty sage smell and showy purple flowers of purple sage. This low shrub looks a bit like sagebrush but is actually in the mint family, so it's not closely related.

The trail ends at a second bench beside Chimney Rock, a 40-foot rimrock tower festooned with cliff swallow nests and bright yellow and green lichen. The view extends across the sinuous chasm of the Crooked River to the distant snowy cones of the Three Sisters.

From this arid perch, the lush green riverbank far below looks like an inviting oasis. To take up that invitation, hike back down the way you came and cross the road to the Chimney Rock Recreation Site. Campsites here cost a mere $8. From a large fishing pier by the entrance signboard, a riverbank path extends both directions. To the left the path leads past campsites 0.2 mile to the grassy tip of an island. To the right the path extends 0.3 mile to a picnic area with restrooms. Watch for redwing blackbirds and zooming swallows against the dramatic backdrop of the far shore's gigantic cliffs.

Hike 17 Steins Pillar

Like a misplaced skyscraper, 350-foot Steins Pillar towers above the forested valley of Mill Creek.

Easy
4 miles round trip
680 feet elevation gain
Open April to mid-December
Use: hikers, horses, bicycles

Steins Pillar.

This odd pink spire remained unscaled until 1950. Skilled climbers still require at least six hours of dangerous work to reach the top. Hikers, on the other hand, can set their sights on a much easier goal: walking the 2-mile trail to the pillar's scenic base.

Getting There— Drive Highway 26 east of Prineville 9.2 miles to the far end of Ochoco Reservoir. Just beyond milepost 28, at a sign for Wildcat Camp, turn left onto Mill Creek Road. Follow this road for 5.1 paved miles and an additional 1.6 miles of gravel. Then, at a pointer for Steins Pillar Trailhead, turn right across a bridge on Road 500. After 2.1 miles, turn left into a well-marked gravel turnaround.

From the parking loop the trail contours 300 feet to a crossing of a small spring-fed creek in a glen. From here the trail climbs up through open woods of small Douglas firs, large ponderosa pines, and some junipers. In spring the slopes are brightened with yellow sunflower-like balsamroot, cushions of lavender phlox, and white death camas.

The path climbs to a viewpoint of the Three Sisters at the 0.4-mile mark and then ambles gradually up and down along a wooded slope. At the 1.8-mile mark the official trail ends at a viewpoint of Steins Pillar. Like Monkey Face at Smith Rock (Page 61), this pink tower is made of rhyolite ash that erupted from a volcano

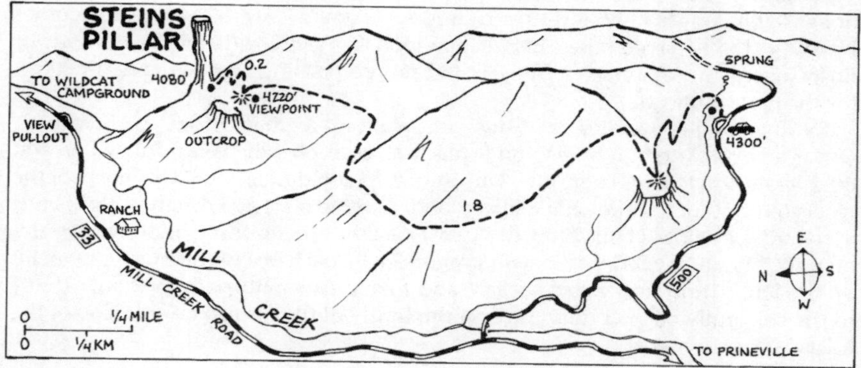

that exploded some 25 million years ago, leaving a large caldera centered on the Prineville area. Erosion has worn away most of the ancient crater.

To continue to Steins Pillar itself, turn sharply right on a smaller path that leads downhill 0.2 mile to the tower's base. Technical gear is required to climb here. But if you walk back up to the viewpoint you'll find a fun rock outcrop nearby where sure-footed scramblers can vent their pent-up mountaineering urges in relative safety, exploring small knolls, caves, and rock windows.

Hike 18 Juniper Hills

Eastern Oregon's colorfully striped Painted Hills are featured in picture books of the state, but did you know this scenery isn't limited to the John Day Fossil Beds National Monument?

Easy (to reservoir)
3 miles round trip
120 feet elevation gain
Open all year

Easy (Painted Hills)
4.8 miles round trip
500 feet elevation gain

Juniper along the trail.

Private ranches throughout the Ochoco Mountains also have "painted" hills. The Nature Conservancy bought one of the best areas and has opened it to respectful hikers. The 13,998-acre Juniper Hills Preserve is on the outskirts of Post, a remote community in the upper Crooked River valley that claims to be the geographic center of Oregon. The Alaska Pacific Ranch once logged pines and ran cattle on a huge spread here. The Nature Conservancy recognized the place as a critical wildlife corridor, both for deer and elk traversing from the Ochocos to the Maury Mountains, and for migratory birds desperate for an oasis on the Pacific Flyway.

Getting There— From Prineville, drive Highway 26 east of downtown's courthouse 0.9 mile to a light and turn right on S. Combs Flat Road (which becomes Hwy 380) for 34 paved miles. Between mileposts 33 and 34 (ten miles beyond the Post General Store), turn left into a wood-fenced parking area with an info kiosk for the first trailhead.

If you are a birdwatcher, start here and walk up a gated gravel road, keeping left at a barn, After 1.5 miles you'll reach a reservoir where tundra swans and other waterfowl tarry. There are some minor "painted hills" outcrops north of the reservoir, but for a more scenic hike, you'll want to start at a different trailhead.

To find the Painted Hills Trail, drive east past the first trailhead another 1.4 miles on paved Highway 380. Just beyond milepost 36, park in a wire-fenced gravel lot on the left. Climb over a locked gate and hike an ancient road track half a mile to the colorfully striped hills. Stay on the trail! Footprints on the soft clay of the hills can last for ages.

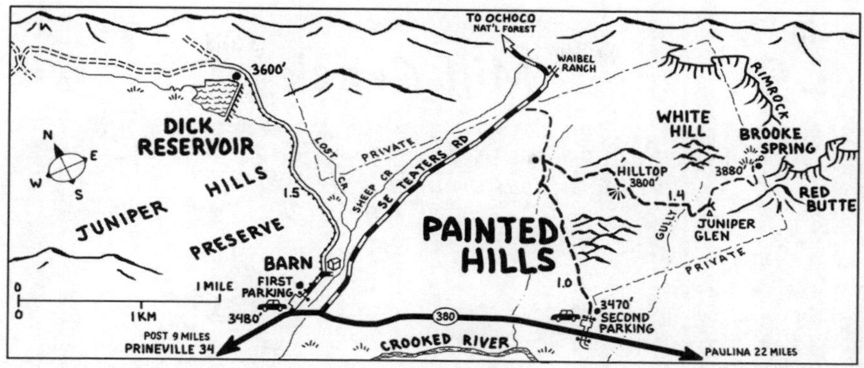

The rounded hills are made of volcanic ash that erupted from the Cascades about 30 million years ago. The ash settled in layers in lakes. When volcanic ash is wet, it gradually turns into clay. Iron, magnesium, and other minerals created the colors. When the Cascades grew tall enough to cut off most rainfall the lakes dried up. The later rise of the Ochoco Mountains exposed the lakebeds to erosion.

Continue half a mile beyond the painted hills and turn right on a faint side track marked "Red Butte". This old dirt road climbs over a hill with a view, crosses a few small dry gullies, and then turns uphill through a glen with a mossy juniper grove. At this point you will have walked 2.1 miles from your car. At a small rock cairn in the juniper glen the ancient road splits three ways and becomes very faint indeed. Keep left, following the gully. The track wanders another 0.2 mile before vanishing in the tall grass of Brooke Spring, where an old cattle trough is backed by rimrock cliffs. Return as you came.

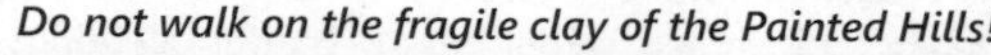

Do not walk on the fragile clay of the Painted Hills!

Hike 19 Mill Creek

Little more than an hour's drive from Bend, the Mill Creek Wilderness is an uncrowded retreat.

Easy (to Ford #4)
2.6 miles round trip
150 feet elevation gain
Open mid-April to early December
Use: hikers, horses

Moderate (to Belknap Trail)
5.8 miles round trip
340 feet elevation gain

Difficult (to Twin Pillars)
11.6 miles round trip
1900 feet elevation gain
Open mid-May to mid-November

Twin Pillars.

For an easy walk, hike up Mill Creek to a meadow. For a longer trip, climb to a viewpoint beside Twin Pillars, a pair of 200-foot volcanic plugs. Part of the route is through woods recovering from a 2000 fire. Cattle are allowed to graze this Wilderness in September.

Getting There — Drive Highway 26 east of Prineville 9.2 miles to the far end of Ochoco Reservoir. Just beyond milepost 28, at a sign for Wildcat Camp, turn left onto Mill Creek Road for 5.1 paved miles and an additional 5.5 miles of gravel. Then fork to the right at an entrance sign for Wildcat Campground and 0.1 mile later turn right into a large gravel parking lot for the trailhead and group camp.

At the parking lot ignore a footbridge to the camp area and instead take the Twin Pillars Trail upstream. In 0.1 mile you'll meet the campground entrance road at a bridge. If you're on horseback, don't cross this bridge; simply cross the road, continue on the main trail a quarter mile, and then splash through the creek at

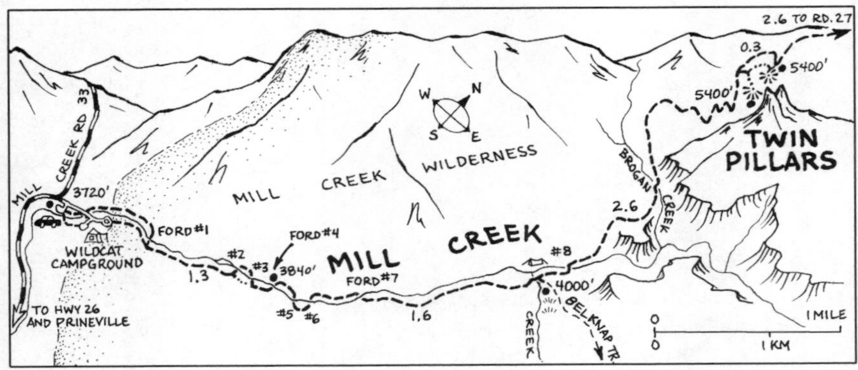

the first ford. If you're on foot, however, cross the bridge into the campground, and keep left 0.1 mile to a "Trail" sign at the far end of the campground loop. This path skips the first and deepest ford of the hike.

The two routes rejoin just beyond ford #1. Then the trail continues upstream through a mixed forest with snowberry, grass, and blue lupine. In early summer, red columbine, purple larkspur, and yellow composites (like balsamroot) bloom in creekside meadows along the way. Butterflies seem to love these meadows too: yellow-and-black swallowtails, blues, coppers, and admirals.

The trail along Mill Creek.

At the 1-mile mark the official trail fords the creek again at the tip of an island. But because the trail recrosses a few hundred feet later, some people simply keep right on a rougher detour path that avoids fords #2 and #3.

Not far ahead, however, is ford #4. This crossing serves as a turnaround point for less adventurous hikers. It's also a great place for kids to play on a small gravel bar. It may be possible to cross dry-footed on a logjam downstream, but fords #5 and #6 generally require an ankle-deep wade. Beyond ford #7 the trail traverses the 2000 fire zone, regenerating nicely with flowers, saplings, and snowbrush.

At the 2.9-mile mark the trail crosses a (sometimes dry) side creek to enter a grassy glade with big ponderosa pine trees and a sign for the faint Belknap Trail. A campsite here makes a good turnaround point *(GPS location 44.4596, -120.5388)*.

If you're headed to Twin Pillars, continue straight on the Twin Pillars Trail. After a quarter mile the path crosses Mill Creek for the eighth and final time (usually an easy rock-hop) and then launches uphill, gaining 1400 feet of elevation in 2.6 hot, shadeless miles. Adventurers with route-finding skills can explore steep, scrambly side trails to the right 0.2 mile to viewpoints beside Twin Pillars. Brightly colored lichens encrust the lava towers. The view across Mill Creek's forests extends to snowy Mt. Bachelor and South Sister.

Other Options — A different 2.6-mile route to Twin Pillars begins on Road 27. This trailhead is also the place for a shuttle car if you want to traverse the Mill Creek Wilderness one way. From Highway 26 in downtown Prineville, turn north on Main Street, which becomes NE McKay Road and then Road 27. Keep right at forks, especially at the 22-mile mark, where Road 27 makes a right-hand turn. In another 6 miles, pavement ends at a fork. Keep right on a dirt road 0.8 mile to the Twin Pillars North Trailhead.

Hike 20 Lookout Mountain

From the wildflower-spangled sagebrush meadows of Lookout Mountain's plateau, views stretch beyond the forested Ochoco Mountains to a string of Cascade snowpeaks.

Moderate
7-mile loop
1220 feet elevation gain
Open June to late November
Use: hikers, horses, bicycles

Mercury mine ruins.

A loop trail here not only visits the summit's old lookout site, but also a rustic shelter and an interesting abandoned mine.

Getting There— From Prineville, drive Highway 26 east toward John Day 16 miles. Just before milepost 35, fork to the right at a sign for Walton Lake. Follow this paved road 8.2 miles to the rentable Ochoco Ranger House (see page 23). A campground behind the building offers campsites for $15.

When you drive 0.1 mile beyond the rental cabin, you'll notice a "Lookout Mountain Trail" sign on the right. This is a much longer, less interesting route to the mountain, so drive on another 0.2 mile to a junction, keep right on paved Road 42 toward Paulina, and continue on this charming two-lane road 6.4 miles to a pass. Here turn right on Road 4205 at a large sign for the Independent Mine.

Just 300 feet up Road 4205 you'll see a giant parking area on the left. If you've brought a horse trailer or a low-slung Ferrari, it's safest to park here at the Round Mountain Trailhead, hike up the road another 50 feet, and take the 0.9-mile trail that angles up to the right to the upper trailhead. Most people, however, choose to shorten the hike by driving up the road a mile to the Motherlode Trailhead. The dirt road is rough and steep, so passenger cars have to take it slow. After 0.7 mile go straight at a junction, ignoring a sign to the old Independent Mine on the left.

At the trailhead, a dirt berm blocks an abandoned road to the old Motherlode mine. Three trails also begin here. Avoid the dusty, steep Motherlode Trail that charges straight uphill. Instead angle up to the left on the gentler Independent Mine Trail for a loop tour. This path climbs gradually through forests that shift from park-like groves of ponderosa pines to thickets of grand fir and finally to storm-stunted subalpine fir.

After a mile the path crests the rocky lip of Lookout Mountain's vast summit mesa. The rimrock is a basalt lava flow that oozed from vents north of the John Day River 25 million years ago, smothering most of the Ochoco Mountains. Today the sagebrush flats atop the old lava bloom each June with yellow desert parsley, mountain bluebells, sunflower-like balsamroot, and wild peony (with reddish bells

Cliffs at Lookout Mountain's lookout site.

on a lush bush). Look for yellowbell lilies where snow patches have just melted.

Continue up and down across the rolling plateau 3 miles, ignoring two side trails to the left, to reach a junction at an old stone corral on a summit's cliff edge. For the loop, you'll turn right on the Lookout Mountain Trail, but first inspect the corral, where the mountain's namesake lookout building once stood.

Then return to the loop trail, following the Lookout Mountain Trail downhill to the right 0.2 miles. Detour on a 100-yard side path to the right to find a 3-sided log snow shelter, built primarily for Nordic skiers and snowmobilers.

Beyond the shelter turnoff 0.3 mile, the loop trail forks. If you're tired you can save a mile by bearing right on the Motherlode Trail. It's more interesting, however, to keep left. The Lookout Mountain Trail descends gently through woods. Just before your car, this path passes a derelict 3-story mine building and a collapsed shaft with ore cart rails. Don't explore off the trail because the red cinnabar ore mined here was processed into poisonous mercury, and the mine may still be contaminated.

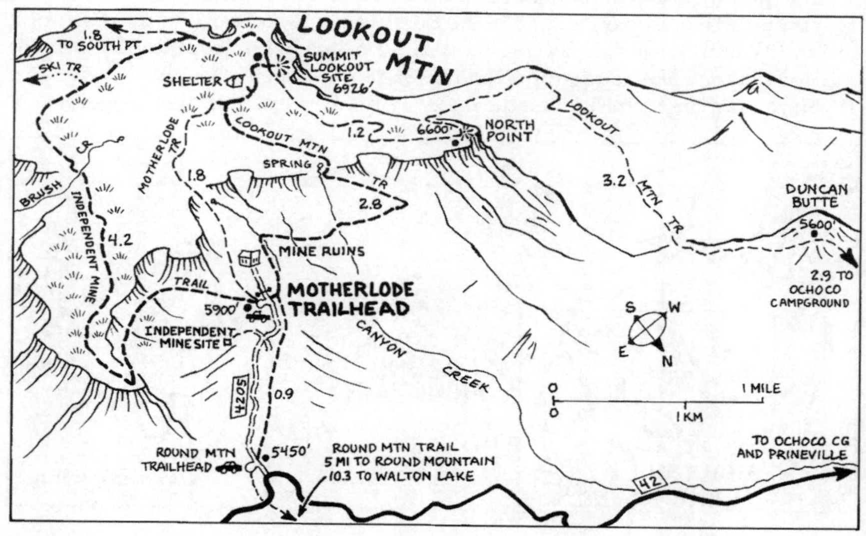

Hike 21 Walton Lake

For a sample of what's great about the Ochoco Mountains, camp beneath the ponderosa pines at Walton Lake, stroll around the shore, and then hike to Round Mountain.

Easy (around Walton Lake)
0.8-mile loop
No elevation gain
Open May to late November
Use: hikers only

Difficult (Road 42 to summit)
10 miles round trip
1720 feet elevation gain
Use: hikers, horses, bicycles

Difficult (entire trail, with shuttle)
10.5 miles one way
1720 feet elevation gain

The Three Sisters from Round Mtn.

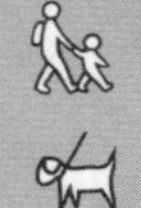

From the sunny wildflower fields atop Round Mountain, views swivel from Big Summit Prairie to the distant snowpeaks of the Cascades.

Getting There— From Prineville, drive Highway 26 east toward John Day 16 miles. Just before milepost 35, fork to the right at a sign for Walton Lake. Follow this paved road 8.5 miles to a junction where a sign for Walton Lake points left onto Road 22.

Note this junction where Road 22 leaves Road 42, because the two roads lead to two trailheads, one on either end of the Round Mountain Trail. For the easy stroll around Walton Lake, turn left on Road 22 for 6.4 paved miles and then turn left into the Walton Lake Campground entrance to an X-shaped junction with a fee box. If you're camping, turn right on the one-way road around the lake, choose one of

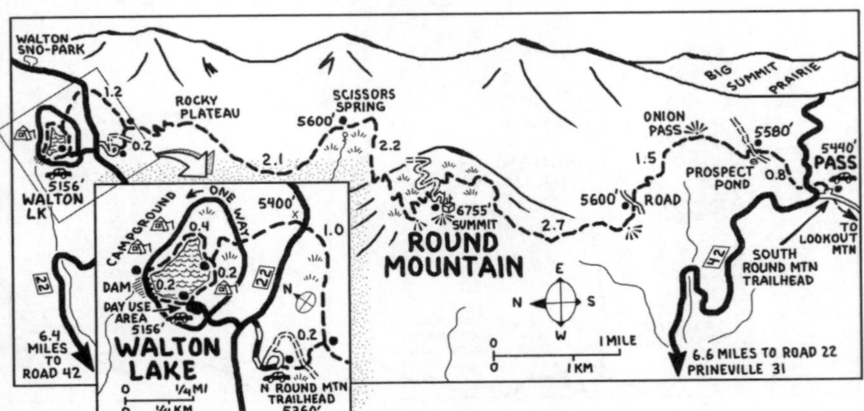

the 31 sites, and return here to pay the $15 fee. If you're just hiking, pay a $5 day-use fee and drive straight ahead to a parking lot by the boat ramp and picnic area.

Walton Lake is actually a shallow 18-acre reservoir, partly covered by duckweed. It was originally dammed to provide water to miners at Scissorsville, a few miles southwest. The Izaak Walton League, a conservation group that promotes fishing, bought the water rights, improved the dam, and renamed the reservoir in 1960.

The 0.8-mile loop around the lake is packed gravel, so it's wheelchair accessible. Pets must be on leash. Just 0.2 mile to the right of the day-use area, a connector trail up through a meadow to the right climbs a mile to the Round Mountain Trail, but this isn't the shortest route to Round Mountain, and it won't work for horses or bikes, because they are not allowed on the lakeshore loop.

If you're headed to Round Mountain, it's better to start at a different trailhead. Remember the junction of Roads 22 and 42? When you drive there from Prineville, simply go straight on Road 42 for another 6.6 miles. At a pass, turn uphill to the right 300 feet on a dirt road and pull into the large, well-marked Round Mountain South Trailhead on the left *(GPS location 44.3492, -120.3481)*.

The path briefly descends to cross the paved road, and then climbs 0.8 mile to cross a gravel mining road. A small, polluted pond remains in the prospect's open pit to the left. Next the path traverses a lovely slope with big ponderosa pines and views east to the giant, crater-like bowl of Big Summit Prairie, once an important Paiute summer camp. Cross a rocky pass where wild onions bloom and descend until you cross a dirt road at the 2.3-mile mark.

For the next 2.7 miles the trail climbs through ever grander meadow openings that blaze with yellow balsamroot in June. When you finally reach a gravel service road, follow it left 0.3 mile to the radio towers on Round Mountain's rocky summit.

If you have left a shuttle car at Walton Lake, it's just as easy to continue there as to return to Road 42. If you're continuing, walk down the summit road 0.1 mile and turn left at a sign for Walton Lake. This path descends with a dozen switchbacks in a steep hellebore meadow. After 2.2 miles the trail passes Scissors Spring, a possible campsite with a series of cattle troughs and a pipe with the only water on the route. After another 2.1 miles the trail forks. Walton Lake is a mile to the right; left is a 0.2-mile path to the North Round Mountain Trailhead, a big gravel loop on a spur road that's almost opposite the Walton Campground entrance.

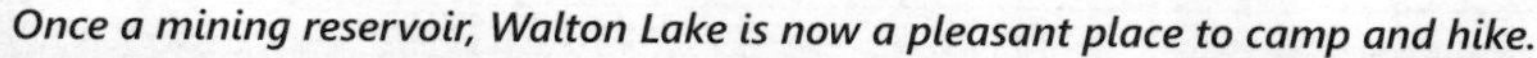

Once a mining reservoir, Walton Lake is now a pleasant place to camp and hike.

Hike 22 Spring Basin

Hedgehog cactus blooms on the panoramic heights of this arid canyonland above the John Day River.

Moderate (to green knoll)
3.8 miles round trip
1060 feet elevation gain
Open all year
Use: hikers, horses

Difficult (to Horse Mountain)
8.2 miles round trip
1590 feet elevation gain

Hedgehog cactus.

If you're eager to hike or backpack early in spring, when Oregon's other mountains are under snow, the Spring Basin Wilderness is often the sunniest, greenest place around. Avoid summer's heat. The name suggests the existence of a spring, but there is essentially no water in this area except during infrequent rainstorms. Day hikers should bring a couple of quarts and backpackers will need a gallon per person per night. The only trails are faint old Jeep tracks, but it's easy to hike cross-country, so bring a map.

Getting There— From Interstate 84, drive 18 miles east of The Dalles to Biggs exit 104 and take Highway 97 south 59 miles. In the "ghost town" of Shaniko, turn left onto Highway 218 for 8 miles to Antelope. (If you're coming from Central Oregon, take Highway 97 north of Madras 18 miles and turn right for 12 miles to Antelope). From Antelope, follow Highway 218 east 15 miles to Clarno. Beyond the John Day River bridge 1.5 miles, turn right onto gravel Clarno Road for 3.2 miles.

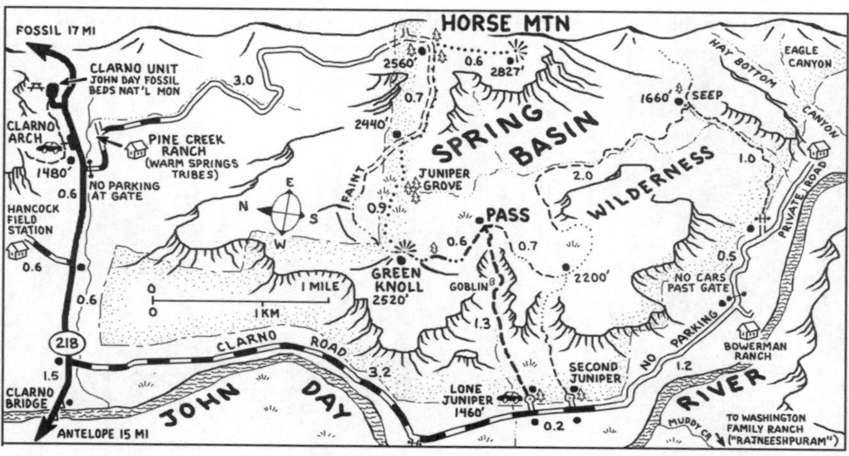

There is a juniper grove in Spring Basin, but no spring.

The trailhead is easy to miss! After driving 2.8 miles along Clarno Road, the road turns sharply left, with private gated roads to the right. Continue 0.8 mile, watching for a faint road that leads 100 feet up to the left to a lone 15-foot-tall juniper tree *(GPS location 44.8728, -120.441)*.

Park by the juniper and hike past a brown "BLM Wilderness" boundary post on a faint trail through the bunchgrass toward a draw on the horizon. The trail ascends a gully where balsamroot sunflowers bloom yellow in April. Purple sage and orange mallows flower in May. Grasshoppers and songbirds are everywhere.

After 1.3 miles you'll crest a pass where a rock cairn marks a faint T-shaped junction amid bunchgrass *(GPS location 44.878, -120.4207)*. Turn left, following a very faint Jeep track up and down along the broad crest of this ridgetop. The hedgehog cactus here has pink blooms from late March to early May.

After half a mile you'll pass a dead juniper snag by some boulders. Continue a tenth of a mile up to the high point of the road and a big rock cairn atop a broad green knoll with views in all directions. This makes a good turnaround point, in part because the track ahead becomes too faint to follow.

If your goal is the grander viewpoint atop Horse Mountain, strike out cross-country, heading due east 0.6 mile to a juniper grove in the heart of Spring Basin *(GPS location 44.8840, -120.4166)*. This is a scenic place to camp, sheltered from the wind. If you continue due east another 0.3 mile up a draw, you'll reach a ridgecrest where the old road is once again clear. Follow it ahead (and to the right) along the ridge 0.7 mile until the road turns sharply left in another juniper grove *(GPS location 44.8832, -120.4016)*. Leave the road here and bushwhack to the right up a ridge 0.6 mile to the rocky summit of Horse Mountain *(GPS location 44.8767, -120.4005)*, overlooking a jumble of buttes and canyons.

Other Options— This wilderness has two other trailheads. One is another 0.2 mile south along Clarno Road, beside another lone juniper—but the faint trail here peters out in a canyon. The other trailhead is the paved Clarno Arch parking area on Highway 218. This pullout is primarily used by people hiking a quarter mile up to a natural rock arch (Hike #23). But you can also walk south along Highway 218 a tenth of a mile and turn left past a locked gate onto a gravel road for the Pine Creek Ranch, owned by the Confederated Tribes of Warm Springs. The tribes allow hikers and equestrians to cross their land on a road that climbs 3 miles to the Spring Basin Wilderness, but ask that you sign in at a kiosk at the ranch.

Hike 23 John Day Fossil Beds

Nearly 100 miles of highway separate the three parts of the John Day Fossil Beds National Monument.

Moderate (Blue Basin overlook)
4-mile loop
800 feet elevation gain
Open all year
Use: hikers only

Easy (4 Painted Hills Unit trails)
2.6 miles round trip
360 feet elevation gain

Easy (2 Clarno Unit trails)
1.2 miles round trip
280 feet elevation gain

Painted Cove Trail.

Stop at each of the national monument's three areas to take short hikes. Collecting fossils is banned here, but it is allowed in the town of Fossil (see page 20).

Getting There— Drive Highway 26 east of Prineville 83 miles (or west of John Day 38 miles) to Picture Gorge's canyon and turn north on Highway 19 for 2 miles to a free visitor center on the left (open daily 9am-5pm in summer, closed Tuesdays and Wednesdays in winter). Here you can watch a short movie, tour dioramas of the fossil beds' history, and see some of the best fossils. Then drive across the highway to the historic Cant Ranch, restored as a museum with indoor ranch house exhibits, a sheep-shearing barn, working hayfields, and an orchard where you can pick fruit.

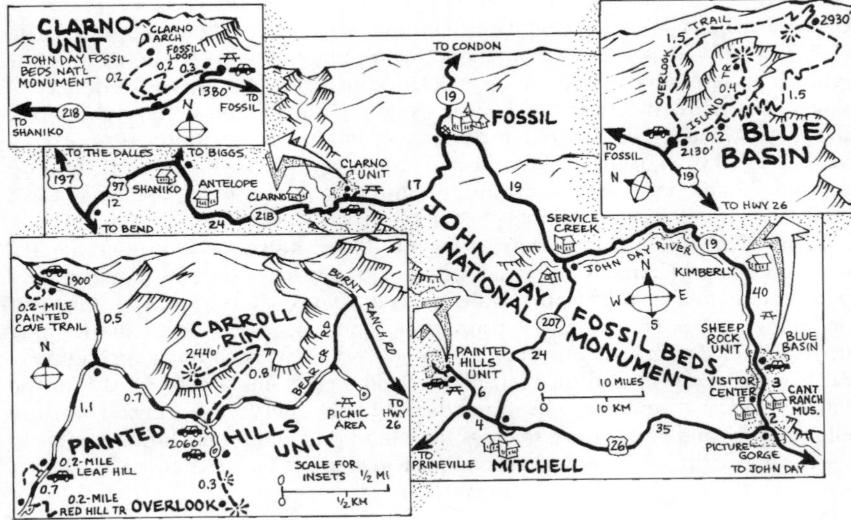

Sheep Rock from the visitor center.

For the first recommended hike, drive north of the visitor center 3 miles and turn right into the Blue Basin trailhead. If you're pressed for time, head to the right on the Island in Time Trail, which ambles 0.6 mile up a green creekbed to trail's end in an eerie badlands canyon of volcanic ash. If you have more time, start by keeping left on the Blue Basin Overlook Trail. This 3.2-mile loop path climbs, steeply at times, around the scenic canyon's rim. Then it descends in 21 switchbacks.

After visiting Blue Basin, drive back 5 miles south on Highway 19 and turn right on Highway 26 for 38 miles. Beyond Mitchell 4 miles (between mileposts 62 and 63), turn north on Bridge Creek Road at a sign for the Painted Hills. After 5.5 miles, turn left on Bear Creek Road for 1.1 mile, mostly on gravel, and then turn left 0.2 mile to the Painted Hills Overlook parking area.

The rounded, colorfully striped Painted Hills began as ash that erupted from the ancestral Cascades 30-40 million years ago. A meandering river deposited the ash in a broad valley here. The resulting claystone was colored red by iron in wetter areas with more organic material. Footprints last for years in the soft soil, so stay on designated paths.

Five trails explore the Painted Hills (see map). First stroll out the 0.3-mile path to the Painted Hills Overlook. Then drive another 1.2 miles to the Painted Cove Trail, a 0.2-mile loop with a boardwalk that crosses the colorful claystone. If you have more time, don't miss the 0.8-mile climb to a viewpoint atop Carroll Rim's lava rimrock. The fourth path, the 0.2-mile Leaf Hill Loop, visits a 30-foot hill of leaf fossils. The fifth, the Red Hill Trail, ends halfway around a 100-foot cone of red and yellow ash.

The third unit of the national monument at Clarno is more than 60 miles away. To find it, drive back to Mitchell, turn north on Highway 207, follow signs 43 miles north to Fossil, and turn left on Highway 218 for 16 miles to the Clarno Unit picnic area on the right. If you reach the John Day River bridge you've driven 3.4 miles too far. From the picnic area the trail parallels the highway 0.3 mile. Then turn uphill to the right on the Trail of the Fossils, a 0.2-mile loop lined with boulders that fell from the rimrock. The rock began as volcanic mud flows 45-50 million years ago. The strata are riddled with leaf fossils from the subtropical forests that were inundated by the eruptions. At the end of the loop, keep right on a path that climbs 0.2 mile to the rimrock itself, where water erosion has carved a tall hollow into the cliff, topped with a dainty 10-foot arch. At this desert viewpoint, crickets chirp, crows squawk, and peregrine falcons swoop past, hunting cliff swallows.

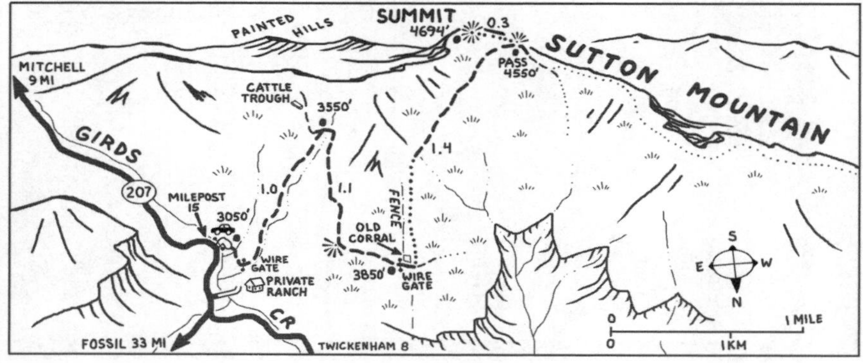

Hike
24 Sutton Mountain

This arid, meadowed mountain beside the Painted Hills is a candidate for a new National Monument. Hike to a cliff-edge summit viewpoint to see what's at stake.

Moderate
7.6 miles round trip
1650 feet elevation gain
Open mid-March thru November
Use: hikers, horses

Sutton Mountain from the Painted Hills.

Spring is the best time to visit, when lupine and even hedgehog cactus bloom on these slopes. The flower show peaks from late April to late June. Fall is also nice. Avoid midsummer's blazing heat. Whenever you come, bring a sense of adventure and sturdy boots because the upper part of the route involves cross-country travel on uneven terrain.

Getting There— Drive Highway 26 east of Prineville 48 miles (or west of John Day 73 miles) to the little city of Mitchell. At the west edge of town, near milepost 66, turn north on Highway 207, and follow this paved two-lane road 9.3 miles. The unmarked trailhead turnoff is on the left 100 feet beyond milepost 15, but that post is easy to overlook. If you reach a signed junction with Girds Creek Road you've driven too far; turn around and drive back 0.3 mile. Then, 100 feet before milepost 15, turn right into a small dirt driveway through the willow brush along Girds Creek. Open a wire gate marked only by a tiny BLM sign: "Report Crime; These Are Your Public Lands." Park in a cow-trampled meadow on the far side of the creek *(GPS location 44.664, -120.1243)*. Camping is permitted here, although there are no facilities.

Blue lupine blooms in Sutton Mountain's meadows

From the parking meadow, walk to the right along a fence on a faint grassy cow track for 400 feet. Walk around a locked metal gate marked "Area closed to all motorized use." The old roadbed beyond, now a cow path, crosses a dry grassland with a few juniper trees. Just before a private horse barn, turn left to follow the grassy old roadbed up a dry wash.

At the one-mile mark, ignore a big cattle trail from the left. Instead, curve to the right across the dry wash on the old roadbed. Another 0.7 mile brings you to viewpoints where the sparse juniper forest yields to slopes of sagebrush and wildflowers. Soon the trail levels out in fields of red and yellow paintbrush, yellow stonecrop, blue flax, and sweet-smelling blue lupine.

At the 2.1-mile mark you'll reach an open wire gate by an old corral. The roadbed appears to end here *(GPS location 44.6666, -120.1436)*, but go straight 60 feet and turn uphill to the left on the far side of an old wire fence. Follow this fenceline straight uphill through a bunchgrass-meadowed slope. After another 0.6 mile the fenceline peters out, atop a broad prairie, but continue straight toward the summit, now the highest point on the horizon ahead.

Eventually the ancient roadbed will again become visible; follow it as it angles up to the right to a pass with views west to Mt. Jefferson. But the views are even better if you bushwhack up to the left along the rimrock cliff edge 0.3 mile to Sutton Mountain's summit, where lichen encrusts the rocks and a stalwart 10-foot juniper tree provides shade. Return as you came.

Hike 25 Spanish Peak

A trail on the crest of the Ochoco Mountains connects the views and wildflowers at Spanish Peak with a historic mining ditch along forested Rock Creek.

Moderate (to Fir Tree Creek)
7.6 miles round trip
620 feet elevation **loss**
Open late May to mid-November
Use: hikers, horses, bicycles

Moderate (to Spanish Peak)
7.9-mile loop
1000 feet elevation gain
Open early June to mid-November

Rock Creek's ditch trail.

For a day hike, try either end of this trail system. If you have a shuttle car, you can hike the entire route one way, mostly downhill.

Getting There— Drive Highway 26 east of Prineville 48 miles to Mitchell and continue 13 miles toward John Day. At a sign for Forest Road 12, turn right on a paved road that passes Barnhouse Campground and turns to gravel. Stick to Road 12 for 15.4 miles. At a crossroads, turn left onto gravel Road 1250 for 3.9 miles. At another 4-way junction turn left onto gravel Road 38 for 1.7 miles to the Rock Creek Trailhead parking area on the left *(GPS location 44.3554, -119.7826)*.

The 23.5-mile Ochoco Mountain Trail starts here. For a day hike along it, amble across a meadow of blue lupine and scattered pines, descend 0.4 mile to a footbridge across 15-foot-wide Rock Creek, and then follow the creek down through lovely meadows and stands of lodgepole pine.

At the 2.4-mile mark, the trail drops to the Waterman Ditch, a flume begun in the late 1800s by E. O. Waterman to supply the Spanish Gulch Gold Mining District to the north. When you reach Fir Tree Creek, in a swale of larkspur and coltsfoot, continue 100 feet to the ruin of the ditch-builders' log cabin, a good turnaround point.

For the hike on Spanish Peak, you'll need to drive to a high trailhead on a much rougher road. Passenger cars can accomplish this if they're driven slowly.

Drive east on gravel Road 38 past the Rock Creek Trailhead 3.1 miles to a 4-way junction and turn uphill to the left on rough, rocky Road 200 for 3.5 slow miles. Park at a trailhead pullout where rock cairns mark the crossing of the Ochoco Mountain Trail *(GPS location 44.3997, -119.7585)*. Road 200 does continue to Spanish Peak's summit, but it becomes too rough for cars.

Start hiking to the left from the trailhead, on a faint, level trail across a lupine meadow, following rock cairns. After 0.8 mile a lush growth of hellebore (corn lily) obscures the tread near the headwater spring of Baldy Creek, but keep traversing. At the 1.4-mile-mark, cairns mark a junction with the spur trail to the summit. Continue straight, traversing around Spanish Peak and down a rim 2 miles to a big clifftop cairn *(GPS location 44.4073, -119.7988)*. Views include most of the Ochoco

Spanish Peak from the rim cairn.

Range and the John Day Fossil Beds canyonlands.

If you have left a shuttle car at the lower Rock Creek Trailhead, simply hike onward 2.5 miles down to the ditch trail and then hike up Rock Creek 7 miles to your car. If you don't have a shuttle, hike back from the rimrock cairn 2 miles to the trail fork on Spanish Peak's flank *(GPS location 44.3993, -119.7769)*. For a loop to the summit, turn uphill to the left, follow cairns 0.4 mile to Road 200, and turn left for 0.4 mile to the summit itself, where four concrete lookout tower foundations remain amidst wind-mown grass, lupine, and sagebrush. After absorbing the view, follow Road 200 back downhill 1.7 miles to your car.

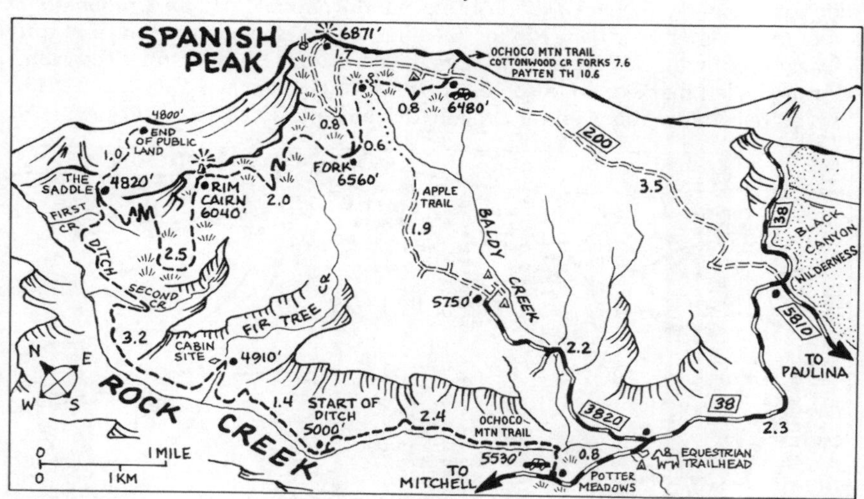

Hike 26 Madison Butte

Any excuse is good for a road trip "to Morrow" — that is, to Morrow County. But this one might get you to pack the car.

Difficult
8.8 miles round trip
2540 feet elevation gain
Open mid-May through November
Use: hikers, horses, bicycles

Madison Butte's lookout tower.

The dry desert canyonlands east of Fossil are hiding a forested mountain with alpine wildflowers, a shady trail, and patches of snow that linger until June. Madison Butte is obviously in a mountain range, but which range is it? Maps don't name it. Locals claim it's part of the Blue Mountains, but the rest of those peaks are 100 miles to the east.

Getting There— If you're coming from The Dalles, drive I-84 east 16 miles, turn right on Highway 97 for 10 miles to Wasco, and turn left on Highway 206 for 51 miles to Condon. At a Y-junction at the southern end of Condon, veer left to stay on Highway 206 toward Heppner. This is an extremely quiet and extremely beautiful paved road, passing ghost towns, wind farms, and canyon ranches. After 32 miles, at a derelict settlement marked "Ruggs", turn right on Highway 207 toward Spray. Follow this paved road 15 miles, climbing into ponderosa pine woods to Anson Wright Memorial Park, a county campground with showers. Continue another 0.3 mile past the park. Then turn left on gravel Sunflower Flat Road for 3.7 miles, fork left onto gravel Tupper Lane 673 for 3.5 miles to an X-shaped junction, and turn left again, following a "Tupper Work Center" pointer for 1.3 miles to a dirt parking spur on the left marked "Madison Butte Tr 3054" *(GPS location 45.068 -119.4949).*

If you're coming from Central Oregon, drive Highway 26 east of Prineville 48

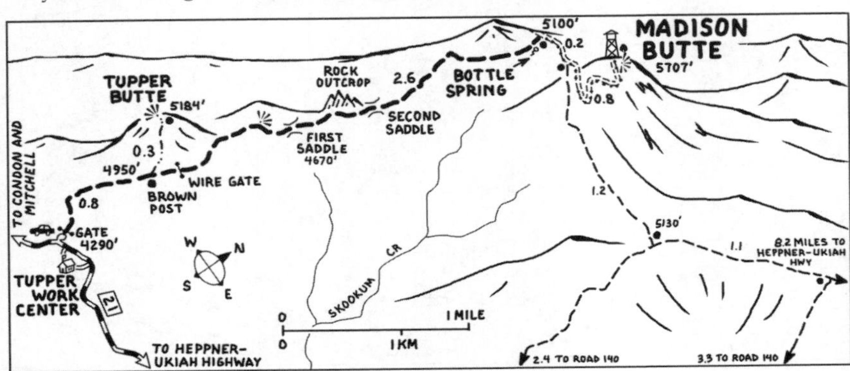

Rock formations along the trail.

miles. Just before Mitchell, turn left on Highway 207. Stick to this paved highway for 51 miles, following signs for Spray and Heppner (if you reach Anson Wright Memorial Park you've gone 0.3 mile too far). Then turn right on gravel Sunflower Flat Road as described above.

If you're coming from the east, drive Highway 395 halfway between John Day and Pendleton. At Ukiah, turn west on paved Road 53 toward Heppner for 22 miles (if you reach Coalmine Hill Campground you've gone 0.3 mile too far). Then turn left on gravel Road 21 for 18.7 miles to the Madison Butte Trailhead on the right, just beyond the Tupper Work Center.

The first 0.8 mile of the trail climbs steeply through sparse ponderosa woods to a rocky meadow slope with a brown post. Theoretically a spur trail to the left climbs 0.3 mile to Tupper Butte, a lesser knoll, but that path is awfully faint.

Madison Butte from the trail near Bottle Spring.

Instead continue straight on the main trail, which soon levels out, crosses a wire gate that leaves all trace of cattle behind, and enters a magical woodland of Douglas fir and larch, with big white ladyslipper orchids, orange paintbrush, and red columbine.

The trail continues up and down and up again another 2.6 miles to a dirt road at Bottle Spring. Parts of this path are just faint enough that some route-finding skill comes in handy. From Bottle Spring (a piped seep amid tall grass), follow a dirt road up to the right for a mile to its end at Madison Butte's summit.

Although the lookout atop the 30-foot tower is usually locked, you can climb the metal staircase most of the way up. Mt. Hood is a dim white ghost on the horizon to the west. To the east, forested hills extend all the way to the Elkhorn Range of the Blue Mountains. To the south, across the arid canyonlands of the John Day River, a faint pyramid on the horizon is Strawberry Mountain. Where else can you see so much of Eastern Oregon at once?

JOHN DAY

With snowy peaks and mountain lakes, the Strawberry Range seems like a chunk of the Canadian Rockies dropped in the midst of Eastern Oregon's ranchlands. One of the prettiest drives in Oregon traces the John Day River from the lava canyon of Picture Gorge through John Day to the base of the range. In downtown John Day, stop for a look at the **John Day Historic Church,** with its white wooden steeple and Carpenter Gothic frills. On the west edge of town, the City Park has the county's only **public swimming pool,** an inexpensive treat on a summer day.

Kam Wah Chung Museum

Chinese gold miners built this two-story stone structure in the late 1860s as a combination pharmacy, cultural center, temple, opium den, and fortress. Now the oldest building in John Day, the museum is filled with artifacts from the fascinating culture of pioneer Chinese immigrants. Open daily 9am-12 and 1-5pm May through October. Tours start on the hour. Admission is free; the suggested donation is $3.

Canyon City

Gold was discovered along Canyon Creek on June 8, 1862, and soon a boomtown of 10,000 sprang up. In two years, $26 million of gold was removed. The young C.H. Miller, later famous as Joaquin Miller, the "Poet of the Sierras," practiced law and wrote poems here 1863-69. A flash flood destroyed much of the town in 1896. Today the town is still the county seat, but its population has declined to about 700, while neighboring John Day has grown nearly three times that large.

Walk a few blocks around **Canyon City's downtown** to see the old stone

Mural of gold rush days in Canyon City.

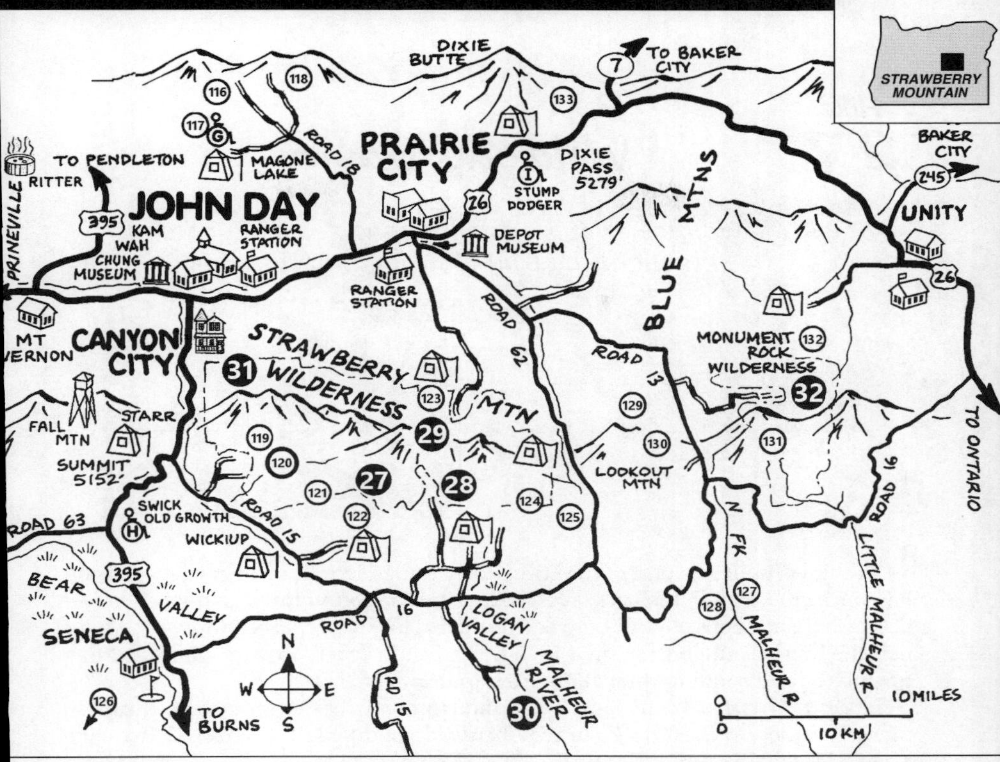

buildings, the city park's historic murals, and the **Grant County Historical Museum,** where Joaquin Miller's 1865 plank cabin has been moved. The museum is open 9-4:30 Tues-Sat from May 1 to September 30. Admission runs $4 for adults, $3.50 for seniors, and $2 for kids 7-16. Then drive up Main Street 0.8 mile and turn left toward the Canyon City Cemetery to see the white crosses of **Boot Hill.** Here, just outside the official cemetery, the gold rush boomtown laid its horse thieves and prostitutes to rest. Each year in early June, Canyon City toasts its heritage at **'62 Days,** a festival featuring a chorus line of can-can girls, a mock hanging, a beard contest, gold-panning demonstrations, and a sawdust-floored saloon.

Prairie City

Stop on Highway 26 to walk along a block of Front Street's original stone and board storefronts from the early 1900s. The **Oxbow Dinner House and Pizza Company** at 128 Front Street features a fabulous wooden saloon bar, steaks, prawns, and a "big game museum" of gigantic stuffed elk heads. Walk a block west to shop for cowboy boots at the **Bar WB**. Then return on the opposite side of Main Street to check out inexpensive **antique shops**.

Prairie City's restored 1910 **Sumpter Valley Railway Depot** houses the DeWitt Museum, featuring the small-gauge railroad that connected this town to Sumpter and Baker City until 1947. Several miles of the old railroad line near Sumpter have been reopened for a steam-powered excursion train, and Prairie City boosters envision extending the tracks 40 miles across the Blue Mountains to the original railhead here. Meanwhile the depot museum also exhibits pioneer artifacts and minerals. In downtown Prairie City, turn south 4 blocks on Main Street to Depot Park. Hours are 10am-5pm Wednesday-Sunday from May 15 to October 15.

Hike 27 Wildcat Basin

Trailside wildflower gardens and pinnacled ash badlands highlight the trail to Wildcat Basin.

Asters.

Moderate
6.9-mile loop
1330 feet elevation gain
Open late July through October
Use: hikers, horses

Lava flows built this part of the Strawberry Range 15 million years ago. Erosion has since cut through the lava layers, exposing the soft volcanic ash sandwiched between them. Seeps emerge between the layers too, watering wildflowers. About half the hike's route burned in a 1996 fire, so snowbrush obscures the tread in a few places and route-finding skills are important.

Getting There— From John Day, take Highway 395 south toward Burns 10 miles. At milepost 10c follow a brown recreation pointer left onto paved, two-lane Road 65 (which becomes Road 15). After 13.6 miles, at a 4-way intersection with a stop sign, turn left on paved Road 16 toward Logan Valley. Drive 2.6 miles, and then turn left again (at a "Strawberry Wilderness" pointer) onto gravel Road 1640. After 9.8 miles, where the road makes a switchback to the right, park in a pullout on the left marked "Roads End Trail 201A" *(GPS location 44.28, -118.7033)*.

At 7870 feet elevation, this trailhead is higher than many Oregon mountaintops, so it's not surprising that the whitebark pines and noble firs here have been dwarfed by storms. The trail itself is actually an old roadbed, now strewn with pearly everlasting, purple aster, and yellow composites. After a mile, when you enter the silver snags of an old burn, huge bushy clumps of wildflowers drape the old roadcut. The display features pink monkeyflower, white cow parsnip, purple

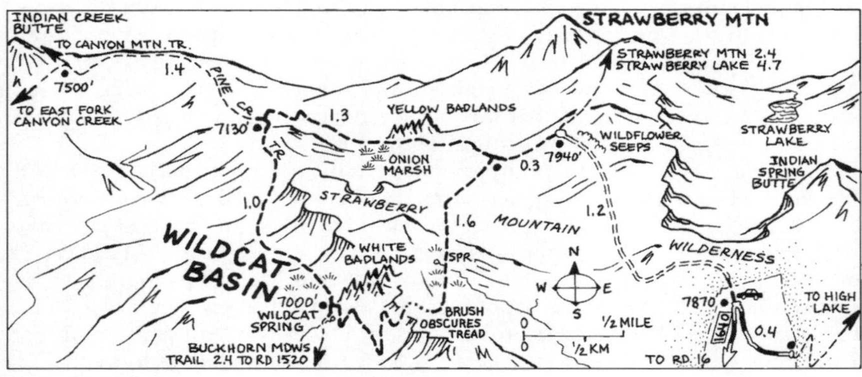

Wildcat Basin's white ash badlands.

penstemon, and white stalks of bog orchid.

When the old road ends at a pass at the 1.2-mile mark, you'll get a first view ahead to the brown pyramid of 9038-foot Strawberry Mountain. At this unmarked junction *(GPS location 44.2902, -118.7178)*, turn downhill to the left along a ridge on a fainter trail for 0.3 mile, crossing a wooded saddle to a fork. Keep left again for 1.6 miles toward Wildcat Basin. After traversing several wildflower glens the path dives down into the old burn through waist-high snowbrush bushes that obscure the tread. Wade straight through, heading downhill. The trail then switchbacks past a white badlands of knobby pinnacles and striped volcanic ash.

In Wildcat Basin itself, a dry meadow below the badlands, you'll reach a T-shaped junction. Here you might detour briefly left 50 feet to see Wildcat Spring, a horse-hoof-damaged font with a few campsites back in the trees. Then take the T-junction's right-hand path to continue the loop. After another mile, fork to the right at a saddle and follow the Indian Creek Trail down into a burned forest of standing snags.

In 0.2 mile, the trail crosses a small creek and begins to climb. Look for cut log ends to find the faint trail. The route climbs steeply half a mile to a surprising marsh of wild onions—an entire meadow of blue, spherical, aromatic wildflowers on tall stalks *(GPS location 44.2892, -118.7328)*. The path is faint but continue to complete the loop and find the road/trail back to your car.

Other Options— The easiest route to the top of Strawberry Mountain also begins at this trailhead. Hike the old roadbed 1.2 miles, veer right to continue on the Onion Creek Trail, and then keep left at junctions. The route gains 1200 feet in a total of 3.6 miles.

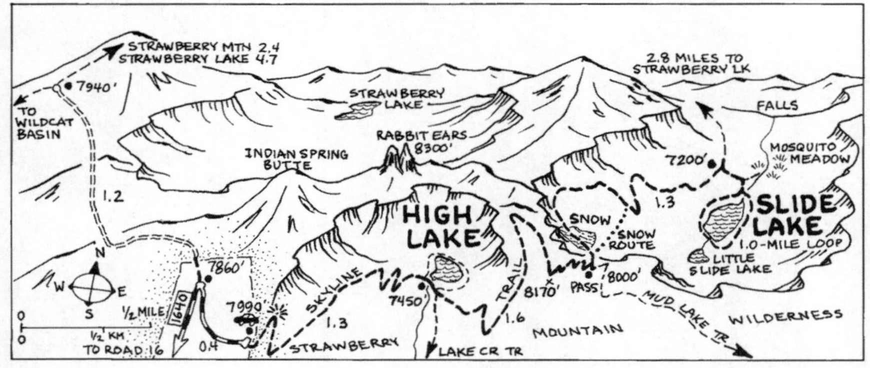

Hike 28 High Lake

It's hard to imagine a better place for a first backpacking trip with kids than High Lake.

Easy ((to High Lake)
2.6 miles round trip
540 feet elevation **loss**
Open late July through October
Use: hikers, horses

Difficult (to Slide Lake)
9.4 miles round trip
2250 feet elevation gain
Open August through October

Slide Lake.

An easy, 1.3-mile path leads past wildflowers and woods to a picturesque lake swarming with small trout. Both High Lake and its neighbor, Slide Lake, are set in giant rock-walled bowls carved into the crest of the Strawberry Range by Ice Age glaciers. The glaciers are gone, but snow lingers until late summer in the scenic pass between the two lakes.

Getting There— From John Day, take Highway 395 south toward Burns 10 miles. At milepost 10c follow a brown recreation pointer left onto paved, two-lane Road 65 (which becomes Road 15). After 13.6 miles, at a 4-way intersection with a stop sign, turn left on paved Road 16 toward Logan Valley. Drive 2.6 miles, and then turn left again (at a "Strawberry Wilderness" pointer) onto gravel Road 1640 for 10 miles to the road's end.

The Skyline Trail sets off toward High Lake by switchbacking down a slope of wildflowers, including blue lupine, pearly everlasting, yellow Oregon sunshine, and pink fireweed. Particularly notice the paintbrush, which usually blooms red, but here is a yellow species.

At High Lake the view extends across the fish-jump rings of the lake to a huge, rounded cliff face topped with the dark crags of Rabbit Ears, a pair of rock spires. The trail forks just before a driftwood logjam that marks the lake's outlet. The left-hand path circles the lake and leads to the quietest campsites. If you're continuing onward, however, keep right across the outlet creek.

At the far end of the footbridge, note that two different trails lead to the right. Don't take the far right path marked "Lake Creek Trail." Instead veer gently to the right on the Skyline Trail. This path climbs more than a mile to a high ridge-end, and then drops to a junction in a rocky pass. Go left across the pass.

For the next 0.1 mile the Skyline Trail traverses a high slope where a dangerously steep snowfield may remain across the trail until August. If snow is still blocking the route, and if you're determined to continue, the safest choice is to head downhill and pick up the trail at its next switchback 0.3 mile below. Once past the snowy slope, follow the trail down a mile to a junction in the woods. Keep right for the loop around Slide Lake. Remarkable cliffs back the lake on three sides. Ice Age glaciers here sliced through ten lava flows, each 50 feet thick, leaving a massive cliff striped like a layer cake.

Other Options— If you're backpacking, consider continuing on a spectacular 13.3-mile loop past Slide Lake to Strawberry Lake and Strawberry Mountain (see Hike #29). The circuit ends at a trailhead on Road 1640 just 0.4 mile from your car. Total elevation gain is 2930 feet.

The tip of Rabbit Ears pokes over the ridge above High Lake.

Hike 29 Strawberry Lake

With alpine lakes, snowy crags, and waterfalls, the Strawberry Range seems like a chunk of the Canadian Rockies dropped onto the sagebrush plains of Eastern Oregon.

Easy (around Strawberry Lake)
4-mile loop
550 feet elevation gain
Open July to mid-November
Use: hikers (Equestrians park at Slide Creek Campground)

Moderate (to Little Strawberry Lake)
6.6 miles round trip
1200 feet elevation gain

Difficult (to Strawberry Mountain)
12.6 miles round trip
3320 feet elevation gain
Open August through October

Strawberry Falls.

For a picture-postcard view of this surprising range, hike 1.3 miles to Strawberry Lake, a mountain pool backed by a palisade of cliffs. For an even better view, continue past Strawberry Falls to Little Strawberry Lake. And for the best view of all, take a well-graded trail all the way to the panoramic summit of 9038-foot Strawberry Mountain.

Getting There— Drive Highway 26 to Prairie City (13 miles east of John Day).

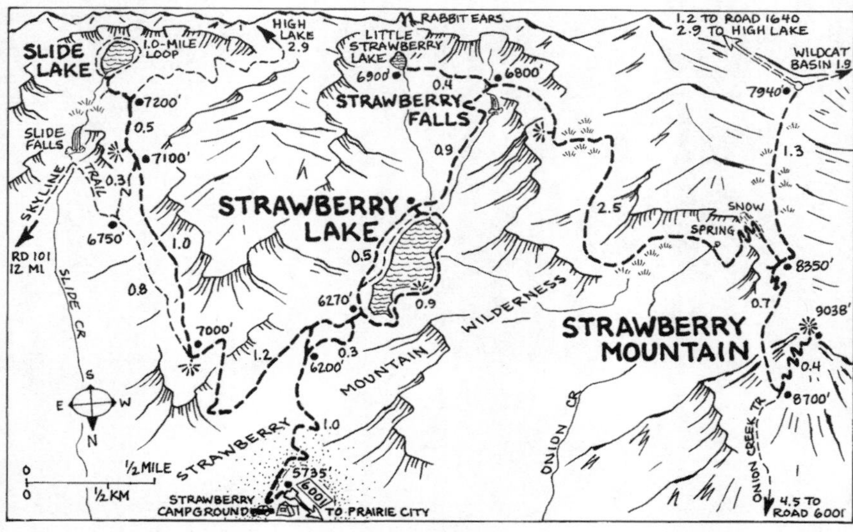

Strawberry Lake.

Turn south in the middle of Prairie City, following a pointer for Depot Park and Strawberry Lake. After 0.3 mile you'll reach a stop sign at a T-shaped junction. Turn left for 200 feet, and then turn right at a (hidden) "Strawberry Campground" arrow onto Bridge Street, which becomes County Road 60 and eventually Forest Road 6001. Continue a total of 11 miles (the last 8 on gravel) to road's end at Strawberry Campground. A campsite here costs about $8, but hikers park free.

The trail begins by a message board at the far end of the parking area and climbs up through a grand fir forest where huckleberries ripen in August.

Keep right at all junctions to the edge of Strawberry Lake at the 1.3-mile mark. Although the main trail turns left here, you'll get better views if you turn right on a smaller path around the quieter, west side of the lake. This path crosses a footbridge over the lake's outlet, a creek that usually flows underground.

Strawberry Lake formed about a thousand years ago when giant landslides dammed the valley. During the Ice Age a glacier filled the valley from wall to wall. When the ice melted, the unsupported cliffs on either hand collapsed. The most recent slide left a red-striped scarp visible on the canyon wall. The lake now mostly drains down a whirlpool, leaving the outlet "creek" gurgling beneath rocks.

If you're strapped for time, you can simply loop counterclockwise around the lake and head back to your car. But a longer trip here is definitely worthwhile. To continue, follow the trail around to the far end of Strawberry Lake. After crossing half a dozen creeks, turn uphill sharply to the right on a steep side path 150 feet and then turn right on a larger trail. This path climbs to Strawberry Falls, a 60-foot fan splashing onto mossy boulders. At the top of the falls you'll reach a junction—and face a choice. You can either turn left for 0.4 mile to Little Strawberry Lake, a dramatic turnaround point for a moderate hike. Or you can keep right for the longer, challenging climb to Strawberry Mountain itself.

The path up Strawberry Mountain climbs through several surprisingly diverse wildflower meadows, where sagebrush mingles with lush pink monkeyflower and red paintbrush. Beyond Strawberry Falls 2.5 miles the path switchbacks up to a windswept pass, where a steep snow cornice often lingers across the trail until August.

Keep taking the uphill fork at junctions and you'll end up atop Strawberry Mountain, a pyramid of shaley, tilted rock strata where only sulfur flowers and alpine butterflies seem to survive. The fire lookout cabin that stood here until the 1950s, anchored to the rock by roof cables, blew out from under its roof in a winter storm. Years later the roof blew away too, leaving only the cables.

From this lofty perch, the creekside forests at the foot of the Strawberry Range look like great green snakes crawling out into the brown desert. To the north, look for the gridiron of Prairie City. To the west, the Strawberry Range humps off toward the crags of Canyon Mountain. To the southeast, above Rabbit Ears' spires, shimmers the distant white stripe of Steens Mountain.

Other Options— Slide Lake is another popular day-hike goal from the Strawberry Campground trailhead. It's 4 miles away and 1500 feet up. Better still, plan a backpack trip to visit three lakes on a grand 15.6-mile circuit of the high Strawberries. Start by hiking past Strawberry Lake to the 8350-foot saddle on Strawberry Mountain's shoulder. If you keep left at all junctions from there on, you'll walk along Road 1640 for 0.4 mile, drop down to High Lake (see Hike #28), and cross a pass to Slide Lake before returning to Strawberry Lake and the trail down to your car. Total elevation gain for the loop is 3470 feet.

Hike 30 Malheur River

The glassy, 30-foot-wide Malheur River gathers its strength at the base of the Strawberry Range to bluster through a rimrock canyon of ponderosa pines before striking off into the desert.

Easy (to gorge viewpoint)
3.8-miles round trip
200 feet elevation gain
Open May to early December
Use: hikers, horses, bicycles

Moderate (with shuttle)
7.6 miles one-way
800 feet elevation gain

Porcupine.

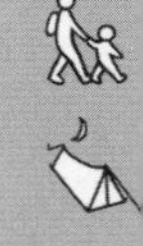

The path through the Malheur River's canyon is a delight.

Getting There— From John Day, take Highway 395 south toward Burns 10 miles. At milepost 10c follow a brown recreation pointer left onto paved, two-lane Road 65 (which becomes Road 15). After 13.6 miles, at a 4-way intersection with a stop sign, turn left on paved Road 16 toward Logan Valley. After 5.1 miles, just before Logan Valley, turn right on gravel Road 1643. Following "Malheur River" pointers, drive 8.6 miles on gravel Road 1643 to a fork and veer left on Road 1651 for 1.3 miles to Malheur Ford's riverside parking area *(GPS location 44.0867, -118.5798).*

The Malheur River.

Malheur Ford really does have a ford—a frightening 50-foot crossing where high-clearance rigs sometimes plow across the river to continue on Road 1651. Fortunately, there's no need to try it because the trail starts on the near side.

The near side of the Malheur River has a lovely meadow with a picnic table at a free campsite, and an all-accessible restroom. The well-maintained trail starts here and heads downstream through an open forest with big ponderosa pine, small lodgepole pines, and scattered Douglas firs. Wildflowers include blue lupine, white yarrow, and red columbine. Watch for stinging nettles by the trail in wet spots. Chipmunks are everywhere.

After 1.9 miles the trail climbs to a clifftop viewpoint in the most rugged part of the Malheur River's gorge. This makes a good turnaround point for an easy hike. You might also look along the trail near here for wild raspberry bushes, with tiny but intensely delicious red fruit in summer.

Beyond this gorge the trail follows the river another 4.5 miles downstream, passing several campable flats and small meadows along the way. Then the path switchbacks uphill for 1.2 miles to the far trailhead at Hog Flat *(GPS location 44.0867, -118.5798).* If you've ridden the trail on a mountain bike, you can return from Hog Flat to Malheur Ford on a pleasant 16.8-mile backroad loop, simply by following the gravel road and keeping right at all junctions. If you want to hike the entire trail, it's best to plan on leaving a shuttle car at Hog Flat. To drive there from Malheur Ford, backtrack 1.3 miles on Road 1651 to a junction, turn left on Road 1643 for 6.5 miles, and turn left on Road 142 for 1.4 miles to its end. Antelope are frequently sighted along the way.

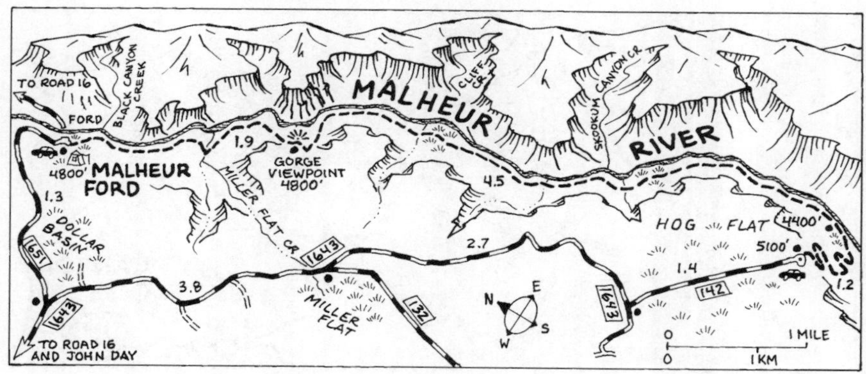

Hike 31 Canyon Mountain

Gold drew 10,000 miners to Canyon City and Canyon Mountain in 1862.

Moderate (to Dog Creek)
6.6 miles round trip
1200 feet elevation gain
Open June to mid-November
Use: hikers, horses

Difficult (to Dean Creek)
11 miles round trip
1700 feet elevation gain

Juniper along the trail.

Today this craggy peak is part of the Strawberry Mountain Wilderness, with a well-graded trail zigzagging along the mountain's flanks. A 2015 wildfire burned the trailhead and the first 3.3 miles of the trail, leaving black snags and opening up new views. Also note that the road to the trailhead is a little rough and confusing because of the area's mining claims.

Getting There— Start in Canyon City, 2 miles south of John Day on Highway 395. At the Grant County Historical Museum turn east on Main Street (which becomes Road 52) for 1.8 miles. Then turn right onto paved Gardner Ranch Lane for 0.3 mile, and curve to the right onto one-lane oiled Canyon Mountain Trail Road for 0.2 mile. At a fork, reset your car's odomoter to zero and go straight on a gravel road for 2.2 miles. This road is very steep and bumpy at times! Ignore dirt spurs. When gravel ends in a saddle at a junction at the 2.2-mile mark, veer left and keep left on a steep, rutted dirt road for 0.1 mile to its end at the trailhead parking area *(GPS location 44.3627, -118.9264).*

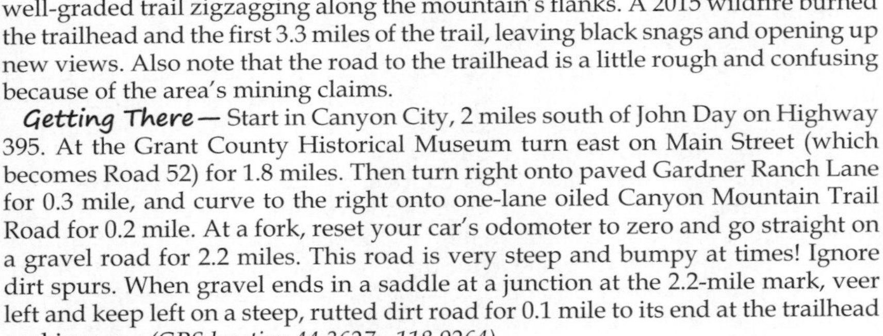

The Canyon Mountain Trail sets off through a forest recovering from fire. Little Pine Creek, at the 1.6-mile mark, is an oasis of green amidst the burn. The creek splashes through a grotto with ferns, red columbine, paintbrush, and purple

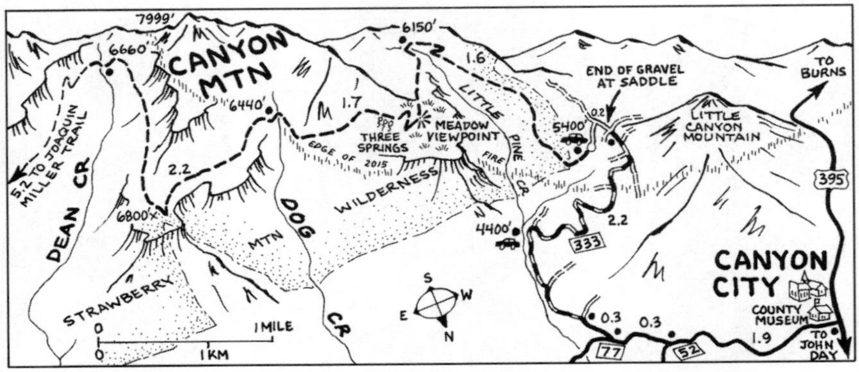

monkshood. The path climbs another 0.6 mile to an arid meadow with a bird's-eye view of the trough-shaped John Day Valley.

Continue to Dog Creek, a good turnaround point for a moderate hike. This is also where the forest fire stopped. The bed of the tumbling stream shows off the colorful rock that attracted miners to this mountain: contorted green serpentine and rough red peridotite, streaked with veins of white quartz and marble. Flecked with faint traces of gold, this rock was originally under the Pacific seafloor, but the advancing North American continent dredged it up like a plow 200-250 million years ago.

If you'd like a longer hike, continue another 2.2 miles to Dean Creek's miniature waterfall, another good goal. A rounded granite ridge above the path here harbors a few small tent sites—the first of the trip. Backpackers can continue up to a total of 37.1 miles along the crest of the Strawberry Range (see Hikes #27-29) to the Skyline Trailhead on Road 101 (Hike #125).

Hike 32 Monument Rock

On this sagebrush mountaintop, white and orange butterflies swarm about the mysterious 8-foot circular rock cairn that gives the Monument Rock Wilderness its name.

Easy (to Bullrun Rock)
4.4 miles round trip
380 feet elevation gain
Open July through November
Use: hikers, horses

Moderate (to Monument Rock)
5.6 miles round trip
550 feet elevation gain

Monument Rock.

No trail climbs to this lithic landmark, visible from far across the wilderness area's alpine mesa. For easier viewpoint goals, hike to Bullrun Rock or drive to the Table Rock lookout, on the two other corners of this scenic triangular plateau.

Getting There— From John Day, drive Highway 26 east 13 miles to downtown Prairie City and turn right at a sign for Depot Park. After 0.4 mile, turn left at a stop sign, and then keep straight on what becomes County Road 62. Continue 8 miles on this paved highway, turn left on paved Road 13 following a "Short Creek" pointer for 11.7 miles, and then turn left onto gravel Road 1370 at a sign for the Little Malheur River. After 4.4 miles, fork to the left to stay on Road 1370. At a junction in another 1.5 miles, turn right following a "Table Rock L.O." sign, still sticking to Road 1370. After just 0.2 mile the road forks. The right-hand branch is the entrance to the primitive Elk Flat Spring Campground, with six excellent, free campsites. For the hike, however, take the left-hand fork. This road quickly deteriorates to a rocky dirt track. Take it slow for 3.8 miles to a switchback with a message board and parking for three cars.

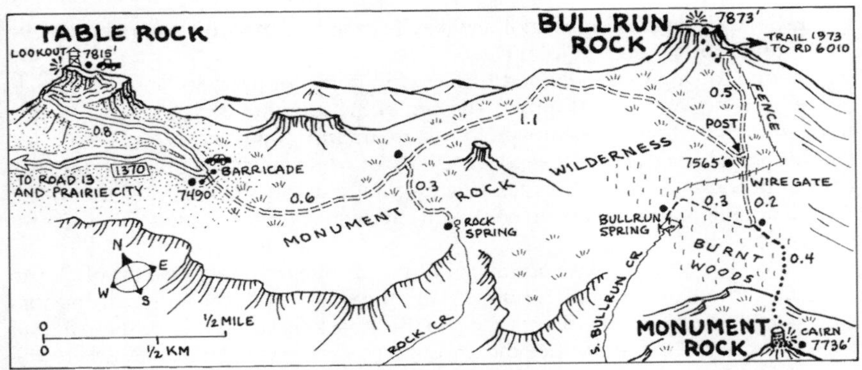

Although the hike begins at this switchback, first consider driving up the road another 0.8 mile to say hello to the Table Rock Lookout staffer. The final 0.2 mile of Road 1370 are so steep and rocky that you'll need to use first gear and drive very slowly. At the top, the 14-foot-square, 1936-vintage fire lookout building has a view sweeping from Strawberry Mountain to the Wallowas. A snowfield lingers here until August. In 1989 the staffer had to evacuate when a forest fire swept over the ridge.

After paying your respects at Table Rock, drive back down to the switchback trailhead and hike out an old road that's closed to motor vehicles by a dirt berm. This nearly level road/trail crosses a sagebrush meadow with blue lupine, red paintbrush, purple aster, and patches of struggling subalpine fir. It's a pleasant stroll across a remote mountaintop prairie.

After 1.7 miles the old road grows faint at a signless, 7-foot post. For the easier hike to Bullrun Rock, walk past the left side of the post 100 feet to find a track that curves left toward Bullrun Rock, the highest rock outcrop on the sagebrush horizon. Follow this old road track 0.4 mile to a pass where a fenceline crosses at a wire gate. Leave the road here and scramble left up a steep rock hill 0.1 mile to the summit of Bullrun Rock *(GPS location 44.3246, -118.2836)*. To the north, the view extends past the distant town of Unity to the craggy Elkhorn Range and the hazy Wallowa Mountains.

Then hike back 0.5 mile to the faint road fork marked by a post. If you're ready for the trickier hike to Monument Rock, continue straight through a fenceline's wire gate 0.2 mile to a small cairn marking a faint junction in a burned forest of snags. Turn left on a dusty elk trail 100 feet to the broad crest of a pass, where the trail peters out. Then bushwhack to the right along the broad ridgecrest, up a steep slope, and across a mountaintop to Monument Rock *(GPS location 44.3116, -118.2879)*.

Lichens encrust only small parts of the shaley andesite in this mysterious cylindrical stack, suggesting that it was built about a century ago. Certainly the region's Paiute Indians did not use this kind of stonework. Perhaps the cairn dates to the gold miners who began prospecting north of Bullrun Rock in 1865. More likely, however, bored Basque shepherds assembled the cairn when they began grazing their flocks across these high meadows in the early 1900s.

If you're backpacking, bring water or a good filter pump, because the summit plateau's two water sources, Rock Spring and Bullrun Spring, have both been badly trampled by cattle and elk.

BAKER CITY

The craggy, granite Elkhorn Range that once drew miners to an 1860s gold rush now attracts hikers and skiers. The range also serves as a dramatic backdrop to several Old West ghost towns and the historic downtown of charming Baker City.

Baker City's historic downtown

Over 100 restored buildings line the streets of Baker City's turn-of-the-19th-century downtown. Pick up a free brochure describing a 1-mile walking tour at **Bettys Books** (1813 Main Street), one of Eastern Oregon's largest bookstores.

Cross the street to the imposing **Geiser Grand Hotel** (1996 Main), a turreted 1889 hotel restored to its Gold-Rush-era glory. Walk inside through the Palm Court, a reasonably priced restaurant beneath the largest stained glass ceiling in the Northwest.

The 1889 Geiser Grand Hotel.

Next cross the street to the US Bank (2000 Main Street), to see its astonishing **gold display,** a glass case filled with gold pebbles, gold dust, and a monstrous 5-pound, fist-sized gold nugget.

Now continue 2 blocks along Main Street to **Barley Brown's Brew Pub,** 2190 Main Street. Dare to order the gigantic Death Burger with a pint of heady Pallet Jack IPA or Jubilee Golden Ale, brewed in honor of Baker City's annual **Miners Jubilee,** held on the third full weekend in July.

Another block down Main Street is the **Adler House Museum,** a restored 1889 home at 2305 Main, packed with original antiques. It's open only on summer weekends (Memorial Day to Labor Day) from 10am-3:30pm. Adults are $6 and kids under 12 are free. Then walk back to **Bella Main Street Market** (2023 Main, open 8am-7pm daily), a wine shop with an upscale grocery and strange kitchen gadgets. Directly across the street is **Sweet Wife Baking** (2028 Main), your source for quiche and an ice mocha.

◄ *Oregon Trail Interpretive Center*

Covered wagons of the Oregon Trail crossed Flagstaff Hill to a dramatic view of the rugged Blue Mountains ahead. Now atop that hill is a world-class interpretive center, renovated in 2022, with walk-through dioramas, a covered wagon camp, a gold mine replica, and hiking trails (see Hike #134 or *oregontrail.blm.gov*). It's open 9-6 daily April-October, 9-4 November-March. Hiking trails are free, but museum admission is $8 for adults and $4.50 for seniors, with kids under 16 free. From Interstate 84 exit 302 at Baker City, drive 5 miles east on Highway 86.

Baker Heritage Museum

Folksier than the better known Oregon Trail Interpretive Center, this Baker City museum has collections of rocks, gems, and pioneer artifacts. A remodeled 1920 natatorium houses the museum at 2480 Grove Street beside the city's Geiser Pollman Park. Admission is $6 for adults and $5 for seniors, but children under

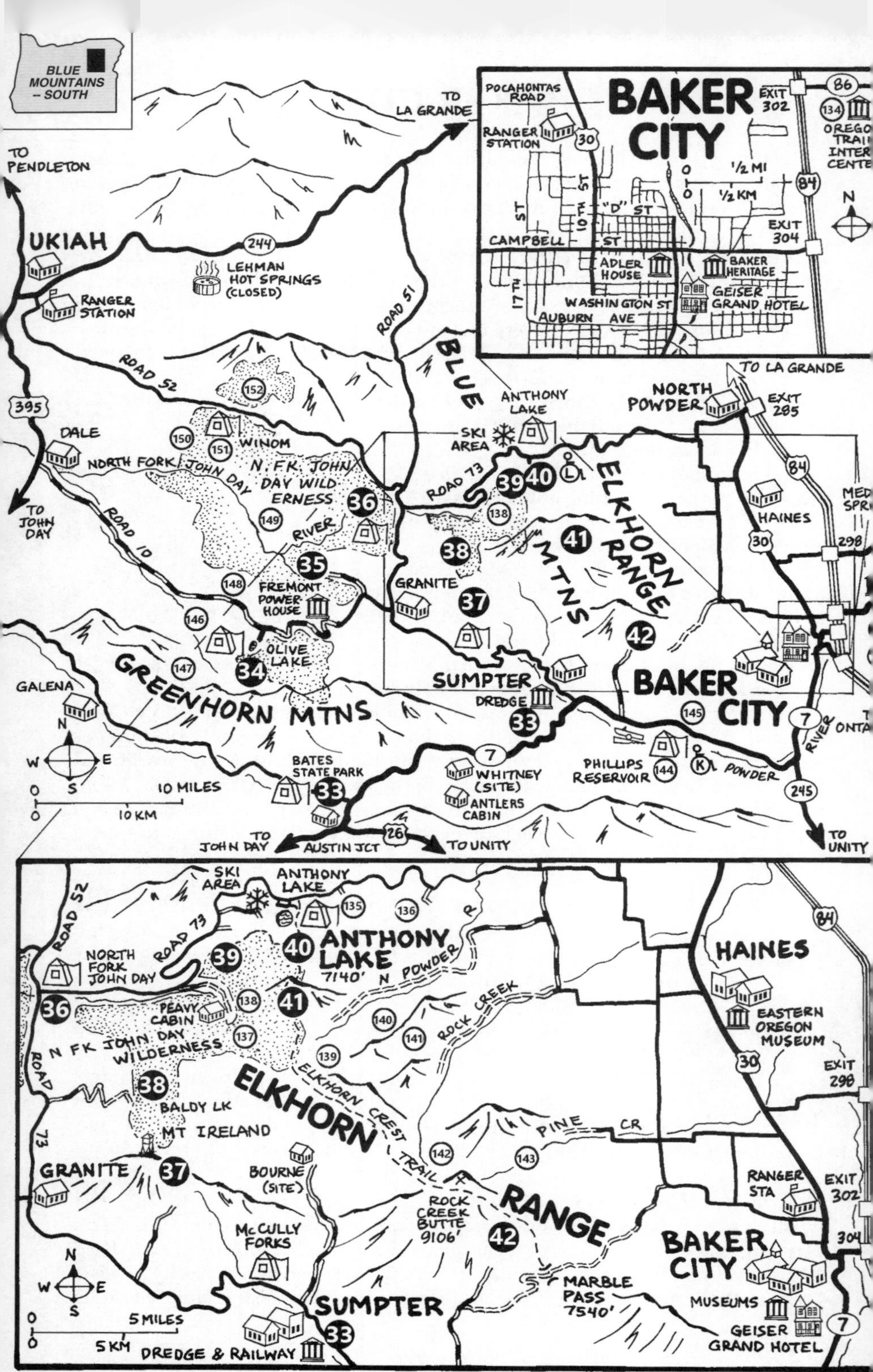

BLUE MOUNTAINS – SOUTH
TO LA GRANDE
TO PENDLETON
UKIAH
244
LEHMAN HOT SPRINGS (CLOSED)
RANGER STATION
ROAD 51
ROAD 52
BLUE
395
DALE
NORTH FORK JOHN DAY RIVER
WINOM
N. FK. JOHN DAY WILDERNESS
TO JOHN DAY
ROAD 10
FREMONT POWER HOUSE
OLIVE LAKE
GREENHORN MTNS
GALENA
0 10 MILES
0 10 KM
BATES STATE PARK
TO JOHN DAY
AUSTIN JCT
26
TO UNITY
ANTHONY LAKE
SKI AREA
ROAD 73
GRANITE
ELKHORN RANGE
MTNS
SUMPTER
DREDGE
WHITNEY (SITE)
ANTLERS CABIN
PHILLIPS RESERVOIR
POWDER
RIVER
BAKER CITY
NORTH POWDER
EXIT 285
84
HAINES
30
298
7
245
TO UNITY
BAKER CITY
POCAHONTAS ROAD
RANGER STATION
EXIT 302
86
134
OREGON TRAIL INTERPRETIVE CENTER
0 1/2 MI
0 1/2 KM
10TH ST
"D" ST
CAMPBELL ST
EXIT 304
ADLER HOUSE
BAKER HERITAGE
GEISER GRAND HOTEL
17TH
WASHINGTON ST
AUBURN AVE
TO LA GRANDE
ROAD 52
SKI AREA
ANTHONY LAKE
NORTH FORK JOHN DAY
ROAD 73
ANTHONY LAKE 7140'
N POWDER R
ROCK CREEK
PEAVY CABIN
N FK JOHN DAY WILDERNESS
ELKHORN CREST TRAIL
ELKHORN
ROAD 73
BALDY LK
MT IRELAND
GRANITE
BOURNE (SITE)
PINE CR
ROCK CREEK BUTTE 9106'
RANGE
McCULLY FORKS
MARBLE PASS 7540'
SUMPTER
DREDGE & RAILWAY
0 5 MILES
0 5 KM
HAINES
EASTERN OREGON MUSEUM
EXIT 298
RANGER STA
EXIT 302
304
BAKER CITY
MUSEUMS
GEISER GRAND HOTEL
7

13 are free. Hours are 9am-5pm daily from mid-March through October, and in winter 10am-3:30pm Fridays and Saturdays.

◄ *Sumpter Valley Railroad*

Nicknamed the "Stump Dodger" because it helped log the area's ponderosa pine forests in the 1890s, the narrow-gauge Sumpter Valley Railroad now runs as a steam train on 5 miles of restored track between Sumpter and McEwen Station, 22 miles east of Baker City on Highway 7. Trains leave McEwen Station at 10am and 1pm (more often on holidays) from Memorial Day through September. The return train leaves Sumpter at 11:45am and 2:45pm. Expect to pay $25 per adult ($15 for kids age 4-17) for the round trip (541-894-2268 or *sumptervalleyrailroad.org*).

Sumpter

Founded by gold miners in 1862, Sumpter boomed to 3500 after the railroad line from Baker City reached here in 1896, but dwindled after a 1917 fire burned nearly every building and even the planked Main Street. Start your visit at the **Sumpter Dredge,** a 1200-ton, 60-foot-tall gold mill floating in a lake of its own making. The odd ship is open 7am-7pm May-Oct for free. See Hike #33.

Walking from the dredge through town you'll pass the **Sumpter Municipal Museum** (open 11am-3pm except Wednesdays), several antique shops, and the remains of a bank vault—one of the few relics from the 1917 fire.

Granite

This 1862 gold boomtown shrank to a population of one in the 1960s, and although it has rebounded to 35, a smattering of weathered, abandoned buildings gives it a ghost-town ambiance. From the town's entrance gateway drive a block uphill and park on the left at **Allen Hall**, the old school/city hall/church, still in use. Behind it is the town's cemetery. Uphill on the corner of Center and Main Streets is the abandoned general store. Half a block farther up on the left, note the empty, crooked log cabin of Otis Ford, the mayor who kept the town alive in the 1960s.

Fremont Powerhouse

This historic stone building has been restored to its original 1907 glory, along with three rentable white clapboard houses (see page 24). To power the area's gold mines, engineers diverted water from Olive Lake (see Hike #34) through a 6-mile redwood pipeline and blasted it through turbines here. The plant generated electricity until 1967. From Granite, drive 5 miles west on Road 10.

Anthony Lake

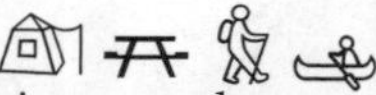

In summer, this picturesque lake high in the Elkhorn Range is a popular spot to hike (see Hike #40), picnic, set up camp (37 sites for $10-14), and paddle (no boat motors allowed). In winter, **Eastern Oregon's largest ski resort** opens beside Anthony Lake, with a triple chairlift (day pass: about $45), 13 kilometers of groomed Nordic trails, and equipment rentals, but no overnight lodging. At 7100 feet, the resort has the highest base elevation of all Northwest ski areas, and perhaps the best powder snow. Ski resort info: (541) 856-3277 or *anthonylakes.com*.

Hike 33 Bates and Sumpter

Sample the history of Eastern Oregon's ghost towns at these two state parks hidden in the Blue Mountains.

Easy (Bates trails)
2.8-mile loop
350 feet elevation gain
Open May through October

Easy (Sumpter Dredge trails)
1.2-mile loop
100 feet elevation gain
Open May through October

The Sumpter dredge.

At Bates a trail from a campground loops around the pond of an abandoned company lumber town. At Sumpter, a loop explores the creekside tailings left by a gold dredge ship. Birds flock to both of these recovering industrial sites. Because the loops are short, and the parks are just 28 miles apart, it's easy to visit both in a day.

Prospectors discovered gold a few miles east of here at Auburn in 1861. The arrival of the Sumpter Valley Railroad in 1890 launched a second rush, this time for timber. The narrow-gauge railroad hauled so much lumber from sawmills at Bates and Prairie City that the line became known as the "Stump Dodger."

Getting There— To see what's left of Bates, drive Highway 26 east of Prairie City 16 miles to Austin Junction, turn left on Highway 7 toward Baker City for 1.1 mile, turn left on Road 20 for 0.4 mile, and turn left into Bates State Park.

If you're coming from Interstate 84, take exit 304 into Baker City a mile, turn left on Main Street, follow signs for Highway 7 toward John Day for 49 miles, and turn right on Road 20 for 0.4 mile to the park entrance.

Drive 0.1 mile down the state park's entrance road and park on the right at a restroom just before a picnic shelter.

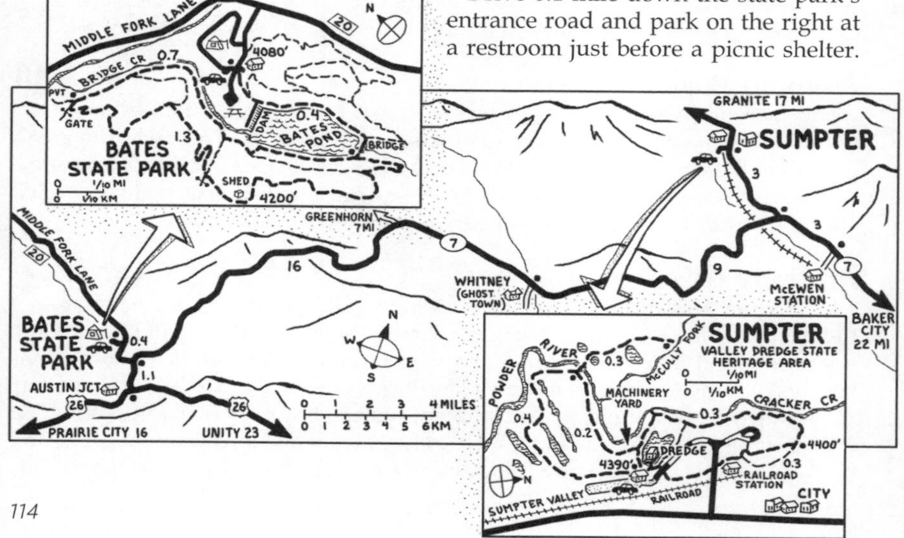

Footbridge at the inlet of Bates Pond.

Start opposite the parking area at a gated road marked "Bates Pond Trail."

After 0.1 mile you'll pass a rock dam. Keep straight along the shore of Bates Pond, a shallow, mucky reservoir. Once a railroad on this trail's route dumped carloads of logs into the pond. The logs floated down a flume to a mill pond where the park's campground now stands, and were cut into lumber at a mill on what is now a picnic area. Workmen often lived in the Bates Hotel (now the campground host's site). Only a lilac bush remains there from that era.

Cross a footbridge at the far end of Bates Pond and keep right around the shore. Just before the dam, the trail swerves up to the left. Continue along the outlet creek half a mile to the end of park property. Keep uphill to the left from the Bridge Creek Trail to the Meadow Trail. After another 0.6 mile, cross a road beside a gate and continue on the Dixie Trail. This path passes an old concrete dynamite shed before looping back to the pond's bridge and the route back to your car.

The Sumpter Valley Railroad carried more than timber. The rail line also made it possible to haul parts to build gold dredges, ships with chains of giant buckets that scoop up river gravel to filter out tiny amounts of gold dust. The 1240-ton ship at Sumpter is 100 miles from a navigable waterway, but it dug its own lake as it churned across the valley. When the dredge stopped in 1954, $4.5 million of gold had been extracted and the valley's farmfields had been destroyed.

To see the dredge, drive back to Highway 7 from Bates and head north toward Baker City. After 16 miles you might stop at a gravel road to the right to see the ghost town of Whitney. This lumber camp died when the railroad folded. A caretaker lives in one of the houses, so view the ruins without leaving the public road.

Another 9 miles beyond Whitney on Highway 7, follow a sign for Sumpter left for 3 miles to a state park sign, turn left past a train station, and keep left for 0.2 mile to a visitor center. First walk 100 feet down to the dredge. After touring the ship, walk back toward the gift shop but veer slightly right onto the "South Trail."

The South Trail is a gravel path beside scummy mining ponds with teasels and willow brush where beavers, ducks, and chipmunks now thrive. After 0.3 mile you might take a detour left across a bridge for 0.3 mile on the McCulley Creek Trail. Then continue on the main loop to a machinery yard near the dredge.

You could return to your car here, but you can see more by turning left on the North Trail. This path accesses a cobble beach of Cracker Creek. After 0.3 mile turn left on the Dredge Overlook Trail, cut across the railroad station parking area, cross the paved road, and take the Walking Trail back to the dredge and your car.

Hike 34 Olive Lake

Campers at this popular lake in the Greenhorn Mountains often hike around the shoreline trail.

Easy (around Olive Lake)
2.7-mile loop
50 feet elevation gain
Open June through November
Use: hikers, horses, bicycles

Difficult (to Lost Creek)
11.9-mile loop
1860 feet elevation gain
Open July through October
Use: hikers, horses

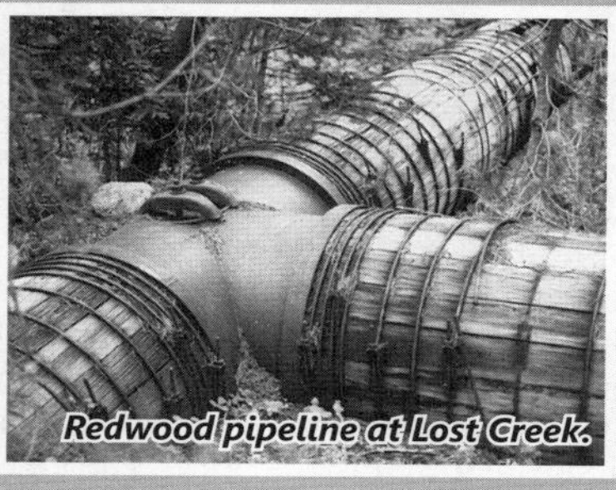
Redwood pipeline at Lost Creek.

Relatively few of the campers at Olive Lake discover the longer, more difficult loop to the alpine viewpoints on Saddle Ridge and the meadows of Lost Creek.

Getting There— From downtown Baker City, drive south on Main Street (which becomes Highway 7) for 25 miles, turn right for 3 miles to Sumpter, continue on the paved road 17 miles to a stop sign at Granite, turn left on paved Road 10 for 3.6 miles, and fork to the right to keep on Road 10, which now becomes gravel. After another 1.4 miles, stop to visit the historic Fremont Powerhouse (see page 113), which operated 1907-1967. Later, on your hike, you'll see the 6-mile redwood pipeline that brought water here from Olive Lake and Lost Creek.

After inspecting the Fremont Powerhouse, drive another 6.5 gravel miles on Road 10 to a pullout on the right for the Lost Creek Trail marked by a message board *(GPS location 44.789, -118.5792)*. If you've brought horses or backpacking gear, this is the place to start your trip. Cross the road, go 0.2 mile to a junction by the old pipeline, and turn right on the Saddle Camp Connect Trail for 1.5 miles to join the path from Olive Lake.

If you're just out for a day hike, however, it's more fun to start at Olive Lake instead. Drive 0.8 mile past the Lost Creek Trailhead to a sign for Olive Lake, turn left on Road 480 for 0.3 mile, and then fork to the right at a "Boat Ramp" pointer for 0.2 mile through the campground to a lakeshore parking lot, picnic area, and dock.

Start at the far left end of the boat ramp parking area beside campsite #1 and walk left around the lake through lodgepole pine woods. Ignore left-hand trails that lead up to campsites—until you've hiked 0.5 mile and the trail climbs away from the shore 50 feet to a walkway across a boggy spring.

Here you'll face a choice. For the easy loop, simply continue around the lake 1.8 miles, cross the 50-foot-tall earthen dam that created the lake, and keep right on a campground road 0.4 mile back to your car. For the much longer loop to Saddle Ridge and Lost Creek, however, turn sharply left on an upper trail that skirts campsite #27 to the campground road turnaround *(GPS location 44.7795, -118.5995)*. As soon as you reach this road, turn uphill to the right past a tree with a sign marking the boundary of the Indian Rock-Vinegar Hill Scenic Area. This

The pipeline's old Upper Reservoir is now a marsh.

path climbs for most of a mile to a small pond at the outlet of the marshy Upper Reservoir. Mosquitoes are a problem in July.

Beyond the Upper Reservoir's marsh, the path climbs 1.9 miles to Saddle Camp, a dry ridgetop meadow *(GPS location 44.7567, -118.6261)*. The tread peters out in the grass, but angle left past a cut log to find a clear ridgecrest trail. Follow this path left 2 miles along the picturesque spine of Saddle Ridge.

Finally the ridgecrest trail descends through lodgepole pine woods to a faint junction at broad, grassy Dupratt Spring Pass *(GPS location 44.7361, -118.6057)*. Ahead is a dirt mining road, but don't take it. Look for a rock cairn on the left by a tree with a "Lost Cr. Trail" sign. No trail is visible here, but turn left and walk straight past this tree 50 feet to the cryptic sign, "3002". Now look left to see a tree blaze and an old roadbed. Follow this track.

After 2.3 miles, when the road/trail reaches a T-shaped junction in a forested pass, turn left on the Lost Creek Trail. In the next 2.7 miles this path crosses five meadows where the tread vanishes. At the first grassy swale, look for a tree blaze on the far lower end of the meadow, on the opposite side. At the second meadow, hop across Lost Creek and follow cairns. When the trail grows faint in the next three grassy openings, simply keep to the meadows' left-hand edge. Finally the path follows the old wooden pipeline down to a junction. Two routes return to Olive Lake from this point. Either turn left on a trail that climbs over a wooded hill, or simply go straight to Road 10 and save 0.6 mile by following the gravel road back to the lake.

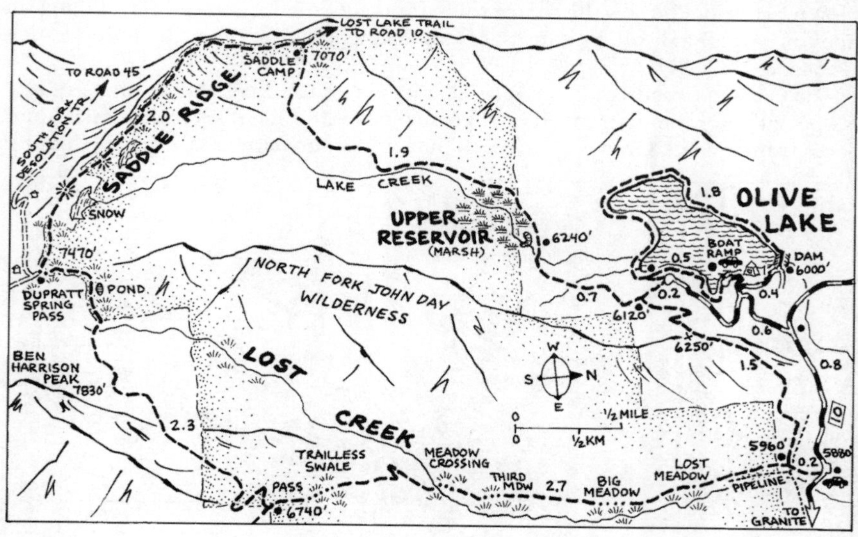

Hike 35 Granite Creek

The Blue Mountains' 1860s gold rush ended long ago, but a few miners still work their claims in the spectacular canyonlands where Granite Creek and the North Fork John Day River collide.

Easy
6.8-mile loop
500 feet elevation gain
Open April to December
Use: hikers, horses

River footbridge.

Footbridges allow the trail to cross from one side to another of the cliff-edged canyon, passing huckleberry patches and old-growth ponderosa pines. To tour the area on a easy loop, hike an upper trail into the heart of the North Fork John Day Wilderness and return on an old mining road past the miners' rustic cabins. Angling is banned in Granite Creek.

Getting There— From downtown Baker City, head south on Main Street (which becomes Highway 7) toward John Day a total of 25 miles, turn right at a sign for Sumpter, drive 3 miles to this rustic gold rush boomtown, continue on the main paved road 17 miles to Granite, turn left on Red Boy Road 24 for 1.4 miles, turn right on gravel Granite Creek Road 1035 for 4.3 miles, and fork left on Road 010 for 0.2 mile to a trailhead parking area. Here you'll see a closed dirt mining road down to the left, but it's the return route for the loop hike. Instead start hiking on the trail straight ahead, by a message board at a pole fence gateway *(GPS location 44.8463, -118.5181).*

The Granite Creek Trail contours 300 feet above the creek, traversing a grassy slope with big, orange-trunked ponderosa pines. After 1.4 miles an unmarked trail joins from the left. On your way back this will be the path to take for the mining

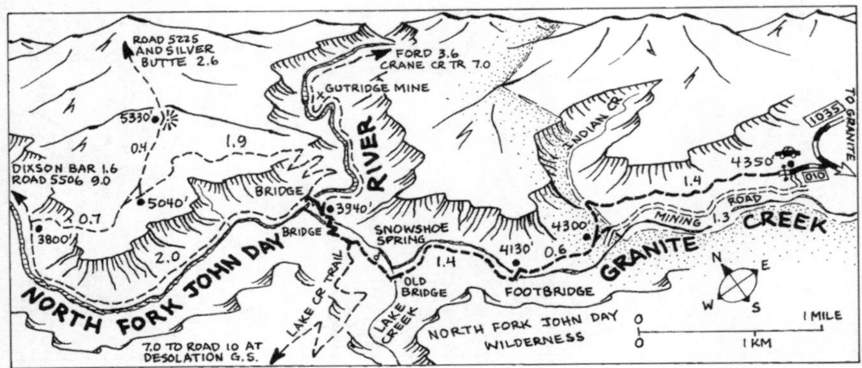

road loop. For now, continue straight 0.6 mile and cross 15-foot-wide Granite Creek on a footbridge that's wide enough for horses. Then the trail follows Granite Creek through a Douglas fir forest where blue huckleberries hang heavy on trailside bushes from late July to mid-August. The narrow canyon twists between cliffs of contorted dark rock.

At the 2.8-mile mark, 0.1 mile beyond the Lake Creek footbridge, note Snowshoe Spring's box to the right, where a pipe delivers cold clear water. In another 0.6 mile the trail bridges Granite Creek again and enters a meadow alongside the North Fork John Day River. Go straight across the meadow to find a large bridge spanning the 60-foot-wide river. Greenish boulders break the stream into whitewater. Flakes of mica shimmer like gold dust in the sandy riverbank.

When you're ready to return, hike back 2 miles, take the trail's right-hand fork, and follow the old mining road 1.3 miles to your car. On this route you'll pass cobble wastelands where a gold mining dredge once churned up the creek. Pits in the hillside were washed out by high-powered hydraulic hoses to find more gold. Little treasure remains for the modern miners whose shacks you'll see. Stay on the road, because trespassing and unauthorized gold panning are not allowed on these private claims.

Other Options— For a longer trip, continue on one of three trails from the riverside meadow. At the start of the meadow, an uphill path to the right follows the river 3.6 miles to a bridgeless crossing and another 10 miles to the North Fork John Day Campground (Hike #36). A second option is to cross the river bridge at the meadow and turn left on the downstream portion of the North Fork John Day River Trail, which continues 11 miles to rough dirt Road 5506. A third choice is to cross the river bridge and turn right. On this route you can make a loop by switchbacking up past canyon viewpoints on the Silver Butte Trail for 1.9 miles, keeping left on a very steep 0.7-mile trail down to the river, and turning left on the North Fork John Day River Trail 2 miles back to the bridge.

Granite Creek from the trail.

Hike 36 North Fork John Day

Deep in the Blue Mountain's gold rush country, the North Fork John Day River Trail traces the river through a rimrock canyon dotted with the decaying log cabins of ancient prospects.

Easy (to Bigfoot Hilton)
5.2 miles round trip
350 feet elevation gain
Open May through November
Use: hikers, horses

Difficult (to Crane Creek)
13.5-mile loop
1280 feet elevation gain

The Blue Heaven cabin.

To sample the scenery, hike 2.6 miles downriver from the North Fork John Day Campground to see four of the cabins, all now public and one still habitable. If you're on horseback, or if you don't mind wading across the chilly river, continue on a 13.5-mile loop that follows a side canyon back to your starting point.

Getting There — From Interstate 84, take North Powder exit 285 (north of Baker City 19 miles or south of La Grande 24 miles), follow "Anthony Lakes" signs 21 paved miles west to the Anthony Lake area, and continue straight on Road 73 another 16.3 paved miles to a stop sign at a 4-way junction. Go straight into the entrance of the North Fork John Day Campground and drive to the far end (beyond an equestrian camping area) to the trailhead parking lot on the left beside tent campsite #16.

If you'd rather drive here from Granite, take paved Road 73 north 9 miles to

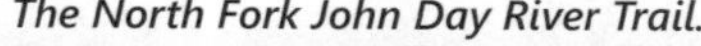
The North Fork John Day River Trail.

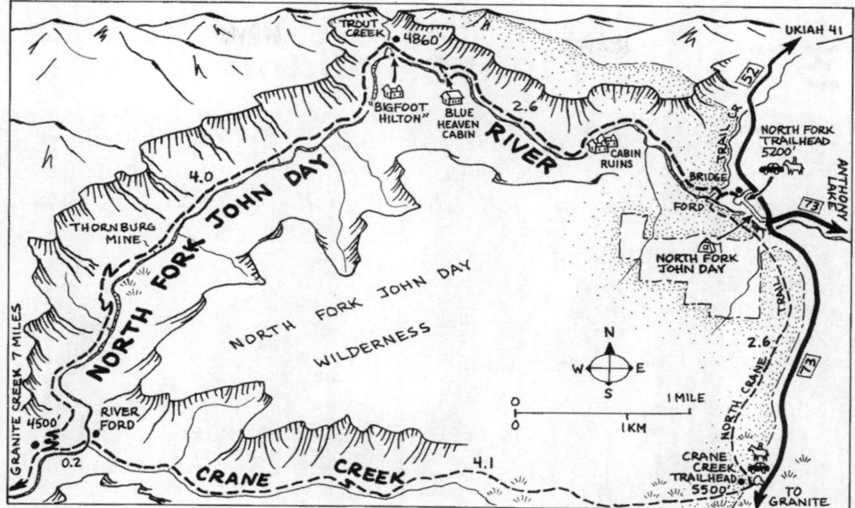

the stop sign and turn left into the campground. Campers should note that the campground lacks drinking water and garbage service, and charges $8 per site.

From the trailhead parking area at the north end of the campground, the trail sets off through a rocky meadow regrowing with lodgepole pines. The area looks as though it has been damaged by floods, and that's almost true. Years ago, the high-pressure water hoses of a hydraulic mining operation washed the riverbank gravels through sluices to separate out gold. After 0.1 mile, turn right to cross Trail Creek on an old log footbridge (or hop across on rocks). Then the trail follows the North Fork John Day River into the Wilderness, where the scenery hasn't changed much since the 1860s gold rush. The forest of Douglas fir and larch is open enough for sunny wildflowers, including blue lupine, red paintbrush, and white mariposa lilies.

After 1.2 miles you'll pass the ruins of two mining cabins on the left. Continue another 1.1 mile and you'll notice a large side trail on the left. This leads 200 feet to the Blue Heaven Mine cabin, now public property and open to visitors. Slide the door handle to unbolt it. The roof and stove are intact, so it's possible to sleep indoors, although there are woodrats, so you might prefer the campsite outside.

If you like exploring cabins, continue on the main trail another 0.3 mile to a collapsed log footbridge across Trout Creek. Immediately before the creek, explore a scramble trail 100 feet to the left to find the ruin of the Home Mine cabin, famed as the "Bigfoot Hilton" in the adventure memoir *Listening for Coyote*.

Backpackers or equestrians interested in a loop trip can continue downstream another 4 miles to the Crane Creek Trail junction. Turn left 0.2 mile to a 30-foot-wide, knee-deep river ford, and hike up Crane Creek 4.1 miles to a parking area on Road 73. If you haven't left a shuttle car here, turn left on the North Crane Trail for 2.6 miles to the North Fork John Day River, where you'll have to cross a 20-foot-wide ford to return to your car.

Other Options— For a longer trip, continue down the North Fork John Day River Trail 3.4 miles to a river ford and another 3.6 miles to the bridge at Granite Creek (see Hike #35). Part of the route follows a historic mining water flume that has been converted to a perfectly level trail.

Hike 37 Mount Ireland

The lookout tower atop 8321-foot Mt. Ireland not only has a terrific view of Baldy Lake and the Blue Mountains, but the tower is actually staffed each summer.

Difficult (to Mt. Ireland)
6.6 miles round trip
2320 feet elevation gain
Open July through October
Use: hikers, horses, bicycles

Difficult (to Downie Lake)
7 miles round trip
2350 feet elevation gain

Mount Ireland's lookout.

A spur of the Mt. Ireland trail descends through the forest to silent Downie Lake. The only person you're likely to meet on either trail is the lonely lookout staffer.

Getting There— From downtown Baker City, drive south on Main Street (which becomes Highway 7) for 25 miles, turn right at a sign for Sumpter, drive 3 miles to this rustic gold rush boomtown, and continue toward Granite on the main paved road for 11.6 miles. Beyond Blue Springs Summit 4.7 miles (and 0.3 mile beyond Milepost 11), turn right on Road 7370. To follow this gravel route, fork left after 0.5 mile and veer steeply left at the 2.2-mile mark. After a total of 2.8 miles, fork up to the right on Road 100 for 0.3 mile to a large wide spot with a "Mt. Ireland LO Trail" sign on the left *(GPS location 44.8127 -118.3287)*.

Berms and pits at the trailhead attempt to keep all-terrain vehicles off the hiking trail, with mixed success. After climbing steeply 0.3 mile you'll reach a junction at a crest with your first view of Mt. Ireland and the tiny white dot that is the summit lookout. Stay on the main trail by keeping left at this fork and right at the next fork, 80 feet later *(GPS location 44.8142, -118.3264)*. The track steepens for 0.3 mile, but then suddenly becomes a lovely footpath traversing left into a shady, uncut forest of 3-foot-thick grand firs. The trail crests a plateau with a lodgepole pine

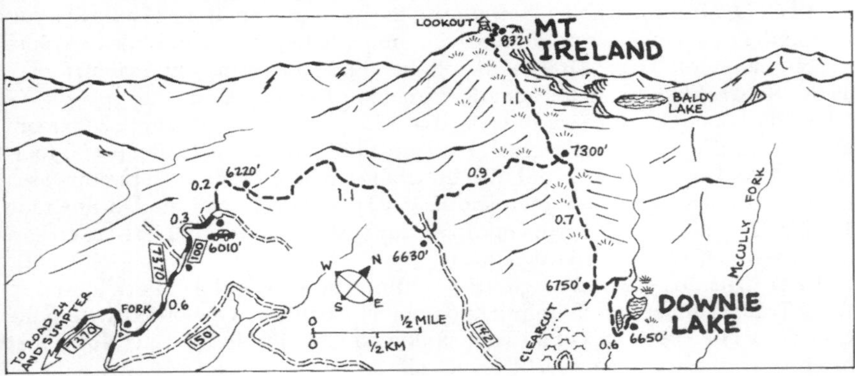

forest, crosses a dirt road, and climbs 0.9 mile to a signpost marking a trail junction in a ridgecrest meadow (GPS location 44.8294, -118.3063). This meadow is full of bastard toad flax, a badly named native plant with drab, 2-foot-tall flower stalks.

At the signpost you'll have to decide whether you want to visit Mt. Ireland's lookout (up to the left), or Downie Lake (down to the right). Most likely you'll choose the lookout. So climb up to the left through meadows on a rocky, gullied path that's confused in places by all-terrain vehicle tracks. Look for cushions of white phlox, yellow sulfur flower, and purple penstemon among the white granite boulders. At the summit you'll find a 13-foot-square metal lookout building, brought here by helicopter in 1957 to replace an earlier wooden structure. The staffers who live here from late June until late September report that only about 50 visitors make the climb each year. Almost directly below, Baldy Lake (Hike #38) looks like a giant sapphire at the head of a long U-shaped valley.

To visit Downie Lake, return to the signpost marking the trail junction. Face downhill from the signpost and then walk to your left, mostly level, on an ATV track for 100 feet to a gap in the trees, where the tread turns downhill. After the trail enters the forest at the 0.7-mile mark and meets an obvious junction, turn downhill to the left on a wide trail for 0.1 mile, and then turn right at a big tree with a notch where a sign used to be. Follow a footpath to the right for 0.6 mile. Expect to step over logs on this infrequently maintained trail. After passing a large pond the trail ends at broad, shallow Downie Lake, just deep enough for a desperate swim. Frogs leap from boulders along the shore. Mt. Ireland resembles a slouching giant, asleep on the horizon. The lakeside forest of lodgepole pines and pointy subalpine firs is too thick for a campsite, but if you bushwhack to the right along the shore 0.1 mile and head uphill, you'll find a campable grassy knoll and views.

Hike 38 Baldy Lake

In an amphitheater of granite cliffs below Mount Ireland, blue-green Baldy Lake is deep enough both for swimmers and large brook trout.

Easy (from Road 7345)
2.4 miles round trip
400 feet elevation gain
Open July through October
Use: hikers, horses

Difficult (from Road 73)
12.6 miles round trip
1600 feet elevation gain

Baldy Lake from Mt. Ireland.

Spire-topped firs circle the lake, while the shore itself sports a grassy fringe of wildflowers. Campsites abound at this scenic wilderness lake, but they're rarely full, and here's why: To reach the lake you have to choose between a short trail with very poor road access, or a very long trail with good road access.

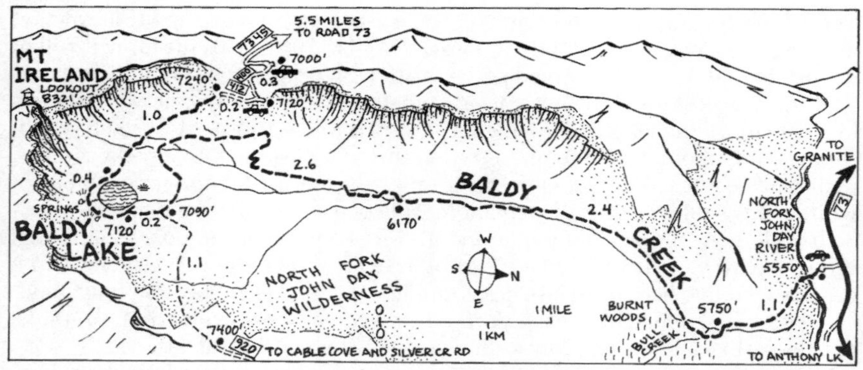

Getting There— For the easy drive but the longer hike, drive Interstate 84 north of Baker City 19 miles (or south of La Grande 24 miles) to North Powder exit 285. Follow "Anthony Lakes" signs 21 paved miles west to the Anthony Lake area, continue straight on Road 73 another 12 paved miles to a sign for the Baldy Creek Trail, and turn left on gravel Road 395 for 0.1 mile to its end.

The trail starts by crossing the swift, 20-foot-wide North Fork John Day River on a log footbridge. The forest here is a mix of lodgepole pine, grand fir, Engelmann spruce, and subalpine fir. After another 1.1 mile the path crosses Baldy Creek on a log—a possible turnaround point. Next the trail crosses Bull Creek and briefly traverses an old fire zone. Beyond this, the next viewpoint is at the 5-mile mark where the path switchbacks up through a grassy swath cleared for an ancient powerline. Built in the early 1900s, the line brought electricity from the Fremont Powerhouse (see page 113) to the gold mines of Cable Cove. Giant rock cairns along the route once held power poles.

After 6.1 miles, keep right at a junction for 0.2 mile to Baldy Lake *(GPS location 44.8464, -118.3132)*. Notice the Mt. Ireland lookout building (Hike #37) atop the cliffs across the lake. A shoreline trail continues left 0.4 mile, passing several springs that spill into the lake through small meadows. Look here for pink heather, purple aster, red paintbrush, and blue gentians.

A much shorter trail to Baldy Lake begins on a rough dirt road. Only high-clearance vehicles can reach this upper trailhead, but passenger cars can park half a mile away if they're driven slowly and carefully. To drive there from the lower trailhead, go back to paved Road 73, continue west on it 4.5 miles to a 4-way junction, turn left to keep on Road 73 for another 4.5 miles toward Granite. Near milepost 30, turn left onto Road 7345 at a sign for the Baldy Lake Trail. (If you're coming from Granite, take paved Road 73 north 3.9 miles to this turnoff.)

Road 7345 is strewn with such large gravel that it has to be driven very slowly and carefully. After 2.3 miles, fork left to keep on Road 7345. Passenger cars should park at the 5.5-mile mark, where the road switchbacks steeply up to the right and becomes Road 400. This steep dirt track has large rocks and ruts. In another 0.3 mile you'll reach a fork in a pass, where even high-clearance vehicles should park. Walk up the right-hand fork (Road 412) for 0.2 mile to its end at the Baldy Lake Trailhead *(GPS location 44.8533, -118.3292)*.

Although the upper trail to Baldy Lake is only a mile long it is poorly designed, diving down and scrambling up slopes for no apparent reason. When you reach the lake follow the shoreline trail to the right for the best views and campsites.

Hike 39 Crawfish Lake

Easy enough for children, this hike traverses high alpine slopes of wildflowers and forest to a pretty mountain lake suitable for swimming.

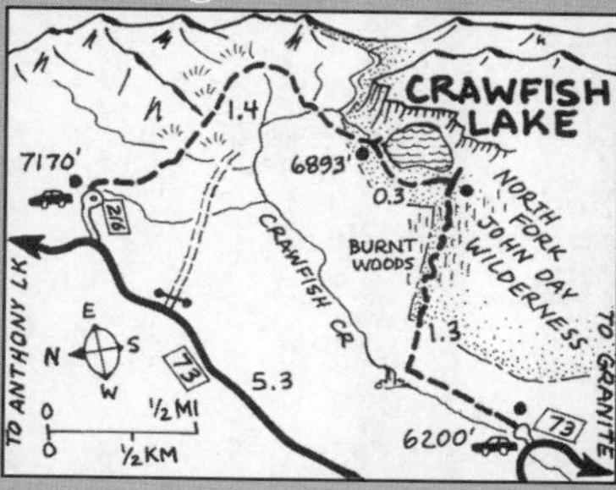

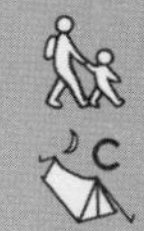

Easy
2.8 miles round trip
350 feet elevation gain
Open July through October
Use: hikers, horses

Getting There— From North Powder exit 285 of Interstate 84, follow "Anthony Lakes" signs 25 paved miles west on what becomes Road 73. Beyond the Anthony Lake Campground 4.5 miles (and 0.7 mile beyond a pass) turn left on Road 216 at a pointer for the Crawfish Lake Trail (avoiding the turnoff for the Crawfish *Basin* Trail). Follow the bumpy dirt road 0.2 mile to its end at a trailhead turnaround.

The trail sets off through mixed subalpine woods, crossing several small creeks lined with pink monkeyflower. Next the trail traverses meadows with sagebrush and views of the white granite peaks of the Elkhorn Range. At the 0.9-mile mark you'll cross a narrow clearcut originally intended as a ski run for a never-completed expansion of the Anthony Lake ski resort.

Then the path reenters subalpine woods, crosses glassy Crawfish Creek on logs, and climbs to a camped-out spot on the lake's shore. A 20-foot granite outcrop to the left seems designed for sunbathing. Fish jump and dragonflies zoom along the piney shore. If you like, continue on a trail to the right 0.3 mile to the lake's shallower end, where a grassy bank has a view of The Lakes Observation Point.

Other Options— If you can arrange a car shuttle, you don't have to hike back the way you came. At the far end of Crawfish Lake turn right at a T-junction to find a continuation of the trail that dives steeply down through a burned forest 1.3 miles to a lower trailhead. To shuttle a car here from the upper trailhead, drive Road 73 downhill 5.3 miles to a switchback loop and a sign for the Crawfish Lake Trail.

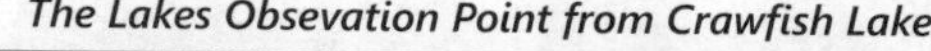
The Lakes Obsevation Point from Crawfish Lake.

Hike 40 Anthony Lake

A glacier scoured Anthony Lake's granite basin from the crest of the Elkhorn Range during the Ice Age.

Easy (to Hoffer Lakes)
2.9-mile loop
460 feet elevation gain
Open July through October

Moderate (to The Lakes Obs. Point)
5.7 miles round trip
1390 feet elevation gain

Moderate (to Dutch Flat Saddle)
8.2-mile loop
1330 feet elevation gain

Anthony Lake's guard station.

Subalpine firs and wildflower meadows now ring the lake, framing its reflection of craggy peaks from a picnic area beside the popular Anthony Lake Campground.

Getting There— Drive Interstate 84 north of Baker City 19 miles (or south of La Grande 24 miles) to North Powder exit 285 and follow "Anthony Lakes" signs 21.3 paved miles west on what becomes Road 73. At an Anthony Lake Campground sign, turn left 300 feet, then fork to the right toward a picnic area and park on the left at a lakeshore picnic gazebo. The gazebo was built in the 1930s by the Civilian Conservation Corps, and so was the guard station across the street, a rentable log cabin (see page 24). A concessionaire charges a $4-per-car fee for day use here.

Start by walking down past the gazebo. Turn left along Anthony Lake's shoreline trail. Flowers here include pink shooting stars, blue gentians, purple asters, and pink heather. After strolling 0.3 mile, cross a boat ramp and continue around the

Lees Peak from the first Hoffer Lake.

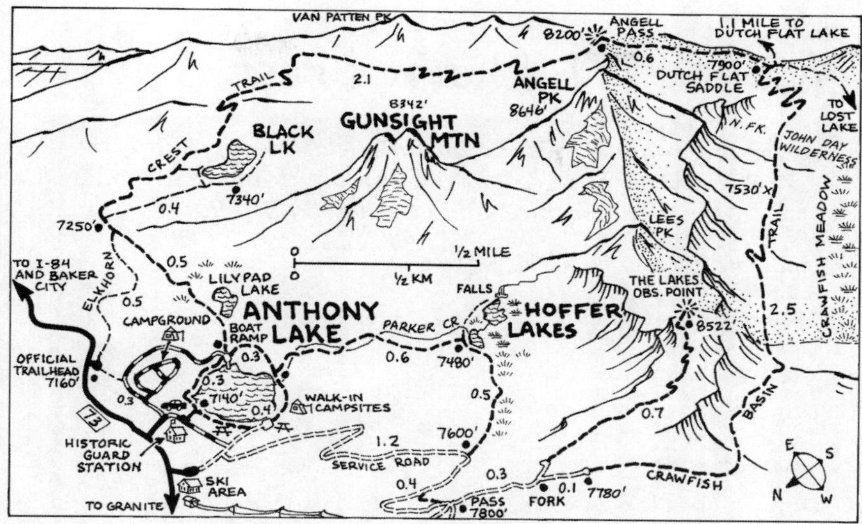

lake on a gravel trail, passing walk-in campsites. At the 0.6-mile mark, look for a sign on the left for the Hoffer Lakes. Turn uphill to the left on this rooty, rocky path along a creek, climbing 0.6 mile to a T-shaped junction at the first Hoffer Lake, an alpine pool backed by the gigantic granite slab of Lees Peak. Detour briefly left 300 feet to see a waterfall beside a second, shallower lake.

Then return to the first Hoffer Lake and continue on the loop trail along its shore, climbing gradually through glorious alpine wildflower meadows for another half mile. The path ends at a gravel service road. For a short loop, simply turn right on the road for 1.2 miles to your car. For a longer trip with grander views, however, turn uphill to the left on this service road 0.4 mile to a pass where four dirt roads meet beside ski area snow fences. Take the left-most dirt road up along the ridge 0.3 mile until the road forks.

Here you face a decision: Would you rather fork left to a viewpoint at The Lakes Observation Point, or fork right for a 8.2-mile loop to Dutch Flat Saddle?

If you go left, you'll climb on what soon becomes a spectacular, well-graded path among sparse whitebark pines. After half a mile the trail switchbacks up through a granite notch dynamited from the ridgecrest. When the trail ends, scramble the final 30 feet up to The Lakes Observation Point, a crag where anchor cables remain from an old fire lookout. The view swings from Crawfish Lake in the west to Anthony Lake in the east, with the distant Wallowa Mountains on the horizon.

For the longer loop hike, however, veer right when you reach the fork in the road. This spur leads 0.1 mile to the Crawfish Basin Trail. The path traverses high above Crawfish Meadow, climbing gradually for 2.5 miles to a well-marked junction at Dutch Flat Saddle, a good lunch stop *(GPS location 44.9299, -118.2265)*. Detour 100 feet ahead for a view of Dutch Flat Lake, a mile below.

Then return to the saddle and head uphill to the north on the Elkhorn Crest Trail for 0.6 mile to another breathtaking viewpoint at Angell Pass. Continue 2.1 gorgeous miles, descending to a junction where the Elkhorn Crest Trail turns right. Instead go straight for half a mile to Anthony Lake and the route to your car.

Hike 41 Elkhorn Crest

One of Oregon's most beautiful backpacking routes, the 22.8-mile Elkhorn Crest Trail contours from pass to pass along the granite spine of the Elkhorn Range.

Moderate (to Dutch Flat Lake)
8.6 miles round trip
1910 feet elevation gain
Open July through October
Use: hikers, horses

Difficult (to Lost Lake)
12.8 miles round trip
1860 feet elevation gain

Difficult (to Summit Lake)
20 miles round trip
2600 feet elevation gain

Difficult (to Marble Pass)
22.8 miles one-way
2820 feet elevation gain

Summit Lake.

Views from this timberline path stretch from the Wallowas to the John Day country. The trail itself passes almost no water sources or flat campsites, so plan to detour to Dutch Flat Lake, Lost Lake, Summit Lake, or Twin Lakes along the way.

Getting There— Drive Interstate 84 north of Baker City 19 miles (or south of La Grande 24 miles) to North Powder exit 285. Then follow "Anthony Lakes" signs 21 paved miles west on what becomes Road 73. Just before the Anthony Lake Campground, turn left into the well-marked Elkhorn Crest Trailhead parking lot.

The trail begins beside a horse-loading ramp on the left side of the parking lot. After 0.5 mile, keep left at junctions with side trails to Anthony Lake and Black Lake. Beyond this the Elkhorn Crest climbs 1400 feet in 2.1 miles to scenic Angell Pass, and then descends 0.6 mile to a 4-way trail junction in Dutch Flat Saddle. If you detour 100 feet to the left, you'll get a birds-eye view of Dutch Flat Lake and its small island. Decide here whether you want to hike down another mile to the lake itself.

If you choose to continue on the Elkhorn Crest Trail you'll contour along an open slope 1.9 miles to Nip and Tuck Pass, where the trail slips through a crack in the granite ridgecrest. A few feet beyond the pass, a side path switchbacks down to the left toward Lost Lake (1.3 miles) and Meadow Lake (2.5 miles). Both are shallow and set among lodgepole pines, but Lost Lake is prettier, with a flowing inlet, while Meadow Lake is stagnant.

If you skip Lost Lake and instead continue on the Elkhorn Crest Trail beyond Nip and Tuck Pass, you'll contour 3.4 miles around Mt. Ruth to Cracker Saddle, where you leave the North Fork John Day Wilderness. Beyond this point motorcycles are permitted, but rare. In the saddle you'll cross a steep, rugged road from the ghost

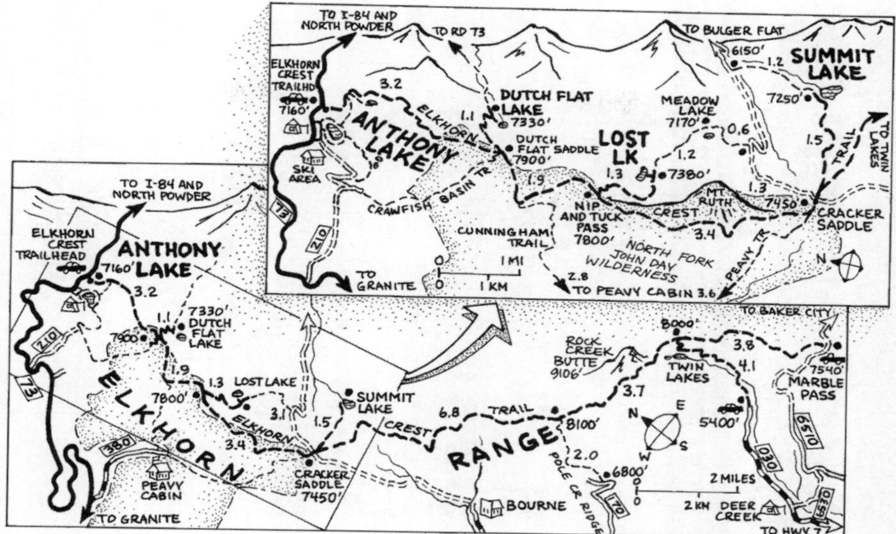

town of Bourne. In another 0.2 mile, a left-hand fork of the trail heads off 1.5 miles to Summit Lake. As large as Anthony Lake, but rarely visited, this beautiful pool borders a 1990s fire zone that left half the shore lined with white snags.

South of the Summit Lake turnoff, the Elkhorn Crest Trail traverses a slope with occasional old mining prospects. After 9.5 miles the route skirts 9106-foot Rock Creek Butte, the range's highest peak. Detour half a mile up to the summit, if you like, with a non-technical scramble.

Then hike onward a mile to a saddle junction, with Twin Lakes sparkling in the cliff-rimmed valley far below. To the right, the Twin Lakes Trail dives down a mile to the lakes and continues 3.1 miles to a trailhead on Road 030 that's accessible by passenger cars. If you go straight at the saddle junction, you'll follow the gentler Elkhorn Crest Trail 3.8 miles to its end at Marble Pass—a trailhead that can be reached only by rugged, high-clearance vehicles. To leave a shuttle car there, drive to Baker City and follow the directions in Hike #42.

Nip and Tuck Pass on the Elkhorn Crest Trail.

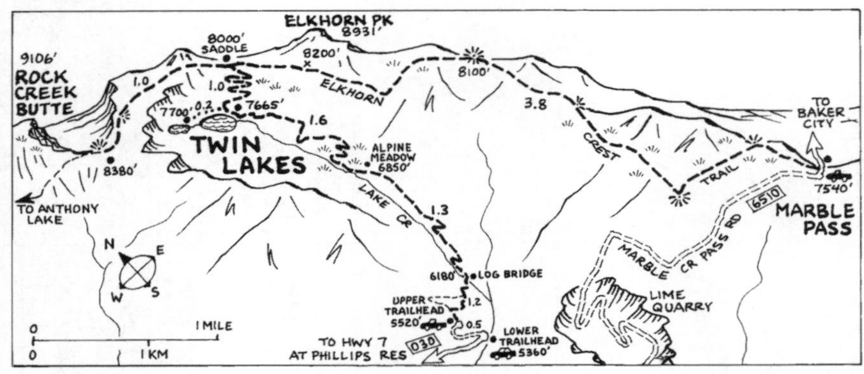

Hike 42 Twin Lakes

Expect mountain goats and wildflowers in the high meadows at Twin Lakes, in a cliff-rimmed cirque at the southern end of the Elkhorn Crest Trail.

Difficult (from Road 030)
8.2 miles round trip
2300 feet elevation gain
Open mid-July through October
Use: hikers, horses, bicycles, motorcycles

Difficult (from Marble Pass)
9.6 miles round trip
1200 feet elevation gain

Mountain goat at Twin Lakes.

Two routes reach Twin Lakes. For a relatively easy drive but a steep hike, start at Road 030. For a longer, gentler trail but a grueling drive, start at Marble Pass.

Getting There— If you choose the Road 030 trailhead, drive west from Baker City on Highway 7 toward Sumpter for 23.3 miles (or east of the Sumpter junction 3.3 miles). Between mileposts 29 and 28 turn north at a sign for Deer Creek Road. This road immediately forks! Do not go straight onto Larch Creek Road. Instead veer left to follow the real Deer Creek Road for 4 good gravel miles to an X-shaped junction. Go straight on Road 030. This track is so rocky that to avoid tire damage you should drive the worst parts no faster than 5 mph.

After 2.4 miles you'll reach a lower parking area at a sign, "Twin Lks Tr ½ ." The rutted road ahead changes names to "095" and looks frighteningly steep. But in fact it's only terrible for the first 100 feet. If your vehicle can handle this, the remaining 0.5 mile to a turnaround at the upper trailhead is easy.

From the upper trailhead the Twin Lakes Trail begins as an all-terrain vehicle track to the left. ATVs have rutted various routes here, but they cannot drive farther than one mile toward Twin Lakes because the route skirts a steep, rocky sidehill.

Twin Lakes and Rock Creek Butte.

Motorcycles are occasionally able to negotiate this obstacle, and are permitted.

Just 0.1 mile from the trailhead the ATV track forks. Follow a "Trail" pointer steeply up to the right. At the 1.2-mile mark you'll cross Lake Creek on a log bridge. After another steepish 1.3 miles the path emerges at a huge alpine meadow. Blooming here in August are orange paintbrush, yellow cinquefoil, and white phlox.

Then the trail switchbacks up 1.6 miles to Lower Twin Lake. The trail misses this lake by 300 feet, and there's no sign, but it's easy to bushwhack over to the shore *(GPS location 44.8083, -118.0857)*. The deep blue pool has a backdrop of huge red cliffs and snowfields. Walk around the shore to the right and head up through a meadow 300 feet to the smaller Twin, where you'll find pink heather and probably a dozen mountain goats. The goats have become so fond of salt that they sometimes nibble on backpackers' tents. Wildlife specialists have put out salt blocks to help.

Getting There— If you'd rather hike to Twin Lakes via the gentler trail from Marble Pass, you must have a high-clearance vehicle that can negotiate the rugged road. From Interstate 84, take Baker City exit 304, drive west into town on Campbell Street for a mile to a traffic light at Main Street, continue straight another 0.5 mile to another light, and turn right on 10th Street for 1.1 mile to a flashing yellow light. Following a pointer for the Marble Creek Picnic Area, turn left on paved Pocahontas Road and follow this road through several zigzags 7.6 miles. Where Pocahontas Road turns right for the third time, go straight on gravel Marble Creek Road. In another 0.3 mile, turn left to keep on Marble Creek Road, and then follow it 7.8 miles to the trailhead in a high pass *(GPS location 44.7735, -118.0437)*. The last 4 miles of the road to Marble Pass are agonizingly slow, with rocks and frequent drainage ditches.

The well-graded Elkhorn Crest Trail sets off across an alpine grassland of sagebrush, blue lupine, white yarrow, and a few whitebark pines. Every mile or so the path passes viewpoints on the range's crest. Each pass has better views—east across the patchwork of ranches surrounding Baker City to the Wallowas, and west across Sumpter's valley to distant Strawberry Mountain. After 3.8 miles you'll reach a saddle with a junction. Turn left to switchback down a mile to Lower Twin Lake.

Whichever way you hike to Twin Lakes, consider adding an extra mile along the Elkhorn Crest Trail to a viewpoint on the shoulder of Rock Creek Butte, the highest peak in the Blue Mountains. Backpackers can continue on the Elkhorn Crest Trail 18 miles to Anthony Lake (see Hike #40).

BLUE MOUNTAINS -- NORTH
PENDLETON
EXIT 207
37
WOOLEN MILL
11
UMATILLA RIVER
AVE
COURT
ROUND-UP GROUNDS
MAIN
MISSION
EMIGRANT
209
84
30
EXIT 213
395
EXIT 210
1MI
1KM
WALLA WALLA
TO LEWISTON
12
WHITMAN MISSION
WASHINGTON
OREGON
WENAHA-TUCANNON WILDERNESS
45
159
158
MILTON-FREEWATER
RD 65
64
WENAHA R
160
MOUNTAINS
ROAD
TROY
62
11
161
157
GRANDE RONDE R
FLORA
6413
TOLLGATE
44
RD
PENDLETON
204
64
156
WESTON
JUBILEE LAKE
SPOUT SPRINGS SKI AREA
43
3
153
11
155
154
WALLOWA
TO THE DALLES
WILDHORSE CASINO
NORTH FORK UMATILLA WILDERNESS
204
WALLOWA
66
EXIT 216
84
RIVER
MEACHAM
RD 62
ELGIN
395
10 MILES
10 KM
82
OREGON TRAIL INTERPRETIVE PARK
68
67
TO UKIAH
LA GRANDE
BLUE
ENTERPRISE
EXIT 248
HILGARD JUNCTION
EXIT 261
232
COVE
WALLOWA MTNS
162
69
HOT LAKE SPR
MOSS SPRINGS
TO UKIAH
244
RED BRIDGE
203
UNION
EAGLE CAP WILDERNESS
LEHMAN HOT SPR (CLOSED)
CATHERINE CREEK
70
71
72
73
LA GRANDE
EXIT 259
30
232
RD 77
"Y" AVE
82
PIONEER PARK
NORTH POWDER
AVE
EXIT 261
ROAD 67
MEDICAL SPRING (SITE)
WALNUT ST
ADAMS
ISLAND
203
HISTORIC HOMES WALKING TOUR
COVE AVE
84
84
RD 70
"N" AVE
AVE
EXIT 298
OREGON TRAIL INTERP CTR
SUNSET DR
2ND ST
4TH ST
ST
86
EASTERN OREGON UNIV
1/2 MI
1/2 KM
30
BAKER CITY
BIRNIE PARK
12TH
"C" AVE
GEKELER LN
TO ONTARIO

Bronze statues on Pendleton's Main Street include Jackson Sundown, the legendary Nez Perce horseman who won the Pendleton Roundup's top prize in 1916 at the age of 53.

PENDLETON

Oregon Trail pioneers once dreaded the northern Blue Mountains' forested canyons and surprise snowstorms. Although Interstate 84 now spans the range from Pendleton to La Grande, there's still plenty of adventure and wild beauty along the mountains' rarely visited back trails.

Downtown Pendleton

Get your bearings in Pendleton's historic downtown district at the **railroad station** at the end of Main Street. Next door is the **Heritage Station Museum** (108 SW Frazier) with exhibits on the Oregon Trail and local history. Hours are 10am-4pm Tue-Sat and admission runs $2-$5. Just down the street, don't miss the **Pendleton Underground Tours,** where you can explore tunnels and opium dens built by Chinese railroad laborers beneath Pendleton's old town in the 1880s. The 90-minute tours cost $20 (no children under 6) and begin at 31 SW Emigrant Street (reservations 541-276-0730). There are no tours on Sundays or Tuesdays.

Then stroll north along Main Street for three blocks, passing bronze statues of famous Pendletoners, to the old-timey **Rainbow Cafe** at 2009 Main, an 1880s saloon where a full ranch breakfast costs just $10. Across the street is **Hamley's Steakhouse,** a posh Wild West eatery with higher prices. Next door is the original Hamley business, a fascinating **leather goods store** that has occupied the same building since 1904 and is now owned by the Umatilla tribe.

Hamleys is a 1904 Pendleton leather goods store operated by the Umatilla tribe.

Continue two blocks north on Main Street to a plaza by a Umatilla River bridge. From here, a **paved pedestrian promenade** extends left and right atop a river dike for a total of 4.5 miles.

The **Pendleton Woolen Mills** factory, founded 1909, weaves Indian-inspired blankets and shawls. At 1307 SE Court Place, the factory offers free tours Monday through Friday year-round. Call 541-276-6911 for an appointment.

Pendleton Round-Up

Pendleton puts on its spurs each year for the **Pendleton Round-Up,** during the second full week of September, when contestants gather from across North America for a professional rodeo competition (tickets $13-30 at 800-457-6336 or *pendletonroundup.com*). The pageantry includes a parade, dance contests, and a Native American beauty contest. If you miss it, check out the **Round-Up Hall of Fame**, a museum of historic photographs, saddles, beadwork, and memorabilia under the rodeo arena's south grandstand at 1114 SW Court Avenue, open Monday-Saturday 10am-4pm in summer. Adults are $5, kids under 11 are $2.

La Grande

The Old Oregon Trail runs through the south edge of La Grande (on B Street), but this city isn't stuck in the past. Catch a play at the McKenzie Theatre on the campus of **Eastern Oregon University** or drop by the **Farmers' Market** for local arts and crafts, open 9am-noon on Saturdays and Tuesdays 3-6pm from the end of May to the third week of October at 4th and Adams. For dinner, try **Ten Depot Street,** a restaurant at 10 Depot Street, of course.

In the evening take your date to the 1952-era **La Grande Drive-In**, one of only

Downtown La Grande.

two drive-in movie theaters left in Oregon. Open on summer weekends, it's on the southeast edge of town off Highway 30 at 404 20th Street.

Wildhorse Resort and Tamastslikt Museum

The Cayuse, Umatilla, and Walla Walla tribes built this elaborate casino (hotel, RV park, golf course, restaurant, slots, gaming tables) and the neighboring Tamastslikt Cultural Institute, a museum with walk-through exhibits describing the tribes' past and present. The museum, on a winding 1-mile entrance road behind the casino, is open 9am-6pm daily from April through September, and 10am-5pm (except Sundays) from October through March. Adults are $10, seniors $9, and kids $7. Drive Interstate 84 east of Pendleton 4 miles to exit 216.

Emigrant Springs State Heritage Area

See Oregon Trail wagon ruts and excellent outdoor interpretive displays on a paved half-mile loop in the Blue Mountain forest. Between La Grande and Pendleton, take I-84 exit 248, follow signs 3.3 miles. Open year-round for day use only.

Hot Lake Springs

This hot spring-fed lake east of La Grande may be Oregon's oldest resort. Known to the Nez Perce tribe as Ea-Kesh-Pa, it became an Oregon Trail stopover and then, in the early 1900s, a sprawling sanatorium spa. Now the Lodge at Hot Lake Springs offers soaks in the hot springs (see page 16), 15 rooms, a pub, and a theater. Take Interstate 84 exit 265 just east of La Grande and drive east 5.2 miles toward Union.

Hat Rock State Park

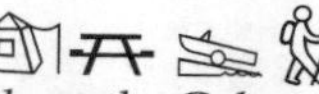

Lewis and Clark described the hat-shaped monolith in this park along the Columbia River. Today visitors flock here to cool off on hot summer days by picnicking on the shady lawns or launching boats onto the river. A hiker/biker path from the boat ramp follows an abandoned railroad grade along the river 4.8 miles to McNary Beach Park. From Interstate 82 in Umatilla, take Hwy 730 east 9 miles.

Hike 43 North Fork Umatilla River

In Pendleton's backyard, the North Fork Umatilla Wilderness resembles a one-third-scale version of Hells Canyon, with jagged canyons carved into tablelands of Columbia River basalt lava.

Easy (to Coyote Creek)
5.4 miles round trip
400 feet elevation gain
Open except in winter storms
Use: hikers, horses

Moderate (to Grouse Mountain)
5 miles round trip
880 feet elevation gain
Open April through November

The North Fork Umatilla River.

The smaller scale of this canyon makes it suitable for day trips. Start with a hike along the river to Coyote Creek, perhaps with a side trip to a viewpoint of the Lick Creek canyon. For a more panoramic view, start at an upper trailhead and follow a canyon rim out to Grouse Mountain.

Getting There— Drive Interstate 84 east of Pendleton 5 miles to the Wildhorse casino at exit 216. Head north toward Walla Walla for 2 miles to a flashing red light, turn right on Mission Road for 1.6 miles, and turn left on paved, two-lane Cayuse Road for 10.9 miles. Between mileposts 15 and 16, turn right across railroad tracks onto Bingham Road. Follow this road for 12 paved miles and an additional 3.2 miles on good gravel to the well-marked trailhead parking turnoff on the left.

Put on your boots, because the trail has a few boggy spots. Then set off straight on the main path, ignoring the Lick Creek Trail to the left for now. The Douglas fir woods here were inundated with mud and boulders in 2020, when a landslide 0.9 mile upstream launched a flood. Even the road was closed for two years. The path upriver is a bit rough until you reach the source of flood, where a slide from

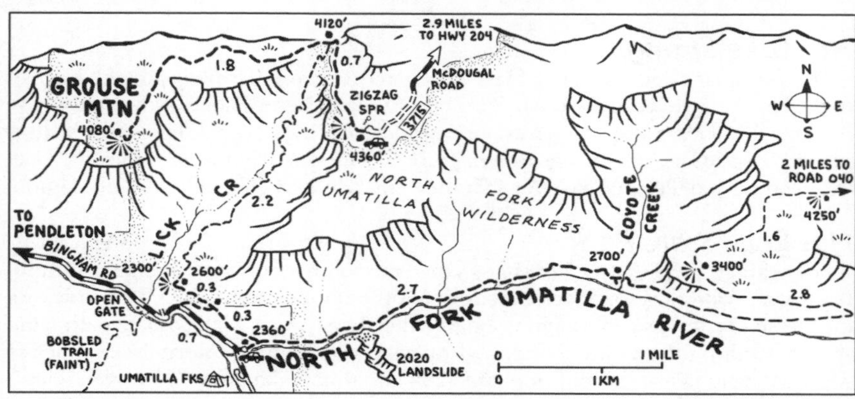

a side canyon briefly dammed the river.

The next 1.6 miles upstream are joyous, tracing the river to its confluence with 4-foot-wide Coyote Creek. Among the riverside cottonwoods and red alders you'll find cow parsnip plants six feet tall, the orange tubes of honeysuckle, and the red glow of columbine flowers. Elsewhere, beneath Douglas fir and grand fir, look for purple Oregon grape, white snowberry, and wild strawberry.

A riverside campsite at Coyote Creek makes a good turnaround point. Beyond Coyote Creek, the North Fork Umatilla Trail leaves the river and climbs 2.8 miles to a viewpoint atop Coyote Ridge, another possible goal.

If you're looking for viewpoints, however, there are two easier options. First, you could hike back to your car, but just before the parking area turn right on the Lick Creek Trail. This path traverses a slope 0.6 mile, where it breaks out of the woods at a canyon vista. Turn back here, because the Lick Creek Trail climbs relentlessly after this, with few views and no water.

For the best views of all, start your hike at the top of the canyon and stroll out to Grouse Mountain. To find this upper trailhead from Interstate 84 in Pendleton, take exit 210 and follow "Milton-Freewater" signs through town and onto Highway 11 for 20.5 miles. Between mileposts 20 and 21, turn right at a sign for Elgin, and in another 0.8 mile fork left to keep heading toward Elgin on Tollgate Road (Highway 204). After 14.6 miles, turn right on gravel McDougall Road for 2.9 miles. The last half mile is rough. At road's end, park at Zigzag Spring and hike a relatively level trail 0.7 mile to a junction with the Lick Creek Trail. Continue straight 1.8 miles along a ridge to the rimrock viewpoint at the edge of Grouse Mountain.

The trail to Grouse Mountain overlooks the North Fork Umatilla River canyon.

Hike 44 Jubilee Lake

A dam created Jubilee Lake in 1968 to provide a recreation goal in the high, rolling forests of the Blue Mountain crest. For an easy walk, stroll around the lakeshore loop.

Easy (around lake)
2.6-mile loop
No elevation gain
Open early June to late November
Use: hikers

Moderate (to S Fk Walla Walla R)
6.6 miles round trip
1880 feet elevation **loss**
Open mid-June to early November
Use: hikers, bicycles, motorcycles

Jubilee Lake's dam.

If the lakeshore loop seems too tame, hike a more rugged trail nearby, down to the South Fork Walla Walla River.

Getting There— From Interstate 84 in Pendleton, take exit 210 and follow "Milton-Freewater" signs through town and onto Highway 11 for 20.5 miles. Between mileposts 20 and 21, turn right at a sign for Elgin, and in another 0.8 mile fork left to keep heading toward Elgin on Tollgate Road (Highway 204). After 19.9 miles (beyond the Tollgate Store 1.2 miles) turn left onto Road 64 at a

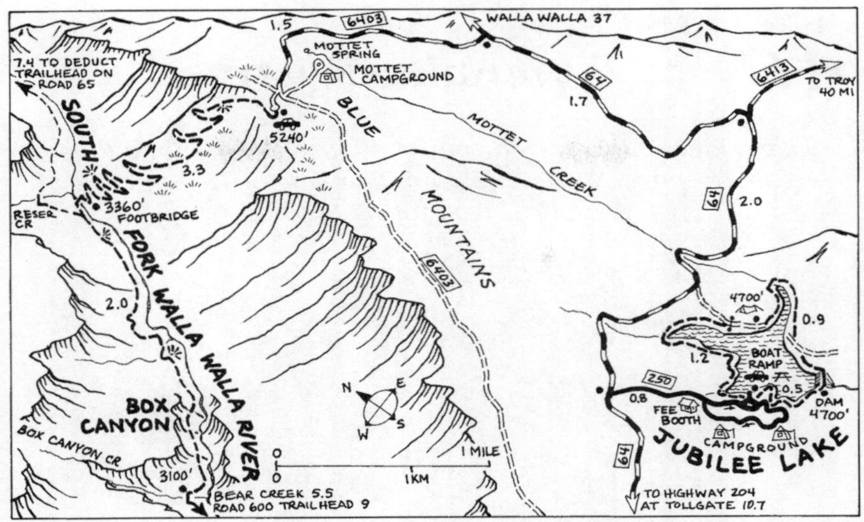

sign for Jubilee Lake. Follow Road 64 north for 3.4 miles of pavement and another 8.1 miles of wide gravel. Then turn right on the paved Jubilee Lake Campground entrance road for 0.6 mile to a fee booth (campsites $17, day use $3), and continue 0.2 mile to the boat ramp parking lot on the left.

Start your hike at the far left end of the parking lot, take a paved path through a picnic area to the shore, and head counter-clockwise around the lake. The high-elevation forest includes lodgepole pine, subalpine fir, and Engelmann spruce. After 0.5 mile you'll cross the lake's earth dam and trade pavement for a dirt path. In another 0.9 mile the path briefly joins a closed road at a free campsite. Continue around the lakeshore 1.2 miles to return to your car.

For the tougher hike to the South Fork Walla Walla River, drive out of the campground, turn north on gravel Road 64 for 2 miles to a fork, veer left toward "Walla Walla" to keep on Road 64 for another 1.7 miles, and turn left on dirt Road 6403 for 1.5 miles to a meadow with a junction. Don't go straight ahead into Mottet Campground, but rather fork slightly to the right on an unmarked road 0.1 mile to a large gravel parking lot *(GPS location 45.869, -117.9673)*.

Set off down "Rough Fork Trail No. 3227," a well-graded path that ducks into a grand fir forest. Before long you'll descend across meadow openings with sagebrush, purple larkspur, blue lupine, and scarlet gilia. Views extend across the sharply crenelated South Fork Walla Walla canyon. After 3.3 miles the trail enters a lush, low-elevation forest, passes a campsite, and crosses the river on a bridge.

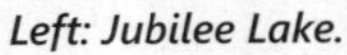
Left: Jubilee Lake.

Hike 45 Wenaha River

Like a jagged crack in the planet's crust, the Wenaha River canyon zigzags from the remote village of Troy into the Wenaha-Tucannon Wilderness.

Easy (to National Forest)
4.6 miles round trip
350 feet elevation gain
Open all year
Use: hikers, horses

Difficult (to Crooked Creek)
12.8 miles round trip
580 feet elevation gain

Wenaha River.

A 31.4-mile trail follows the river from the start of its desert canyon to its source high in the Blue Mountains. For an easy day trip, explore the first few miles of the path. For a longer trip, continue to a campsite near the Crooked Creek footbridge.

Getting There— From Interstate 84 in La Grande, take exit 261 and follow signs for Wallowa Lake 65 miles to Enterprise. At a pointer for Lewiston in the middle of Enterprise, turn left on First Street (alias Highway 3) for 35 miles to a sign for Flora. Turn left 3 miles to this interesting ghost town, which peaked as a wheat farming center in the 1910s. The town's schoolhouse has been restored as a cultural center.

Next drive on past Flora for 4.1 paved miles and an additional 7.2 miles of steep, winding, 1-lane gravel road (past a sign "Not recommended for trucks or passenger cars") down to a bridge across the Grande Ronde River. On the far side of the bridge turn left on a paved road for 2 miles to the edge of Troy. A block before "downtown," (a cafe, store, laundry, gas station, and inn), turn right toward Pomeroy on Bartlett Road. Up this road 0.4 mile, where the road switchbacks to

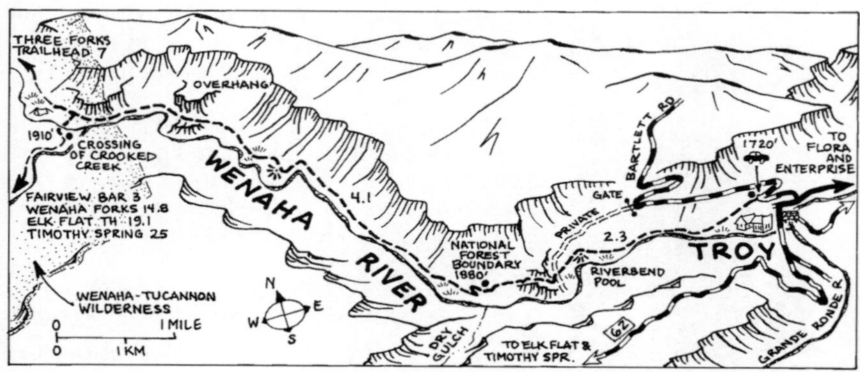

the right, park at a pullout straight ahead beside a trailhead message board *(GPS location 45.9474, -117.4544).*

The Wenaha River Trail sets out through sparse ponderosa pine woods with teasels, elderberries, and salsify. In spring look for the sunflower-like blooms of balsamroot. After 0.7 mile you'll reach the first access to the river itself, a 60-foot current of boulder-strewn whitewater. After this the trail climbs past the first of several patches of poison ivy. Beware these triple-leafletted shrubs!

The Wenaha River.

After 1.8 miles you'll climb to a viewpoint above a riverbend pool where you can watch giant fish idling far below. Then the trail crosses a crude, private roadbed and climbs around a scenic cliff between layers of rimrock. White mariposa lilies dot the slope, along with Oregon sunshine and wild clematis.

In another 0.4 mile you'll pass a sign marking the National Forest boundary—a turnaround point for casual hikers. Beyond this, the trail continues upriver 4.1 miles, occasionally ducking under cliffs, to a rock cairn at a possibly unmarked junction. Ahead the trail passes a meadow with campsites along Crooked Creek. To the left, the Wenaha River Trail dips to a crossing of Crooked Creek, another good turnaround goal *(GPS location 45.9775, -117.5553).* A footbridge here collapsed in 2016, but it's usually easy to wade.

Backpackers and equestrians can continue upriver two or three days to trail's end at Timothy Springs (Hike #157). To drive a shuttle car there from Troy, go south through downtown past the cafe, go straight toward "Long Meadows Ranger Station" for 0.3 mile, fork right toward Elgin on what becomes Road 62 for 27 miles, and turn right on Road 6415 for 6.9 miles.

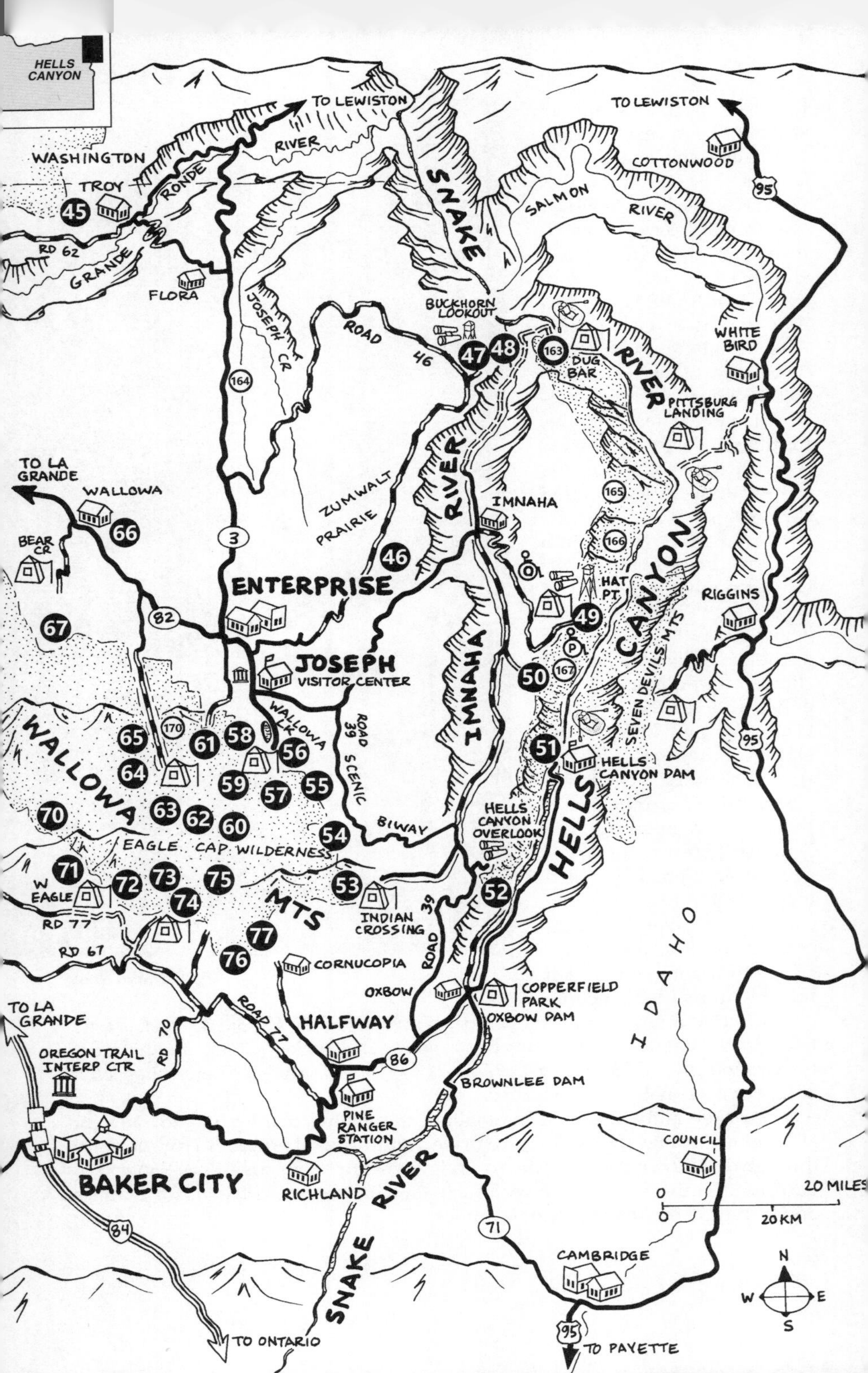

HELLS CANYON
TO LEWISTON
TO LEWISTON
WASHINGTON
RIVER
RONDE
GRANDE
TROY
45
RD 62
FLORA
SNAKE
COTTONWOOD
SALMON
RIVER
95
JOSEPH CR
164
ROAD 46
BUCKHORN LOOKOUT
47
48
163
DUG BAR
RIVER
WHITE BIRD
PITTSBURG LANDING
TO LA GRANDE
WALLOWA
66
BEAR CR
ZUMWALT PRAIRIE
RIVER
IMNAHA
165
166
CANYON
3
46
ENTERPRISE
HAT PT
49
82
67
RIGGINS
JOSEPH
VISITOR CENTER
SEVEN DEVILS MTS
50
167
P
WALLOWA LK
ROAD 39 SCENIC
BIWAY
IMNAHA
WALLOWA
170
65
61
58
56
64
59
57
55
51
HELLS CANYON DAM
95
70
63
62
60
54
HELLS CANYON OVERLOOK
HELLS
EAGLE CAP WILDERNESS
71
72
73
75
53
52
W EAGLE
74
MTS
RD 77
INDIAN CROSSING
ROAD 39
IDAHO
RD 67
77
76
CORNUCOPIA
OXBOW
COPPERFIELD PARK
OXBOW DAM
TO LA GRANDE
RD 70
ROAD 77
HALFWAY
OREGON TRAIL INTERP CTR
86
BROWNLEE DAM
PINE RANGER STATION
COUNCIL
BAKER CITY
RICHLAND
SNAKE RIVER
0
20 MILES
0
20 KM
84
71
CAMBRIDGE
N
W
E
S
95
TO ONTARIO
TO PAYETTE

HELLS CANYON

Deeper than the Grand Canyon, this colossal river gorge looks like the ragged edge of a broken planet, with rimrock tiers stacked to the sky. The canyon is so deep that it has two completely different climate zones. Snow drapes the subalpine forested rim from November to June, but shimmering summer heat bakes the desert landscape of the Snake River's rocky banks 6000 feet below.

Hells Canyon Viewpoints

For such a monumental canyon, Hells Canyon has remarkably few convenient viewpoints. At only four places can passenger cars drive to canyon vistas on the Oregon side. At the south end of the gorge, drive a paved road along the Hells Canyon Reservoir and across the **Hells Canyon Dam** to a riverside visitor center, described in Hike #51. For a paved route to the rim's crest, take the Hells Canyon Scenic Byway route north from Halfway toward Joseph and follow signs to the **Hells Canyon Overlook**. For a better view, take a long, steep gravel road up from the town of Imnaha to the **Hat Point lookout tower** (see Hike #49), where observation decks, trails, and a picnic area add to the attraction. Some claim the most attractive panorama of all is at **Buckhorn Lookout** (see Hike #47), a quieter pullout beside an old lookout building north of Joseph.

Snake River whitewater trips

Drifting the Snake River through Hells Canyon is a 2- to 8-day voyage through some of the biggest scenery on earth. From the Hells Canyon Dam launch site it's 32 miles downriver to the boat ramp at Pittsburg Landing, 51 miles to Dug Bar, 79 miles to the mouth of the Grande Ronde River, and 104 miles to Lewiston, Idaho. Be forewarned that the most dangerous rapids are packed into the first 17 miles of the trip. For this thrilling stretch, ranger-issued permits are required from the Friday before Memorial Day through September 10. Applications for the permit lottery can be made between December 1 and January 31 each year at *recreation.gov* under "permits". Check with rangers for advice on suitable floatcraft, river levels, weather, and the canyon's strict campfire restrictions. If you need help shuttling a vehicle between your launch and take-out sites, check with Hells Canyon Shuttle in Halfway (800-785-3358 or *hellscanyonshuttle.com*).

Guided jet boat tours are a simpler but noisier alternative. Tours leave from the dock at the visitor center just below Hells Canyon Dam. Expect to pay about $155 for a 3-hour tour to Sheep Creek (leaves at 11am Pacific Time) or $205 for a 6-hour, 65-mile tour with lunch (leaves at 9am). Longer trips in rubber rafts are also available. For details and reservations, check 800-422-3568 or *hellscanyonadventures.com.* Other tour companies offer jet boat trips from Lewiston into Hells Canyon.

Imnaha

 ▶

Where pavement ends on the road to Hat Point's viewpoint, stop in the village of Imnaha to visit its rustic **tavern/general store.** The store features cigar-store Indian statues and an eclectic sampling of wares, but has no gasoline.

Hike 46 Zumwalt Prairie

Raptors soar above this rolling grassland between the snowy Wallowa Mountains and the ragged cliffs of Hells Canyon.

Harsin Butte.

Easy (Patti's Trail)
2.3-mile loop
80 feet elevation gain
Open all year

Moderate (Harsin Butte scramble)
1.6 miles round trip
690 feet elevation gain

Zumwalt Prairie has one of the highest concentrations of breeding hawks and eagles in the world—largely because the native bunchgrass prairie here teems with their favorite prey, ground squirrels.

Oregon State University researcher Marcy Houle celebrated the area's rich ecosystem in her 1995 book, *The Prairie Keepers*, and marveled that a century of careful cattle grazing may actually have improved raptor habitat. This intrigued The Nature Conservancy, a nonprofit group that bought 51 square miles here, making this the state's largest private nature preserve.

Most of the preserve is off limits, but you're allowed to stroll a loop trail to a quaking aspen grove or scramble up Harsin Butte for a look around. For the best wildflowers, visit between late April and June. Avoid the freezing winds of winter and the heat of August. Pets, horses, fires, vehicles, and camping are banned.

Getting There— Drive Highway 82 east of Enterprise 3.2 miles (or north of Joseph 3 miles). At a pointer for Buckhorn Springs between mileposts 68 and 69, turn north onto paved Crow Creek Road for 1.2 miles to a fork. Veer right to stay on Crow Creek Road for another 3.9 miles to another fork. This time veer right onto Zumwalt Road, which is paved for the first 2.3 miles. Continue on a good gravel

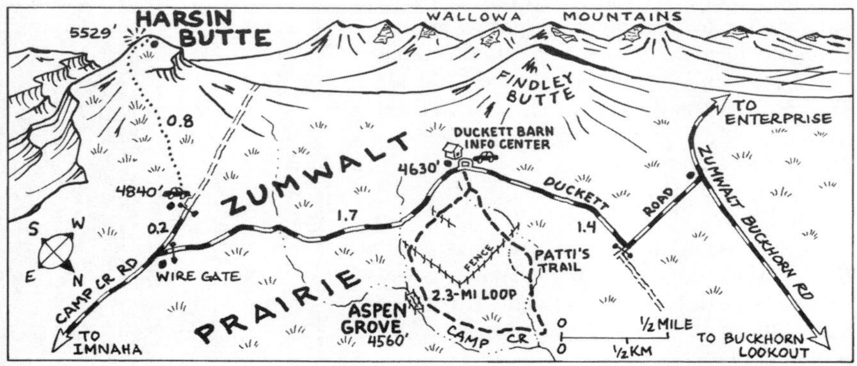

Park at an information kiosk in front of the explorable 1920s Duckett barn.

road an additional 11.5 miles. Then, at a sign for the Zumwalt Prairie Preserve, turn right on on one-lane gravel Duckett Road for 1.4 miles. Park at the Duckett Barn Information Center on the right.

Patti's Trail begins on the opposite side of the road and strikes off across the prairie. The big horizon is empty, save for the humps of Harsin and Findley Buttes. The real view is at your feet, where you'll see six kinds of native grasses, including 5-foot clumps of basin wildrye. Look for the blooms of yellow bells in April, pink Nootka roses and yellow lupine in May, and pink Clarkia and white mariposa lilies in June. The Nature Conservancy burns this area periodically to boost native plants, including the threatened Spaldings catchfly, an inobtrusive white-petaled flower that can catch flies with its sticky leaves.

After 0.2 mile the trail forks. Keep right, on a path that crosses two fence stiles before turning left along mostly dry Camp Creek. You'll pass a fenced stand of quaking aspen. At the 1.3-mile mark, at a blue post with an arrow, the loop trail turns left and follows a dry gulch back toward Duckett Barn.

For the second hike, drive Duckett Road east another 1.7 miles and turn right on gravel Camp Creek Road for 0.2 mile. Cross a cattle guard and park by a trailhead sign on the left *(GPS location 45.5358, -116.9564)*.

Although there is no established trail to Harsin Butte, this rounded knoll to the left (south) is the only high ground for miles, so there's not much chance of confusion. It's easy to walk across the prairie. The scramble route steepens beside a ponderosa pine grove where elk like to bed. The wildflowers bloom later on this butte than on the prairie below, with blue gentians and other alpine favorites. When you puff to the summit you'll find a solar-powered antenna and a 360-degree view.

After hiking back down to your car you might drive back by way of Imnaha through a very rough but very beautiful canyon—if you have plenty of gas. From the trailhead, take gravel Camp Creek Road east 11 miles to paved Highway 350. Imnaha's quaint store is a mile to your left, and Joseph is 28 miles to your right.

Other Options— The Nature Conservancy has two other trails open to the public at Zumwalt Prairie. The **Canyon Vista Trail** begins on Camp Creek Road, east of the Harsin Butte trailhead 2 miles, and climbs 1.8 miles to a viewpoint of the Imnaha canyonlands. The **Horned Lark Trail** begins on the Zumwalt Buckhorn Road, 3.1 miles north of the Duckett Road junction, and loops 1.9 miles through the prairie.

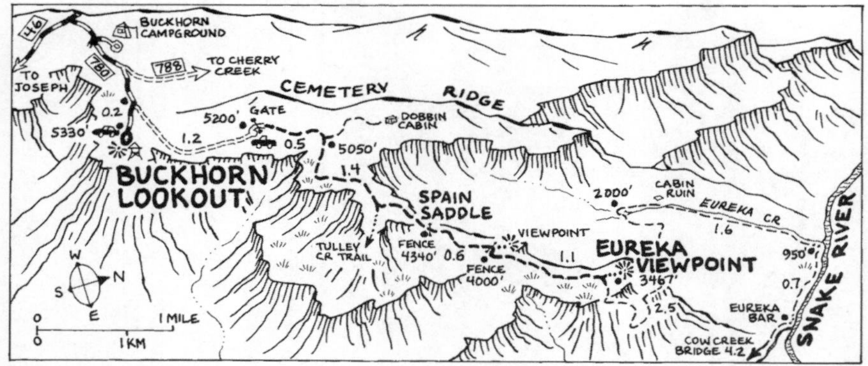

Hike

47 Buckhorn Lookout

The panorama is breathtaking from the historic Buckhorn fire lookout, perched on the lip of Hells Canyon's colossal chasm.

Moderate (to Eureka Viewpoint)
7.2 miles round trip
1780 feet elevation **loss**
Open June to mid-November
Use: hikers, horses, bicycles

Very Difficult (to Eureka Bar)
15.4 miles round trip
4150 feet elevation **loss**
100 feet elevation gain

Buckhorn Lookout.

The view actually improves the farther you hike from the lookout, following a well-graded trail down across slopes of wildflowers. The danger here is that you'll be tempted to romp too far down this trail into Hells Canyon. Remember that you will have to regain every step of lost elevation (perhaps thousands of feet!) later in the hot afternoon sun.

Getting There— Drive Highway 82 east of Enterprise 3.2 miles (or north of Joseph 3 miles). At a pointer for Buckhorn Spring between mileposts 68 and 69, turn north onto paved Crow Creek Road for 1.1 mile to a fork. Veer right to stay on Crow Creek Road for another 3.9 miles to another fork. This time veer right onto Zumwalt Road, which is paved for the first 2.4 miles. Continue on a good gravel road an additional 30 miles across high, scenic Zumwalt Prairie (see Hike #46). Weathered barns remain from the homesteaders who tried to settle this arid upland—including Henry and Josie Zumwalt, who opened a post office here in 1903.

At a sign for Buckhorn Overlook (9 miles after Zumwalt Road becomes Forest Road 46), turn right on Road 780. After 0.3 mile ignore a rough spur road that

The view from Buckhorn Lookout..

descends to the left to the primitive, free, 5-site Buckhorn Campground. Go straight at this junction and then keep right at the next two forks to reach the Buckhorn Lookout parking turnaround *(GPS location 45.7539, -116.8233).*

The vast canyons of the Imnaha River and its tributaries steal the show at Buckhorn Lookout because the Snake River itself is hidden. Look for Idaho's snow-capped Seven Devils above Hat Point's plateau, and the long white horizon of the Wallowa Mountains above Zumwalt Prairie. With a view like this, the 14-foot-square lookout building never needed a tower. Built in the 1930s, the building is no longer staffed.

The actual trailhead is 1.4 miles from the lookout turnaround, but if you're driving a passenger car, it's probably best to park here. Walk back from the turnaround 0.2 mile to a fork and turn right on a rutted, rocky track for 1.2 miles to a green metal gate marked "Road Closed." If you have a high-clearance vehicle with good tires, park in a gravel pullout just before the gate and start your hike here.

Beyond the gate, the old road becomes a wide trail along a ridge with scattered Douglas firs, wild rose bushes, yellow desert parsley, scarlet gilia, and orange paintbrush. After 0.5 mile, fork to the right in a grassy saddle. The path now traverses a view-packed bunchgrass slope speckled with countless colors of wildflowers from early June to mid-July. After another 1.4 miles the trail crosses a wire fence and enters a partially burned forest at Spain Saddle. Continue at least another 0.6 mile to the next wire fence crossing, where a cliff edge 300 feet to the left offers a first view down to the Snake River.

For an even better view, continue down the trail another 1.1 mile to a rock cairn, where the trail turns sharply right. To the left 50 feet you'll notice a fenceline ending in a small saddle. Leave the main path here and bushwhack left up amid 6-foot lava formations for 0.2 mile to Eureka Viewpoint, a ridge-end summit where prickly pear cactus blooms *(GPS location 45.8001, -116.7804).* From this eerie vantage point, teetering in the midst of Hells Canyon, you can see the Snake River in three different places.

Most hikers should turn back at Eureka Viewpoint. Beyond this point the trail continues downhill 4.1 miles to the Snake River, and then follows a canyon bottom with bushy poison ivy for 0.7 mile to Eureka Bar (see Hike #48).

Hike 48 Eureka Bar

Where the Imnaha River rages through a jagged rock gorge to Eureka Bar, it looks like a giant has jackhammered a crack into the earth's crust and inserted a river sideways.

Difficult
9.8 miles round trip
350 feet elevation gain
Open all year
Use: hikers, horses, bikes

Mine entrance at Eureka Bar.

Incredibly, a well-built, nearly level trail clings to the cliffs for the river's final 4.2 miles. At trail's end hikers emerge from the gorge to find themselves at the cobble-banked Snake River, amidst the ruins of an improbable mining boomtown, deep in Hells Canyon. Wear long pants because the path is occasionally crowded with blackberry vines and poison ivy—obstacles that block nearly all horse, mountain bike, and motorcycle users.

Getting There— Start by topping off your tank at the gas station in downtown Joseph. Then turn east beside the station at a large "Hells Canyon Scenic Byway" sign and follow signs 29 paved miles to the village of Imnaha. One block past the Imnaha store/tavern, turn left on Lower Imnaha Road for 6.6 paved miles to Fence Creek.

At this point the Lower Imnaha Road suddenly becomes a rutted, steep one-lane dirt road strewn with rocks. Although most passenger cars can handle it, turn back if you don't like the first 200 feet, because this is perfectly typical of what lies ahead: 15 miles of road so rough it takes a full hour to drive. Three miles beyond the Thorn Creek Guard Station you'll reach the Cow Creek Bridge—which spans

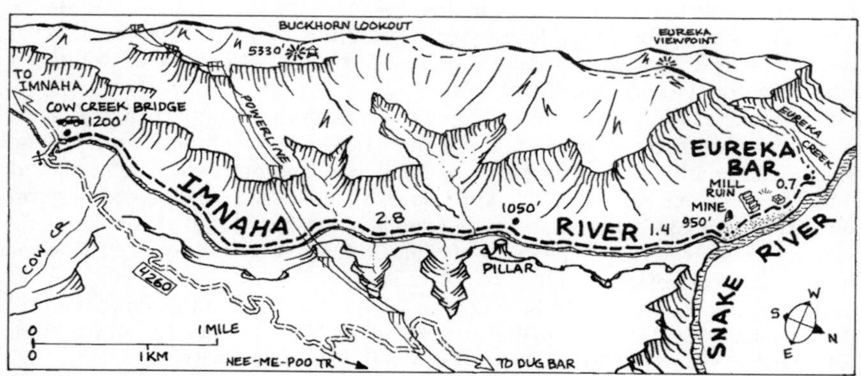

The trail down the Imnaha River hugs the base of canyon cliffs.

the Imnaha River near Cow Creek. Just before the bridge turn left on a dirt spur road 100 feet to a small, unmarked turnaround and parking area *(GPS location 45.7638, -116.7483)*.

Set off downstream along the Imnaha River, a 100-foot-wide torrent with car-sized boulders turning up whitewater. Enormous orange cliffs on either hand shoulder out most of the sky, leaving the trail shady even on hot days. Make sure you recognize—and step around—the shiny triple leaflets of poison ivy. What look like dwarf palm trees along the trail are actually sumac, a harmless relative of poison ivy and poison oak. Sumac has a 6-foot woody stalk with compound leaves that turn scarlet in September. You're also likely to see ducks starting up from the river, 3-inch crickets hopping out of the path, and countless fluttering butterflies—yellow swallowtails, orange monarchs, and black admirals.

When you reach the Snake River at Eureka Bar's long, gravelly beach, keep left along the base of the cliffs to find a campsite beside an explorable, 30-foot-long mining tunnel *(GPS location 45.8173, -116.7667)*. From the campsite a trail continues past the stonework ruins of a 7-story gold stamp mill and a house. These are the remains of the mining boomtown of Eureka.

In 1899 a group of cagey local miners announced they had found copper ore in the granite of Hells Canyon's inner gorge. They made good money for two or three years, selling shares of stock back East. When investments lagged, the miners claimed the copper ore contained gold. Bedazzled stockholders financed a 125-foot sternwheeler that could claw its way up the Snake River rapids from Lewiston to the new El Dorado. A town of 2000 sprang up on this remote gravel bar to build a huge gold processing mill. But on the day the steamer sailed upriver with the machinery that would finally enable Eureka to produce gold, the ship lost control in the rapids, bridged the canyon,, and broke in two. The investors lost their money. And the city of Eureka vanished as swiftly as a stranger who writes bad checks.

Beyond the ruined mill the trail follows a stonework roadbed toward the old steamboat landing. The trail now vanishes near Eureka Creek at a cairn with a signpost—a good turnaround point for your hike.

Hike 49 Hat Point

Perhaps the most difficult day hike in Oregon descends 5600 feet from Hat Point to the bottom of Hells Canyon and back.

Easy (Granny View and Hat Point)
0.3-mile and 0.4-mile loops
100 feet elevation gain
Open early June to mid-November
Use: hikers

Difficult (to Elk Ridge viewpoint)
10.2 miles round trip
2600 feet elevation **loss**
Use: hikers, horses

Very Difficult (to Snake River)
15.4 miles round trip
5600 feet elevation **loss**

Meadow below Hat Point.

Fortunately, Hat Point also offers easier hikes. If you venture just halfway down into the canyon, you can get a bird's-eye view of the Snake River. And if you just stroll a few short nature loops you'll see many of Hells Canyon's wildflowers and views without losing any elevation at all. Fires burned some of the trees at Hat Point in 1989 and 2007, but crews saved the tower by wrapping it in fireproof Kevlar.

Getting There— Start by topping off your tank at the gas station in downtown Joseph. Then turn east beside the station at a "Hells Canyon Scenic Byway" sign and follow signs 29 paved miles to the village of Imnaha. Drive straight through

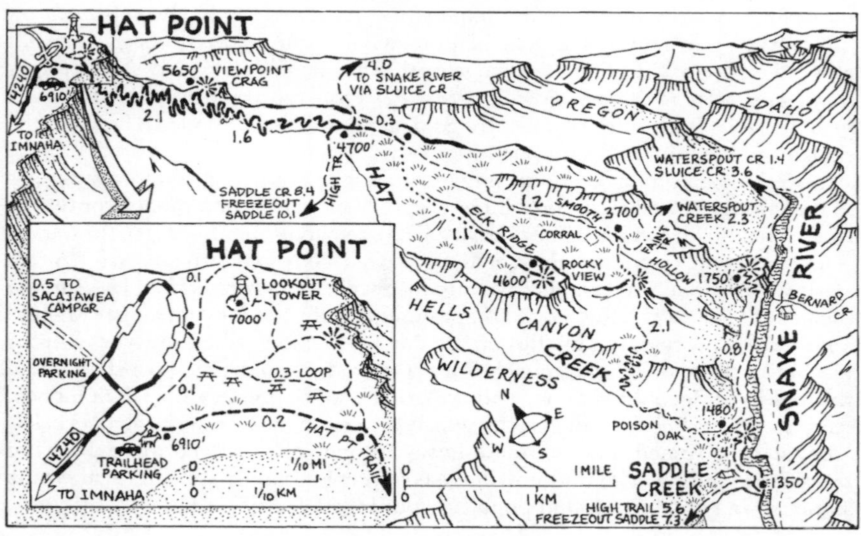

The Snake River at Saddle Creek.

Imnaha onto Hat Point Road 4240, which promptly becomes gravel. Although this steep, narrow road has blind curves and washboard, passenger cars do just fine if driven carefully. The first 5 miles climb so relentlessly that you may need to pause in the shade and let your car's engine idle a while to keep it from overheating. After this the road widens a bit and begins to level out.

Beyond Imnaha 16.6 miles turn right at a sign for Granny View Vista and park by the restroom for this short nature trail. Astonishing views of the vast Imnaha River canyon open up at each turn on a 0.3-mile loop (not shown on map). Expect dense alpine wildflowers in June and July, including red paintbrush, blue penstemon, purple larkspur, and yellow balsamroot.

After a quick walk at Granny View Vista, get back in your car and drive on up the Hat Point Road another 6 miles to a series of parking areas below the Hat Point lookout tower. If you only have time for a short walk, park at a display board nearest the tower, take a gravel 0.3-mile loop to the right through a picnic area to a viewpoint, and then climb up to the lookout tower itself. Public stairs climb 60 feet up the tower to an observation deck. Only lookout staffers are allowed the final 30 feet up to the historic, 8-foot-square cabin.

If you have the energy for a longer hike, park instead at the official "Trailhead and Loading Dock," the first parking lot on your right at Hat Point *(GPS location 45.4368, -116.6638)*. The trail traverses left across a meadow of blue lupine, purple larkspur, and scarlet gilia. Soon the path begins switchbacking down amid Douglas fir snags. After 3.7 miles you'll reach a T-shaped junction in a flat of live ponderosa pine trees *(GPS location 45.4277, -116.6389)*.

Turn left at the T-shaped trail junction for 300 feet to a fork, and veer right. This path leads across a grassy benchland with views to the snow-capped Seven Devils in Idaho. After 0.3 mile the trail starts to descend into Smooth Hollow, but beware of losing any more elevation, because you will have to regain it all later. Instead consider leaving the trail and veering to the right along a nearly level grassy ridgecrest. An elk path traces this ridge 1.1 mile to its end at a panoramic rocky viewpoint in the midst of Hells Canyon, overlooking the Snake River at Saddle Creek. Declare victory at this knoll and turn back.

If you opt to take the very steep and faint trail down Smooth Hollow to the Snake River, continue 1.2 miles until the path crosses a dry wash beside an old corral and vanishes in the grass. Head for a rock cairn with a signpost just above a half dozen dead cottonwood trees. Here head downhill to the right on a faint path that traverses to a small pass beside a rock knoll. Next the path switchbacks faintly down an extremely steep, rocky slope to Hat Creek, and then follows a rugged canyon bottom through knee-deep patches of poison ivy to the Snake River Trail. Turn right on this large, well-built path 0.4 mile to a campable, grassy field at Saddle Creek, where a path descends to a boulder bar beside the Snake River *(GPS location 45.3917, -116.6241).*

Other Options— To return on a loop from Saddle Creek, head north along the Snake River Trail through a particularly dramatic whitewater gorge. Don't attempt to find the virtually abandoned trail up Waterspout Creek. Continue a total of 4.8 miles and turn left up the well-built Sluice Creek Trail 4 miles to the junction below Hat Point. A longer loop option heads up Saddle Creek 5.6 miles and turns right on the High Trail for 10.1 miles to the junction.

Hike 50 Freezeout Saddle

The lowest point on the Oregon rim of Hells Canyon, this balmy saddle is usually free of snow a month before Hat Point.

Moderate (to Freezeout Saddle)
5.6 miles round trip
1950 feet elevation gain
Open early May through November
Use: hikers, horses

Difficult (to Summit Ridge)
11.9-mile loop
3470 feet elevation gain

Freezeout Saddle.

Equestrians and backpackers prefer the Saddle Creek Trail through Freezeout Saddle as a more reliable, and better graded, route to the Snake River. For a day hike here, climb to the views at Freezeout Saddle or continue on a difficult loop through the wildflower meadows of Summit Ridge.

Getting There— Begin at the gas station in downtown Joseph to top off your

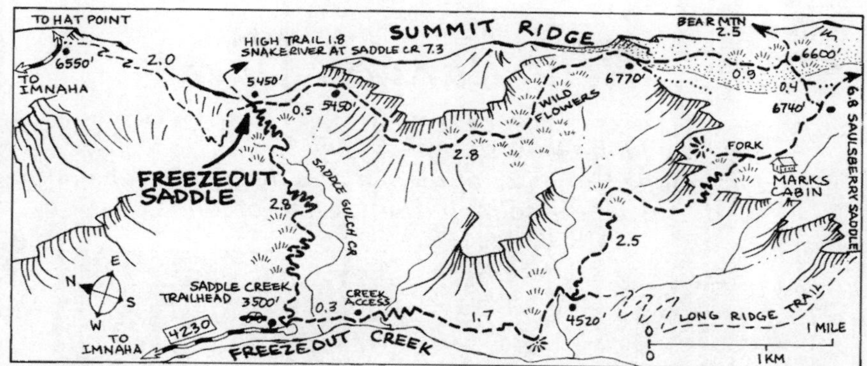

tank. Then turn east beside the station at a "Hells Canyon Scenic Byway" sign and follow signs 29 paved miles to the village of Imnaha. Following a sign for Halfway at the Imnaha store, turn right onto Upper Imnaha Road. Drive this wide gravel road 12.3 miles to a fork just before a bridge. Veer steeply up to the left on a one-lane gravel road marked "Freezeout" and "Dead End." If you see a "No Trespassing" sign, it refers to adjacent property and not this public road. Drive 2.7 miles to a large gravel parking lot at road's end, where a Northwest Forest Pass or other parking permit is required *(GPS location 45.3756, -116.7617).*

Two trails start at a message board and a horse watering trough on the left. Head up to the left on the Saddle Creek Trail. This path switchbacks up past old-growth ponderosa pines to a grassy slope with salsify blooms, mulleins, and wild roses. You'll pass a few shady Douglas firs, but the trail mostly stays in the open. Near the pass the wildflowers become profuse. Masses of clarkia line the trail with their pink crosses in June and July. Also expect yellow balsamroot, blue flax, orange paintbrush, and blue lupine.

When you reach Freezeout Saddle's large rock cairn, you'll gain a view down the Saddle Creek canyon to the rugged inner gorge of the Snake River. To the west, a long row of snowy Wallowa Mountains rises above Morgan Ridge and the Imnaha River's chasm. Even if you're not doing the longer loop, you might want to amble to the right on the level trail along the saddle's crest 0.5 mile, enjoying the views and the flowers, before heading back.

If you're continuing on the rugged loop, sally southward another 2.8 miles to a junction at the edge of Summit Ridge's plateau. Keep left on the main trail through a young forest regrowing from an old fire. After 0.9 mile you'll reach an ugly meadow junction, where cows and elk have churned a spring to mud. Although this is now in the official Wilderness, set aside by the U.S. Congress for preservation, the Forest Service allowed salvage logging and intensive grazing here after a 1970s fire, leaving blackened stumpfields of cow pies.

At the desolate meadow junction, turn right on an old logging road, keep right at a fork, and follow a cow trail across the crest of a ridge until the path peters out. Continue downhill and slightly left 300 feet to a rock cairn with a signpost at a real trail *(GPS location 45.3347, -116.7287).* Turn right on this path 0.4 mile to Marks Cabin, a private cowboy camp. Continue another 0.2 mile to a fork and veer downhill to the left across a steep meadow. This cattle-drivers' path descends steeply another 1.9 miles through woods to a T-shaped junction with the relatively level Long Ridge Trail. Turn right for 1.7 miles to return to your car.

Hike 51 Hells Canyon Dam

Built by the Idaho Power Company in 1956, this 330-foot-tall dam flooded 20 miles of the nation's deepest gorge and destroyed the salmon runs for half of Idaho.

Easy (to Stud Creek)
2.4 miles round trip
180 feet elevation gain
Open all year

Easy (to Deep Creek)
0.4 miles round trip
150 feet elevation gain

Hells Canyon Dam.

Today, surrounded on three sides by the Hells Canyon Wilderness, the colossal concrete structure remains a monument to the threats facing America's most scenic places. But the dam's paved access road also offers hikers a back door into the midst of Hells Canyon's mile-deep chasm. From road's end, an easy trail follows the whitewater Snake River into the canyon's wondrous wilds. At the dam itself, a railed catwalk descends the fearsome cliffs to Deep Creek. There are no easier paths to the spectacular scenery of Hells Canyon.

Getting There— If you're coming from the west, leave Interstate 84 at exit 302 just north of Baker City, drive Highway 86 east 65 miles to Oxbow, follow signs another 23 miles to Hells Canyon Dam, and continue 1.1 mile to a parking lot by the visitor information center at road's end. If you're coming from the south, leave Interstate 84 at exit 374 in Ontario, drive north 48 miles through Weiser to Cambridge on Highway 95, turn left 40 miles to Oxbow, keep right for 23 miles to the Hells Canyon Dam, and continue 1.1 mile to road's end.

Start by perusing the displays in the visitor center. Then go out the building's

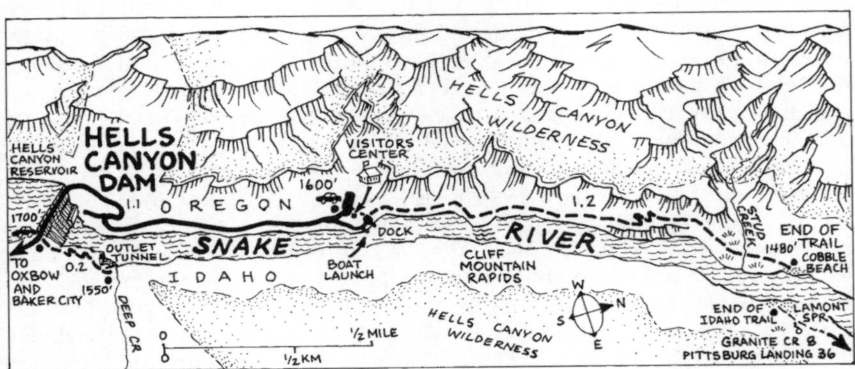

The end of the trail at Stud Creek offers a view into the heart of Hells Canyon.

back door to the deck and take the stairs down to the boat launch area. Special permits, equipment, and skills are required to pilot rafts down the churning Snake River 32 miles to the next take-out point, Pittsburg Landing. Jet boat tours are also available. At a dock beside the launch site, a private operator offers rides that range from $155 for a three-hour trip to $205 for a six-hour outing with lunch.

But the quietest way to explore the canyon is on foot. From the boat dock, follow a walkway past a railed archeological site—a prehistoric pit house depression where poles once supported a roof made of reed mats. Continue another 300 feet along the trail and you'll pass a cave-like overhang in the cliffs. Scratches on the cliff face here may be evidence of prehistoric visitors. Today the markings are guarded by a dense stand of poison ivy. Take a moment to identify these triple-leafleted plants, so you can avoid them when they appear along the edges of the trail ahead.

A friendlier plant to spot along the trail is mock orange, a bushy tree with sweet-smelling white blossoms in June. If you're hiking in fall, you'll probably notice another attractive, bushy tree—the sumac, whose leaflets turn fiery red in autumn.

After a mile the riverside trail enters Stud Creek's outwash plain, a gravelly slope of bunchgrass, mullein stalks, and a few ponderosa pines. Just beyond the creek crossing the path ends at a cobble beach. Ahead, sheer 500-foot cliffs rise from the Snake River, blocking further foot travel. And although a rough trail does start on the Idaho shore at this point, the Snake River is far too deep and swift to cross without a boat. So enjoy the view from the beach and then return as you came to your car.

If you'd like to do another short hike nearby, drive back 1.1 mile and park on the shoulder at the far end of the Hells Canyon Dam. A sign here marks the start of the Deep Creek Trail, a perilous-looking series of steel catwalks and railed stairs that descends 0.2 mile down the misty cliffs beside the spillway to a rocky creek near the outlet of the dam's diversion tunnel.

Hike 52 Hells Canyon Reservoir

The Oregon side of the Hells Canyon Reservoir has waterfalls in side canyons, slopes of wildflowers, and cliffs where you can watch giant fish idling in the Snake River's still green waters.

Easy (to Spring Creek)
5.2 miles round trip
600 feet elevation gain
Open all year
Use: hikers, horses

Swallowtail butterfly.

Perhaps the greatest treasure along the trails here is solitude. Power boats rarely venture this far north, and traffic is so light on the highway across the reservoir in Idaho that hours can pass without the sound of a motor. Because occasional patches of poison ivy grow beside the shoreline trail, be sure to wear long pants.

Getting There— From Baker City, leave Interstate 84 at exit 302 just north of town and follow Highway 86 east 65 miles through Richland and Halfway to Oxbow. Just before reaching the Snake River keep left onto Homestead Road at pointers for Homestead and the Hells Canyon Trail. Follow this increasingly bumpy gravel road 9.2 miles to its end on a grassy slope beside the reservoir. Impromptu campsites and parking places abound. (If you're driving here via Ontario or Boise, take Highway 95 north through Weiser to Cambridge, turn left on Road 71 for 40 miles to Oxbow, and then take Homestead Road to its end.)

Start at a trailhead message board a few feet before road's end, where the track forks three ways. Follow the left-hand road to a colorful rock outwash plain of red, purple, black, green, and white boulders. Hop across Copper Creek to a register box marking the start of the actual trail.

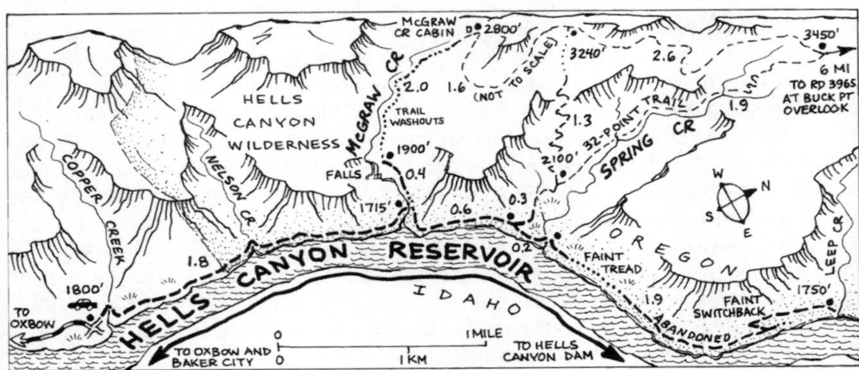

Hells Canyon from the reservoir trail.

In early summer, wildflowers brighten the slopes of dry bitterbrush above the reservoir. Look for stalks of yellow four-o'clocks, purple asters, white yarrow, yellow salsify, and tiny purple penstemons. The pretty little pink flowers with four elegant, cross-shaped petals are clarkias. The name honors Lewis and Clark, who first identified the flower in 1805-06 when they passed the northern end of Hells Canyon.

The upper Snake River's native salmon runs died when the Hells Canyon Dam impounded this reservoir in the 1950s. The hundreds of brown, 2-foot-long fish you see lazing in the water are unappetizing crappies or catfish, whose O-shaped mouths suck scum from rocks. Look in the shadows near shore to spot dozens of livelier, 8-inch rainbow trout.

After 0.9 mile the path crosses Nelson Creek in a gully, and at the 1.8-mile mark the trail appears to end at the broad, gravel outwash plain of McGraw Creek. In spring this 15-foot-wide stream is deep enough that you may have to wade, but by summer it's possible to cross on rocks or logs. Every few years, flash floods strip this canyon bottom of vegetation and repave the plain with fresh gravel.

For a worthwhile side trip, follow McGraw Creek up the canyon 0.2 mile and look for a rock cairn on the right. The abandoned McGraw Creek Trail begins here amid small trees and climbs a quarter mile to a clifftop viewpoint of a 15-foot waterfall in a canyon of house-sized boulders. Keep an eye out for the triple-leafletted poison ivy crowding this path. Beyond the falls, flood washouts have eliminated this old trail, so turn back to the reservoir.

If you're continuing on the reservoir's shoreline trail beyond the mouth of McGraw Creek, be prepared to make short detours where patches of poison ivy have overgrown the trail. After 0.6 mile keep right at a signed junction with the 32-Point Trail. Then continue another 0.2 mile down to Spring Creek, a braided stream in an outwash plain of willows and alders. Plan to turn back here. Although the Hells Canyon Trail once continued 1.9 miles to Leep Creek, the final portion has become so faint and overgrown that it's only suitable for adventurous pathfinders.

Other Options— Explorers can extend this hike by taking the 32-Point Trail up Spring Creek's canyon. The trail soon forks. To the right, a faint path follows Spring Creek up the canyon. To the left, a new trail switchbacks steeply up to a high bench crossed by the old trail to McGraw Creek Cabin.

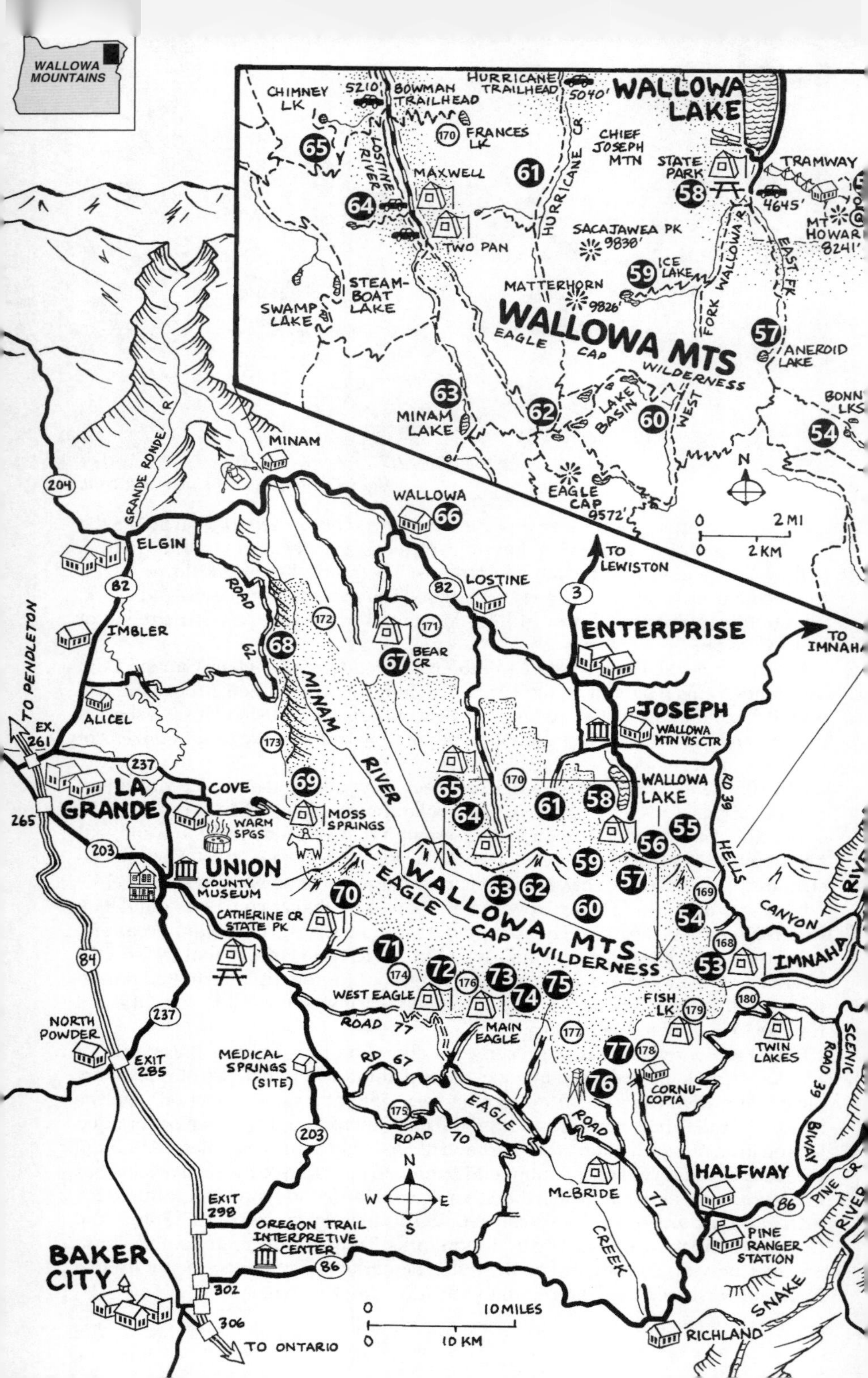

WALLOWA MOUNTAINS
WALLOWA LAKE
HURRICANE TRAILHEAD
5040'
CHIMNEY LK
5210'
BOWMAN TRAILHEAD
LOSTINE RIVER
FRANCES LK
CHIEF JOSEPH MTN
STATE PARK
TRAMWAY
4645'
MAXWELL
TWO PAN
HURRICANE CR
SACAJAWEA PK 9838'
MT HOWARD 8241'
ICE LAKE
MATTERHORN 9826'
STEAMBOAT LAKE
SWAMP LAKE
WEST FORK WALLOWA R
EAST FK
WALLOWA MTS
EAGLE CAP WILDERNESS
ANEROID LAKE
LAKE BASIN
WEST
MINAM LAKE
BONNY LKS
EAGLE CAP 9572'
0 2 MI
0 2 KM
TO LEWISTON
MINAM
GRANDE RONDE R
WALLOWA
ELGIN
LOSTINE
ENTERPRISE
TO IMNAHA
IMBLER
ROAD 62
BEAR CR
MINAM RIVER
JOSEPH
WALLOWA MTN VIS CTR
TO PENDLETON
EX. 261
ALICEL
LA GRANDE
COVE
WARM SPGS
MOSS SPRINGS
WALLOWA LAKE
RD 39
HELLS CANYON
UNION
COUNTY MUSEUM
CATHERINE CR STATE PK
IMNAHA
WEST EAGLE
ROAD 77
MAIN EAGLE
FISH LK
TWIN LAKES
NORTH POWDER
EXIT 285
MEDICAL SPRINGS (SITE)
RD 67
CORNUCOPIA
SCENIC ROAD 39 BIWAY
EAGLE ROAD
ROAD 70
EAGLE CREEK
HALFWAY
McBRIDE
PINE CR
EXIT 298
OREGON TRAIL INTERPRETIVE CENTER
PINE RANGER STATION
BAKER CITY
302
306
TO ONTARIO
0 10 MILES
0 10 KM
SNAKE RIVER
RICHLAND
N
W E
S

Bronze sculpture in downtown Joseph.

ENTERPRISE

The Wallowa Mountains form an alpine backdrop to the country that was home to Chief Joseph's Nez Perce band until 1877. Stop in Enterprise to see the 1909 **Wallowa County Courthouse,** built of local stone. For dinner, try a buffalo burger and a pint of fresh IPA at **Terminal Gravity Brewing** at the east end of town (803 SE School Street), open daily in summer but only Sundays, Mondays, and Wednesdays in winter.

Joseph

Monumental **bronze sculptures** line Joseph's scenic main street, the work of local foundries and artists (also represented in this charming little town's many art galleries). The **Wallowa County Museum**, in a 1888 bank building at 110 S. Main in the middle of downtown, includes a Nez Perce room with a tepee and is open daily (except Tuesday) 11am-9pm from late May to mid-September. Admission is $5, with kids under 7 free. For information about the backcountry, stop at the Forest Service's **Wallowa Mountains Office**, a visitor center on 2nd Street, two blocks east of Main. If you're hungry, try a calzone and microbrew on the spacious deck of **Embers Brewhouse** at 204 N. Main Street.

Wallowa Lake

Wedged against spectacular alpine peaks, this beautifully blue, 3-mile long lake fills the footprint of a vanished glacier. As you drive here from Joseph, stop at the lake's near end to see the **grave of Old Chief Joseph,** moved here in 1925. At the far end of the lake, **Wallowa Lake State Park** features a picnic area, marina, boat ramp (motors OK), chilly swimming beach, and popular 201-site campground with two yurts ($50-60, reservations 800-452-5687). Beyond the park entrance 0.3 mile, the gondolas of the **Wallowa Lake Tramway** zoom visitors up 3700 feet of elevation in 15 minutes to panoramic views atop Mt. Howard (see Hike #56). The tramway is open 10am-4pm daily from mid-May to Labor Day, and costs about $38 for adults, $35 for kids age 12-17, and $28 for kids age 4-11.

Cove and Union

At the western foot of the Wallowa Mountains (14 miles east of La Grande on Highway 203), the quaint little town of Union preserves its early 1900s charm. Visit the **Union County Museum's** excellent exhibit on cowboys (333 S. Main). Hours are 11am-3pm Wed-Sat from May through November. Admission is $5 for adults and $3 for students. Nearby is the surprisingly grand 1921 **Union Hotel**. Then drive 9 miles north to the even smaller town of Cove. By the white-steepled church, turn right on French Street and follow "swimming pool" pointers 0.4 mile to **Forest Cove Warm Springs,** an old-timey bathhouse and 9-foot-deep concrete pool built over a bubbling 86° F spring. Admission is $6 for adults, $5 for seniors and students, and $2.50 for kids. It's open noon-6pm Tuesday to Sunday in summer.

Eagle Cap Excursion Train

A passenger train travels 79 miles along the roadless Grande Ronde and Wallowa Rivers on most Saturdays from late June to mid-October, departing from Elgin at 10am. Adults are $70, seniors $65, and kids 3-16 $35. Trips for fishermen run in February and March. Check *eaglecaptrainrides.com* or call 541-437-3652.

Hike 53 Imnaha Falls

The Imnaha River roars out of the Eagle Cap Wilderness 40 feet wide, but upstream it squeezes through spectacular, 10-foot rock slots at Blue Hole and Imnaha Falls.

Easy (to Blue Hole)
4 miles round trip
200 feet elevation gain
Open mid-May to mid-November
Use: hikers, horses

Difficult (to Imnaha Falls)
11.4 miles round trip
800 feet elevation gain

Blue Hole.

Children do well on the easy 2-mile walk to Blue Hole, where the riverbank is full of skipping rocks. For a longer hike, continue to Imnaha Falls.

Getting There— From the gas station in downtown Joseph, turn east on the Hells Canyon Byway, follow Imnaha Road 8.3 miles to a sign for Halfway, and turn right onto paved Wallowa Mountain Road 39 for 32 miles. A mile beyond Blackhorse Campground turn right on paved Road 3960. After 9 miles, at the entrance sign for Indian Crossing Campground, park by a restroom on the right. *Do not* drive across a bridge to the end of the road, where a different trail begins.

If you're driving here from Baker City, leave Interstate 84 at exit 302 just north

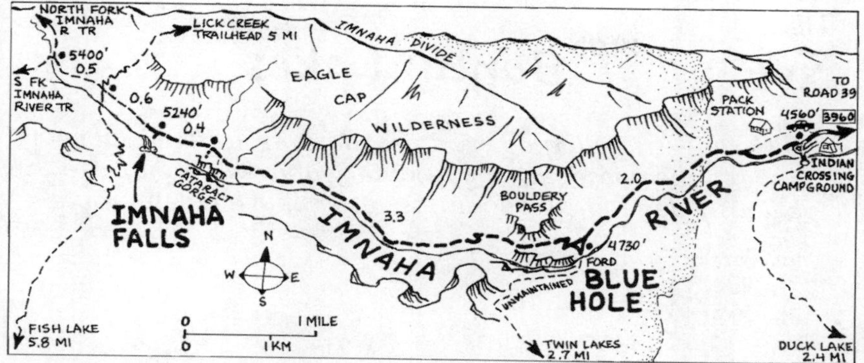

of town and follow Highway 86 east for 58 miles through Richland and Halfway. At a pointer for Joseph between mileposts 63 and 64, turn left onto paved Road 39 for 23.7 miles. Just beyond Ollokot Campground, turn left on paved Road 3960 for 9 miles to Indian Crossing Campground. Parking permits are required.

The trail sets off near the river through an open forest of grand fir, Douglas fir, and lodgepole pine. After 0.8 mile you'll enter a 1996 fire zone with the blooms of pink fireweed, pearly everlasting, and white yarrow among the snags. You're almost certain to see red-shafted flickers, the robin-sized woodpeckers that swoop from tree to tree, flashing reddish-brown wings. With luck you'll also spot a pileated woodpecker, a foot-tall bird with a bright red head.

When the trail forks at the 2-mile mark, detour left 0.1 mile to visit Blue Hole, where the Imnaha River emerges from a narrow rock gorge to a beach of white marble pebbles. The straight, 50-foot-deep slot follows a geologic fault.

If Imnaha Falls is your goal, return to the main trail and continue upriver into unburned forest. Notice that the exposed bedrock and bluffs along the way have been rounded by the glacier that filled this valley during the Ice Age. The trail does not pass within sight of Imnaha Falls, so listen for the roar of rushing water. The first such roar you'll hear, beyond Blue Hole 3.3 miles, is made by Cataract Gorge. If you follow the sound and bushwhack 200 feet to the left you'll find a 100-yard-long river chasm, but no waterfall. To find Imnaha Falls, continue on the main trail 0.4 mile to the next roar. Here, 0.6 mile before the trail reaches a marked 4-way junction, look for a short path to the left. This path leads to an 8-foot falls where the river squirts into a blue pool with the shadows of fish.

The Imnaha River at Indian Crossing Campground.

Hike 54 Bonny Lakes

The crowds struggling up the steep, dusty trail from Wallowa Lake to the gorgeous alpine country above Aneroid Lake obviously don't know about this easier, much quieter route.

Moderate (to Bonny Lakes)
7.8 miles round trip
1300 feet elevation gain
Open mid-July through October
Use: hikers, horses

Difficult (to Dollar Lake)
11.8 miles round trip
2000 feet elevation gain

Difficult (around Imnaha Divide)
16.3-mile loop
3000 feet elevation gain

Dollar Lake.

If you park at the little-used Tenderfoot Trailhead, you can trim a mile and nearly 2000 feet of elevation gain from the hike to dramatic Dollar Lake. Along the way you'll climb through wildflower fields at the Bonny Lakes, a good goal in itself. And because the trail really is less steep, you may have enough energy to continue on a grand loop around the Imnaha Divide.

Group size is limited to six. Campsites must be at least 100 feet from lakeshores, tethered horses must be at least 200 feet from lakes, and campfires are strongly discouraged. The use of snags for firewood is banned.

Getting There— From the gas station in downtown Joseph, turn east on the Hells Canyon Byway, follow Imnaha Road 8.3 miles to a sign for Salt Creek Summit, and turn right onto paved Wallowa Mountain Loop Road 39 for 13 miles. Beyond the Salt Creek Recreation Site 3 miles, where the road crosses a creek on a concrete bridge, turn right onto gravel Road 100 for 3.2 miles to the

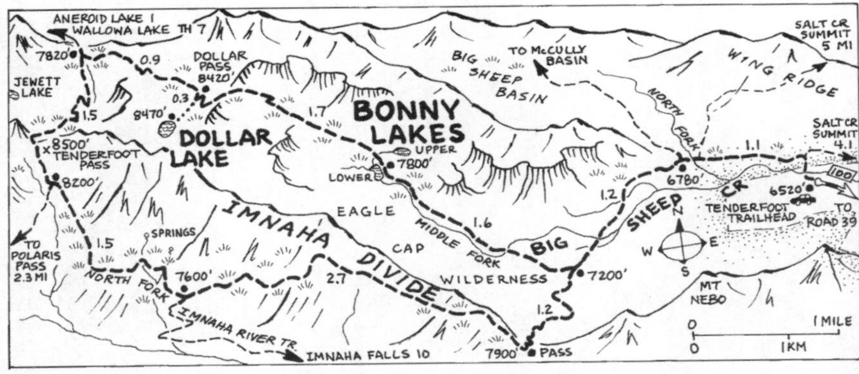

Upper Bonny Lake..

Tenderfoot Trailhead, a large gravel parking area at road's end. Parking permits are not required.

The trail sets off through a young lodgepole pine forest recovering from a 1989 fire and an errant clearcut. Grass, white yarrow blooms, pearly everlasting, pink fireweed, and chipmunks have helped refill the woods. After 0.1 mile the path fords Big Sheep Creek, but look for a nearby log that allows you to cross dry-footed.

Keep left at the next couple of junctions, following the main trail as it leaves the burned area and climbs through occasional sagebrush meadows. At the 2.3-mile mark you'll reach a fork—the start of the long loop around the Imnaha Divide. Veer right, following an "East Fork Wallowa River" pointer. This path follows a creek up amid a parade of colorful wildflowers. Look for blue lupine, white bugbane, red paintbrush, purple asters, and tall stalks of purple monkshood. A special treat are the delicate mariposa lilies, whose three large, creamy petals each have a lavender dot.

At the 3.9-mile mark the trail passes between the two Bonny Lakes, shallow pools fed by meandering marshy meadows that harbor mosquitoes during the last weeks of July. For the best view of the lakes, continue across their connecting creek 0.1 mile to a marble outcrop.

For a better mountain panorama, continue up the trail another 1.7 miles to Dollar Pass, a grassy alpine saddle. Ahead is the craggy white crest of Bonneville Mountain, with the rounded tops of the Matterhorn and Sacajawea looming beyond. Allow enough time in the Dollar Pass area for an easy cross-country detour to Dollar Lake. Leave the trail at Dollar Pass and amble 0.3 mile to the left (due south), through a level ridgecrest meadow toward a cliffy peak with snowfields. At the peak's base you'll discover a dramatic blue lake, round as a dollar coin.

Dollar Lake is an excellent spot to declare victory and head back the way you came. But backpackers (or athletic day-hikers) may want to return on a longer loop. Go back to Dollar Pass, follow the trail left 0.9 mile to a junction by a creek fork, and turn left again. If you keep turning left at every junction for the next 6.9 miles, you'll climb across scenic Tenderfoot Pass, traverse fabulous alpine meadows along the Imnaha Divide, cross another pass, and descend to a junction at the end of the loop, near Big Sheep Creek. From there on you'll have to keep right at junctions for the final 2.3 miles back to your car.

Hike 55 McCully Basin

Question: Why is this delightful trail, just 10 miles from Joseph, virtually unused? Answer: McCully Basin doesn't have a lake.

Moderate (to creek crossing)
9.2 miles round trip
1910 feet elevation gain
Open mid-July through October
Use: hikers, horses

Difficult (to McCully Basin)
11.6 miles round trip
2260 feet elevation gain

Difficult (to pass)
12.8 miles round trip
3160 feet elevation gain

The creek crossing after 4.6 miles.

If you can't live without fishing or swimming, forget McCully Basin. Come here if you love alpine brooks, meadows, and high country where you can roam all day without seeing another human. It's also the best base camp for a non-technical climb of Aneroid Mountain, Oregon's ninth tallest peak. Parking permits are required and group size is limited to 12.

Getting There — From the gas station on Main Street in downtown Joseph, turn east on Wallowa Avenue at a sign for Ferguson Ridge. After 5.4 miles, turn right onto Tucker Down Road for 3.1 miles of pavement and another 0.6 miles of good gravel to a ski area parking area. Then continue 1.4 miles on rough gravel (keeping right at junctions) to a turnaround at road's end *(GPS location 45.2772, -117.1359).*

The trail starts beside an outhouse and soon joins a (gated) service road that

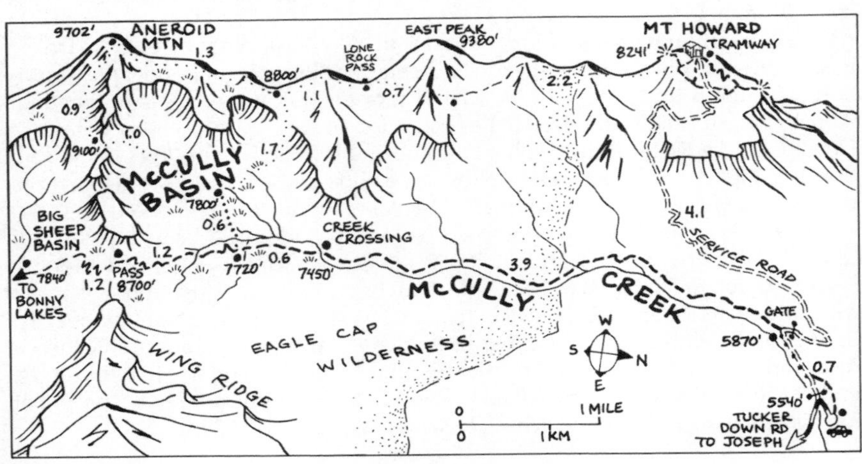

climbs to the tramway atop Mount Howard—a popular loop route for mountain bikers who have taken their bikes up the tram. After 0.7 mile the service road turns right, but fork to the left on an old roadbed that becomes the trail up McCully Creek. The forest here is mostly lodgepole pine, with Engelmann spruce, Douglas fir, scrub alder, red huckleberry, and blue lupine. You'll also find some pink fireweed, because fires have burned a few patches in these woods.

At the 4.6-mile point the trail crosses 12-foot-wide McCully Creek, a ford that's usually passable dry-footed on rocks. Beyond is the hike's first big meadow. This is a possible turnaround point for day hikers.

If you're still going strong, continue 0.6 mile, crossing two small side creeks along the way, to another meadow where you face a choice. Both choices require a sense of adventure. Ahead, the trail suddenly begins to climb. If you charge on ahead for 1.2 miles you'll climb on an increasingly faint trail through increasingly spectacular meadows until you puff to a high pass overlooking Big Sheep Basin and a fair share of the high Wallowas. This is a very nice goal.

If, however, you want to see McCully Basin's main meadows, you'll have to leave the trail and bushwhack a bit. Where the trail suddenly steepens *(GPS location 45.2172, -117.1453)*, strike off to the right across a meadow for 200 feet, cross a creek, scramble up a sandy slope 60 feet, and continue 200 more feet to the first of McCully Basin's three large meadows *(GPS location 45.2167, -117.1487)*. From here, Aneroid Mountain is but one blip in a wall of stripey red-brown cliffs ringing the horizon. A creek burbles out from the meadow amid purple aster, blue gentian, and white grass of parnassus.

The meadows here are heavenly, and even if you come in August you might well be the first visitor of the season. Where else in the Wallowas can you say that?

Other Options— McCully Basin is the best base camp for a climb of 9702-foot Aneroid Mountain. Because there are two non-technical routes to the summit from this side, it's possible to hike there from McCully Basin's main meadow on a 4.9-mile loop that gains only 1900 feet. The map shows these routes, but attempt them only with topo maps and off-trail experience. Even so, you'll have to use your hands, and there is a danger of rockfall, so helmets are a good idea. Turn back if you're in doubt or if the weather is iffy. At the top an ammo can holds a summit register, but no camera can hold the view.

Aneroid Mountain from McCully Basin.

Hike 56 Mount Howard

For a quick sample of the Wallowa Mountain's high country, ride a tramway's gondola up from Wallowa Lake to Mt. Howard.

Easy (summit tour)
1.9-mile loop
300 feet elevation gain
Open July to early September
Use: hikers

Moderate (to East Peak springs)
5.5 miles round trip
1140 feet elevation gain

Wallowa Lake Tramway.

Crowds of tourists follow an easy loop trail from the tramway station to Mt. Howard's summit, where the panorama includes a jagged horizon of snowpeaks. For a more adventurous outing, continue on a faint ridgecrest path to East Peak's wildflower meadows.

Getting There— From Interstate 84 at La Grande, take exit 261 and follow Wallowa Lake signs on Highway 82 through Enterprise and Joseph a total of 78 miles. At the far end of Wallowa Lake, at milepost 6 where the main road veers right into Wallowa Lake State Park, turn left for 0.3 mile and park on the left at the Wallowa Lake Tramway station. The tramway is open 10am-5pm daily from mid-May to September 30. The ride up gains 3700 feet of elevation in 15 minutes and costs about $38 ($35 for children age 13-17 and $28 for kids age 4-12). Expect impressive views north to 3-mile-long, cucumber-shaped Wallowa Lake. An Ice Age glacier left the curving moraine hill of sandy debris that rims the lake.

At tramway's top you'll step out onto the patio of the Summit Grill, a cafe that serves sandwiches and hamburgers. After exclaiming at the view from the patio, most people remark on the fat Columbia ground squirrels begging for handouts.

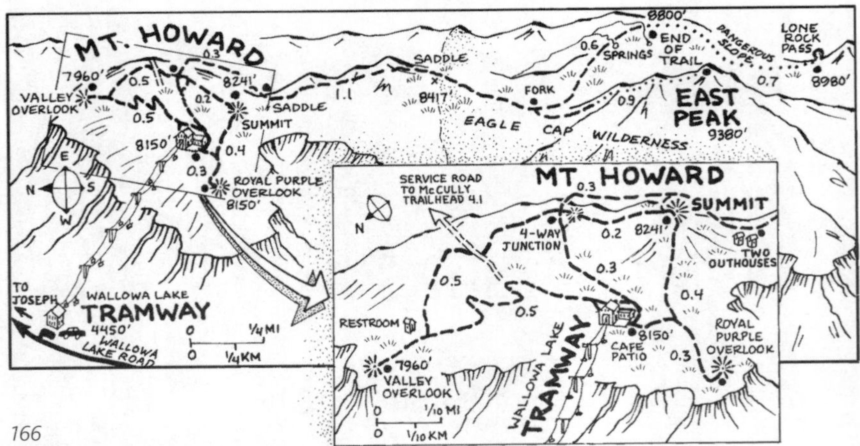

The view from Mt. Howard.

For a while these native squirrels were getting so many leftover French fries that the mountain's chipmunks, Clark's nutcrackers, and golden-mantled ground squirrels began pestering people too. Don't feed any of these wild animals, no matter what! They are truly healthier and happier gathering the plentiful seeds of grasses and wildflowers growing nearby.

The best way to see all three of the viewpoints on the edges of Mt. Howard's broad top is to set off from the patio and keep right at all trail junctions. The path leads past storm-bent limber pines, fields of pink heather, and yellow desert parsley. After 0.3 mile you'll climb a rocky knoll to the Royal Purple Overlook. The snowy peak in the distance is Eagle Cap. Somewhat closer to the right is a taller summit, the 9826-foot Matterhorn, capped with white marble.

Turn around at the Royal Purple Overlook and continue keeping to the right for 0.4 mile to reach Mt. Howard's summit. The view stretches east across distant Hells Canyon to the jagged blue horizon of Idaho's Seven Devils Mountains.

Continue on the well-marked loop trail from the summit for 0.2 mile to the Highlands Overlook, and keep right for 300 feet to a four-way junction. If you turn left here you'll shortcut back to the tram. If you go straight you'll take a one-mile loop past viewpoints before returning to the tram.

If you'd rather extend your hike with an adventurous scramble toward East Peak, you could turn right at the 4-way junction, but there's a shortcut. After you hike to Mt. Howard's summit, continue 30 feet on the loop trail and turn right on a smaller path down to the right. After a few hundred feet, turn right on a trail that leads 0.1 mile to a grassy saddle with two outhouses. Beyond this the trail continues 1.1 mile to a fork. If you fork uphill to the right you'll follow a trail 0.2 mile up to a ridgecrest viewpoint. It's possible to scramble another 0.7 mile to the summit of East Peak, but the route is rough and you should turn back when unsure.

If you veer left on a level trail at the fork, you'll contour 0.6 mile to a spring on a grassy bench where yellow monkeyflowers, blue gentians, and white grass-of-parnassus bloom. This is a pleasant spot to rest before turning back—but don't rest too long, because the last gondola may leave as early as 4:45pm.

Other Options— The trail ends at the springs on East Peak's flank, but sure-footed pathfinders can scramble onward 0.7 mile, across a dangerously steep talus slope, to Lone Rock Pass. Ahead is a tempting view of Aneroid Lake, 2.2 miles away and 1500 feet down. The route is not easy, but explorers sometimes bushwhack there and hike down the East Fork Wallowa Trail (see Hike #57) to the bottom of the tramway.

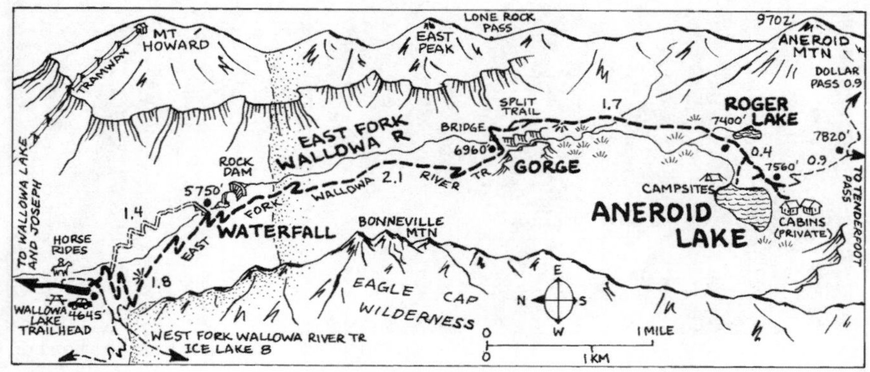

Hike

57 Aneroid Lake

Admittedly, the trail to Aneroid Lake is long and steep. Granted, the path is dusty from countless boot soles and horse hooves.

Moderate (to waterfall)
3.8 miles round trip
1150 feet elevation gain
Open June through October
Use: hikers, horses

Difficult (to Aneroid Lake)
12 miles round trip
2950 feet elevation gain
Open mid-July through October

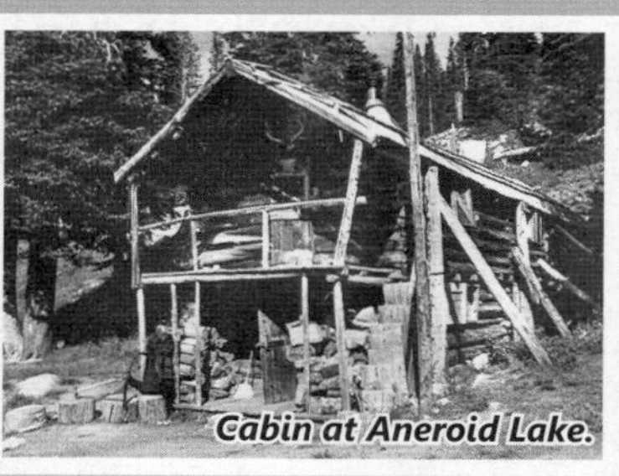
Cabin at Aneroid Lake.

Despite these drawbacks, if you're staying at Wallowa Lake State Park, this is the shortest route to the Wallowa high country's famous alpine lakes. The trail's final miles traverse gorgeous wildflower meadows backed by 9000-foot peaks. If you decide to turn back earlier, there's a consolation prize: a cool, cascading waterfall.

Note that group size is limited to 12. Tents must be at least 100 feet from the lakeshore, horse grazing is banned within 200 feet of the lake, and campfires are strongly discouraged. Firewood cutting from standing trees or snags is banned.

Getting There— From Interstate 84 at La Grande, take exit 261 and follow Wallowa Lake signs on Highway 82 through Enterprise and Joseph a total of 78 miles. At the far end of Wallowa Lake, at milepost 6 where the main road veers right into Wallowa Lake State Park, turn left for a mile to road's end at the Wallowa Lake Trailhead. On the right is a state park picnic area. The trail itself begins on the left, beside a message board and wilderness registration box.

Up the trail 150 feet, a dusty path joins from nearby horse rental corrals. A few feet later, veer left onto the East Fork Wallowa River Trail. This path climbs up amid a mixed forest of Douglas fir, grand fir, and larch, with an understory of

Bonneville Mountain from Aneroid Lake.

golden currant and thimbleberry. Ignore a gravel service road that joins from the left. You'll also want to ignore a dusty side trail that heads down to the right at the 0.8-mile mark—a return loop for the rental horse tours. After the fourth switchback, when the trail crosses a rockslide with a view across Wallowa Lake, pause to listen to the flutter of quaking aspen leaves and the cheeping of pikas, the little round-eared "rock rabbits" that live under the boulders.

After 1.8 miles the path reaches a river bridge at the upper end of the old service road. Continue up the trail for two more quick switchbacks to the base of a 100-foot waterfall, a pleasant turnaround point for a moderate hike.

Above the waterfall the trail passes an old rock dam that diverts water through a flume to generate electricity. Then the path leaves the river, climbs steadily for 2 miles, recrosses the river on a footbridge below a dramatic gorge, and ambles up past two large meadows. Mosquitoes are a problem here in July.

The first lake you see, through the trees to the left, is Roger Lake. Continue 0.4 mile on the main trail, passing two side trails to camping areas, to a bench overlooking Aneroid Lake. The deep, blue-green lake, with its dramatic backdrop of Bonneville Mountain's white crags, was named by a fish surveyor who brought an aneroid ("liquid-free") barometer here in 1897 to measure elevation.

Just beyond the bench viewpoint, the trail forks. If you turn right, past a sign "Camp Halton; Private Property; Please Respect," you'll find a collection of eight log cabins that began as a 1920s silver mining camp. By the 1950s a colorful character named Charley Seeber had turned one of the rickety cabins into a store, supplying thirsty hikers with cold cans of soda pop. Since then the property has changed hands several times and the rustic store has closed, but the cabins remain. Since the 1990s the owners have employed a caretaker who welcomes respectful visitors.

Other Options— If you've backpacked into the Aneroid Lake area, you might spend the next day exploring the high country with a day pack. One option is to continue up the main trail 0.9 mile and fork left for 0.9 mile to Dollar Pass, where you can bushwhack 0.3 mile to Dollar Lake (see Hike #54).

Hike 58 Wallowa Lake

Wallowa Lake State Park is one of Eastern Oregon's most popular recreation destinations, so it's surprising how few easy trails start here.

Easy (to BC Falls)
2.6 miles round trip
680 feet elevation gain
Open June to mid-November

Moderate (from campground)
4.7-mile loop
1050 feet elevation gain

Lake view on Chief Joseph Trail.

Perhaps the best short family hike crosses a river gorge footbridge to a viewpoint at BC Falls. If you start at the campground, you can do the hike as a longer loop.

Getting There— From Interstate 84 at La Grande, take exit 261 and follow Wallowa Lake signs on Highway 82 through Enterprise and Joseph a total of 78 miles. At the far end of Wallowa Lake, at milepost 6 where the main road veers right into Wallowa Lake State Park, turn left for a mile to road's end at the Wallowa Lake Trailhead. On the right is a picnic area. The trail itself begins on the left, beside a message board.

Up the trail 150 feet, a dusty path joins from nearby horse rental corrals. A few feet later the trail forks. Keep right on the West Fork Wallowa River Trail. After

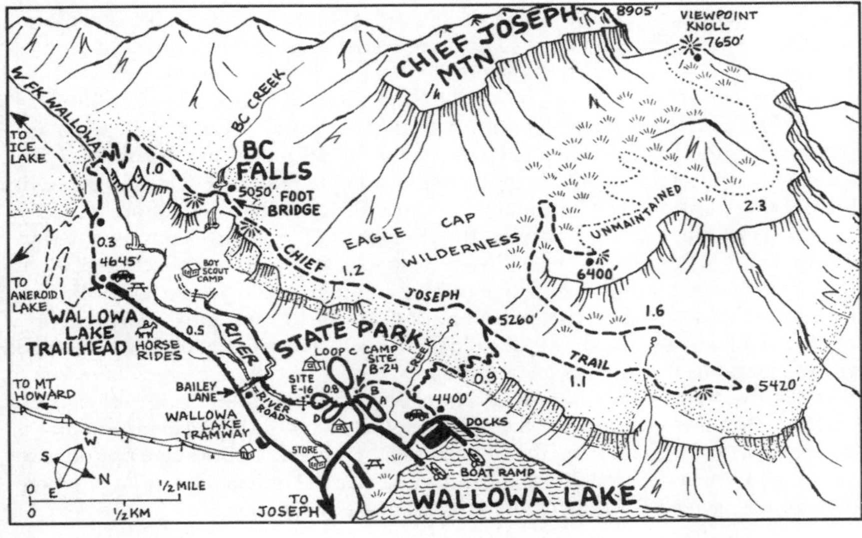

another 0.3 mile, fork to the right again—this time on the Chief Joseph Trail. This path heads up the gorge of the West Fork Wallowa River (ignore scramble paths to the right). The trail crosses the river on a footbridge, switchbacks uphill, and traverses through the woods to a footbridge at BC Falls, a nice spot for lunch. The 50-foot corkscrewed waterfall here gets so wild in winter that the Forest Service has replaced the bridge twice.

Would you rather start your hike at the campground? If so, you can hike to BC Falls on a loop. When you drive into the entrance of Wallowa Lake's campground, keep straight for a quarter mile and curve right toward the boat ramp until you're almost to the lake. Then turn left 0.1 mile and park by a fish-cleaning log shelter on the left. Walk another 200 feet along the road toward the docks to find the trail, which climbs left into the woods just beyond a brown concrete block shed. Follow this pet-exercise trail 0.1 mile to a footbridge at a creek and turn uphill to the right on a small steep path.

The path climbs along the route of a buried water line for a micro hydro plant that powers the park and the surrounding area. Look for remnants of the line's original wooden pipe. Also look for white (inedible) snowberries amid the ponderosa pines.

After 0.4 mile you'll switchback up to a junction with the Chief Joseph Trail. Turn left for 1.2 miles to the bridge at the waterfall on BC Creek. Continue another mile, keeping right at junctions, to a marked junction with the West Fork Wallowa River Trail. Then turn left and keep left for 0.3 mile down to the Wallowa Lake Trailhead.

To complete the loop, you'll have to walk down along the road 0.5 mile. Then turn left on Bailey Lane, cross the river on a bridge, and take the next street to the right—River Road—which takes you back to the campground at site E-16. Walk campground roads to site B-24, where a trail climbs to the micro hydro power plant. Continue past it on a trail that contours 0.4 mile back to the big parking lot by the lakeshore fish cleaning station.

Other Options— For a longer hike with wider views, take the Chief Joseph Trail up Chief Joseph Mountain. From the poorly marked junction with the campground waterline trail, it's 1.1 easy mile to a nice lake viewpoint just before a major switchback. Or continue another 1.6 miles to a viewpoint at the trail's third switchback, at the 6400-foot level. Beyond, the trail is unmaintained and faint, but continues 2.3 miles to its end atop a knoll. Cliffs block access to the mountain's actual summit.

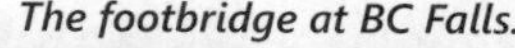

The footbridge at BC Falls.

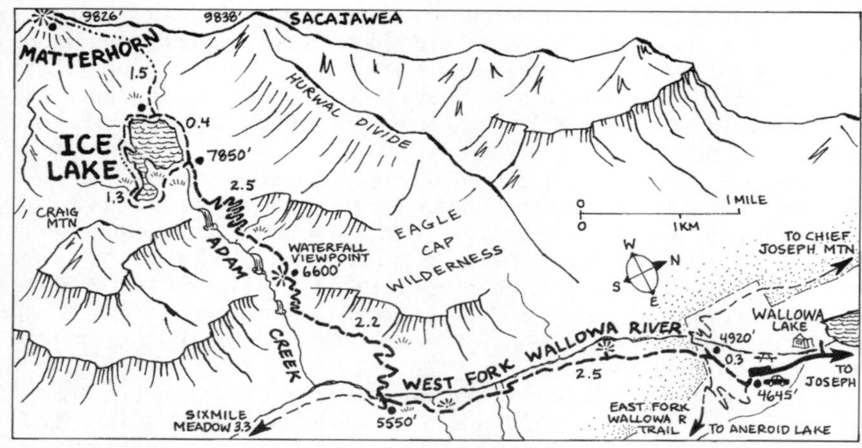

Hike
59 Ice Lake

Backed by the two tallest peaks in Eastern Oregon, Ice Lake belongs to an alpine world halfway to the sky.

Difficult
15 miles round trip
3300 feet elevation gain
Open mid-July through October
Use: hikers, horses

Waterfall on Adam Creek.

You'll feel like you've climbed to the sky, too, after hiking up the seemingly endless switchbacks from the Wallowa Lake Trailhead. Although the round-trip distance is 15 miles, the scenery is so great that this is one of the most popular hikes in the Eagle Cap Wilderness.

Note that group size is limited to six. To protect the fragile lakeshore, tents must be kept 100 feet away, grazing horses must be kept 200 feet from shore, and campfires are not allowed within a quarter mile.

Getting There— From Interstate 84 at La Grande, take exit 261 and follow Wallowa Lake signs on Highway 82 through Enterprise and Joseph a total of 78 miles. At the far end of Wallowa Lake, at milepost 6 where the main road veers right into Wallowa Lake State Park, turn left for a mile to road's end at the Wallowa Lake Trailhead. On the right is a state park picnic area. The trail itself begins on the left, beside a message board and wilderness registration box.

Up the trail 150 feet, a dusty path joins from nearby horse rental corrals. A few

The Matterhorn from Ice Lake.

feet later the trail forks. Keep right on the West Fork Wallowa River Trail for 0.3 mile to another fork. Go left for 50 steps and then keep straight, ignoring a dusty loop trail on the left used as a return route for rental horse tours.

For the next 2.5 miles the West Fork Wallowa Trail climbs steadily through the woods, with occasional viewpoints down into the churning river's whitewater gorge. Don't touch the stinging nettles, identified by their serrated leaves on tall stalks beside the trail. Then turn right at a fork, following an "Ice Lake" pointer. This trail promptly crosses the river and begins to switchback uphill.

Winter avalanches on these slopes have cleared stripes of steep meadow where you'll find purple aster, red paintbrush, and white pearly everlasting. After nine switchbacks the path traverses nearly a mile to an overlook of cascading Adam Creek. There the path launches up another 14 switchbacks to a viewpoint by a spectacular 60-foot waterfall. A final set of 12 switchbacks brings the trail to a fork at Ice Lake's outlet, the hike's goal. If you're backpacking, most sites are to the left, across the outlet creek. If you have time, continue on a 1.7-mile loop around Ice Lake, although this involves 0.2 mile of boulder hopping along the far south shore.

Other Options— The 9826-foot Matterhorn is a non-technical climb from Ice Lake. Keep right around the lakeshore trail 0.4 mile to an inlet creek at the far end of the lake. From there a sometimes faint path climbs steeply 1.5 miles up a broad ridge to the summit. The only requirements for scaling this relatively gentle, eastern face of the Matterhorn are stamina, strong knees, and excellent weather—turn back if lightning or clouds threaten. The mountain earns its name for the startling, 3000-foot white marble cliff on its far side, to the west.

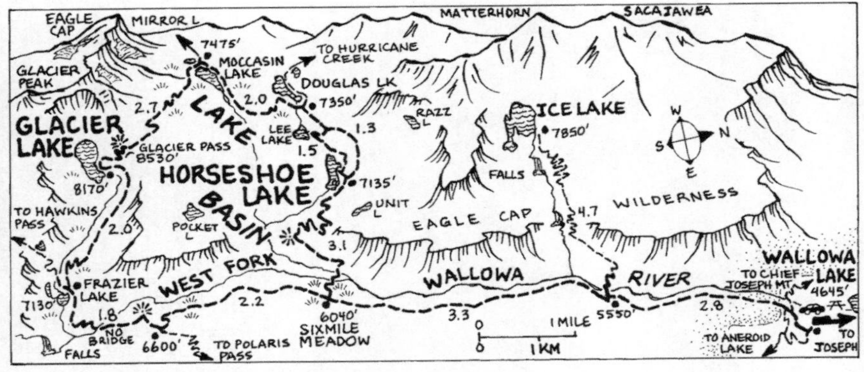

Hike
60 Horseshoe Lake

In the high Wallowas' wondrous Lake Basin, a dozen alpine lakes shimmer among wildflower meadows and polished granite outcrops, while ragged peaks rim the horizon.

Difficult (to Horseshoe Lake)
18.4 miles round trip
2500 feet elevation gain
Open mid-July through October
Use: hikers, horses

Difficult (to Glacier Lake)
27.3-mile loop
4000 feet elevation gain

Horseshoe Lake.

The price of admission here, however, is steep indeed: a dusty, 9-mile trudge up one of the most heavily used paths in the Eagle Cap Wilderness. As a result, only backpackers and equestrians can tour the miraculous high country between Horseshoe Lake and Glacier Lake.

The area's popularity has led to some restrictions. Group size is limited to 12 on trails and six in camps in the Lake Basin. Tents must be kept at least 100 feet from lakeshores and grazing horses must be at least 200 feet from lakes. Campfires are banned within a quarter mile of lakes, so bring a stove to cook.

Getting There— Drive Interstate 84 to La Grande exit 261. Then follow Wallowa Lake signs on Highway 82 through Enterprise and Joseph a total of 78 miles. At the far end of Wallowa Lake, at milepost 6 where the main road veers right into Wallowa Lake State Park, turn left for a mile to road's end at the Wallowa Lake Trailhead. The trail begins on the left, beside a message board.

Up the trail 150 feet, a dusty path joins from the horse rental corrals on the left.

Glacier Peak from Glacier Lake.

A few feet later the trail forks. Keep right on the West Fork Wallowa River Trail for 0.3 mile to another fork. This time go left, and then ignore a dusty loop trail that peels off to the left 50 steps later—a return route for rental horse tours.

The West Fork Wallowa Trail climbs steadily through mixed woods of Douglas fir and lodgepole pine, with occasional viewpoints into the churning river's whitewater gorge. Near the Ice Lake junction at the 2.8-mile mark, you'll start traversing small meadows of pearly everlasting, thimbleberry, white cow parsnip, and purple aster. Watch out for stinging nettles—the serrated leaves on tall stalks beside the trail.

After 6.1 miles you'll reach a junction beside Sixmile Meadow, a broad field heavily used by backpackers. If you have to stay in this crowded area, pack used toilet paper out in a plastic bag rather than attempting to burn or bury it. To hike onward, turn right beside Sixmile Meadow to a horse ford at the swift, 30-foot-wide river. The hiker footbridge is gone, but logs usually allow you to cross dry-footed. Beyond the river the trail climbs a hot slope 3.1 miles to Horseshoe Lake, a pool with a small island and a huge reflection of a 1000-foot-tall white granite ridge. Horseshoe Lake is a common goal, but it would be a shame to turn back here. Much of the lake's shore is roped off for restoration, and the prettiest scenery lies ahead, on the grand loop to Glacier Lake. So sally onward if you can.

The trail forks beside Horseshoe Lake. Go right, although the two routes rejoin in about a mile. Beyond that point, follow "Glacier Pass" pointers. These will aim you to the left on a trail that skirts Douglas Lake. The path crosses 2 more miles of glorious alpine country to Moccasin Lake and a close-up view of Eagle Cap. The meadows here blaze with giant blue gentian, delicate pink heather, and the aromatic, ball-shaped purple flowers of wild onion.

At a junction beside Moccasin Lake, turn left across a scenic isthmus between the lake's two parts. Next the loop trail climbs steeply over Glacier Pass to Glacier Lake. A century ago this spectacularly stark, rocky cirque was home to the Benson Glacier, the last in Eastern Oregon. From Glacier Lake, simply follow the trail downstream 6 miles to complete the loop to Sixmile Meadow. Along the way you'll pass grass-rimmed Frazier Lake, a 100-foot waterfall on the canyon cliffs, and a tricky, bridgeless river crossing on stepping stones.

Hike 61 Hurricane Creek

Pioneers named Hurricane Creek because they thought the broken trees in this otherwise picturesque valley must be the work of violent windstorms.

Easy (to Falls Creek Falls)
0.6 miles round trip
200 feet elevation gain
Open May to mid-November
Use: hikers, horses

Moderate (to Slick Rock gorge)
6.2 miles round trip
750 feet elevation gain
Open mid-June through October

Difficult (to Echo Lake)
15.4 miles round trip
3400 feet elevation gain
Open late July through October

The Matterhorn's west face.

In fact the valley is not particularly windy, but its sides are so steep that snow avalanches crash down through the forests in winter. In summer the avalanche clearings provide views up the valley to the startling, 3000-foot white marble face of the Matterhorn, the second tallest peak in the Wallowas.

For a quick sample of the valley's scenery, take a short walk to Falls Creek Falls, in a side canyon stripped by flash floods. For a longer hike, continue 3 miles up Hurricane Creek to a slot-like gorge with a pair of waterfalls. For an athletic challenge, tackle the steep trail up to Echo Lake's snowy cirque.

Getting There— From Interstate 84, take La Grande exit 261 and follow

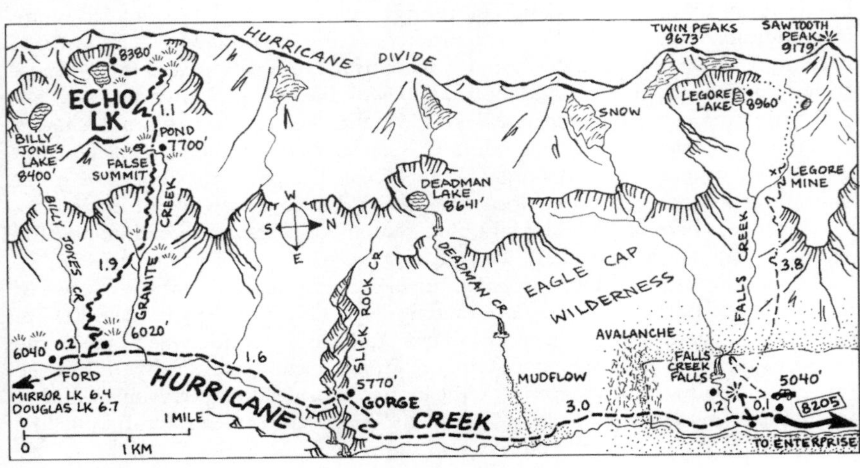

Wallowa Lake signs 65 miles on Highway 82 to downtown Enterprise. Beyond the county courthouse 0.3 mile, where the highway jogs left toward Joseph, follow a "Hurricane Creek" pointer right onto Hurricane Creek Road 8205, which is gravel at first, and then paved. At the 4.9-mile mark fork to the right to stay on Road 8205, once again on gravel. Continue another 3.8 miles to the Hurricane Trailhead at road's end, where parking permits are required *(GPS location 45.3114, -117.3072).*

The trail sets off through an oddly mixed stand of quaking aspen, lodgepole pine, Douglas fir, and juniper. After just 0.1 mile a fork up to the right is the side trail to Falls Creek Falls. Don't miss this quick detour to see a 60-foot waterfall in a rock canyon stripped by winter floods. It's just 0.2 mile up to a viewpoint.

Echo Lake.

Then return to the main trail and continue up alongside Hurricane Creek. This route occasionally emerges from the forest to cross barren boulder fields where avalanches or mudflows have roared out of side canyons. At the 3-mile mark you'll switchback up beside a 200-foot-deep rock slot where Hurricane Creek churns through a series of waterfalls. At the top of the gorge, the path crosses Slick Rock Creek, a side stream barreling down a bedrock chute.

If you're getting tired, this is a good place to have lunch before turning back. Take a moment to notice the bluebells, red paintbrush, and white yarrow blooming here amid sagebrush and subalpine fir. Also note two kinds of purple flowers: penstemon (shaped like trumpets) and aster (shaped like daisies).

If you're headed for Echo Lake, continue another 1.6 miles to a large rock cairn with the junction sign. But before you turn right on the Echo Lake Trail, you might want to continue straight 0.2 mile to a gorgeous meadow where the Hurricane Creek Trail fords its namesake stream. There is no bridge.

Then return to the Echo Lake Trail and follow this extremely steep, infrequently maintained track straight up the canyon wall. After 1.9 miles you'll crest what appears to be a summit. It's actually the lip of a basin with a pond. Here the trail briefly peters out in a meadow crowded with blue gentian blooms. Continue straight toward the lowest point on the horizon to find the continuation of the tread. Another 1.1 mile of climbing brings you to deep, blue Echo Lake. Listen here for the cheep of pikas, the little "rock rabbits" on the far shore's rockslide. If you're backpacking, remember to tent at least 100 feet from the lake.

Other Options— If you wade across the Hurricane Creek Trail's ford you can continue up the valley 5.3 miles to a junction in the Wallowas' popular Lake Basin. From there, one trail goes left to Douglas Lake and the Wallowa Lake Trailhead (Hike #58), while another goes right to Mirror Lake and the Two Pan Trailhead (Hike #62). Both routes make good trips for backpackers with a shuttle car.

Hike 62 Eagle Cap

Eight valleys radiate from 9572-foot Eagle Cap, the rock hub of the Wallowa Mountains.

Moderate (to meadow crossing)
10.2 miles round trip
1500 feet elevation gain
Open mid-July through October
Use: hikers, horses

Difficult (to Mirror Lake)
14.8 miles round trip
2020 feet elevation gain

Difficult (to Eagle Cap)
19.6 miles round trip
4000 feet elevation gain
Open late July through October

Mirror Lake from Eagle Cap.

Although Eagle Cap is not quite the tallest peak in this range, its 360-degree view is unmatched, and a surprisingly well-graded trail climbs to the summit from the East Lostine River's meadows. If your goal's the summit, plan on a two-day trip. If you're out for a day hike, settle for the view from Lostine Meadows or Mirror Lake.

Note that group size is limited to 12 on trails and six in camps. Tents must be at least 100 feet from lakeshores, grazing horses must be at least 200 feet from lakes, and campfires are banned within a quarter mile of Mirror Lake.

Getting There— Drive Interstate 84 to La Grande exit 261 and follow Wallowa Lake signs 55 miles on Highway 82 to Lostine. In the center of town, where the highway turns left, go straight on Lostine River Road, following a pointer for "Lostine River Campgrounds." This route is a two-lane paved road for the first 7 miles, followed by 5.2 miles of washboard gravel to the Lostine Guard Station and another 6.1 miles of narrow gravel to road's end at the Two Pan Trailhead. Parking permits are required.

At the trailhead you'll find a large parking area for horse trailers on the left. Continue down to the right another 0.1 mile to a smaller parking area at the actual trailhead with a registration box. Start here and hike 0.1 mile to a major fork. Veer left on the East Fork Lostine River Trail. This path climbs through a mixed forest of fir, lodgepole pine, and spruce for 0.8 mile to a footbridge across the river, just above an 8-foot waterfall. Beyond this the trail steepens, climbing 11 switchbacks in 2 miles. As you pass rockslides listen for the cheep of pikas, the "rock rabbits" that gather grass to store in their rockslide burrows.

Finally the path levels off beside several ponds at the start of a long, beautiful meadow. Here at last is a grand view ahead to Eagle Cap. During the Ice Age, a glacier from Eagle Cap filled this high valley, sculpting it into a long U-shaped trough. When the glacier melted, it left a shallow lake that filled with sediment to become a meadow traced with the river's looping meanders. Ground squirrels scurry across

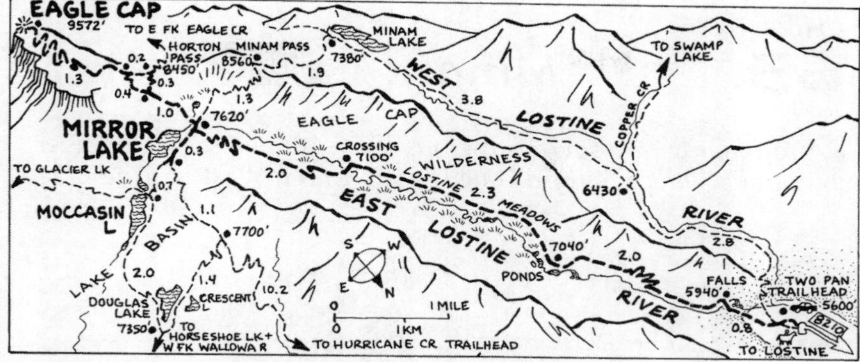

the fields and then stand on their hind legs like prairie dogs to watch you pass. The trail along this meadow is nearly level for 2.3 miles to a stream crossing at the far end—a good turnaround point for a moderate hike.

If you're continuing, hop across the stream at a collapsed bridge. Beyond, the trail climbs 2 miles to a rock cairn at a junction within sight of Mirror Lake. Here the old glacier has left patches of bare, polished granite amid fields of brilliant alpine wildflowers—especially the thumb-sized blue blooms of gentian.

Detour briefly left to see Mirror Lake's reflection of Eagle Cap's snowy cliffs. Then return to the rock cairn and keep left at all trail junctions. After a mile the trail forks at a signless post. Horton Pass is to the right, while the left-hand path is shorter and snowier. The two trails rejoin on a ridgecrest and climb left 1.3 miles to Eagle Cap's summit, a wind-swept knoll where only a mat of tortured whitebark pines and fuzzy alpine dandelions survive. A green ammo can holds the summit climbers' register. Peer over a cliff to the east for a breathtaking look down at barren Glacier Lake. To the left, lakes dot the forested Lake Basin beneath the white cliffs of the Matterhorn. Still farther left, meadows roll down the barrel-shaped East Lostine River valley toward the Two Pan Trailhead where you began.

Other Options— Several backpacking loops return from the Mirror Lake area. If you can arrange a car shuttle, hike east through the Lake Basin and down the West Fork Wallowa River to the Wallowa Lake Trailhead (Hike #58) for a total of 20.6 miles. If you don't have a shuttle, hike west to Minam Lake (Hike #63) and down the West Lostine River for a total of 16.9 miles.

Eagle Cap from Mirror Lake.

Hike 63 Minam Lake

A range of white sawtooth crags looms above the wildflower meadows where Minam Lake spills into the West Lostine River.

Difficult (to Minam Lake)
11.6 miles round trip
1800 feet elevation gain
Open mid-July through October
Use: hikers, horses

Difficult (to Blue Lake)
15 miles round trip
2150 feet elevation gain

Minam Lake.

The view at Minam Lake is just pretty enough to help you forget the long, steep, dusty trail you've just hiked from the heavily used Two Pan Trailhead. To make the most of your time in this glorious high country, consider continuing around Minam Lake and up another 0.9 mile to Blue Lake, a smaller pool in a cirque ringed with snowy cliffs. Group size is limited to six.

Getting There— Drive Interstate 84 to La Grande exit 261 and following Wallowa Lake signs 55 miles on Highway 82 to the village of Lostine. In the center of town, where the highway turns left, go straight on Lostine River Road, following a pointer for "Lostine River Campgrounds." This route is a two-lane paved road for the first 7 miles, followed by 5.2 miles of wide washboard gravel to the Lostine Guard Station, a log cabin visitor information center. Stop here to fill your water bottles from the valley's only tested water supply, an outdoor drinking fountain. Then continue on a rougher, one-lane gravel road another 6.1 miles to road's end at the Two Pan Trailhead. Parking permits are required.

At the trailhead you'll find a large parking area for horse trailers on the left. Continue down to the right another 0.1 mile to a smaller parking area at the actual

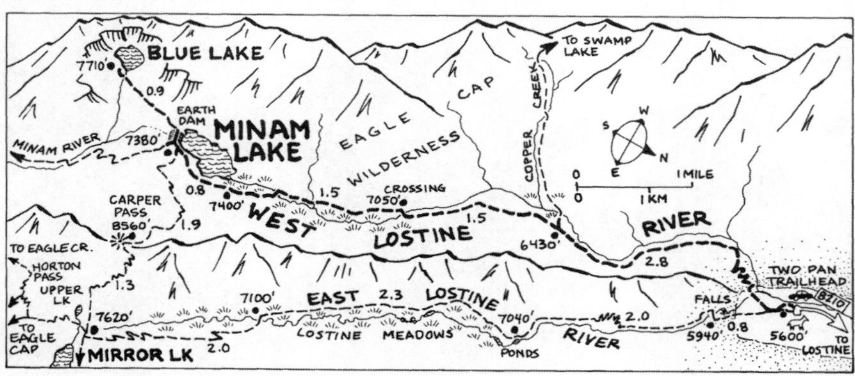

trailhead with a registration box. Start here and hike onward 0.1 mile to a major fork. Veer right on the West Fork Lostine River Trail. This path crosses a fork of the river on a concrete footbridge and climbs through a forest of Douglas fir, lodgepole pine, and grand fir. Views of the river or the mountains are rare at first. After 2.8 miles, turn left at a junction marked by a signpost in a rock cairn, and follow the path uphill across a rockslide of white boulders. Another 1.5 dusty miles brings you to an easy crossing of the 30-foot-wide West Lostine River on stepping stones.

The final 1.5 miles from this river crossing to Minam Lake are a delight, following the meandering river through meadows of blue gentian, red paintbrush, pink heather, and purple aster. At the lake itself, remember that campsites are banned within 100 feet of the shore and horse grazing is not allowed within 200 feet. Campfires are not permitted within a quarter mile of Minam and Blue Lakes.

Minam Lake used to be the headwaters of the Minam River, not the Lostine. If you continue 0.8 mile to the far end of the lake you'll discover an old, grassy dam built by early Wallowa County irrigators. This earth dike is only 15 feet tall, but it sufficed to send the lake spilling north instead of south. If you're headed for Blue Lake, walk across the dam and continue 0.9 mile to trail's end.

Other Options— If you're out for a 2- or 3-day backpack, try the spectacular 16.9-mile loop that returns from Minam Lake via Mirror Lake and the East Lostine River. Hike to the far end of Minam Lake, but just before the dam, switchback up to the left at a "Lake Basin" pointer. This path climbs 3.2 miles over scenic Minam Pass to a pair of trail junctions 200 feet apart, both marked by large rock cairns. If you turn right at the first one, you'll be headed up Eagle Cap. If you go straight at both, you'll visit Mirror Lake. If you keep left at both, you'll descend the East Lostine River back to your car.

The West Lostine River.

Hike 64 Maxwell Lake

Most of the Wallowa Mountains' beautiful alpine lakes are simply too far away to visit on a day hike—but not this jewel.

Difficult
7.8 miles round trip
2420 feet elevation gain
Open late July through October
Use: hikers, horses

Maxwell Lake.

Maxwell Lake sits in a glacially carved notch high on the side of the Lostine River canyon, with mountain crags and wildflowers. Although the trail starts out gently, it steepens later on. Maximum group size is 12.

Getting There— From Interstate 84, take La Grande exit 261 and follow Wallowa Lake signs 55 miles to Lostine. Where the highway turns left in Lostine, go straight on Lostine River Road at a sign for "Lostine River Campgrounds." Follow this two-lane paved road for 7 miles, followed by 5.2 miles of wide washboard gravel to the Lostine Guard Station and another 5.6 miles of rougher gravel to the Maxwell Lake Trailhead on the left, where parking permits are required.

The trail immediately crosses the road, passes some Shady Cove Campground sites, and crosses the Lostine River on a bridge. Just beyond is Maxwell Creek, and although the bridge here has washed out, it's usually easy to cross on big granite boulders. Then the path climbs 2.5 miles on seven long switchbacks.

At this point the trail suddenly scrambles straight up a dusty, rocky slope 0.8 mile to a pass, and then ambles 0.2 mile down to its end beside Maxwell Lake. Almost the entire hike is on open slopes with views across the valley to high Wallowa peaks. As you climb higher you'll trade Oregon grape, wild strawberry, and

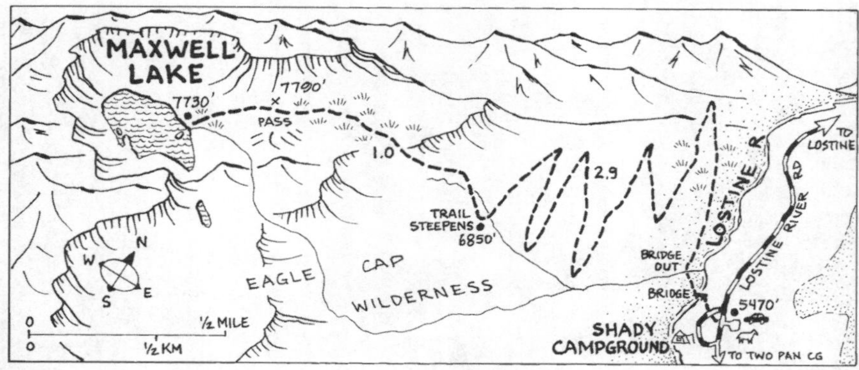

bracken fern for monkshood, pink monkeyflower, and Christmas-tree-sized firs.

The lake itself is a deep blue pool with a cute little island and a backdrop of boulder rockslides below gigantic gray crags. Look for the blue blooms of gentians in the narrow heather meadow along the shore. Tents are banned within 100 feet of the lake, grazing horses must be kept 200 feet from the lake, and campfires are prohibited within a quarter mile.

Hike 65 Chimney Lake

Here are the Wallowa Mountains at their best: heather-rimmed alpine lakes, granite peaks, and wildflower meadows.

Difficult (to Chimney Lake)
10.2 miles round trip
2420 feet elevation gain
Open late July through October
Use: hikers, horses

Difficult (to Steamboat Lake)
29.3-mile loop
5920 feet elevation gain

Chimney Lake.

Despite the splendor, this is not the famous, crowded Lake Basin below Eagle Cap's cliffs. It's a quieter corner of the Eagle Cap Wilderness. For a strenuous day hike, explore Chimney Lake, in a basin with four other lakes. For a three-day trip, continue across passes to Steamboat and Swamp Lakes.

Getting There— From Interstate 84, take La Grande exit 261 and follow Wallowa Lake signs 55 miles on Highway 82 to the village of Lostine. Where the highway turns left in Lostine, go straight on Lostine River Road at a sign for "Lostine River Campgrounds." Follow this road for 7 miles of pavement and 5.2 miles of washboard gravel to the Lostine Guard Station, a visitor information center. Then continue on a rougher, one-lane gravel road another 2.9 miles and turn left into the parking area of the Bowman/Frances Lake Trailhead. Parking permits are required, and maximum group size is 12.

Walk back down to the parking lot's entrance to find a sign marking the Bowman Trail on the right. Follow this path across the road to a footbridge over the Lostine River. Then the trail climbs through a forest of lodgepole pine, fir, and spruce. After 0.8 mile the path switchbacks beside a 100-foot slide waterfall. Continue uphill another 2.8 miles to a trail junction at a rock cairn above Brownie Basin.

For the day hike, turn right at this junction for 1.5 miles to Chimney Lake, a large, swimmable lake with two small islands, set in a huge bowl of white granite rockslides and heather meadows. Campfires are banned within a quarter mile of all lakes in this area. If you have the time and energy, continue up the well-graded trail another 1.2 miles to a high pass with a terrific view across Chimney Lake to the high Wallowas' snowpeaks. From this pass, a 0.4-mile trail climbs up to the

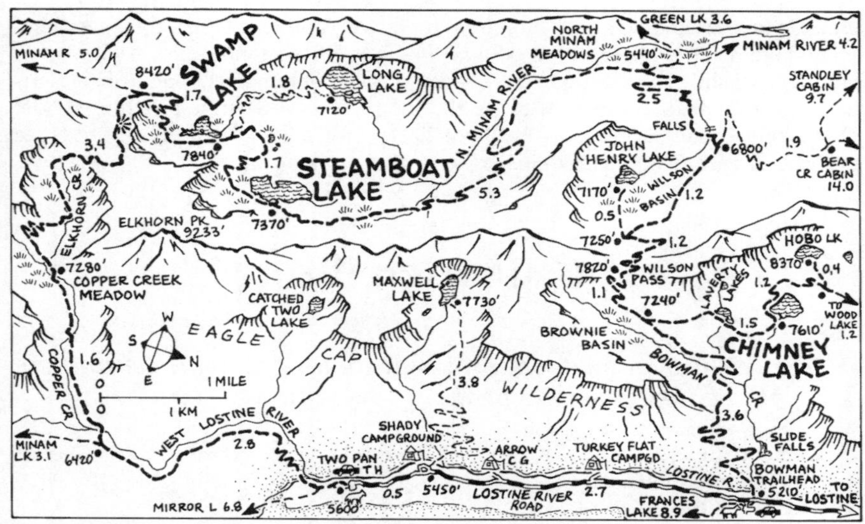

left to end at Hobo Lake, in a windy, barren cirque, while a 1.2-mile trail descends through the forest to the right to end at Wood Lake.

If you're prepared for the 3-day trek to Steamboat Lake, you might skip the detour to Chimney Lake altogether, and instead camp at less-visited John Henry Lake. To find it from the junction above Brownie Basin, follow a "Wilson Basin" pointer up 1.1 mile to Wilson Pass and continue down the far side of the pass 1.2 miles to the fourth switchback. When the trail turns sharply right, go straight on an unmarked side trail for 0.5 mile. John Henry Lake is shallow, and has mosquitoes until early August, but a low rise north of the lake has good campsites.

Swamp Lake.

For the trip's second day, return to the main trail and continue west 3.7 miles down to a junction at North Minam Meadows. Turn left, following a "Copper Creek" pointer. After climbing 5.3 miles you'll reach Steamboat Lake, a large lake with several sandy coves. The few good campsites here may be taken, so consider continuing 1.7 miles to Swamp Lake. This misnamed, gorgeous alpine lake is surrounded by granite hillocks where tents can hide. Shaped like a silhouette of Bullwinkle the moose, the lake features an island "eye" and "antler" inlets. Fish are so scarce that bats skim insects off the surface in the evening. Campfires are banned within a quarter mile of either Swamp or Steamboat Lakes.

On the third day, climb from Swamp Lake to a high, granite upland and keep left at all junctions for 9.5 miles to descend along Copper Creek and the West Lostine River to the Two Pan Trailhead. If you haven't left a shuttle car here, you'll face a 3.2-mile walk down the road to your car at the Bowman Trailhead.

Hike 66 Wallowa Homeland

The Wallowa Band of Nez Perce was driven out of Oregon by the U.S. Army in 1877, but the band's descendants have bought their old winter campsite and now welcome visitors.

The Wallowa Homeland.

Easy
4.3-mile loop
600 feet elevation gain
Open all year
Use: hikers, horses, bicycles

Start at the homeland's visitor center, where excellent displays tell the story of the band's forced removal, their 1000-mile flight toward political sanctuary in Canada, and their subsequent internment at the Fort Leavenworth prison. You will also learn that the French term *nez percé* means "pierced nose" and was based on the mistaken assumption that the tribespeople wore ornaments in their noses. The word "Nee-Me-Poo" (or *nimipu*) means "the real people" in the Nez Perce language, and is the tribe's own name for itself.

Getting There— From Interstate 84, take La Grande exit 261 and follow Wallowa Lake signs 47 miles on Highway 82 to the city of Wallowa. In the center of town turn left on Storie Street a block to the visitor center at 209 E. Second Street.

After touring the museum, leave your car where it is and walk north on Storie Street for a block, away from the highway. When the street turns left, go straight on a wide trail that curves to the right over a Wallowa River bridge. On the far side you'll see a huge circular dance arbor, the site of the annual Tamkaliks Celebration, held the third weekend in July, one week after the "Chief Joseph Days" cowboy rodeo in Joseph.

In front of the dance arbor, walk a gravel road 0.1 mile to the base of a huge cliff, fork to the right 0.1 mile to a boulder, and veer left on a trail that soon switchbacks uphill. After a mile the path crosses a road and climbs to a gazebo with a view of the Wallowa Mountains. On your way back, veer right on a trail that recrosses the dirt road, passes a radio tower, and switchbacks down to a gravel road along the Wallowa River. Turn left on this road to complete the loop back to your car at the visitor center.

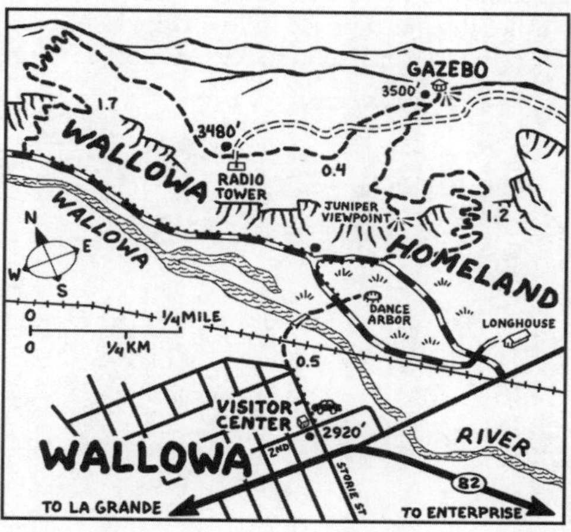

Hike 67 Bear Creek

The Wallowa Mountains are known for their alpine lakes. But here's another side of the range: trails to historic log cabins.

Moderate (Bear Cr Guard Station)
10 miles round trip
900 feet elevation gain
Open May through November
Use: hikers, horses

Moderate (to Standley Cabin)
10.2 miles round trip
1400 feet elevation gain
Open mid-July through October
Use: hikers, horses

Standley Cabin.

The first route follows Bear Creek through a low-elevation forest, while the other traces the higher ground of Standley Ridge. For a longer adventure, connect the two routes with a 3.5-mile trail up Dobbin Creek. Maximum group size is 12.

Getting There— From La Grande, take Interstate 84 exit 261 and follow Wallowa Lake signs 46.5 miles on Highway 82 to the village of Wallowa. Just as you are about to enter the town's city limits, turn right at a sign for North Bear Creek Road. Follow this road (which becomes Road 8250) for 3.2 paved miles and another 5 miles of good gravel to a fork. Following a "Boundary Campground" pointer, go straight on Road 040. In the next 0.8 mile you'll pass a string of campsites (some for equestrians) along 20-foot-wide Bear Creek. The road ends at a large trailhead parking lot. If you don't have a parking permit, you can buy one here for $5.

The wide, nearly level trail sets off through a fir forest with snowberry and the white blooms of solomonseal. Big cottonwood trees line the bouldery creek. After 0.2 mile you'll cross the creek on a 60-foot bridge beside mossy cliffs. For the next 4 miles the path simply follows the creek, occasionally climbing above it on bluffs. Then the trail crosses a rocky meadow to a trail sign cairn and a bridge across Goat

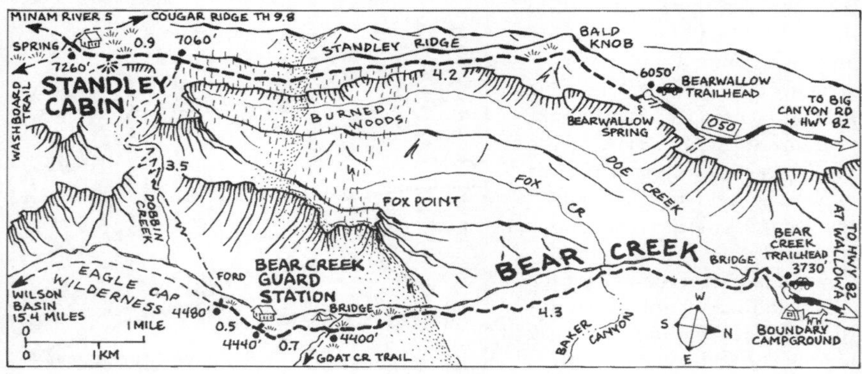

Bear Creek.

Creek. Some nice, large campsites are in the forest to the right.

To find the log cabin, continue on the main trail 0.7 mile beyond Goat Creek and turn right on a large, unmarked side trail 0.1 mile. The early 1900s Bear Creek Guard Station *(GPS location 45.4107, -117.535)* is a masterfully built 18-by-24-foot structure with dovetailed corners. Although it's locked and closed to the public, the large porch makes a good place for lunch. Telephone wire connectors on the outside wall once tied this station to a network of outposts like Standley Cabin. Horse hitchrails and campsites are nearby. A side trail crosses a gravel bar 200 feet to a placid portion of Bear Creek.

Beyond the guard station 0.5 mile the main trail forks. To the right, a path fords Bear Creek (which can be crossed dry-footed by August) and climbs along Dobbin Creek toward Standley Cabin.

If Standley Cabin is your goal, however, you might start at a closer trailhead. From La Grande, drive Highway 82 toward Wallowa Lake for 35 miles. At milepost 35, turn right onto Big Canyon Road 8270 for a slow, hour-long drive. After 10.8 miles of gravel, veer left at a fork onto Road 050, a bumpier road that's passable for passenger cars if driven carefully. Take the largest road at junctions for the next 6.9 miles to a parking turnaround and horse ramp at the Bearwallow Trailhead *(GPS location 45.4499, -117.5885)*.

The trail to Standley Cabin sets off through an open forest of lodgepole pines and subalpine firs.. Beyond the Dobbin Creek trail junction continue on the main trail 0.9 mile up to Standley Cabin *(GPS location 45.3820, -117.5751)*. The 18-by-24-foot log building is locked and closed to the public, but has a nice porch. Beside the cabin, a muddy spring launches a moss-lined creek across a meadow of coneflowers and hellebore (corn lily). Camping is banned within 150 feet of the spring.

Although the Standley Cabin is the logical turnaround point for a day hike, it lacks a view. To find a better vantage point, head back down the trail 0.3 mile to the far end of the meadow and bushwhack up to the right 100 feet to a clifftop rim. From there you can survey the green cirque bowl of Dobbin Basin, the immense gorge of Bear Creek, and the distant summits of high Wallowa peaks, including the Matterhorn's white cliff and Sacajawea's brown pyramid.

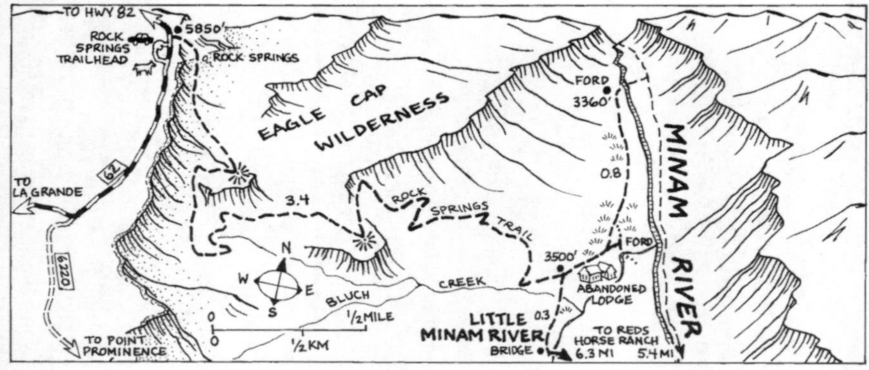

Hike

68 Rock Springs

The Minam River gathers its forces high in the Wallowa Mountains and barrels down a 2500-foot-deep rimrock canyon for 40 miles. This is the easiest path to that mighty torrent.

Difficult
8.4 miles round trip
2500 feet elevation **loss**
Open mid-June through October
Use: hikers, horses

The Minam River.

Admittedly, the path from Rock Springs is still pretty difficult. It loses 2500 of elevation that you will have to regain on the return trip, which is why most visitors here are on horseback. A big meadow beside the Minam River includes the explorable ruins of an old lodge. There's plenty of room for camping nearby.

Getting There— From Interstate 84, take La Grande exit 261 and follow Wallowa Lake signs on Highway 82 toward Elgin for 8 miles to the grain elevator silos at Alicel. Turn right on paved Alicel Lane for 0.6 mile to a T-shaped junction, and turn left to keep on Alicel Lane through several zigs and zags for another 3.4 miles. Then turn right on gravel Gray's Corners Road for exactly 1 mile and turn left on an unmarked gravel road that climbs steeply uphill. After 10.2 miles you'll cross a bridge to another T-shaped junction. Turn left on gravel Road 62. After 6.8 miles veer right at an unmarked fork and then continue on Road 62 for another 3 miles to the Rock Springs Trailhead, between mileposts 12 and 13.

At the trailhead you'll see a horse trailer parking area on the left, but the trail itself starts at a sign 200 feet farther along the road on the right, and you may want

View of the Minam River canyon from the Rock Springs Trail.

to park your car on the shoulder there *(GPS location 45.4049, -117.7065)*. Note that group size on the trail is limited to 12 people and/or 18 head of stock.

The woods along the canyon rim are full of huckleberry bushes, so if you're here during the last three weeks of August, stock up on the blue fruit. The trail marches downhill through an open forest of lodgepole pine, subalpine fir, grand fir, and larch. Twice the path emerges from the woods at ridge-end viewpoints where you can look up the Minam River's canyon to the snowy peaks of the high Wallowas.

At the bottom of the trail keep left at a junction to a collection of mostly roofless log cabin ruins from an old lodge *(GPS location 45.3989, -117.6754)*. Beyond the cabins the trail traverses a large grassy field. The main trail appears to go right, but it merely ends at the bank of the 20-foot-wide Little Minam River, a popular spot to water horses. To find the larger Minam River you'll need to keep straight (and level) through the meadow. After more than half a mile this path reaches a ford of the boulder-strewn, 80-foot-wide river. Horses can manage this bridgeless crossing, but hikers should plan on turning back here. In early summer the dangerously swift current is waist deep. By late summer it's still knee deep and cold.

Other Options— You don't need to risk fording the Minam River to continue into the Eagle Cap Wilderness. Instead go back to the junction by the ruined lodge and veer left on the trail up the Little Minam River. After 0.3 mile you'll cross the stream on a bridge. Continue another 5.2 miles and you'll reach a trail junction in a pass (see Hike #69). Turn left for 1.1 mile to Reds Horse Ranch (another old lodge), where a bridge crosses the Minam River to the Minam River Trail.

Hike 69 Moss Springs

Popular with equestrians, the trails radiating from Moss Springs Campground can seem long and dusty to hikers. The top goals are two lodges.

Bridge at Little Minuam River.

Difficult
15.2 miles round trip
2300 feet elevation gain
Open mid-June through October
Use: hikers, horses

Reds Horse Ranch is an old, closed resort that's owned by the Forest Service. It's beside a vast meadow with the area's only Minam River bridge. A mile beyond, farther downriver, is privately owned Minam Lodge, where reservations are essential for pricey cabins and meals. It's most often accessed by private airplane.

Make a special note of Eagle Cap Wilderness rules: Maximum group size on the trail is 12 people and/or 18 head of stock. Horses may not be hitched or tethered to trees at campsites, or within 100 feet of any stream. Any extra horse feed brought along must be certified to be free of weed seeds that might introduce alien plants.

Getting There— From La Grande, take Interstate 84 exit 261, follow Wallowa Lake signs 1.8 miles to a stop at a major intersection, and go straight on Highway 237 for 14 miles to Cove. In Cove follow the highway as it turns right on Main Street for a block, but then turn left at a white steepled church onto French Street at a sign for Moss Springs Campground. After 3 blocks turn right on Second Street. Follow this paved street (which becomes Mill Creek Lane and then Road 6220)

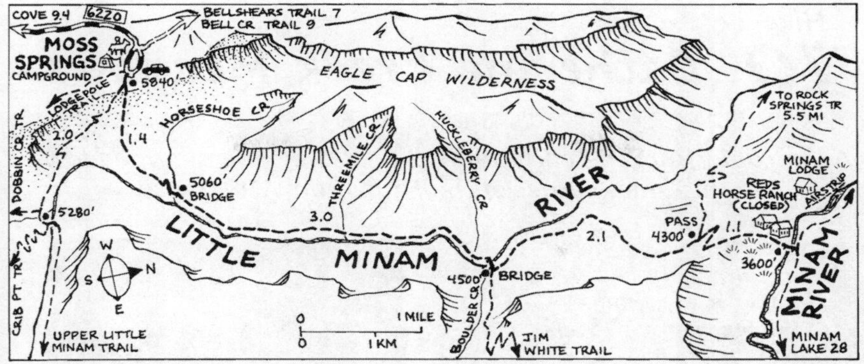

for a total of 9.1 miles to the campground. The last 6.9 miles are relentlessly uphill on gravel. Fork to the right through the campground for 0.3 mile to the trailhead parking area at the far end of a long loop. A fee box is provided for purchasing a trailhead parking permit. You don't need a trailhead permit if you're staying in the campground ($5 per site), a horse-friendly area with corrals and hitching rails.

Start at a message board at the far end of the parking area and follow a broad, very dusty track 300 feet to a major fork. Keep left on the Horse Ranch Trail. After descending gradually 1.4 miles through a forest of grand fir, subalpine fir, and larch, you'll cross Horseshoe Creek on a bridge and start following the 15-foot-wide Little Minam River downstream. Blue huckleberries ripen along the trail in August. In another 3 miles you'll cross the river on a bridge, a possible turnaround point for hikers.

Beyond the Little Minam bridge turn left at a junction, traverse 2.1 miles to a pass, and fork to the right for a mile down to the broad grassy field at Reds Horse Ranch. The caretaker who lives here sometimes offers tours of the old resort compound. Perhaps the nicest campsites are across the river bridge and to the right along the Minam River Trail—a wilderness thoroughfare that continues 28 miles to the river's head in the high country at Minam Lake (Hike #63).

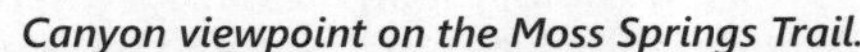

Canyon viewpoint on the Moss Springs Trail.

Hike 70 Catherine Creek Meadows

A log cabin from the early 1900s sits at the edge of a meadow in this quiet corner of the Eagle Cap Wilderness.

Difficult
10.8 miles round trip
1450 feet elevation gain
Open June to mid-November
Use: hikers, horses

The Catherine Creek cabin.

The well-graded trail to the meadow follows the North Fork of Catherine Creek up a long, curving valley gouged from the mountains by an Ice Age glacier.

Getting There — If you're driving from La Grande, take Interstate 84 exit 265 and follow Highway 203 for 14 miles to Union. In the center of town, turn left on Beakman Street at a sign for Medical Springs and continue on Highway 203 for 11.4 miles. Between mileposts 11 and 12, turn left on Catherine Creek Lane (Road 7785) for 6.1 gravel miles, keeping left at junctions, to the Catherine Creek Trailhead. Parking permits are required. Maximum group size on the trail is 12.

If you're driving from Baker City, take Interstate 84 north 6 miles to exit 298 and follow Highway 203 through Medical Springs a total of 29 miles. Between mileposts 12 and 11, turn right on Catherine Creek Lane for 6.1 gravel miles.

The trail doesn't begin at the official trailhead parking area, but rather 0.1 mile farther up to the left on Road 7785, where the road ends at a primitive 6-site campground by the creek. Parking is tight, so only leave your car here if you're planning to camp.

From the campground message board *(GPS location 45.1541, -117.6155)*, the trail climbs gradually through a grand fir forest along the river. After 1.3 miles, when the trail crosses the 30-foot-wide creek on a bridge, take a moment to look for

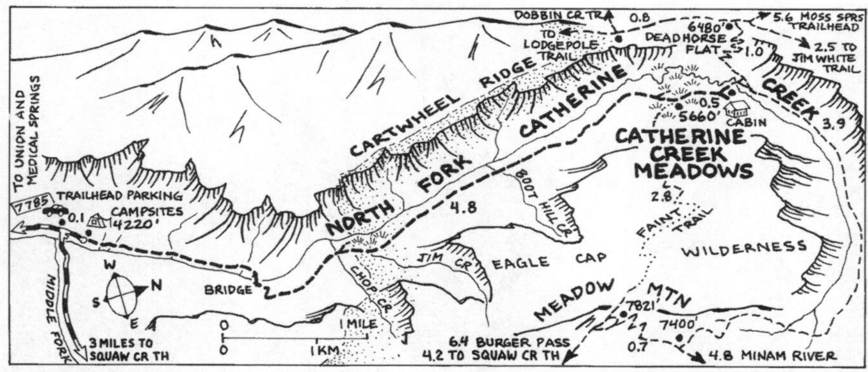

Catherine Creek Meadows.

water ouzels, the dark, robin-sized birds that whir from boulder to boulder before diving underwater to search for insect larvae on the creek bottom.

For the next mile the trail climbs through a zone of huckleberry bushes, where hikers can pick ripe blue berries during the latter half of August. Finally the path enters Catherine Creek Meadows, a broad, half-mile-long field of grass and wildflowers. Grasshoppers jump out of your path. Fat ground squirrels stand on their hind paws to watch you pass. In the midst of the meadow, a rock cairn marks a junction with the faint Meadow Mountain Trail. Continue on the main trail to the end of the meadow and through a spruce grove to a smaller meadow with an unsigned but obvious trail fork where the main trail goes left to cross the creek.

Veer right at this fork for 0.1 mile to find the cabin *(GPS location 45.2205, -117.61).* The 14-by-18-foot log building has a shake roof, two glass windows, 3 cots, a box stove, and a cupboard. Graffiti on the cupboard and door date to 1944, with comments such as "Dam Mosquitoes" (1994), "10 feet of snow" (December 23), and "Fishing bad, Borbon perfect" (1961).

Other Options— Just before the cabin, the main trail forks to the left, crosses the creek, and continues into the Wilderness. For a 17.2-mile loop, keep right for 4.6 miles to the summit of Meadow Mountain, turn left on the China Ridge Trail 1.6 miles, and turn right for 2.6 miles down to the poorly marked Squaw Creek Trailhead. If you don't have a shuttle, walk left on the gravel road 3 miles to your car.

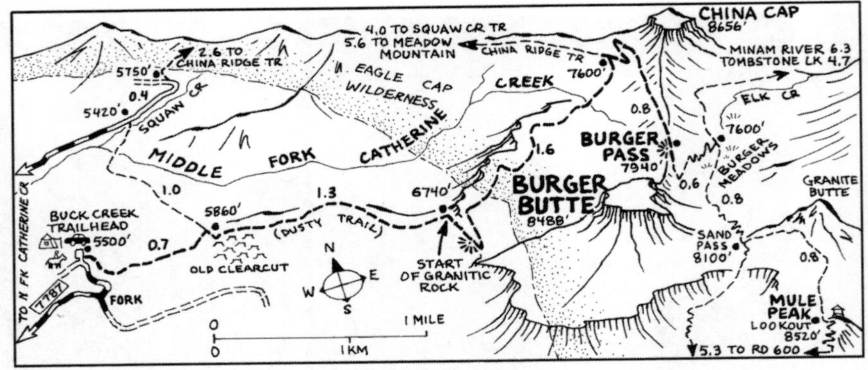

Hike

71 Burger Pass

In this scenic alpine pass you stand on a Wallowa Mountain divide separating the craggy granite snowpeaks of the east from the basalt canyonlands of the west.

The view from Burger Pass.

Difficult
8.8 miles round trip
2440 feet elevation gain
Open mid-July through October
Use: hikers, horses

The route to Burger Pass includes what may be the dustiest mile of trail you've ever seen. The dust is a result of the Wallowas' schizophrenic geologic past. The range began as a string of Pacific Ocean islands nearly a billion years ago. Currents in the Earth's molten mantle gradually "rafted" the islands eastward and scraped them off onto the North American continent. Later additions to Oregon's shore left the Wallowas inland, and erosion wore the islands down to their granite roots.

About 17 million years ago enormous floods of basalt lava buried most of Eastern Oregon and Washington. But then the Wallowas rose again, exposing the white granite underneath. Today Burger Pass balances between the granite peaks and the basalt tablelands. The dust of the trail is volcanic ash sandwiched in between.

Getting There— If you're driving here from La Grande, take Interstate 84 exit 265 and follow Highway 203 for 14 miles to Union. In the center of town, turn left on Beakman Street at a sign for Medical Springs and continue on Highway 203 for 11.4 miles. Between mileposts 11 and 12, turn left on Catherine Creek Lane (alias Road 7785) for 4.2 gravel miles, turn right on Road 7787 for 3.9 miles to a fork, and veer left for 0.3 mile to the Buck Creek Trailhead on the right, where parking permits are required *(GPS location 45.1474, -117.571)*.

If you're driving from Baker City, take Interstate 84 north 6 miles to exit 298 and follow Highway 203 through Medical Springs a total of 29 miles. Between mileposts 12 and 11, turn right on Catherine Creek Lane for 4.2 gravel miles, turn right on Road 7787 for 3.7 miles, and fork left for 0.3 mile.

The trail begins at a message board at the far end of a big horse campgound parking loop. Parking permits are required, but you can buy them here for $5. The path crosses an old logging road and skirts a regrowing clearcut. By the 0.9-mile mark you'll be in cooler woods, but the dust is still 2 inches deep, puffing at each step like cocoa powder. It comes as a relief at the 2-mile mark when the trail switchbacks up from the volcanic ash into less dusty granite terrain. Hop across the 4-foot-wide Middle Fork of Catherine Creek and climb to a junction with the China Ridge Trail. Turn right for a 0.8-mile climb through pink heather and spire-shaped subalpine firs to Burger Pass *(GPS location 45.144, -117.5136)*, a good turnaround goal. For the best views, scramble 100 feet up to the right from the pass.

***Other Options*—** Beyond Burger Pass the trail dives 0.6 mile down into the white granite canyon of Burger Meadows. For a longer hike, continue to the right on a steep, dusty 0.8-mile path to Sand Pass (in the ashy contact zone between granite and basalt), and traverse another 0.8 mile to the view at the historic Mule Peak fire lookout cabin, now shuttered closed.

Hike 72 Tombstone Lake

Snowy crags surround Tombstone and Traverse Lakes like castle walls, yet within these alpine fortresses are delightful gardens— gentle lakeshore meadows of pink heather and white phlox.

Difficult (to Traverse Lake)
13.4 miles round trip
2290 feet elevation gain
Open mid-July through October
Use: hikers, horses

Difficult (to Tombstone Lake)
17.8 miles round trip
3550 feet elevation gain

Echo Lake.

Crowds aren't likely, and not just because these lakes lie on the less-visited, southern side of the Wallowa Mountains. The price of admission here is steep: long trails with lots of switchbacks.

Because the gardens are so fragile, campsites must be at least 100 feet from any lakeshore, horses may not be grazed within 200 feet of lakes, and fires are banned within a quarter mile of Tombstone or Traverse Lakes. The use of snags for firewood is prohibited, and downed wood is scarce. Group size is limited to 12.

***Getting There*—** From La Grande, take Interstate 84 exit 265 and follow Highway

Tombstone Lake from the trail's pass.

203 for 14 miles to Union. In the center of town, turn left on Beakman Street at a sign for Medical Springs and continue on Highway 203 for 14.2 miles to the highway's summit. At a pointer for "West Eagle" turn left on gravel Road 77 for 15.7 miles to the West Eagle Trailhead parking area on the left (*GPS location 45.0797, -117.4767*). The final 5.4 miles of this road are so rough that cars creep along at 10 miles per hour.

If you're driving from Baker City, take Interstate 84 north 6 miles to exit 298 and follow Highway 203 for 18 miles to Medical Springs. Following signs for Boulder Park, turn right on Eagle Creek Drive, which soon becomes gravel. After 1.6 miles, fork left onto gravel, one-lane Big Creek Road 67. In another 14 miles, turn left

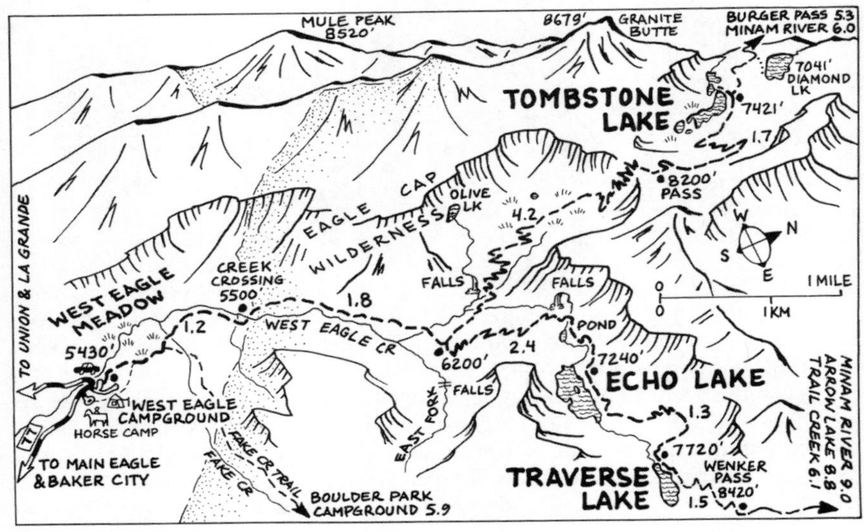

on Road 77 for 0.7 mile, and then turn left to keep on Road 77 for 4.5 miles to the West Eagle Trailhead. The final 3.2 miles are bumpy and very slow.

The trailhead area has 24 campsites and a large equestrian campground. Look for nice walk-in tent sites where the creek meanders out into West Eagle Meadow, a broad field visited by elk and deer at dusk. Expect to pay $5 per car at a fee box if you don't already have a Northwest Forest Pass.

The trail launches into a forest of grand fir, Douglas fir, Engelmann spruce, and larch. Douglas squirrels scold from the trees and red-shafted flickers swoop from trunk to trunk. After 1.1 mile the path meets 15-foot-wide West Eagle Creek. There is no bridge, but logs and boulders upstream make a dry crossing possible. Then continue 1.8 miles up the scenic canyon to a signpost at a fork.

Here you have to choose between the tough trip to Traverse Lake (to the right) or the even tougher trip to Tombstone Lake (to the left). If you take the left-hand fork toward "Elk Creek" you'll switchback up past falls and meadows 4.2 miles, gaining 2000 feet to a pass with a view of Tombstone Lake—but to actually reach the lakeshore you'll still have to hike another 1.7 miles, losing 780 feet of elevation. Whew! You may be ready for a swim when you get there, and if so, note that the lowest (and farthest) of Tombstone Lake's four connected pools is least icy. Granite boulders around the lake really are as white and smooth as cemetery slabs.

If the trip to Tombstone sounds like a killer, keep right at the trail's fork and switchback up a mere 1040 feet in 2.4 miles to Echo Lake. With echoing cliffs and a little island, this lake would be an excellent destination but for the fact that Traverse Lake, another 1.3 miles up the trail, is an even more spectacular goal.

Hike 73 — Eagle Lake

The Ice Age glaciers that scalloped the southern Wallowa Mountains left granite lake basins around the rim of Eagle Creek's spectacular valley like cupboards in a giant's kitchen.

Difficult (to Arrow Lake)
10.6 miles round trip
2720 feet elevation gain
Open mid-July through October
Use: hikers

Difficult (to Eagle Lake)
19.1-mile loop
4080 feet elevation gain

Refer to map on page 199.

Eagle Lake.

Day hikers only have time to peek into one of those cupboard doors, but backpackers can visit one alpine lake after another on a loop. The difficult route is impassable for horses, making this one of the few hiker-only Wallowa tours.

Getting There— From Baker City, take Interstate 84 north 6 miles to exit 298 and drive 19 miles on Highway 203 to Medical Springs, an old stagecoach stop.

(If you're coming via La Grande, take Interstate 84 exit 265, follow Highway 203 for 14 miles to Union, and turn left to continue on Highway 203 for 21 miles to Medical Springs.) At Medical Springs turn east on Eagle Creek Drive, following the first of many signs for Boulder Park. The road soon becomes gravel. After 1.6 miles, fork left onto one-lane Big Creek Road 67. After another 14.6 miles, turn left on Road 77 for 0.8 mile and then keep straight on Road 7755 for 3.7 miles to its end at the Main Eagle Trailhead, where parking permits are required. A landslide obliterated the old Boulder Park Resort near here, but the name lives on at the 10-site Boulder Park Campground and horse unloading site just before the trailhead. Maximum group size on the trail is 12 people and/or 18 head of stock. Tents and fires are banned within 100 feet of lakeshores.

The trail sets off across the debris of the landslide, launched from a white scar on the opposite canyon wall. The path crosses 30-foot-wide Eagle Creek on a footbridge after 0.6 mile and on an impromptu log at the 2.5-mile mark. Then you'll hop on rocks across Copper Creek and glimpse the 60-foot fan of Copper Creek Falls to the left. In another 0.2 mile, look for a sign marking the small Bench Trail that forks uphill to the left.

The Bench Trail begins so steeply that it resembles a bobsled chute. It climbs across slopes of sagebrush and wildflowers for 1.5 miles to a crest. Continue 0.1 mile downhill to a confusing turn beside Bench Canyon Creek. Instead of going straight to a small campsite, cross the creek to the left on the less-obvious main trail. This path climbs another 0.8 mile to Arrow Lake *(GPS location 45.1102, -117.3923)*, in a spectacular granite bowl with pink heather and blue gentians.

To continue on the loop, follow the Bench Trail past Arrow Lake over a pass 0.8 mile, turn right for 1.6 miles to another pass with a panoramic view, and continue 2 miles down to a 4-way trail junction. To the right is Cached Lake (*GPS location 45.1179, -117.369)*, a lovely pool rimmed with alpine wildflower meadows and rockslides. Straight ahead is a clifftop viewpoint and campsite. Turn left, however, to continue the loop route. In another mile, veer left to detour 1.1 mile up to the 20-foot-tall stonework dam that has converted the otherwise immensely scenic Eagle Lake into a reservoir. Fires are banned at Eagle Lake, but the bare rock bluff at its outlet makes a dramatic campsite. To complete the loop from Eagle Lake, return 1.1 mile to the main trail and follow it 6.2 miles back to your car.

Eagle Creek Meadow.

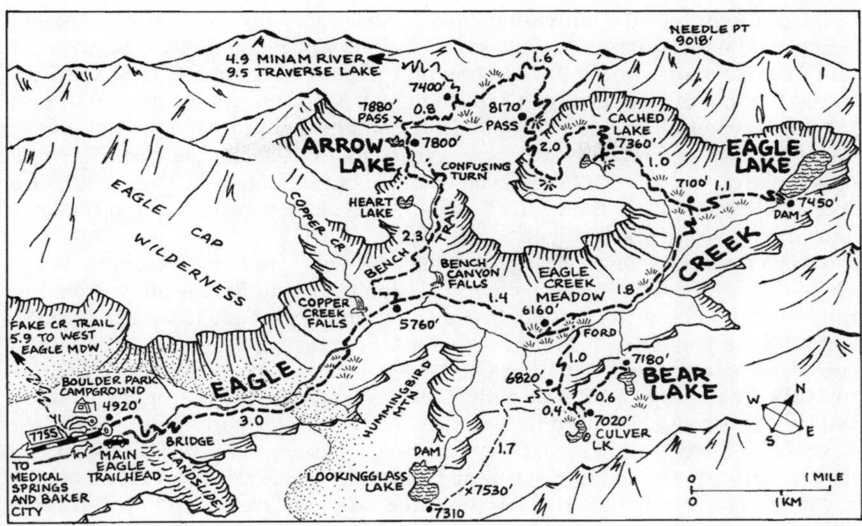

Hike 74 Bear Lake

Even families with children can generally manage the trek to Eagle Creek Meadow, a creekside field surrounded by granite canyon walls reminiscent of the Swiss Alps.

Moderate (to Eagle Creek Meadow)
8.8 miles round trip
1250 feet elevation gain
Open early July through October
Use: hikers, horses

Difficult (to Bear Lake)
12.8 miles round trip
2240 feet elevation gain
Open mid-July through October

Bear Lake.

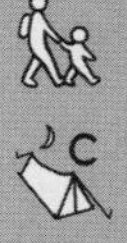

From Eagle Creek Meadow, hardier hikers can climb a side trail up the canyon wall 2 miles to beautiful Bear Lake, one of the few large alpine lakes in Northeast Oregon that has never been dammed to serve as an irrigation reservoir.

Getting There— Start by driving to the Main Eagle Trailhead described in Hike #73, at the end of gravel Road 7755 near the free Boulder Park Campground. Parking permits are required. Remember that group size on the trail is limited to 12 people and/or 18 head of stock. Campsites must be at least 100 feet from any lakeshore, tethered horses must be at least 100 feet from water or campsites, and fires are strongly discouraged. Firewood may only be gathered from downed, dead trees.

The trail begins on the outwash plain of a landslide, whose source is visible as a white scar on the opposite canyon wall. After crossing Eagle Creek at the 0.6-mile and 2.5-mile marks, you'll have to hop on rocks across Copper Creek. Look for the 60-foot fan of Copper Creek Falls to the left. Continue on the main trail past the 8-foot waterfall of Bench Canyon Creek and hike another mile to the start of Eagle Creek Meadow's vast opening. Where the trail enters the clearing you'll cross an exceptionally well preserved example of glacial polish. This valley's Ice Age glaciers smoothed the bedrock granite here as they ground past 6000 years ago, and the shiny finish still gleams as if wet.

At a well-marked fork, veer right on the Bear Lake Trail into the grassy flat of Eagle Creek Meadow. If this is your goal, don't camp in the meadow itself, but rather in the trees at the far end. If you're continuing to Bear Lake, head for the creek, where you'll find a 30-foot-wide ford. By mid-August you may be able to complete this crossing dry-footed. On the far shore the path climbs most of a mile to a fork. To the right a 1.7-mile path climbs over a ridge to Lookingglass Lake, a reservoir. Instead go left 0.4 mile, where two different side paths detour to Culver Lake, backed with a ring of snow and a spectacular amphitheater of cliffs. Keep left for another 0.6 mile to reach Bear Lake *(GPS location 45.1006, -117.3485)*. A substantial fir forest abuts this lake on three sides, but the far end opens onto a large meadow with a colossal backdrop of cliffs. There's plenty of room to camp on the sparsely wooded rise overlooking Eagle Creek's canyon.

Hike 75 Hidden Lake

Deep in the Wallowas, this lake is a hidden Eden. Snowy crags surround a high valley of wildflower meadows, subalpine firs, brooks, and tarns.

Hidden Lake.

Difficult
16.4 miles round trip
2650 feet elevation gain
Open mid-July through October
Use: hikers, horses

From rocks beside the still green waters you can dive into the depths or sit and watch fish. The gate protecting this secret glen is distance: 8.2 miles of trail that bar all but backpackers, equestrians, and the most determined of day hikers.

If you venture here, remember that groups cannot be larger than 12. Campsites must be at least 100 feet from any lakeshore, tethered horses must be at least 200 feet from lakes, and campfires are strongly discouraged. Firewood cutting from standing trees or snags is prohibited, and downed wood is scarce.

Getting There — From Interstate 84 at the north edge of Baker City, take exit 302

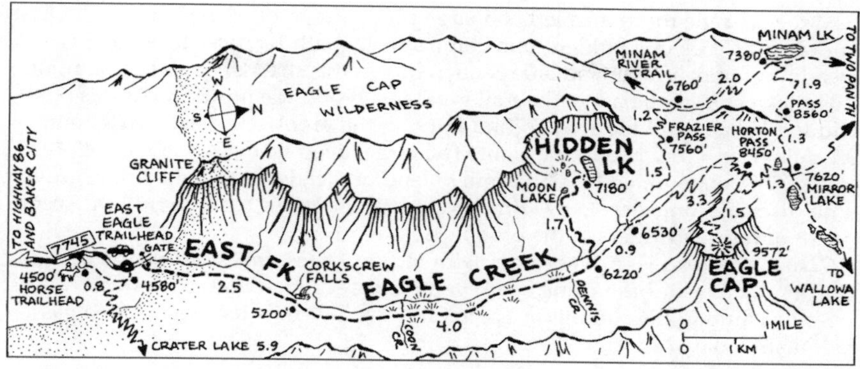

and follow Highway 86 east toward Richland 23.2 miles. At a pointer for Sparta just beyond milepost 23, turn uphill to the left on gravel Sparta Lane for 4.9 miles. Then turn left on East Eagle Creek Road for 5.8 miles to a 5-way road junction. Veer right on Empire Gulch Road 7015 for 4.8 miles and cross a bridge to a T-shaped junction. Turn left on Road 77 for 2.8 miles and fork to the right on East Eagle Road 7745 for another 6.4 miles. Only if you're pulling a horse trailer should you heed the "Eagle Creek Trailhead" pointer and turn right into an equestrian staging area. Otherwise, continue straight another 0.8 mile to a parking turnaround loop at the end of the gravel road *(GPS location 45.0565, -117.3225)*. Parking permits are not required.

Although there is no official campground near the trailhead, you'll pass plenty of free creekside campsites as you drive in. This area was used in the filming of the 1968 Lee Marvin movie, *Paint Your Wagon*.

Start at an "East Eagle Trail" sign on the left side of the parking loop and hike along a rough dirt extension of Road 7745 for 0.2 mile. Before you reach a gate in the road, fork to the right onto a real trail. This path heads up the canyon past the 2400-foot face of Granite Cliff. After 2.5 miles the creek in the gorge below the trail twists through a corkscrew-shaped slot and emerges sideways as a rooster tail of spray. For the next 4 miles the path crosses meadow openings cleared by the avalanches that roar down this canyon's steep walls in winter. Look here for brown coneflower, red paintbrush, fuzzy blue mint, purple aster, and quaking aspen.

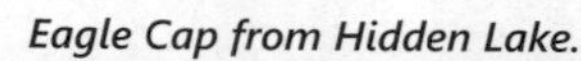
Eagle Cap from Hidden Lake.

At the 6.5-mile mark turn left at a large rock cairn, cross the 15-foot-wide East Fork Eagle Creek on boulders, and climb a rocky path 1.4 miles to Moon Lake. A meadow of pink heather and blue gentian fringes this shallow pool. Then continue 0.3 mile over a small pass to the trail's end in a brookside meadow. At this point, Hidden Lake is still hidden. To find it, cross the brook and head cross-country 0.1 mile over a low rise to the right. The large, deep lake *(GPS location 45.1415, -117.329)* is surrounded by a charming blend of meadows and subalpine groves with discreet campsites. Leave time to explore the lake's basin to find the scenic ponds at the headwaters of the brook.

Other Options— Adventurers with strong knees and stout hearts can use Hidden Lake as a base camp for several large-scale adventures—notably, the 7.4-mile climb to the summit of Eagle Cap or a 17.7-mile loop over three passes to Minam Lake.

Hike 76 Summit Point Lookout

You'll see timberline meadows even at the start of this hike, because the trailhead is one of the highest in the Wallowas.

Easy (to lookout)
2 miles round trip
550 feet elevation gain
Open late July through October
Use: hikers, horses

Difficult (to Pine Lakes pass)
11.8 miles round trip
2120 feet elevation gain

Difficult (to Pine Lakes)
16.2 miles round trip
2950 feet elevation gain

The Summit Point Lookout.

For a quick trip, climb an ancient roadbed to the Summit Point fire lookout tower. For a more substantial day hike, traverse the length of Little Eagle Meadows to a spectacular, high pass overlooking the Pine Lakes. Backpackers can continue onward to the lakes themselves, although that goal is slightly easier to reach via the Cornucopia Trailhead described in Hike #77.

Getting There— From Baker City, drive Interstate 84 north 2 miles to exit 302 and follow Highway 86 east toward Halfway 49 miles. Beyond Richland 6 miles (between mileposts 48 and 49), turn left on gravel Road 77, following a green "Summit Pt. L.O." sign. After 11 miles you'll reach a X-shaped intersection. If you're looking for a place to spend the night, you might turn left into the entrance of McBride Campground, a quiet camp with seven free sites. Otherwise turn right on one-lane Road 7715 for 4.8 slow, steep miles to the Summit Point Trailhead parking area at road's end.

The trail begins as a steep, rough road that's closed to vehicles but used

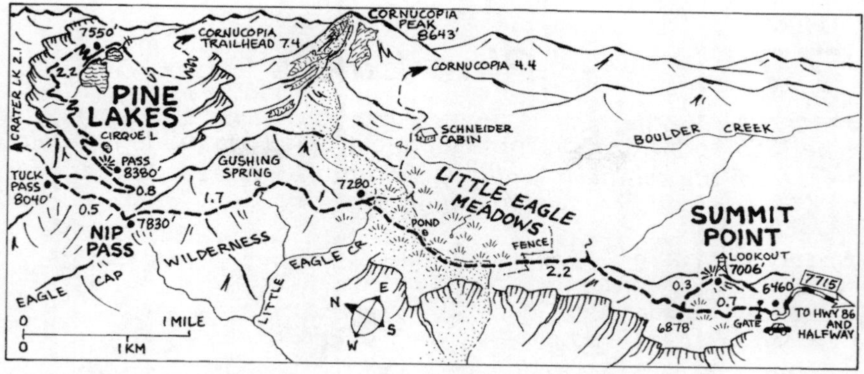

occasionally by cattle. The sagebrush slope is punctuated by the spires of subalpine firs and a variety of wildflowers: blue lupine, scarlet gilia, fuzzy white mint, and red paintbrush. After 0.7 mile the dusty road forks at a ridgecrest. For the short hike, turn right 0.3 mile to the 14-by-14-foot lookout building, perched on a 20-foot tower atop a summit knoll. The lookout is staffed only in times of high forest fire danger. The view extends from the craggy Elkhorn Range on the far western horizon to the rumpled brown badlands toward Hells Canyon. The metal rooftops of Halfway glint from a patchwork of ranchfields.

For a more substantial hike, take the other ridgecrest fork and follow a genuine trail 2.2 miles to the far end of Little Eagle Meadows. Backed by the massive white granite face of Cornucopia Peak, the mile-long meadows cover a gorgeous plateau with grass, lupine, and aster. Expect to see Clark's nutcrackers, blue butterflies, and some cattle. At the far end of the meadows cross a small creek to a trail junction signpost and turn left. In the next 2.2 miles you'll traverse a steep slope past a gushing spring, climb through Nip Pass, and reach a trail junction in Tuck Pass. Switchback up to the right for 0.8 mile to an even higher pass with a view of a small cirque lake and the two large, green Pine Lakes in a gigantic granite bowl.

This scenic, unnamed pass makes a good lunch stop—and a wise turnaround point for day hikers. Backpackers can continue on down 2.2 miles to the Pine Lakes, confident that the climb back up to this pass can be left for another day.

Pine Lakes.

Hike 77 Pine Lakes

The 1885 boomtown of Cornucopia extracted $15 million of gold from the southern Wallowa Mountains before its mines closed in 1941.

Easy (to Chute Falls)
4.2 miles round trip
480 feet elevation gain
Open June through November
Use: hikers, horses

Difficult (to Pine Lakes)
14.8 miles round trip
2720 feet elevation gain
Open late July through October

Pika at the pass above Pine Lakes.

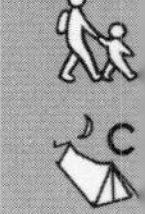

Today Cornucopia's derelict buildings, with their spookily tilted porches and gaping windows, seem strangely out of place so near the Eagle Cap Wilderness. A trail from the ghost town climbs to the Pine Lakes, a pair of deep green pools in a gorgeous alpine basin of heather, wildflowers, and granite cliffs.

Getting There — From Baker City, drive Interstate 84 north 2 miles to exit 302 and follow Highway 86 east through Richland a total of 52 miles to the village of Halfway. Turn left on the Halfway Business Loop and keep straight through town on Main Street (which becomes Cornucopia Road 4190) for 7.2 miles of pavement and another 5.1 miles of gravel to a junction at a sign for Cornucopia Lodge. Most of the ghost town's ruins are half a mile ahead, but to find the trailhead, turn right

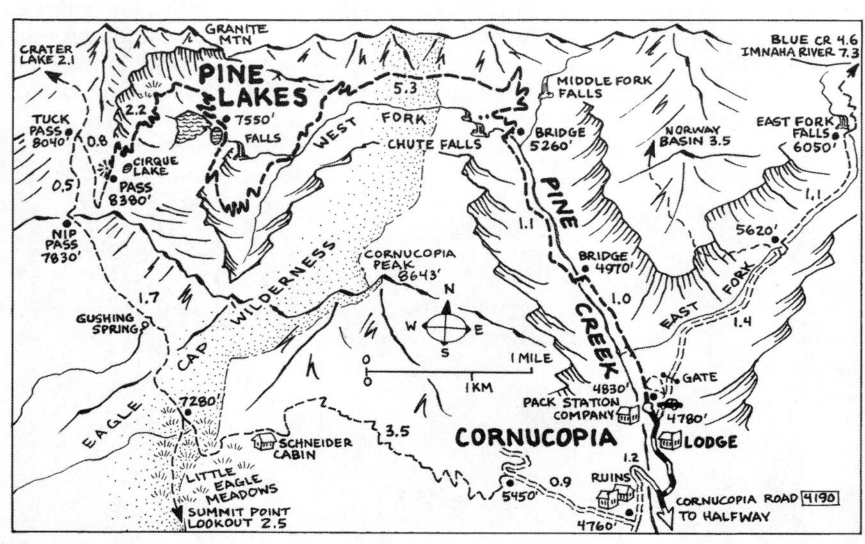

Pine Lakes.

for half a mile to the lodge and keep left 0.1 mile to the lodge's pack station. The station often allows hikers to park in their private lot, but if you drive 300 feet past the station you'll find a small pullout on the right with public parking.

From the mapboard at the pack station's parking area, keep left on the Pine Lakes Trail (an ancient mining road) past the horse corrals and red buildings of the pack station. Soon the route enters meadows of brown coneflower and blue mint beside the creek's big cottonwood trees. To the left the cliffs of Cornucopia Mountain rise 3000 feet, marked by the caverns and white debris fans of old mines.

After 1 mile the trail crosses Pine Creek. A footbridge here was destroyed by an avalanche in 2005. The replacement was damaged by a flood in 2019, but is expected to be repaired. Cross the river and continue upstream 1.1 mile to a second bridge, where the old roadbed narrows to a genuine trail. Beyond this bridge 0.3 mile you'll come to a right-hand switchback where you can hear a waterfall. To find the falls, bushwhack straight 100 feet. The creek plunges 10 feet before sliding through a 30-foot bedrock chute. This makes a good turnaround point.

If you're continuing to Pine Lakes, the trail switchbacks up a mile through a Douglas fir forest and then traverses several miles across hot, shadeless rockslides. You'll see quaking aspen and sagebrush, as well as entire fields of red paintbrush and fireweed. Finally the path switchbacks up to a small cement dam that turned the lower Pine Lake into a reservoir. Continue 0.3 mile to the undammed and very beautiful upper lake, rimmed with meadows and white cliffs.

Campsites must be at least 100 feet from any lakeshore, tethered horses must be at least 200 feet from lakes, and campfires are strongly discouraged. Firewood cutting from standing trees or snags is prohibited. Maximum group size is 12.

Other Options — For an 18.2-mile loop, continue on the trail past the Pine Lakes, switchbacking up through alpine meadows to a 8380-foot pass. Continue 0.8 mile to Tuck Pass, turn left for 1.7 miles to the start of Little Eagle Meadows, and fork to the left on a faint, confusing route among cowpaths. Don't disturb Schneider Cabin, a cowboy outpost that's still in use. When you reach a rough, rocky road, follow it 0.9 mile down to Cornucopia and turn left to return to your car.

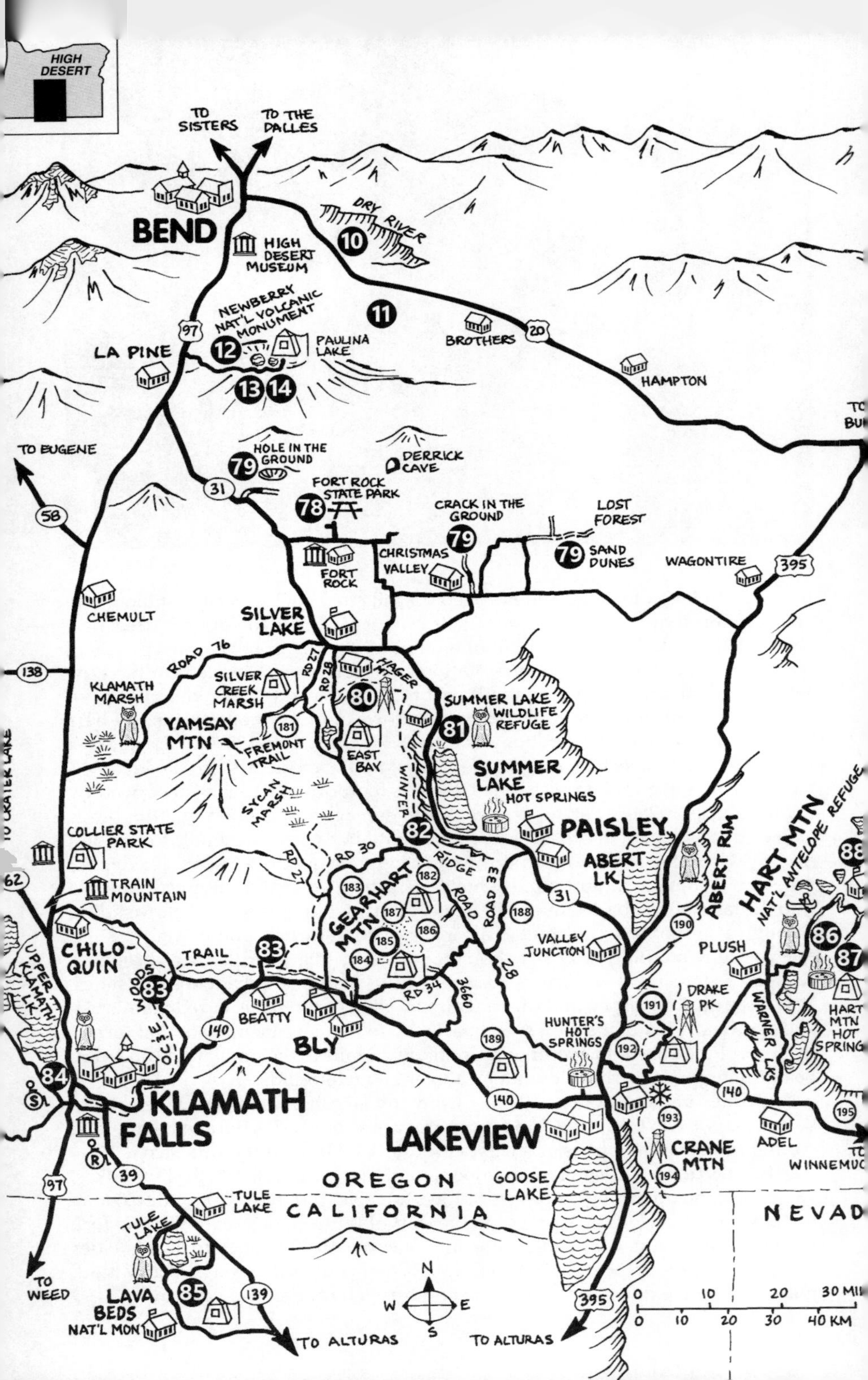

HIGH DESERT
TO SISTERS
TO THE DALLES
BEND
HIGH DESERT MUSEUM
DRY RIVER
10
11
NEWBERRY NAT'L VOLCANIC MONUMENT
12
13
14
PAULINA LAKE
LA PINE
BROTHERS
HAMPTON
97
20
TO EUGENE
58
HOLE IN THE GROUND
79
DERRICK CAVE
31
FORT ROCK STATE PARK
78
CRACK IN THE GROUND
79
LOST FOREST
79
SAND DUNES
FORT ROCK
CHRISTMAS VALLEY
WAGONTIRE
395
CHEMULT
SILVER LAKE
ROAD 76
138
RD 27
RD 28
HAGER MTN
KLAMATH MARSH
SILVER CREEK MARSH
80
SUMMER LAKE WILDLIFE REFUGE
81
YAMSAY MTN
181
FREMONT TRAIL
EAST BAY
SUMMER LAKE
WINTER
SYCAN MARSH
HOT SPRINGS
HART MTN
NAT'L ANTELOPE REFUGE
PAISLEY
82
COLLIER STATE PARK
RD 30
RD 27
RIDGE
ROAD 33
ABERT LK
ABERT RIM
88
TRAIN MOUNTAIN
62
183
182
GEARHART MTN
187
186
185
184
ROAD
31
188
190
CHILOQUIN
TRAIL
83
VALLEY JUNCTION
PLUSH
86
87
UPPER KLAMATH LK
WOODS
83
28
3660
RD 34
DRAKE PK
WARNER LKS
HART MTN HOT SPRINGS
BEATTY
140
BLY
HUNTER'S HOT SPRINGS
191
189
192
OC&E
84
140
140
195
KLAMATH FALLS
LAKEVIEW
193
ADEL
CRANE MTN
194
97
39
OREGON
GOOSE LAKE
WINNEMUCCA
TULE LAKE
CALIFORNIA
NEVADA
TULE LAKE
85
139
LAVA BEDS NAT'L MON
N
W
E
S
395
TO ALTURAS
TO ALTURAS
TO WEED
0 10 20 30 MI
0 10 20 30 40 KM

The Homestead Village Museum in Fort Rock.

KLAMATH FALLS

In the rain shadow of the Cascade Range, Oregon's high desert country is strewn with curiosities—lava caves, fault-block mountains, hot springs, and oasis lakes.

Fort Rock

This landmark resembles a castle in a sea of sagebrush. Visit the picnic area and loop trail at the rock (Hike #78). Next, stop in the nearby hamlet of Fort Rock to see the **Homestead Village Museum** (open Thursday-Sunday 10am-5pm in summer), a collection of buildings salvaged from early 1900s dry-land farms. Museum admission $5 for adult and $3 for kids age 6-17. Then tour Fort Rock's valley to find an enormous crack in the ground and other geologic oddities (Hike #79).

Summer Lake

The marshes of the **Summer Lake Wildlife Area** attract pelicans, Canada, andand bald eagles. To see the birds, walk along a dike (Hike #81), or drive an 8.5-mile gravel road tour (open February through September), following "Wildlife Viewing Loop" signs from Highway 31. The Summer Lake Store sells required parking permits for $10 a day or $30 a year.

Drive Highway 31 south 22 miles to **Summer Lake Hot Springs** (near milepost 92), a funky resort with hot spring pools available to those who rent a cabin ($130-325) or a campsite ($20-60/person). Call 541-943-3931 or *summerlakehotsprings.com.*

Downtown Klamath Falls

Linkville updated its name to Klamath Falls in 1893, but the city's downtown preserves an old-time charm. Start at the **Klamath County Museum** at 1451 Main Street. Originally built as an armory, this 1935 art deco building features displays of Klamath tribal history and Klamath Lake wildlife. It's open Tue-Sat 9-5 for a $5 admission. Then head west on Main Street past the 1927 Balsiger Ford Building (with Egyptian revival palm motifs), and the **Baldwin Hotel Museum** at 31 Main Street, a 1906 brick building with displays of Klamath history, open Wed-Sat 10-4 from Memorial Day to Labor Day for $10. After a mile, turn back on the far side of the Link River at the **Favell Museum,** a private collection of Western theme art and Indian artifacts, including 60,000 arrowheads, open Tue-Sat 10-5 (closed January) for a $10 admission ($5 for children age 6-16). See also Hike #84.

Collier State Park and Logging Museum

A 2020 wildfire damaged this park's outdoor museum of logging equipment and its "pioneer village" of relocated log cabins. When the park reopens, it will once again offer two streamside picnic areas and a 64-site campground. Drive Highway 97 north of Klamath Falls 30 miles (or north of Chiloquin 5 miles).

Train Mountain Railroad Museum

This free museum *(tmrr.org)* features 37 cabooses. Next door, the **Klamath & Western Railroad** *(knwrr.org)* has 36 miles of miniature track and free train rides on summer Saturdays. From Highway 97 just south of Chiloquin, turn west 0.8 mile.

Hart Mountain

Pronghorn antelope, bighorn sheep, and mule deer roam the 430-square-mile **Hart Mountain National Antelope Refuge** (see Hikes #86-88). The free Hot Springs Campground is a treasure, with streamside sites near a free, natural hot springs pool. To the west, below a 2000-foot fault scarp cliff, the marsh-rimmed alkali Warner Lakes offer canoe routes through bird habitat.

Fort Klamath Museum

South of Crater Lake on Highway 62, this free, historic Army fort includes the graves of four Modoc tribal leaders. Open 10-6 Thurs-Mon, June to late September.

Hike 78 Fort Rock

An easy stroll explores the inside of this fortress-shaped outcrop in the arid bed of a vanished Ice Age lake.

Easy (around the inside)
1.7-mile loop
250 feet elevation gain
Open all year
Use: hikers, horses, bicycles

Moderate (around the outside)
1.9-mile loop
200 feet elevation gain

Fort Rock.

If you're feeling adventurous, a rougher route loops around the outside of the desert ring's rock cliff.

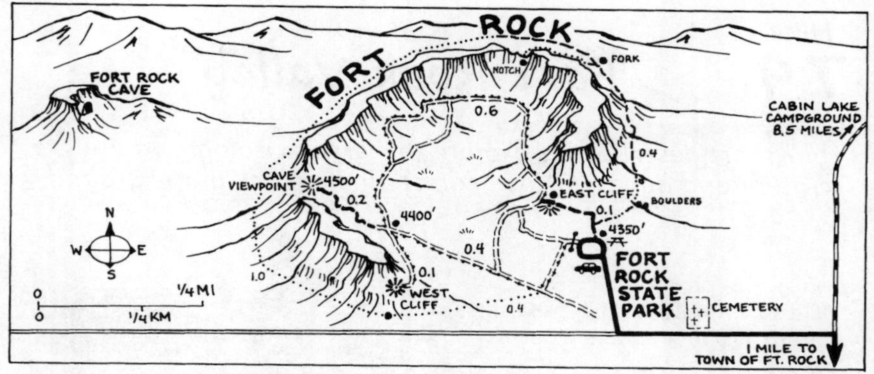

Near here, in a cave overlooking what is now the sagebrush country of arid Fort Rock Valley, archeologists in 1938 unearthed a 9000-year-old cache of more than 70 sandals woven from sagebrush bark. Originally, Fort Rock had the gently sloping sides of a *maar*—a volcanic explosion crater. When Ice Age rainstorms filled the valley with a vast, 250-foot-deep lake 13,000 years ago, Fort Rock became an island, battered by storm waves from the south winds. The surf wore the outer slopes back to steep cliffs and then breached the crater's south wall.

Amidst Fort Rock's sagebrush you'll find brilliant red paintbrush in June, yellow clumps of sunflower-like Oregon sunshine in summer, and yellow-tipped rabbit brush in fall. Cliff swallows swoop from mud nests high on the guano-stained rock walls, watched by prairie falcons. Avoid the heat of July and August. Winter months are windy and very cold.

Getting There— From Bend, drive 29 miles south on Highway 97. Beyond LaPine, turn left at a "Silver Lake" pointer for 29.2 miles on Highway 31, and then turn left at a "Fort Rock" sign for 6.5 miles. Turn left again just beyond the Fort Rock store, following signs 1.7 paved miles to Fort Rock State Natural Area.

For the easy tour around the inside of Fort Rock, take a paved path from the far end of the picnic area's parking lot for 100 feet and continue uphill on a rougher trail 0.1 mile to a viewpoint beside Fort Rock's east cliff. Notice the 10-foot-tall notch in the cliffs, carved by the vanished lake's surf. Then keep right at all junctions, following a broad trail around the inside of Fort Rock 0.6 mile to a 4-way junction. Take two viewpoint detours from here. First climb to the right on a faint path 0.2 mile to a cliff-edge notch overlooking the historic sandal cave (a dark spot on a knoll a mile away). Then return to the 4-way junction and turn right 0.1 mile to Fort Rock's west cliff. Finally return to the 4-way junction and turn right for 0.4 mile to your car.

If you've already seen the inside of Fort Rock and you're ready for a wilder exploration, try bushwhacking around the outside of the rock instead. Long pants are essential. From the parking lot, walk 100 feet up the paved path to a plaque commemorating Reub Long and turn right for 50 feet to a turnstile in a wire fence. A faint, braided path climbs past several boulders, becomes a real trail for 0.3 mile, and then forks. To the left is a scramble route that deadends at a viewpoint notch high on Fort Rock's rim. So keep to the right. This route squeezes past a wire fence and scrambles across a slope of rocks. Then the trail mostly vanishes, but it's easy to walk around the spectacular cliffs of Fort Rock's outer wall. It's a mile to the west cliff viewpoint, and another 0.4 mile across a sagebrush flat to your car.

Hike 79 Fort Rock Valley

Four short desert walks explore this area's geologic oddities: a crater, sand dunes, a "lost" forest, and a crack in the ground.

The Lost Forest from Sand Rock.

Easy (4 short hikes)
0.4 to 1.4 miles each, round-trip
50 to 170 feet elevation gain
Open all year

Because you'll need to drive from site to site, you might not have time to visit all four attractions in one day. Start at Hole in the Ground, a half-mile-wide pit that looks like a meteorite crater, but is in fact a volcanic *maar*. As at Fort Rock itself, a bubble of magma rose to the surface here and exploded.

Getting There— From Bend, drive Highway 97 south 29 miles and turn left at a "Silver Lake" pointer onto Highway 31 for 22 miles. At milepost 22, follow a "Hole in the Ground" pointer left onto gravel Breakup Road 3125 for 3 miles. Then fork right onto washboard gravel Road 3130 for 1.2 miles to a powerline, and turn left on bumpy Road 200 for 0.2 mile to the crater rim *(GPS location 43.4128, -121.2053).*

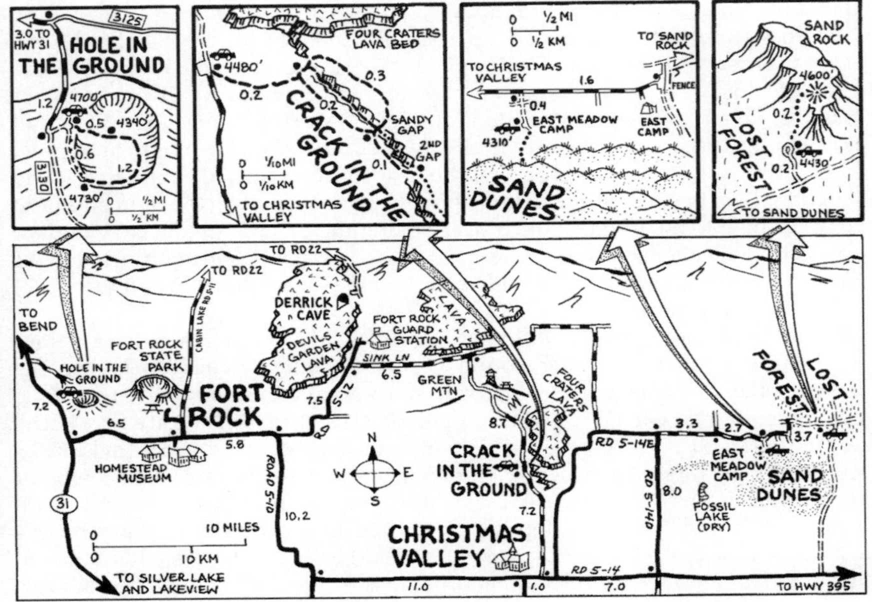

Park here and hike straight ahead on a steep, dusty trail 0.5 mile down to a small central playa. Continue straight on an ancient roadbed for 1.2 miles, spiraling up to the right through ponderosa pine woods. Then continue 0.6 mile to the right around the rim on a dirt road back to your car.

The next attraction, Crack in the Ground, appeared a few thousand years ago when four cinder cones erupted, emptying an underground magma chamber. As the ground settled, a crack formed along the edge of a valley. To get there from Hole in the Ground, drive back to Highway 31, follow it south 7.2 miles, and turn left 6.8 miles to the town of Fort Rock. Continue straight, following signs for 27 zigzagging miles to Christmas Valley. At the far edge of this sprawling desert town, turn left (north) off the main paved road at a "Crack in the Ground" pointer. Follow a gravel road 7.2 miles to a signed parking area.

Crack in the Ground.

A wide trail leads 0.2 mile to the 70-foot-deep lava slot. The rock chasm is so narrow that boulders hang wedged overhead. Snow sometimes lingers in the shade until May. Walk 0.2 mile along the bottom of this slot to a sandy gap. The next 0.1 mile of the crack is much tougher to follow, requiring the use of hands three times to scramble over boulders and reach a second gap. Then return along the rim—or, explorers can follow the crack's rim another mile south before turning back.

The third attraction, the Sand Dunes, is evidence that a 1500-square-mile lake filled the Fort Rock Valley during the Ice Age. Desert winds corralled the old beaches into 60-foot dunes. To drive there, return to Christmas Valley and turn left (east) for 7 paved miles to a 4-way junction. Turn left on paved Road 5-14D for another 8 miles to a T-shaped junction and turn right on gravel Road 5-14E for 3.3 miles to a junction with an information kiosk. Go straight on the main road another 2.7 miles. Beyond a "Helipad" sign 0.9 mile, turn right on a dirt track with the small signposts, "East Meadow Camp" and "Open Road." Park here, or if you have 4-wheel drive, drive this sandy road 0.4 mile to a message board at a grassy flat where primitive camping is possible *(GPS location 43.3492 -120.4014)*. Hike ahead on the undrivably sandy road 0.1 mile to the 20-foot face of a sand dune where the sagebrush plain ends. All-terrain vehicles are allowed, but are rare here. Wander as far as you like in the Sahara ahead, always remembering how to return to your car.

Next, to visit the Lost Forest, return to the gravel road and drive 1.6 miles east to a T-shaped junction at a rail fence in a big primitive RV camping area. Turn left for 0.2 mile to another T-junction at a rail fence. Turn right on much rougher dirt Road 5161 for 2.1 miles and fork uphill to the left for 0.2 mile to a turnaround and a "No Camping" sign at the base of Sand Rock *(GPS location 43.3643 -120.3291)*. Park here and scramble up the trailless knoll 0.2 mile to a viewpoint of the forest.

The five-square-mile Lost Forest survives on a mere nine inches of annual rainfall, half of what ponderosa pines usually require. Here the pines' taproots have found an underground water source. The buried hardpan of Fort Rock's ancient lakebed collects rainfall that might otherwise sink into the subsoil.

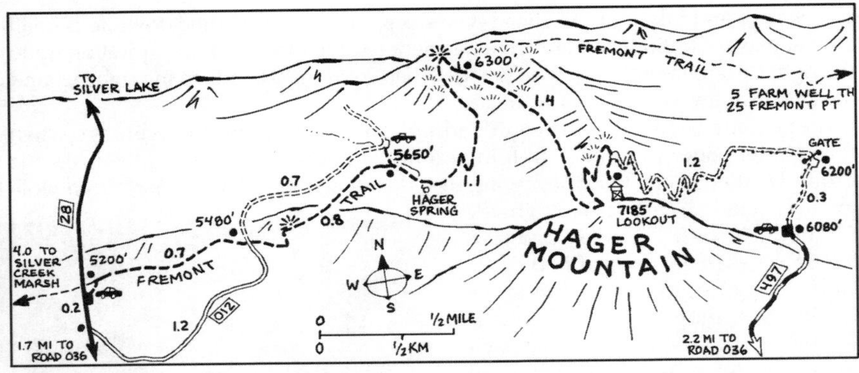

Hike 80 Hager Mountain

Like its more famous cousin Black Butte, Hager Mountain is a charming little volcano with a summit trail that climbs through wildflowers to a panoramic fire lookout.

Easy (from Road 497)
3 miles round trip
1105 feet elevation gain
Open June to early November
Use: hikers, horses, bicycles

Moderate (from Road 012)
5 miles round trip
1535 feet elevation gain

Difficult (from Road 28)
8 miles round trip
1990 feet elevation gain

Hager Mountain's lookout.

Because Black Butte is near Bend, however, several hundred people hike there each day, while only a few make their way to Hager Mountain's scenic summit.

Getting There— From Bend, drive Highway 97 south 29 miles and turn left on Highway 31 for 47 miles to Silver Lake. Near milepost 47 (just after the Silver Lake Ranger Station), turn right on paved Road 28 for 8.9 miles to the Hager Mountain Trailhead, a parking pullout on the left. Although this is the official trailhead, there are two other possible trailheads—both of them involving easier hikes. If you park here you'll have to climb 4 miles to the summit.

If you're short on time, you might opt for the shortest possible route to the top: Hager Mountain's lookout service road. To find it, drive past the official trailhead on Road 28 another 1.8 miles, turn left on gravel Road 036 for 1.8 miles, and turn left on Road 497 for 2.2 miles to a parking area where the road steepens and becomes too rough for cars. Park here and walk the road another 0.3 mile up to a smaller parking area at a locked gate. Then continue on the service road 1.2 miles to the lookout staff's parking area, just below the summit buildings—an outhouse, a propane shed, a woodshed, and the 14x14-foot lookout, staffed each year from June until early October. In the off-season from November 15 to May 15 it's unlocked, and can be rented at *recreation.gov*. Inside you'll find 3 bunks with mattresses, a wood heat stove, a propane light, a propane cook stove, a sink, and a box full of interesting old guest log books.

The prettiest route to the top begins at a less obvious trailhead. From the official trailhead on Road 28, drive another 0.2 mile south, turn left on faint dirt Road 012, and keep right for 1.9 miles on an increasingly rough, brushy road to a small parking area with a "Trail" sign on the right *(GPS location 43.0078, -121.0589)*. After hiking the trail 200 feet, turn left on the Fremont Trail past fenced Hager Spring. The path then switchbacks up past a 1990s clearcut, and traverses a meadowed slope of wildflowers. Views here extend from Mt. Shasta (above Thompson Reservoir) to Mt. Thielsen and even Mt. Jefferson. Then keep straight at a trail junction for 1.4 miles to the summit lookout.

Hike 81 Summer Lake

When explorer John C. Fremont struck south from The Dalles to California in 1843, he crested a snowy ridge on December 16, saw this sunny alkali lake 2700 feet below, and named the features Summer Lake and Winter Ridge.

Easy
4.6 miles round trip
No elevation gain
Open all year
Use: hikers, horses, bicycles

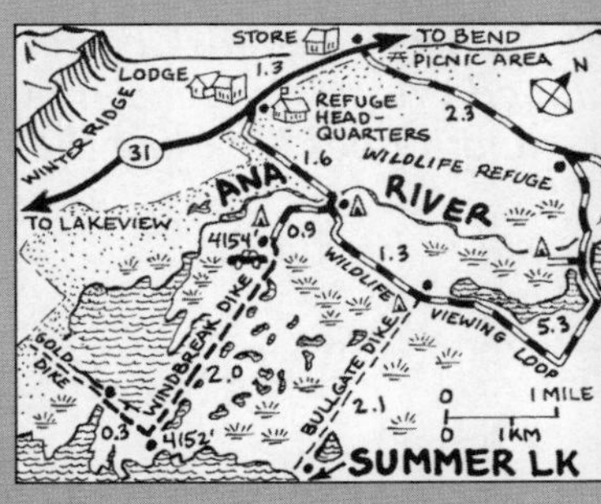

Since 1944 the Oregon Department of Fish and Wildlife has bought 19,000 acres of marshland as a wildlife preserve where the Ana River meanders into the landlocked lake. Great flocks of birds arrive here in March and April, en route to the arctic from Central America. White pelicans, Canada geese, and ducks linger through summer. Herons, egrets, and terns are common. Bald eagles, ducks, and swans remain in the winter.

Getting There— From Bend, take Highway 97 south 29 miles and turn left at a "Silver Lake" pointer on Highway 31 for 70 miles. Near milepost 70, opposite the Lodge at Summer Lake, turn left through the wildlife area headquarters

Winter Ridge from Summer Lake.

compound, following "Wildlife Viewing Loop" pointers onto a gravel road. At a T-shaped junction after 1.6 miles, turn right for 0.9 mile to the Windbreak Campground, which consists of a gravel parking lot with outhouses and garbage cans. Parking permits are required here, and cost $10 a day or $30 a year at the Summer Lake Store.

From the parking lot, hike onward along a dike-top road that's cabled closed to motor vehicles most of the year (March 15 to August 15 and early October to late January). On either hand are large patches of open water surrounded by reeds and cattails. Redwing blackbirds, mallards, avocets, black-necked stilts, and long-billed curlews are everywhere. Ignore short side dikes that deadend to left and right.

After 2 miles the dike road turns right alongside a wave-lapped lake rimmed with rounded cobbles. Continue 0.3 mile to three large culverts that release the Ana River to Summer Lake. This makes a good turnaround point. White pelicans start up reluctantly with a few flaps. To the south, alkali duststorms dim the horizon across the lake. Ahead, the dike road ends at a private ranch.

Hike 82 Winter Ridge

The long, fault-block mountain that Captain John Fremont dubbed Winter Ridge is known by the locals as Winter Rim—and it does look like the rim of gigantic broken bowl.

Easy (to Currier Spring)
5.4 miles round trip
320 feet elevation gain
Open late May to mid-November
Use: hikers, horses, bicycles

Moderate (to pine viewpoint)
7.8 miles round trip
420 feet elevation gain

Ponderosa pine on Winter Ridge.

Tracing this rim of this 3000-foot-tall scarp is the Fremont Trail, a 147-mile route that traverses the entire Fremont National Forest. Much of the Fremont Trail is best toured on horseback, but the scenic section along the rim north of Government Harvey Pass makes a good day hike—if you can handle faint tread and a few fallen trees.

Wildflowers bloom amidst the sagebrush and ponderosa pines here throughout

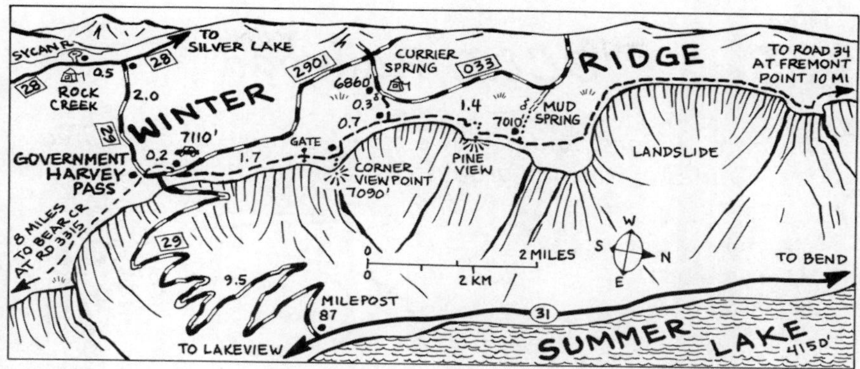

June. Of course, June is also when mosquitoes swarm across the Fremont National Forest. Fortunately, a reliable ridgecrest breeze helps keep the bugs at bay. Expect to meet grazing cattle along the route in August and September.

Getting There— Drive Highway 97 south of Bend 29 miles and turn left at a "Silver Lake" pointer on Highway 31 for 87 miles. At milepost 87 (northwest of Paisley 12 miles), turn right on gravel Road 29 at a sign for Government Harvey Pass and drive 9.5 miles up to a T-shaped junction at the pass. Turn right on Road 2901, driving slowly for just 0.1 mile until you spot a tiny trail marker on a pine tree to the right. Park on the shoulder here *(GPS location 42.7031, -120.7984)* and hike up to the right.

Summer Lake from Winter Ridge.

The ponderosa pines along the trail are two feet in diameter, but grow only 60 feet tall before they're trimmed by winds. Fires have left patches of snags. Four-foot stumps recall older trees, skidded out on winter snow in the 1920s. Swallowtail butterflies abound. Flowers include red paintbrush, purple penstemon, blue lupine, white yarrow, and arrowleaf balsamroot (a wild yellow sunflower).

After 1.5 mile you'll pass a gate. Just 0.1 mile later, when the trail turns downhill to the left at a sharp corner, you might bushwhack up to the right 200 feet to a viewpoint on a rimrock promontory. Far below, dust devils swirl along the alkali shore of Summer Lake.

Then continue on the main trail 0.7 mile to a big signpost marking a side path to Currier Spring. It's worth detouring downhill 0.3 mile to see the spring. The trail cuts through a lovely aspen grove with hellebore (corn lily) and purple larkspur on its way to Road 033. Across the road is a horse camp, while the spring is in a fenced area to the left. Mosquitoes can be fierce here, so you might turn back to the main trail on the breezy rim before settling down for lunch.

If you're not yet ready to return to your car, continue north along the rim another 1.2 miles to a clifftop viewpoint beside a pine tree. Beyond this point the trail traverses away from the rim and connects with an old road that leads down to Mud Spring.

Hike 83 OC&E Railroad

The state's longest and narrowest park consists of a hundred miles of railroad grades east of Klamath Falls.

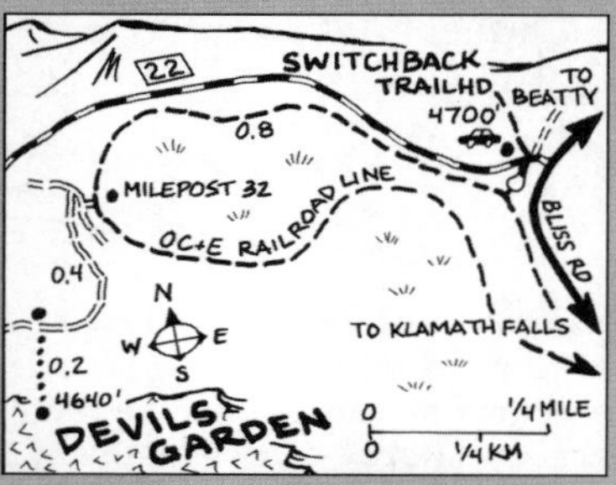

Easy (Switchback Trailhead tour)
2.8 miles round trip
80 feet elevation gain
Open all year
Use: hikers, horses, bicycles

Easy (to Brown Cemetery)
4.8-mile loop
130 feet elevation gain

Open to hikers, bicyclists, and equestrians, the OC&E Woods Line State Trail follows an abandoned logging railroad from Klamath Falls over a mountain to the Sprague River. The railroad's story begins in 1917, when Klamath Falls entrepreneurs dreamed of building east to connect with railroad lines in Lakeview and Burns. Although the tracks stopped in Bly in 1929, the steam locomotives of the Oregon, California, & Eastern Railroad kept busy by hauling away Klamath County's forests. Up to a million board feet of ponderosa pine rode the steel rails to Klamath Falls each day. When the big trees were gone the line fell into disuse. In 1992 the route became a linear park as part of the "Rails to Trails" movement.

Only the first 7 miles of the old railbed have been paved, on the outskirts of Klamath Falls. The most interesting sections for day trips are unpaved—at a mountain switchback where trains backed over a pass, and at Beatty where the rail line forks beside the Sprague River. If you have time, you can do both in one day.

Getting There — Drive Highway 140 east of Klamath Falls toward Lakeview 17 miles. At the Yonna Valley Store, turn left on Bliss Road for 12 miles to a forested pass, turn left on Road 22, and immediately pull into the Switchback Trailhead parking area on the left *(GPS location 42.4148, -121.5498)*. Trains crossing this pass used to loop around a switchback, stop on a deadend spur, and then back over

Sprague River trestle.

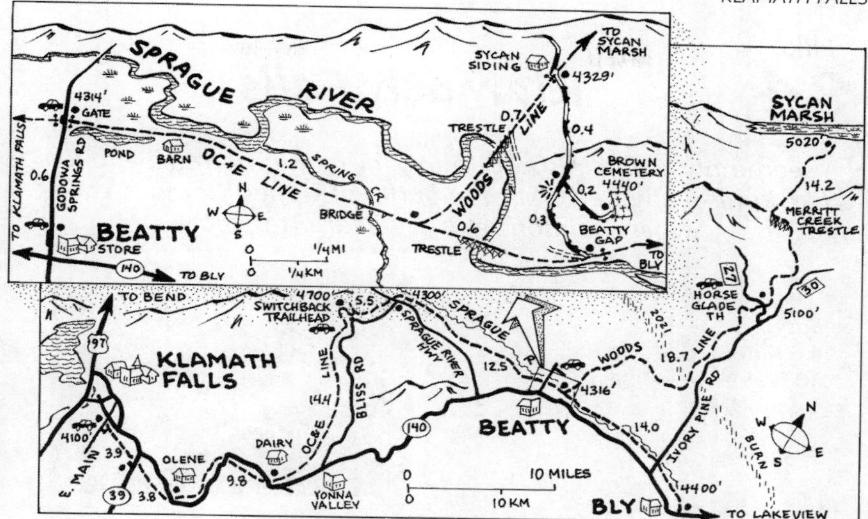

the summit. Just beyond the switchback is the Devils Garden, a mile-wide patch of weird lava formations filling the caldera of an ancient volcano.

Hike to the right down the railroad grade 0.8 mile to the switchback. There is no trail to the Devils Garden, but if you're feeling adventurous you can bushwhack there through the sagebrush and ponderosa pines. Near a milepost labeled "32" at the far end of the switchback loop, turn right on a faint dirt road for 300 feet. Then turn left on another dirt road for 0.4 mile, and finally strike off cross-country to the left (due south) across a small gully for 0.2 mile to the Devils Garden *(GPS location 42.411, -121.564)*. Ash from Crater Lake's eruption has left this lava field riddled with sandy openings that make for easy walking, but it's also easy to get confused. Note your route so you can find your way back!

For the hike near Beatty, drive Bliss Road north 4 miles from the Switchback Trailhead, turn right on the Sprague River Highway 10 miles, and turn left on Highway 140 for 5 miles to Beatty (pronounced BAY-tee). In the middle of Beatty turn north on paved Godowa Springs Road for 0.6 mile. When the road dips to cross a slough, look for a green metal gate on the right with signs banning motor vehicles and hunting. This is the railroad trail, but there's only enough space for one car to park here without blocking the gate. If your vehicle won't fit, drive back 0.6 mile to a shoulder pullout just before Highway 140 and walk back to the trail. Wear long pants because of tall weeds along the trail.

The trail sets off alongside a pond with cattails, redwing blackbirds, and snowy egrets. After 0.3 mile the glassy, 80-foot-wide Sprague River meanders up beside the path. After crossing Spring Creek on a bridge, the line forks. Keep straight for 0.6 mile, crossing the river on a low, 250-foot-long trestle.

Two roads join from the left at a river narrows called Beatty Gap. Turn left on the larger, uphill road for 0.3 mile. Then detour to the right 0.2 mile on a spur road to Brown Cemetery, a panoramic final resting place for Modoc families.

After exploring the Indian cemetery, return to the main road for another 0.4 mile to Sycan Siding, an abandoned railyard. At a ranch house by the siding, turn left through a green metal gate onto a red cinder road that becomes the railroad trail and crosses another river trestle to complete the loop.

Hike 84 Klamath Falls

A seemingly magic resource allowed the Klamath tribe to live like kings—a waterfall at the outlet of Upper Klamath Lake, where salmon returned year after year.

Easy
4.8 miles round trip
60 feet elevation gain
Open all year

A dam drowned the falls.

The tribe called the falls *Tiwishkeni,* or the "rush-of-falling-waters-place." Its spirit has not been entirely lost amidst the city of Klamath Falls. Along the Link River Trail from Upper Klamath Lake you can still expect to see pelicans and ruddy ducks. Although the path passes a freeway, a walk here still seems sheltered by wildness and magic.

Getting There— Drive Highway 97 a mile north of downtown Klamath Falls, take the Lakeshore Drive exit, and follow signs toward Lakeshore Drive (which starts out as Nevada Avenue) for 0.8 mile. Immediately after crossing the Link River on a bridge, turn left into a paved parking lot for the Link River Nature Trail.

The wide gravel trail starts at a pedestrian turnstile with a "Pets On Leash Only" sign. The Link River here has been dammed, creating a lake popular with birdlife. Giant white pelicans glide past, lanky black cormorants line up on the dam's boom logs, seagulls squawk, and blackbirds warble. Hikers who venture off trail may find stinging nettles among the willows and juniper of the shore, so stay on the main path. The trail passes the dam, bridges a 30-foot canal, and then follows the green canal along the edge of a remarkably wild river canyon. If you'd like to get down to the actual shore of the Link River, wait for the 1.4-mile mark and climb

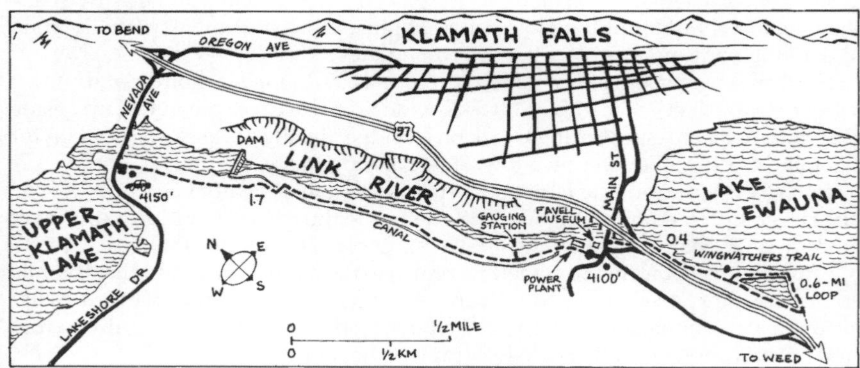

The Link River.

down a steel staircase to a small gauging station in jungly riverbank woods. This makes a good turnaround point for hikers with children.

If you continue on the main trail you'll soon pass a power station and a parking turnaround. Turn left on Main Street a few feet to the Favell Museum, a private collection of Western theme art and Indian artifacts (see page 208). In front of the museum, carefully cross busy Main Street to a gravel parking lot with a small brick building beside the Link River. Then continue on the gravel Klamath Wingwatchers Nature Trail to Lake Ewauna, ducking underneath three freeway bridges. After 0.4 mile turn left on a dike beside a cattail slough. Then keep right along the dike to circle the slough and start heading back to your car.

Hike 85 Modoc Lava Beds

Riddled with lava caves, this volcanic landscape was the setting for one of the West's most famous Indian wars.

Easy (the top 3 short hikes)
1.3 miles total
100 feet elevation gain
Open all year

Moderate (3 more short hikes)
6.4 miles total
770 feet elevation gain

Catacombs Cave.

Here in Northern California, a defiant band of 52 Modoc men held off a thousand US Army troops for five months in 1872-73. Today hiking trails tour the Lava Beds National Monument's geologic and historic sites. If you just have one day, explore the visitor center's Mushpot Cave, hike the 0.5-mile loop to Captain Jack's Stronghold, and visit the rock art at Petroglyph Point. Otherwise spend

Schonchin Butte from the Cave Loop.

the night at the campground and hike three more trails. Pets are banned on trails.

Getting There— From Klamath Falls, follow signs for Reno. You'll end up on Highway 39, which turns into Highway 139 at the California border. Turn right in Tulelake, south of the border 3.6 miles. Following "Lava Beds" signs, drive 0.4 mile through town, turn right on "E" Street for 4.6 miles, turn left on Hill Road for 9.2 miles, turn right at a T-shaped junction to an entrance fee booth (expect to pay about $25 per car), and then continue 9.7 miles to the Lava Beds visitor center.

Park here to tour the center's indoor displays. Then take a paved path from the end of the parking lot 100 feet to Mushpot Cave, a railed pit with a steel staircase. This is the only lava tube in the national monument that is lighted inside. The 700-foot-long cave features *lavacicles* (where superheated gas remelted the rock walls), *cauliflower lava* (a chunky lava flow that puddled up on the floor), and a *mushpot*, where liquid rock bubbled up from a lower cave. Like all lava tubes, Mushpot Cave formed when a liquid basalt lava flow formed a crust but the hotter lava underneath kept on flowing, draining tube-shaped caves.

If Mushpot Cave catches your fancy, you can explore two dozen other lava tubes nearby. Simply drive the 1.3-mile paved loop road from the visitor center and stop at one of the many parking pullouts. Especially for these less developed caverns you'll need to remember some safety rules. Bring battery-powered flashlights (available for free at the visitor center). Gas lanterns and fires are banned. Never explore alone. Wear warm coats because the caves are cold even on hot days. Wear a helmet because many caves have low ceilings. Remember that several hours may be needed to explore a single cave, and that the gate on the loop road closes at 5pm (6pm in summer). Also note that Labyrinth Cave, Hercules Leg - Juniper Cave, and Sentinel Cave have more than one entrance.

Even if you're just here on a day trip, be sure to save time for one or two short walks above ground. Drive back toward Klamath Falls 9.8 miles to the Hill Road junction, but then keep right another 3.2 miles to a large pullout for Captain Jack's Stronghold. An interpretive trail here winds through a lava moonscape where pressure ridges and caves served as a natural fortress for Keintpoos ("Captain Jack") and his Modoc warriors. The Modocs had been forced to leave their homeland here in 1864 to join their enemies the Klamaths on an Oregon reservation.

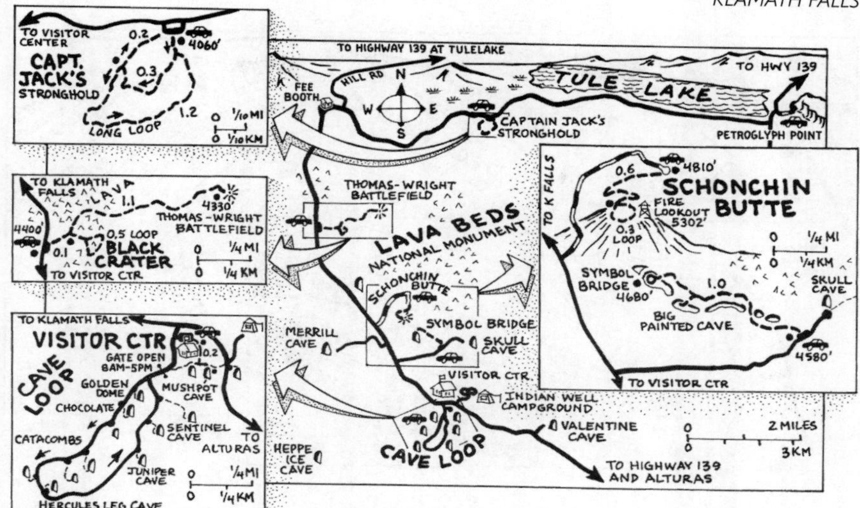

After more than 100 of the Modocs returned, the US Army arrived in November, 1872 to take them to the reservation by force. Keintpoos stymied the troops and killed General Canby in a parley — the first US general to die in an Indian war. After Keintpoos' surrender on June 1, 1873, he and three other Modoc leaders were hanged. At the 0.3-mile mark you'll reach a T-shaped trail junction. Turn right to complete a short loop back to your car, or turn left for a longer loop tour.

After visiting Captain Jack's Stronghold, drive back toward Klamath Falls a different way. Head east on the paved road 5.4 miles, turn left at a T-junction for 0.8 mile to a railroad crossing, and turn right on gravel 0.9 mile to Petroglyph Point's parking area. Stroll 0.3 mile along the railed cliff here to see thousands of petroglyphs, carved into the soft rock when Tule Lake was higher and this sacred site was an island. Then drive back to the railroad tracks and turn right on the paved road to return to Highway 139 and the route to Klamath Falls.

If you're staying overnight at the national monument, set up at the Indian Well Campground across the road from the visitor center. Then use your extra day to hike three other interesting trails. For the first, drive 1.6 miles north from the visitor center toward Klamath Falls. At a sign for Skull Cave, turn right for a mile to a pullout on the left for Symbol Bridge. This 1-mile path follows a partly collapsed lava tube to a natural arch with prehistoric petroglyphs.

For the next hike, return to the main road, drive another 0.7 mile north, and turn right toward Schonchin Butte for a mile. From here a trail climbs 0.6 mile up the cinder cone to its crater. A 0.3-mile loop around the rim visits a fire lookout tower (staffed in late summer) with a view from Mt. Shasta to Mt. McLoughlin.

For the final recommended hike, return to the main road and drive another 2.5 miles north to the Black Crater parking pullout. This path sets off across a sagebrush prairie with penstemon, larkspur, and other wildflowers in May and June. After 0.1 mile, fork to the right for a half-mile loop tour of Black Crater, a giant spatter cone with contorted, red-and-black lava outcroppings along its walls. Then return to the main trail and hike another 1.1 mile to trail's end at an overlook of the Thomas-Wright battlefield, where Captain Jack's warriors wiped out most of a 64-man Army patrol on April 26, 1873.

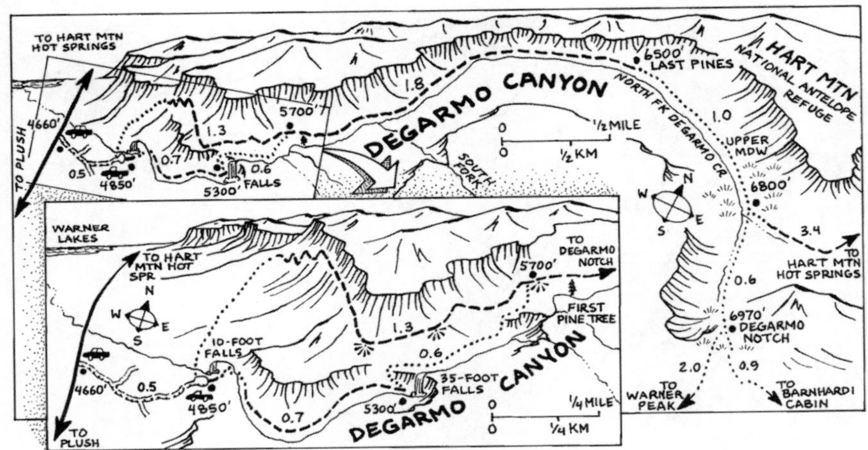

Hike

86 DeGarmo Canyon

Like a secret door in a 2000-foot-tall wall, DeGarmo Canyon's spectacular slot offers adventurers a route into the high desert country of the Hart Mountain National Antelope Refuge.

Easy (to 35-foot falls)
1.4 miles round trip
450 feet elevation gain
Open late April through November

Moderate (to first pine tree)
2.6-mile loop
850 feet elevation gain

Difficult (to DeGarmo Notch)
9.4 miles round trip
2120 feet elevation gain
Open June to mid-November

The 35-foot waterfall.

For a quick look at the canyon, follow a 0.7-mile trail to an oasis-like grotto at the base of a 35-foot waterfall. If you don't mind some steepish scrambling, you can return on a 2.6-mile loop trail with far-ranging views. If you want to explore the trailless upper end of the canyon, hike or backpack 5.7 miles to DeGarmo Notch.

Getting There— Drive Highway 395 north of Lakeview 5 miles and turn east on Highway 140 toward Winnemucca for 16 miles to a fork. Following a pointer for Plush, veer left onto paved Road 3-13 for almost 20 miles to Plush's store/cafe/tavern/gas station. Continue straight through town 0.8 mile and turn right on paved Road 3-12 toward the Hart Mountain Refuge for 8.6 miles to a "DeGarmo Canyon" pointer. Here a very rough dirt road leads up to the right past an old "No

Camping" sign. Unless you have a high clearance vehicle, park and walk! Follow the track 0.5 mile uphill, keeping right at the 0.2 mile mark and left at the 0.3-mile mark, to an upper parking area at road's end *(GPS location 42.4788, -119.7897).*

From this upper parking area the trail climbs immediately into the canyon's mouth, a red rock chasm with tall sagebrush and a tangle of quaking aspen. After just 300 feet the trail meets rushing DeGarmo Creek at a dangerous ford just above a 10-foot waterfall. Don't cross here. Instead follow rock ledges along the right-hand bank of the creek another 150 feet to an easier creek crossing. On the far side, scramble a few feet up to a clear trail. This path follows the creek upstream 0.6 mile to a cliff-lined grotto with a 35-foot waterfall. Listen here for the *zeet!* of water ouzels, dark, robin-sized birds that dive underwater in search of insects.

The trail ends at this waterfall, but adventurers can continue up the canyon by backtracking 100 feet to a steep scramble route that climbs around the end of the waterfall's cliffs. Then bushwhack half a mile upstream to another lava layer cliff that chokes the canyon. Detour around this one the same way, on a steep scramble route to the left. But then keep angling up the canyon's side 500 feet until you meet a well-built, relatively level trail at a viewpoint overlooking the canyon's first ponderosa pine tree. You may hear or even see a rattlesnake in this part of the canyon. If you do, stop a moment to let it retreat to safety.

The canyon's mouth overlooks Hart Lake.

The upper trail is an old cattle drive route from the days when the refuge allowed grazing. To return to your car on a loop, follow the trail left, traversing high above DeGarmo Canyon's rugged inner gorge. Dramatic views extend out the canyon mouth to Hart Lake. After 0.9 mile the trail suddenly dives down a sagebrush slope with a confusion of steep switchbacks. The path peters out at the slope's base *(GPS location 42.4834, -119.7882).* At this point, however, you can see your car at the canyon mouth, so it's easy enough to bushwhack through the sagebrush and scramble across the creek to the trailhead.

If you'd like to explore the upper canyon, turn right when you first meet the old cattle trail. This part of the path has a few faint spots, but is generally easy to follow for 1.8 miles, passing groves of quaking aspen and big ponderosa pines. The trail ends when you pass the last pines, but the treeless upper canyon makes for easy walking. A range fire in the late 1990s replaced most sagebrush with the blooms of orange paintbrush. A mile past the last pines the canyon forks at a grassy meadow of corn lilies (hellebore). If you veer left, you can follow a faint old road 3.4 miles to the Hart Mountain Hot Springs campground. If you keep right you'll hike past a quaking aspen grove to the canyon's end at DeGarmo Notch. Both routes are described in Hike #87. If you're backpacking, you'll need a self-issued backcountry permit, available free at all hours at the refuge's headquarters, 15 miles up the main road from the DeGarmo Canyon turnoff.

Hike 87 Hart Mountain Hot Springs

At this hot springs in the high desert you can soak in a free 102° F rock pool, watching bubbles rise from the rocks below while songbirds zoom overhead.

Moderate (to Barnhardi Cabin)
5.3-mile loop
750 feet elevation gain
Open late May to mid-November
Use: hikers, horses

Difficult (to DeGarmo Notch)
7.4-mile loop
1600 feet elevation gain
Open June to mid-November

Difficult (to Warner Peak)
11.1 miles round trip
2320 feet elevation gain

The campground's free pool.

Nearby, the Hart Mountain National Antelope Refuge provides free campsites, scattered along grassy streambanks amid groves of silver-leaved quaking aspen.

Most visitors here take a dip in the hot springs, camp, and then drive on. But to see the refuge's wildlife and mountain scenery up close, use the campground as a base for some exploration afoot. Although the only trails are animal paths, bushwhacking is easy through the high desert's sagebrush meadows. For a moderate hike, follow an old road to a sheepherder's cabin at Barnhardi Basin. For a longer loop, continue through a high pass to DeGarmo Canyon. For an even tougher day hike, bushwhack to the area's highest viewpoint, 8017-foot Warner Peak.

Getting There— From Lakeview, drive 4.7 miles north on Highway 395 and

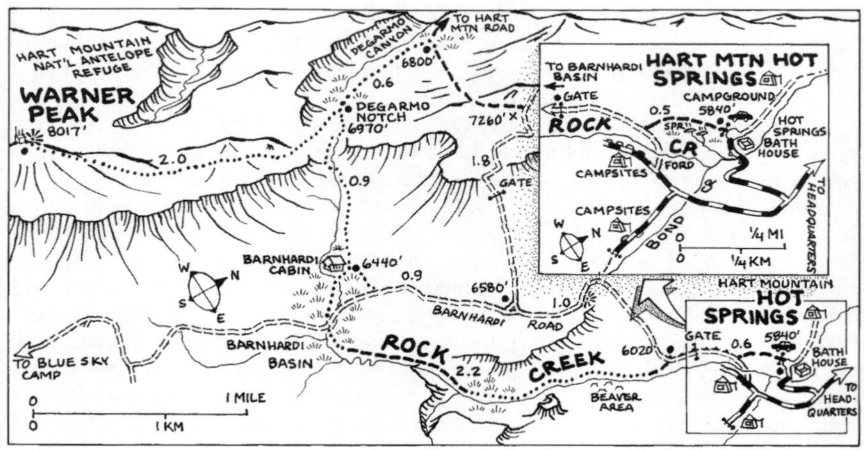

Warner Peak from Rock Creek.

turn east on Highway 140 toward Winnemucca for 15.8 miles to a fork. Following signs for the Hart Mountain Refuge, veer up to the left onto a two-lane paved road for 18.6 miles to Plush.

A rustic ranching hamlet, Plush has a combination store/cafe/tavern/gas station. Check your gas gauge here. Then continue straight through town 0.8 mile and turn right on Hart Mountain Road 3-12 for 24 miles (the last 10 miles on good gravel) to the refuge headquarters. A visitor room here, always open, has displays, brochures, restrooms, and the free, self-issuing backcountry permits required for overnighting anywhere except at designated campgrounds.

Beyond the refuge headquarters, keep right at road forks for 4.5 miles to a parking area at the hot springs bath house, where a rock-faced wall surrounds a deep, natural 8-by-10-foot rock pool. Rules of courtesy: No glass containers. No soap. No more than six people. Maximum stay 20 minutes if others are waiting.

For the hike, cross the parking area from the bath house, step over a pole barricade, and walk along a closed old road that curves left through a meadow past a shallower hot springs pool. Continue across the meadow to an outhouse and turn right on Barnhardi Road for 0.3 mile to a rusty green gate (locked to vehicles December 1 to August 1). Continue walking up the road a mile, keep left at a fork, and hike another 0.8 mile until the road enters the broad meadow bowl of Barnhardi Basin. Leave the road and bushwhack up to the right around the edge of the marshy meadow to reach the cabin, a dilapidated 10-by-16-foot plank shack in a grove of giant aspens *(GPS location 42.4797, -119.72)*.

It's simplest to return as you came, but adventurers can return on a loop by bushwhacking downstream along Rock Creek 2.2 miles to the campground. If you do, be sure you wear long pants to protect your legs from sagebrush.

If you'd like a longer hike, bushwhack upward and onward from Barnhardi Cabin. Skirt the boggy area directly behind the cabin and follow a little creek up through aspen groves 0.9 mile to DeGarmo Notch, a broad, grassy saddle *(GPS location 42.4849, -119.7319)*.

From DeGarmo Notch it's not difficult to return to your car on a loop. Continue straight 0.6 mile down the sagebrush meadows and aspen groves of DeGarmo Canyon. Where the canyon forks, turn right on a faint old roadbed up a side valley. After climbing 0.7 mile to a windy ridgecrest, turn right on a larger dirt road that descends 1.1 mile to the Barnhardi Road and the route back to your car.

A detour to Warner Peak's summit adds 4 trailless miles to your trip, but it's mostly easy walking along an open alpine ridge. From DeGarmo Notch, traverse uphill to the south, angling below an outcrop of cliffs, to a bare ridge shoulder above a grove of mountain mahogany trees. Then simply continue south along the ridge. Soon you'll see your goal: a small concrete building and radio towers on the summit *(GPS location 42.4596, -119.7412),* where views extend from Steens Mountain to California's South Warner Mountains.

Other Options— Those who arrange a car shuttle can connect Hikes #86 and #87 into a single 9.4-mile trek from Hart Mountain Hot Springs through DeGarmo Notch and down the length of DeGarmo Canyon.

Hike 88 Petroglyph Lake

Short, trailless walks lead to two mystic rock art sites in the Hart Mountain National Antelope Refuge.

Easy (Petroglyph Lake)
4.4 miles round trip
80 feet elevation gain
Open early May to mid-November

Easy (Flook Lake)
2.8 miles round trip
120 feet elevation gain

Antelope Spring petroglyphs.

The precise meaning of the circles, zigzags, and animalistic figures etched into Oregon's desert cliffs thousands of years ago has been lost, but petroglyphs may have been an attempt to communicate with the spirit world at sacred sites. Nearly 100 drawings decorate the basalt ledge ringing Petroglyph Lake, a rare water source where antelope come to drink. Flook Lake is a dry alkali playa, but an adjacent box canyon has petroglyphs near a hidden rock pool.

To be sure, these are not destinations for the disrespectful, nor for the ill prepared. Even the touch of a finger can damage the ancient art. And the sagebrush desert has no trails. Bring long pants, boots, and some routefinding skills.

Getting There— Start by driving to the refuge's headquarters and visitor center, described in Hike #87. From there, drive one mile west on the main gravel road toward Plush. At a "Petroglyph Lake" sign, park beside a gated dirt road on the right. Walk this track through the sagebrush for 1.7 miles to the lake. Then head cross-country, following the grassy shore of the lake to the left for half a mile. Turn around at the far end of the lake. On your return route, explore the base of the basalt cliff above the shore to find the scattered petroglyphs. Don't touch!

To find Flook Lake, drive back to the refuge headquarters and continue east 6.7 miles on the main gravel road toward Frenchglen. Just before the highway curves right, turn right at a small "Flook Lake" pointer onto a rough dirt road. Do not drive this road in wet weather because rain makes it dangerously muddy. After 1.2 miles, stop at the edge of Flook Lake's alkali flat to make sure the lakebed is completely dry. Then follow the road another 0.6 mile straight to the center of

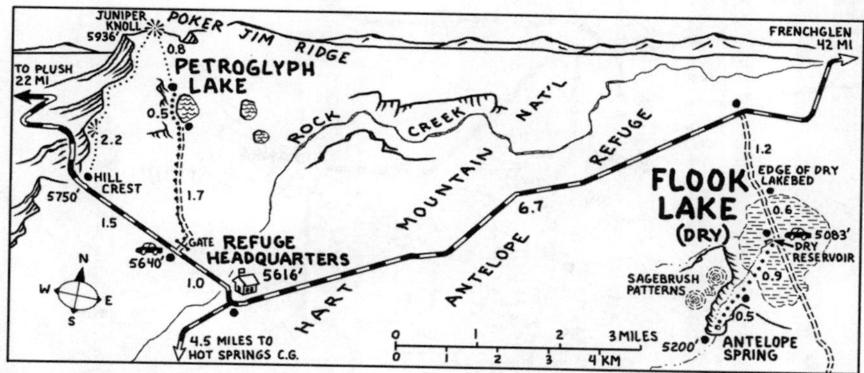

the playa and park beside the bulldozed ramparts of a dry reservoir *(GPS location 42.576, -119.5304)*. Do not drive off of the road, even if other vehicles have. The refuge's ban of off-road driving is particularly important here because the playa has soft spots that trap vehicles, and tires destroy the playa's struggling bunchgrass.

From the dry reservoir, hike southwest across the playa toward the rockiest canyon mouth in the low cliffs beyond the lakebed, following an outwash channel lined with bunchgrass. After 0.9 mile you'll reach the canyon entrance. Obsidian chips amidst the sagebrush show that this was a prime site to make arrowheads and hunt. Do not collect anything. It is a federal crime to remove an artifact.

Bushwhack half a mile up the canyon until it ends at Antelope Spring, encircled by 20-foot cliffs *(GPS location 42.5599, -119.5409)*. The spring is actually a small pool of brackish green water in a rock basin at the base of a dry waterfall. Most of the site's petroglyphs are on a wall 200 feet away.

Seen from the air (or Google Earth), the plateau north of Antelope Spring is covered with quarter-mile-wide circles and other gigantic shapes. The puzzling patterns appear to mimic the petroglyphs, but are evidently part of an old government range management project, removing sagebrush to encourage grass.

Other Options— The area's best views are atop Poker Jim Ridge's 1300-foot cliff. Adventurers can bushwhack there by heading west from Petroglyph Lake 0.8 mile, or by following the rim north from the crest of the refuge's main gravel road (see map).

Do not touch the rock art on the rimrock walls at Petroglyph Lake.

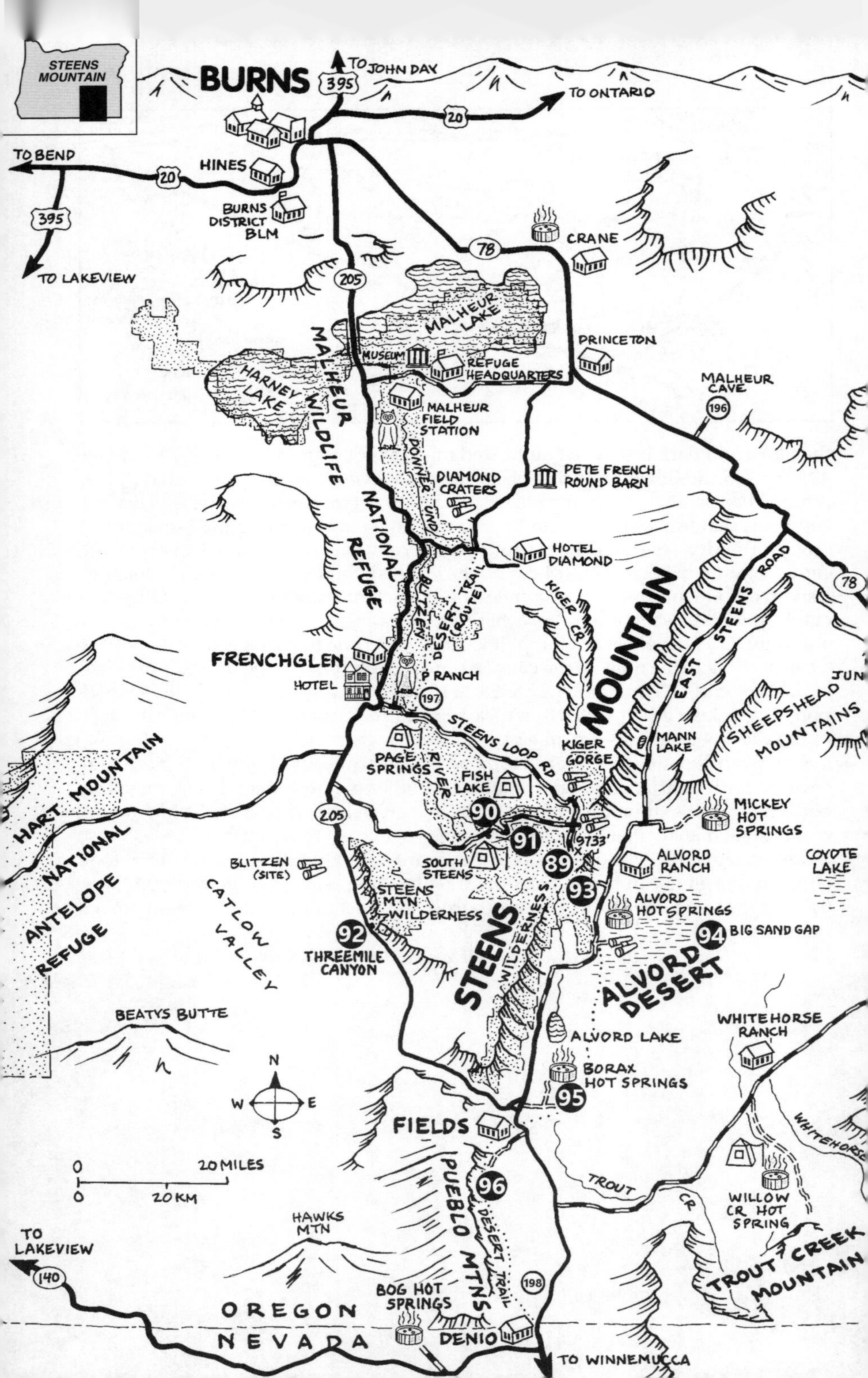
STEENS MOUNTAIN
BURNS
TO JOHN DAY
395
TO ONTARIO
20
TO BEND
HINES
BURNS DISTRICT BLM
TO LAKEVIEW
CRANE
78
205
MALHEUR LAKE
MUSEUM
REFUGE HEADQUARTERS
PRINCETON
HARNEY LAKE
MALHEUR WILDLIFE NATIONAL REFUGE
MALHEUR FIELD STATION
MALHEUR CAVE
196
DONNER UND BLITZEN
DIAMOND CRATERS
PETE FRENCH ROUND BARN
HOTEL DIAMOND
KIGER CR
DESERT TRAIL (ROUTE)
MOUNTAIN
EAST STEENS ROAD
FRENCHGLEN
HOTEL
P RANCH
197
STEENS LOOP RD
PAGE SPRINGS
RIVER
FISH LAKE
KIGER GORGE
MANN LAKE
SHEEPSHEAD MOUNTAINS
JUN
HART MOUNTAIN NATIONAL ANTELOPE REFUGE
90
91
89
93
9733'
MICKEY HOT SPRINGS
ALVORD RANCH
COYOTE LAKE
BLITZEN (SITE)
SOUTH STEENS
STEENS MTN WILDERNESS
CATLOW VALLEY
92
THREEMILE CANYON
STEENS
WILDERNESS
ALVORD HOTSPRINGS
94
BIG SAND GAP
ALVORD DESERT
ALVORD LAKE
WHITEHORSE RANCH
BEATYS BUTTE
N
W
E
S
BORAX HOT SPRINGS
95
FIELDS
WHITEHORSE
0
20 MILES
0
20 KM
PUEBLO MTNS
96
TROUT CR
WILLOW CR HOT SPRING
DESERT TRAIL
HAWKS MTN
TO LAKEVIEW
140
TROUT CREEK MOUNTAIN
198
BOG HOT SPRINGS
OREGON
NEVADA
DENIO
TO WINNEMUCCA

The Frenchglen Hotel.

BURNS

Landmark for all of southeast Oregon, 50-mile-long Steens Mountain looms a vertical mile above the Alvord Desert's stark alkali flats. Nights are crisp and starry in this quiet corner of Oregon. Days are pungent with the scent of sage. Burns, the area's commercial center, has a population of just 3000.

Steens Mountain

Congress protected much of this 9733-foot-tall fault-block mountain with the 170,202-acre **Steens Mountain Wilderness** in 2000. Most visitors begin in Frenchglen (see below) and drive the **Steens Mountain Loop Road,** a 56-mile gravel circuit that slices through the Wilderness almost to the mountain's summit. Because this is the highest road in Oregon, cresting at 9550 feet, snow gates close the upper part of the loop from November through June, depending on snow levels. Highlights along the loop, clockwise from Frenchglen, include the **Page Springs Campground** (open all year, $8 per site), the **Fish Lake Campground** (open July 1 to October 30, $8 per site, no motorboats allowed on lake), the **Jackman Park Campground** (open July 1 to October 30, $6 per site), the **Kiger Gorge and East Rim viewpoints** (see Hike #89), the narrow **Rooster Comb**, and the **South Steens Campground** (open late May through October, $6 per site, see Hikes #90 and #91). Expect to see wild horses, deer, and antelope.

Malheur Wildlife Refuge

Most of Steens Mountain's winter snow melts into creeks that flow westward down gigantic U-shaped gorges to the marshlands of the Malheur National Wildlife Refuge. Huge flocks of migrating birds stop here from March through May: sandhill cranes, snow geese, egrets, swans, grebes, herons, pelicans, songbirds, and many kinds of ducks. Bring binoculars or a spotting scope to watch birds from your car without disturbing them. From Burns, drive east 1.7 miles on Highway 78, turn right toward Frenchglen on Highway 205 for 23.2 miles, and turn left 6 miles to

the Malheur Refuge Headquarters. A worthwhile museum here (open dawn to dusk) has some 200 mounted specimens of birds. A nearby visitor center offers road tour maps, brochures, and tips on recent bird sightings.

Left: Irrigation gate on the Donner und Blitzen River.

Frenchglen

An hour south of Burns, this frontier hamlet consists of a few dozen buildings. The 1916 **Frenchglen Hotel** (open March 15 to November 1), restored by the Oregon State Parks, still has no public telephone or television. For meals, hotel guests pack family-style around two large tables. Typical dinner fare is herb-baked chicken with garlic roast potatoes and marionberry pie. Reservations are required (see page 25), but drop-ins are welcome for lunch and breakfast.

P Ranch Headquarters

The P Ranch and Frenchglen were named for Peter French, sent to Oregon in 1872 by ranching mogul James Glenn. French ruthlessly amassed ranchland, including much of the present Malheur Wildlife Refuge. In 1897 French was shot dead by a homesteader, but a local jury acquitted the murderer. To see the ranch headquarters, drive the Steens Mountain Loop Road east of Frenchglen 1.5 miles, turn left on a gravel road 0.2 mile, and turn left to a parking area beside the Donner und Blitzen River. First walk the left-hand road 0.1 mile to a 200-foot-long horse barn built with juniper trunks. A square winch outside hoisted slaughtered cattle. Then stroll along the glassy river to spot redwing blackbirds and ducks.

Diamond

Less well known than Frenchglen, the village of Diamond is dominated by the **Hotel Diamond,** a rambling, weathered wood building with a cafe and eight hotel rooms (see page 25). Drive Highway 205 south of Burns 44 miles (or north of Frenchglen 17 miles), and turn east for 13 paved miles to Diamond.

Nearby **Diamond Craters** is a 2500-year-old lava field strewn with volcanic craters, domes, and cracks. Drive west of Diamond 6 miles, turn right on paved Lava Beds Road toward Highway 78 for 3.2 miles, and turn left to the craters on a 4.7-mile cinder road suitable only for high-clearance vehicles. Next continue north toward Highway 78 on the paved road another 9 miles to a sign for **Peter French's Round Barn,** a 100-foot-diameter building with a circular stone corral inside. French built the unusual barn about 1880 to train horses.

Crystal Crane Hot Springs

Commercialized but practical, this resort 25 miles southeast of Burns on Highway 78 offers a hot pool for $6, private hot tubs for $10, tent sites for $25, and five simple cabins for $85-90. Call 541-493-2312 or check *cranehotsprings.com.*

Alvord Desert and hot springs

For a spectacular drive along the base of Steens Mountain's abrupt eastern cliff, follow East Steens Road to hot springs and desert viewpoints. Start at the rustic cafe/store/gas station that is **Fields,** where you'll want to stop for one of their famous milkshakes. Take the paved road 1.3 miles north toward Frenchglen and keep right onto East Steens Road. (This junction is also the turnoff for **Borax Hot Springs,** Hike #95). Drive north 10.8 miles on pavement and an additional 8.1 miles on excellent gravel to the turnoff for the **Alvord Desert** on the right *(GPS location 42.509, -118.5344)*. Look for this unmarked side road 1.7 miles after your first view of the Alvord Desert's 9-mile-long dry alkali lakebed. A rough dirt spur descends 0.3 mile to the alkali flat, which is open to hiking or driving except on the rare occasions when the playa actually fills with water. Annual precipitation here is just 6 inches.

From the Alvord Desert turnoff, continue north on the main road another 2.3 miles to a sign for **Alvord Hot Springs.** At the caretaker's office, pay $10 per person (kids under 10 are free) and walk a gravel path 300 feet to an ancient tin shed where natural springs are piped into two 8-by-8-foot concrete pools at about 102°F. Clothing is optional. Shadeless campsites nearby are $50, but include bathing.

North of Alvord Hot Springs 2.2 miles the road passes Pike Creek (Hike #93). To find **Mickey Hot Springs,** continue another 8.3 miles, passing the Alvord Ranch and two big highway curves. Near the end of the second big curve, at a small "Mickey Hot Spring" sign, turn sharply back to the right on a gravel road with no gate or cattle guard *(GPS location 42.6756, -118.4513)*. If you're driving here from the north, you'll find this turnoff 7 miles south of the Mann Lake Recreation Site, 0.1 mile beyond a "40 MPH" curve sign. Follow the washboard side road through several zigzags. Keep left at forks after 1.9 and 3.0 miles, staying on the larger road. Continue on a dirt road another 3.9 miles and park at a railed turnaround on the right.

Very dangerous for children or pets, the moonscape at Mickey Hot Springs features boiling pools, steam jets, mudpots, and the scalding, 30-foot-deep turquoise Morning Glory Pool. All pools are far too hot for humans, with the possible exception of a single bathtub-sized basin carved into the ground by frustrated bathers.

Steens Mountain's summit in April.

Hike 89 Steens Summit

The windswept cliffs at the summit of Steens Mountain seem perched on the edge of a broken planet.

Easy (to three viewpoints)
1 mile total
250 feet elevation gain
Open mid-July to late October

Moderate (to Wildhorse Lake)
2.4 miles round trip
1100 feet elevation **loss**

Moderate (Little Wildhorse Lake)
2.6 miles round trip
550 feet elevation **loss**

Little Wildhorse Lake.

From the summit, the Alvord Desert shimmers faintly more than a vertical mile below, a mirage in the void. At 9733 feet, this is the eighth tallest mountain in Oregon, and the easiest to climb. In fact, after strolling through an otherworldly landscape 0.4 mile to the top, you're likely to have enough energy left over to scramble down into the hanging valleys of wildflowers at Wildhorse Lake or Little Wildhorse Lake.

Getting There — From Burns, drive 1.7 miles east on Highway 78 toward Crane and turn right on paved Highway 205 for 61 miles to Frenchglen. Just beyond the Frenchglen Hotel, fork left onto the gravel Steens Mountain Loop Road for 2.9 miles to the Page Springs Campground entrance. Keep left, past a snow gate that's closed from about mid-November until Memorial Day.

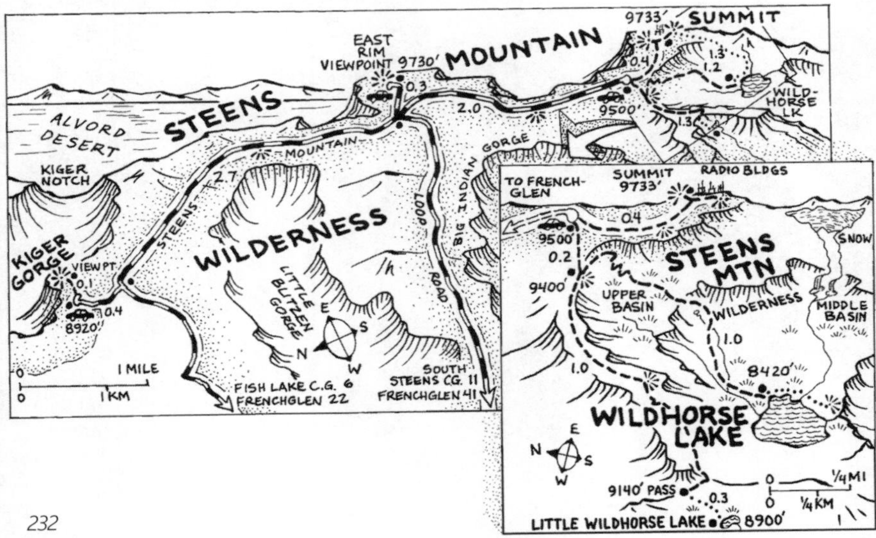

Wildhorse Lake.

Driving up Steens Mountain is like climbing a 20-mile ramp. This fault-block mountain has risen up in the past five to seven million years. During the Ice Age, seven glaciers gouged 2000-foot-deep, U-shaped canyons into the western slope.

After driving 13.4 miles up from the gate, detour to the right into the Fish Lake Recreation Site. Mountain lakes are rare in southeast Oregon and this pool's a beauty, with a campground and picnic area among silvery-leaved quaking aspen. Then continue up the main road another 5.7 miles, passing a snow gate that's closed from about November 1 until July 1, depending on snow levels. At a pointer for the Kiger Gorge Viewpoint, detour 0.4 mile to the left and walk 300 feet to a cliff-edge panorama of Kiger Creek's gorge. This colossal trough breaches the mountain's crest, leaving a gap called Kiger Notch.

Return to the main gravel road and drive another 2.7 miles to a 4-way junction. First turn left for a 0.3-mile side trip up to the East Rim Viewpoint and a dizzying look down to the Alvord Desert. Then return to the 4-way junction and follow a "Wildhorse Lake" pointer left on a rough dirt road for 1.9 miles to a parking lot at road's end. The sparse blooms of white yarrow, pink desert buckwheat, and white phlox struggle here in a field of lava rocks encrusted with black, green, and orange lichens.

If you're headed for Steens Mountain's summit, simply hike up a gated, steep, rocky roadbed 0.4 mile to the top, with views and five small communications buildings. If you have a little more time and energy, however, try the other trail from the parking lot. This path heads downhill past a hiker registration box for 0.2 mile to a rimrock cliff overlooking Wildhorse Lake. Here the trail forks.

For Wildhorse Lake, take the fork that turns sharply left, traversing down a precariously steep rocky slope. Soon the path begins following a brook through increasingly lush meadows, ablaze with pink monkeyflower, orange paintbrush, and yellow Oregon sunshine. At the 1.2-mile mark, the narrow sand beach of Wildhorse Lake makes a good turnaround point. If you're backpacking, do not camp on the fragile meadow plants, and bring a cookstove, because fires are not allowed.

From the trail fork atop the ridge, a much rougher, fainter path continues straight along the scenic ridgecrest toward Little Wildhorse Lake. After 0.8 mile this path scrambles to a rocky summit. Then it descends and switchbacks faintly to the right to a pass. The trail ends here, but it's easy to hike 0.3 mile down to the lake.

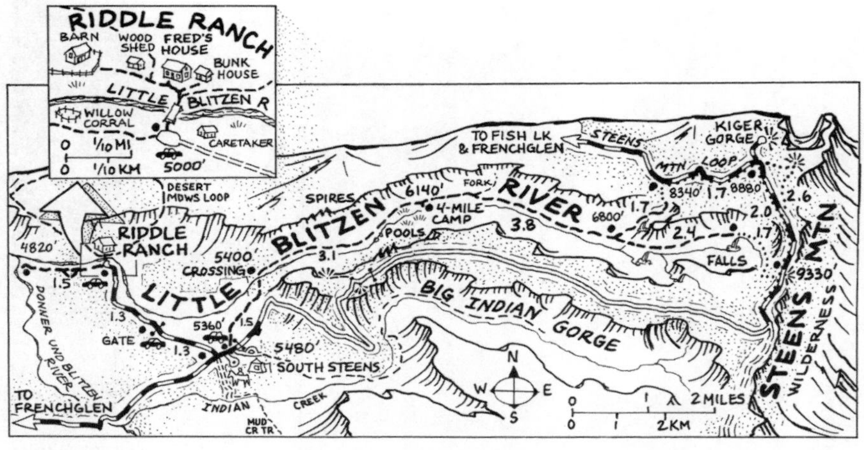

Hike

90 Little Blitzen River

Riddle me this: How many bachelor cowboys does it take to create a historic ranch district?

Easy (to Donner und Blitzen River)
3 miles round trip
200 feet elevation **loss**
Open late May to late November
Use: hikers, horses

Moderate (to 4-Mile Camp)
9.2 miles round trip
800 feet elevation gain
Open June to mid-November
Map: Fish Lake (USGS)

Fred Riddle's ranch house.

The answer is three, if we're talking about the Riddle Brothers Ranch along the Little Blitzen River. Three brothers—Fred, Ben, and Walt Riddle—built plank-and-log ranch houses on Steens Mountain in the early 1900s. The trio died childless, and the Bureau of Land Management later bought the area. The partially restored ranches recall a simpler, Old West lifestyle, with kerosene lamps, woodstoves, and barns full of horse gear.

The ranch area also serves as a starting point for hikers exploring trails along the Little Blitzen River. An easy 1.5-mile path downstream from Fred Riddle's cabin is popular with fly fishermen and hikers with children. A longer route up Little Blitzen Gorge prowls the rugged high country of Steens Mountain.

The Riddle brothers were the third generation of the pioneer family that founded the town of Riddle, south of Roseburg. Fred, Ben, and Walt raised mules, herded them south to the rail line at Winnemucca, and sold them to the US Army cavalry. They raised cattle and irrigated hayfields. They brewed moonshine, read books,

Little Blitzen Gorge near 4-Mile Camp.

played records on a Victrola, and complained about who had to do the cooking. Fred kept 40 cats, feeding them six gallons of milk a day.

Getting There— From Burns, take Highway 78 east toward Crane for 1.7 miles, turn right on Highway 205 for 61 miles to Frenchglen, continue towards Fields another 10 paved miles, and then turn left onto the gravel Steens Mountain Loop Road, closed by a gate from about Thanksgiving to late May. Drive 19.2 miles to a sign for Riddle Ranch (0.3 mile before South Steens Campground), and turn left on a dirt road for 1.3 miles to a parking area by a gate. When the gate is open (9am-5pm Thursday through Sunday from June to October) you can drive the next 1.3 miles to a parking lot at road's end.

Cross a footbridge over the Little Blitzen River to tour Fred Riddle's ranch house. Then return to the parking lot and set out on the Levi Brinkley trail, which begins near an outhouse. This 1.5-mile path heads downriver past a corral of woven willow branches, forks briefly, rejoins, and ends at a meadow by the Donner und Blitzen River. This is a lovely spot to lie in the grass and watch the glassy rivers merge. Butterflies flit past. Trout dart in the water. It's easy to see why the Riddles liked the place.

For a longer hike up Little Blitzen Gorge, drive back to the Steens Mountain Loop Road and turn left 0.3 mile. Immediately before the South Steens Campground entrance pull into a trailhead parking area on the right. The trail begins across the road and contours through sagebrush for 1.5 miles to a bridgeless crossing of the 20-foot-wide Litle Blitzen River. Sometimes logs allow a dry-footed crossing, and sometimes you have to wade. Then turn right on a fainter, brushier route that enters a spectacular canyon lined with 1000-foot cliffs. At the 3.6-mile mark you'll pass two deep little pools in the river and enter a broad meadow with wildflowers among the sage. A mile upriver is 4-Mile Camp, with a ruined corral and big cottonwood trees (*GPS location 42.6907, -118.6751).*

Other Options— If you tent at Four-Mile Camp you can explore the rest of Little Blitzen Gorge the next day. It's 3.8 increasingly rough miles up to a fork at a knoll that divides the canyon. To the left a steep, rough path climbs to the Steens Mountain Loop Road. To the right the trail continues faintly upriver 2.4 miles to a 20-foot waterfall at the lip of the valley's bowl-shaped cirque, filled with alpine flowers and rimmed with headwall cliffs. Climbing out of this mile-wide bowl is tricky and requires the use of your hands, even at the easiest spot, alongside a cascade to the right.

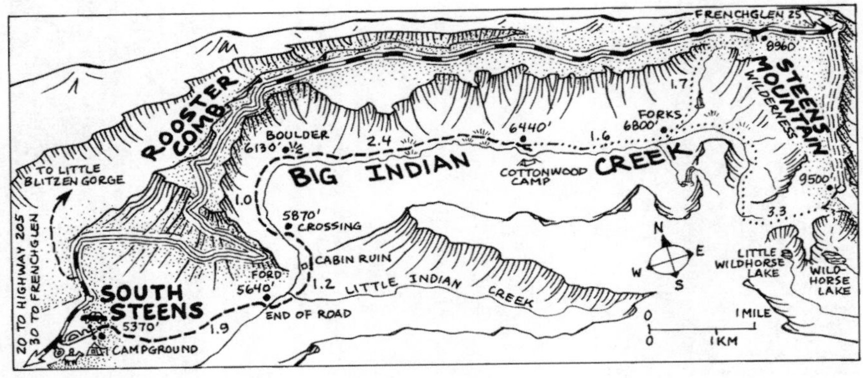

Hike 91 Big Indian Gorge

Snow fell so heavily on Steens Mountain during the Ice Age 10,000 years ago that glaciers crept 10 miles down to the west.

Moderate (to boulder)
8.2 miles round trip
960 feet elevation gain
Open June to mid-November
Use: hikers, horses

Difficult (to cottonwood camp)
13 miles round trip
1270 feet elevation gain

Big Indian Gorge.

The rivers of ice gouged seven colossal 2000-foot-deep gorges, each with the U-shaped cross section typical of glacial valleys. Because the climate has become relatively dry since then, the canyons still have their elegant curving silhouette, and not the V-shape of valleys cut by rivers.

One of the most accessible of these scenic canyons, Big Indian Gorge, has a modern campground at its mouth. To be sure, you'll still have to hike 1.9 miles to reach the creek, and then negotiate three creek crossings, but that's the price of admission to this quiet world of quaking aspen groves and wildflowers in the Steens Mountain Wilderness.

Getting There— From Burns, drive 1.7 miles east on Highway 78 toward Crane and turn right on paved Highway 205 for 61 miles to Frenchglen. Continue on the paved highway towards Fields for another 10 miles and turn left onto the gravel Steens Mountain Loop Road for 18.9 miles to the South Steens Campground on the right. The first campground entrance is for equestrians. The second entrance has family campsites amidst junipers and sagebrush. Cold drinking water is available from a spigot at a well house. The trail begins at the far end of this camp loop at a trailhead/picnic area parking lot.

The wide gravel trail (an old roadbed narrowed by rocks) ambles through juniper woods 1.9 miles to a ford of Big Indian Creek. If there's no log across the creek here, you'll have to wade. On the far shore, the trail continues 0.2 mile to Little Indian Creek, a 15-foot-wide stream that skillful hoppers can cross on rocks. In another 0.4 mile you might notice a ruined log cabin on the left, and in another 0.6 mile you'll reach a final, awkward crossing of Big Indian Creek. Scramble across on logs downstream or look upstream for stepping stones.

After a mile the trail curves around a bend in the canyon to a 5-foot boulder where weary hikers can declare victory and turn back. This is the first viewpoint of the canyon's distant headwall, where snow patches cling to the cliffs of Steens Mountain's summit ridge. The canyon's flora changes here too. Junipers have begun to yield to white-barked quaking aspen and tall cottonwoods. Flowers among the sagebrush include yellow senecio, blue lupine, and the beautiful, 3-petaled lavender blooms of mariposa lily.

If you're up for a longer hike, continue 2.4 miles through grassier meadows to a campsite near the gravelly 15-foot-wide creek in a cottonwood grove. Beyond this point the increasingly faint trail is easy to lose. Adventurers who continue 1.6 miles will reach a fork in the creek below a castle-shaped outcrop in the canyon wall, with several waterfalls in view. Tempted to continue still farther? Stamina, balance, and route-finding skills are required to climb out of this steep-walled canyon to the road more than 2000 feet above, following either the left- or right-hand fork of the creek.

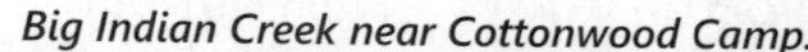

Big Indian Creek near Cottonwood Camp.

Hike 92 Threemile Canyon

From a new Steens Mountain trailhead, explore a canyon and climb a historic cattle trail to the scenic Catlow Rim.

Easy (Threemile Canyon)
3.4 miles round trip
650 feet elevation gain
Open April through November
Use: hikers, horses

Moderate (Huffman Trail)
5 miles round trip
1320 feet elevation gain

Columnar wall.

This lower, western portion of the Steens Mountain Wilderness had no convenient access until 2020, when the Bureau of Land Management opened the Threemile Trailhead on Highway 205, exactly halfway between the Old West outposts of Frenchglen and Fields. So far, the trail network here consists of two paths with wide-ranging views and desert canyon scenery. You might well hike both in one day.

Getting There— From Burns, drive 1.7 miles east on Highway 78 toward Crane and turn right on paved Highway 205 for 61 miles to Frenchglen. Continue on the paved highway towards Fields for 25 miles to a gravel parking lot on the left with a trailhead signboard. (If you're coming from Fields, drive 25 miles toward Frenchglen to find the parking lot on the right.) The highway has no signs marking this turnoff, but it's the only pullout for miles on the Steens Mountain side of the highway without a gate or a "No Trespassing" sign. If you have GPS on your phone or in your car, the location 42.5131 -118.9126.

From the parking area, open a wire gate and follow a relatively level trail amid sagebrush, bunchgrass, and 20-foot-tall junipers. Behind you, the view extends to a small reservoir and a few green fields that fade to brown in the flat expanse of the arid Catlow Valley. When the U.S. government offered free land here to

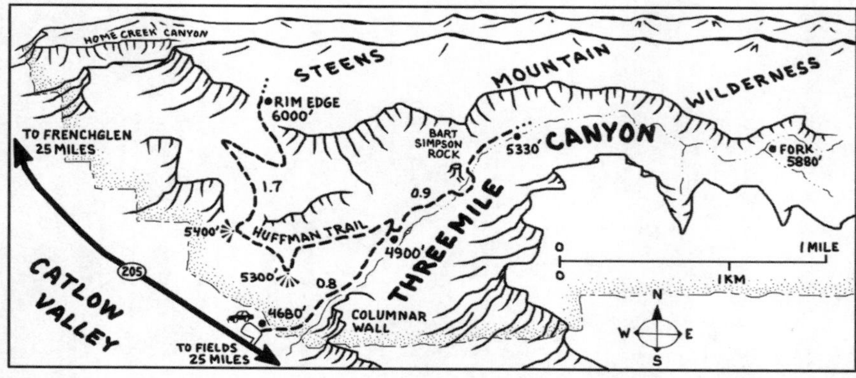

homesteaders in the early 1900s, the valley filled with hopeful farmers. The ghost towns of Catlow, Blitzen, and Beckley, now closed to the public, remain from those dried-up dreams.

After 0.3 mile the trail crosses an old stone wall and enters the gigantic V-shaped mouth of Threemile Canyon. The creek here is mostly dry, but the canyon bottom seems lush anyway, with willows, pink geraniums, and lots of bird song. Crowding the canyon on the right is a 120-foot cliff composed of a dozen stacked layers of columnar basalt, evidence of the massive lava flows that buried all of the Steens Mountain country 15-20 million years ago. Later tectonic pressure cracked this corner of Oregon diagonally, tilting up ranges like the Steens.

At the 0.8-mile mark the trail forks, and you face a decision. The Threemile Trail to the right continues up the canyon bottom for 0.9 mile, crossing the mostly dry creekbed twice to avoid a basalt pinnacle that looks like Bart Simpson when seen from the right angle. Beyond the end of the completed trail, bushwhacking further up the canyon is tough in the rocky brush, so go back to the trail junction.

If you want a quiet spot for lunch, explore 80 feet directly toward the creek from this trail junction. You'll find a small, hidden pool in a grove of quaking aspen.

If you're ready for a longer hike, take the other fork at the junction. The Huffman Trail climbs 1.7 miles out of the canyon, steeply at times, to wider views. Rockwork banks remain along portions of this old cattle drive route. Mules ear wildflowers on slopes bloom yellow in June. The path curves around two broad ridge-ends with views of the Catlow Valley, crosses a rockslide, and switchbacks up to its end at the edge of the Catlow Rim *(GPS location 42.5262 -118.9121)*. Ahead stretches a plateau of bunchgrass and low sage. Explore as far you want, but be sure you can find your way back, because the trail back is not at all obvious from the plateau.

View of the Catlow Valley from the Huffman Trail.

Hike 93 Pike Creek

At first glance, it hardly seems possible for a hiking trail to be hiding on Steens Mountain's east face, a snowy, mile-high cliff above the Alvord Desert's alkali flats.

Easy (to creek crossing)
3.4 miles round trip
700 feet elevation gain
Open April through November

Moderate (to forks)
6.6 miles round trip
1700 feet elevation gain

Needle hole caves.

At Pike Creek, however, an ancient mining road gives hikers a secret entryway into a spectacular box canyon of colorful rock formations and wildflowers.

Getting There— Drive here via the East Steens Road, a wide gravel route with some of the best scenery in Oregon. Just be sure to top off your gas tank before leaving civilization behind. From Burns, drive east through Crane on Highway 78 for 65 miles. At a pointer for Fields near milepost 65, turn right onto East Steens Road for 10.9 miles of pavement and another 27.9 miles of excellent, wide gravel. Beyond the Alvord Ranch 2.2 miles, park in a pullout on the right with a trailhead message board at the gated Pike Creek road *(GPS location 42.5711, -118.5222).*

If you're coming from Fields instead, you'll want to take the paved road north toward Frenchglen for 1.3 miles and then go straight onto East Steens Road. After 10.8 miles of pavement and an additional 12.6 miles of excellent gravel (and beyond the sign for Alvord Hot Springs 2.2 miles), park in the trailhead pullout on the left.

From the gate, walk up a public dirt road 0.6 mile to a private campground at a crossing of Pike Creek. If you want, you could pay $50 to the caretaker at Alvord Hot Springs for a campsite here, attempt to drive up the awful road, and shorten your hike by 0.6 mile.

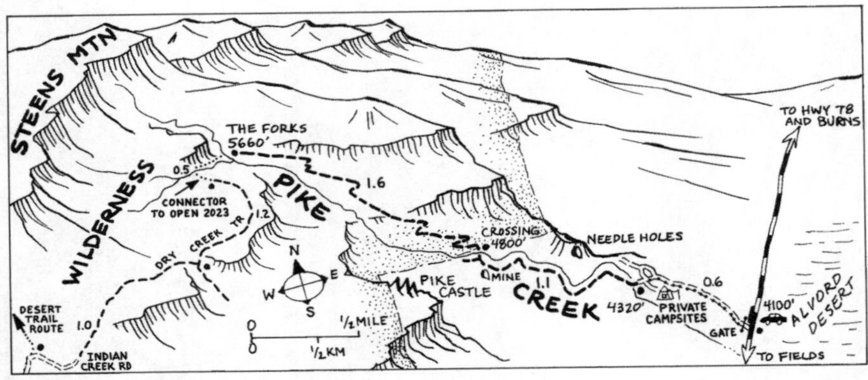

Steens Mountain from Pike Creek Canyon.

Hop across the creek beside a house-sized boulder. Then follow the old mining road—now a trail strewn with colorful rocks—up the far bank through the sagebrush. Wildflower patches along the way are prettiest in May, with sunflower-shaped balsamroot, yellow lupine, purple penstemon, and red paintbrush. As you climb, you'll gain a view back through two small caves toward the Alvord Desert.

At the 1.1-mile mark you'll pass a Wilderness boundary sign, a dynamite shed by a cliff, and then the collapsed entrance of an unsuccessful uranium prospect. The path then forks beside a creek crossing. For a short hike, go straight on the overgrown old road 200 feet to a a small creekside opening, a possible lunch spot before turning back.

For a longer hike, take the right-hand fork, cross the creek on boulders, and switchback up a hill. Just 100 feet before the crest of the trail, you'll see fist-sized, red rock nodules on the slope. Rockhounds have cracked many of these open in search of quartz crystals or the colorful jasper of thundereggs.

For the next 1.6 miles the trail traverses the canyon slope above Pike Creek's right bank. Views keep improving of Steens Mountain's snow-streaked summit cliffs ahead. Finally you descend to trail's end at the east fork of Pike Creek, a tumbling brook with flat rocks on the bank where you can rest before heading back.

In 2023 an extension of this trail is planned to cross the forks of Pike Creek and climb to the Dry Creek Trail, a track that connects with the Oregon Desert Trail.

Hike 94 Big Sand Gap

On the far side of the Alvord Desert's vast alkali playa, wild horses have beaten a trail from a desert spring to Big Sand Gap, a sandy notch in a palisade of cliffs.

Moderate
5.2 miles round trip
400 feet elevation gain
Open except in wet weather
Use: hikers, horses

Greasewood at the "trailhead".

During the Ice Age, when this desert's basin filled with a 30-mile-long lake, the water finally spilled out here, launching a colossal flood that roared down the Snake and Columbia Rivers to the sea.

Today, a trip to Big Sand Gap is still an otherworldly experience—driving across a dry lakebed and scrambling to one of the loneliest viewpoints in the country. Although the hike is not difficult, it is only for adventurers with routefinding skills, two quarts of water, long pants, a hat, sunglasses, and sunscreen.

Getting There— From Burns, drive east through Crane on Highway 78 for 65 miles. At a pointer for Fields near milepost 65, turn right onto East Steens Road for 10.9 miles of pavement and another 32.4 miles of excellent gravel to an ungated dirt road to the left signed "Frog Spring: Alvord Desert" *(GPS location 42.509, -118.5344)*. The turnoff is 2.3 miles beyond the sign for Alvord Hot Springs.

If you're coming from Fields, drive 1.3 miles north of town. Where the main road to Frenchglen curves left, go straight on East Steens Road for 10.8 miles of pavement and an additional 8.1 miles of excellent gravel to the "Frog Spring" turnoff on the right, 1.6 miles beyond a crest with your first view of the Alvord Desert.

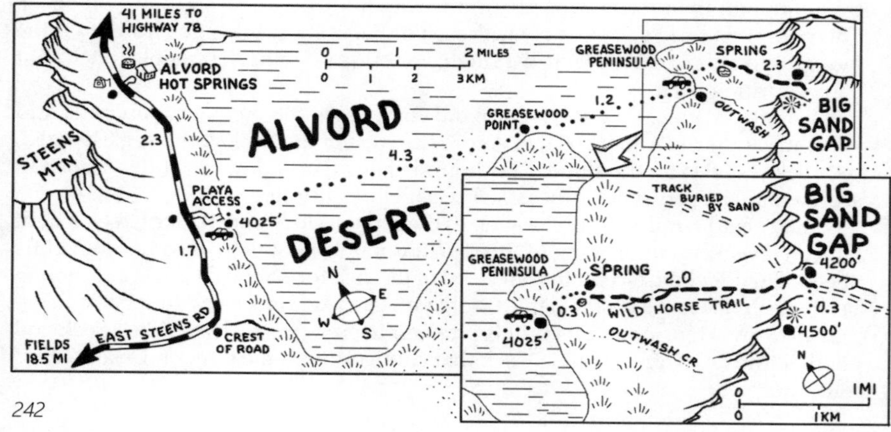

Drive down the ungated dirt road 0.2 mile to a parking area with a signboard explaining that the Alvord Desert is a Wilderness Study Area. Vehicles are currently allowed on the playa if they are not driven near vegetation along the lakebed's shore. So continue on a very rough dirt road 0.1 mile down to the alkali flat. Stop here to check that the surface really is drivable. This area gets only 6 inches of rain a year, but rain can turn the playa to mud.

Then drive directly across the playa, heading straight toward a small notch in the low white rimrock beyond the far shore. After 4.3 miles you may need to swerve slightly left to skirt some greasewood bushes. At the 5.5-mile mark, you'll approach the green line of vegetation marking the far shore. You want to park on the right-hand side of a "peninsula" of greasewood bushes, by a dry outwash creekbed with tire tracks *(GPS location 42.4946, -118.4225)*.

Your first hiking goal is Big Sand Gap Spring, visible as a slight rise with tall bushes, directly beneath Big Sand Gap's notch. Bushwhack toward it 0.3 mile, skirting the left-hand side of a marshy pool to find the start of the wild horse trail *(GPS location 42.4956, -118.4165)*. Follow this braided route straight toward the notch on the horizon for 2 miles. The trail splits often, but rejoins. Finally crest a sand dune to Big Sand Gap *(GPS location 42.4872, -118.3867)*.

An ancient roadbed extends east from the Gap toward even wilder desert lands, but the most satisfying viewpoint is close at hand, atop the cliff immediately to the right of Big Sand Gap. Veer right, looking for horse trails that climb the gentlest route up the steep slope. After 0.2 mile you'll scramble to a breathtaking brink *(GPS location 42.4848, -118.3895)*, with a view of an alien world.

Big Sand Gap.

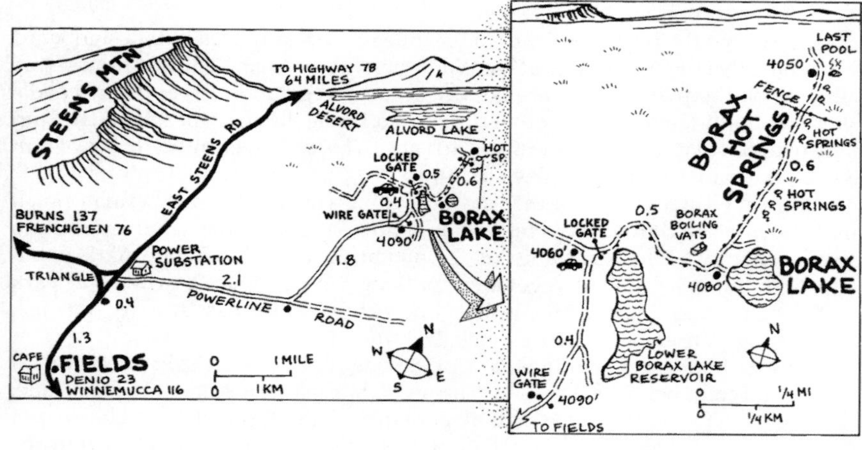

Hike
95 Borax Hot Springs

At Borax Lake, fish thrive in warm alkaline water. Steam rises from boiling turquoise pools.

Easy
3 miles round trip
60 feet elevation gain
Open all year

Borax vat by the lake.

Curlews with curling bills swoop through the sagebrush, screaming. In the distance beyond the hot pools, the snowy crest of Steens Mountain shimmers above the desert like a mirage.

The strange desert springs at Borax Lake are fired by the same active fault system that hoisted Steens Mountain a mile above the surrounding plains. Here, groundwater seeps into the planet's crustal cracks and boils back to the surface through deep, trumpet-shaped pools.

During the wetter climate of the Ice Age, a gigantic lake filled this valley 200 feet deep, spilling north to the Snake River. As the rains lessened, the lake evaporated, leaving an alkali playa at the Alvord Desert. Incredibly, not all of the fish perished. At Borax Lake, one minnow-like species evolved to suit the increasingly warm, alkaline water. Today the Borax Lake chub lives in 600-foot-wide Borax Lake, and nowhere else on earth. Arsenic levels in the lake are 25 times higher than the limit considered fatal for humans, but the diehard chubs don't seem to mind.

Borax Lake fell into private hands in the late 1800s, when entrepreneurs hired Chinese laborers to collect sodium borate crusts and dissolve them in huge vats to produce borax. Mule-drawn wagon caravans hauled the chalky borax more than a hundred miles to the railroad in Winnemucca. To preserve the area's fragile ecosystem, the non-profit Nature Conservancy bought the lake in the 1990s. Today hikers pass the rusted remains of the old vats beside the lake.

Getting There— Start by driving to Fields, a remote roadside settlement that consists of a combination cafe, store, motel, garage, and gas station. A wall chart records annual sales of the cafe's famous hamburgers and milkshakes since the 1980s. The milkshakes are winning. To find Fields from Burns, drive east 1.7 miles toward Crane on Highway 78, turn right on Highway 205 for 59 miles to Frenchglen, and continue another 50 miles on the paved road toward Winnemucca.

Check your gas gauge in Fields. Then drive back toward Frenchglen 1.3 miles, heading north on the paved road. When the main road curves left at a fork, go straight on a paved road, following a pointer for Highway 78. After 0.4 mile, turn right beside a power substation *(GPS location 42.2895, -118.6655)* onto a dirt road that follows a large powerline. At the first fork, after 2.1 miles, veer left away from the powerline for 1.8 miles to a wire gate that is usually open *(GPS location 42.3201, -118.611)*. A sign here reads, "Danger! Hot Springs. Scalding Water. Ground May Collapse. Control Children and Pets." In fact, dogs and other pets are banned to protect the area's birdlife. Fishing, boating, and swimming are not allowed either.

Heeding those cautions, drive onward along the road 0.5 mile and park at a turnaround with a locked metal gate *(GPS location 42.3264 -118.6109)*. Hike past the gate on a sandy old road 0.5 mile to Borax Lake. Along the way you'll pass a (usually dry) lower reservoir and the old boiling vats. Alkali deposits have left Borax Lake perched 20 feet above the surrounding flats.

Dozens of smaller hot springs, strung out in a line to the north for 0.6 mile, are visible from here as wisps of steam rising from the grass. For a closer look, walk back 100 feet toward the vats, turn right on an old road, and keep straight toward distant Steens Mountain. The pools are to the right of the road, but be careful if you leave the track, because these deep, sheer-sided springs are dangerously hot at 180°F. After 0.5 mile a wire fence crosses the road. Beyond the fence 0.1 mile, where the road veers left, turn back at two large, final hot spring pools on the right. The Nature Conservancy prohibits visitors from attempting to swim in any of the area's pools, not only because of the obvious danger, but also to protect the fragile ecology of this eerie place.

Steens Mountain from Borax Hot Springs.

Hike 96 Pueblo Mountains

Most Oregonians have never heard of the Pueblo Mountains, a commanding fault-block range between Steens Mountain and the Nevada border.

Moderate (to cairn #5)
3.2 miles round trip
1200 feet elevation gain
Open mid-July to mid-November
Use: hikers, horses

Difficult (to cairn #14)
7.2 miles round trip
2200 feet elevation gain

Cairn at the trailhead.

The Pueblo crest hiking route described here has no trees, no water sources, and no trail tread. But the starkness of this remote desert range conceals charms that can haunt adventurers' souls: silent top-of-the-world viewpoints, herds of antelope, huge blue skies, and unexpected wildflowers. Wear long pants because of sagebrush.

Although views extend for 50 miles in all directions throughout much of this cross-country route, the only man-made artifacts visible are 15 rock cairns. Often hard to find, these 4-foot stacks have been spaced at roughly quarter-mile intervals to mark the general course of the Desert Trail and its more recent variant, the Oregon Desert Trail. The original route was mapped as part of a planned 2000-mile hiking corridor from Mexico to Canada in the 1980s. The newer version, promoted by the Oregon Natural Desert Association (ONDA), winds 750 miles through southeast Oregon. Both proposed trails follow the same route the length of the Pueblo Mountains. Because hikers are left to find their own path through the sagebrush from one cairn to the next, it is important to bring a topographic map, available at *onda.org*.

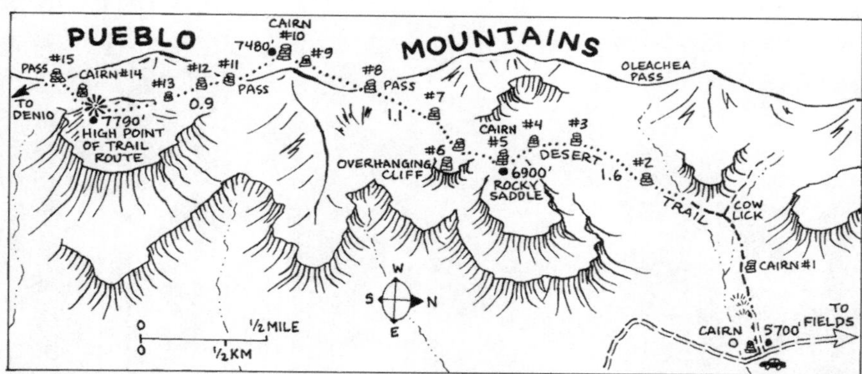

The Pueblo Mountains from cairn #14.

Getting There— From Burns, take Highway 78 east toward Crane 1.7 miles, turn right on Highway 205 for 59 miles to Frenchglen, and continue south on the paved road toward Winnemucca another 50 miles to the tiny settlement of Fields. Check your gas gauge here. Then, carefully watching the mileage on your car's odometer, continue south on the paved road 3.0 miles. At a pointer for Domingo Pass *(GPS location 42.2268, -118.6475)*, turn right across a yellow cattle guard onto a one-lane gravel road for 4.7 miles, sticking to the main, larger road when in doubt.

After 4.7 miles, cross another cattle guard and fork to the left *(GPS location 42.2041, -118.7228)*. This rocky, bumpy road is passable only by high-clearance vehicles. After 0.9 mile the road bends 90° to the left around a fence corner. Turn the corner and continue another 1.3 miles. Just 0.2 mile after the road's high point, park in a grassy flat with a rock cairn marking a very faint side road to the right *(GPS location 42.1778, -118.7216)*.

Hike up this faint side road 0.6 mile through the sagebrush to a barren area (an old cow lick) and veer left, heading cross-country up the leftmost branch of the valley. Scramble up past a grove of shrub-sized mountain mahogany trees to find cairn #3 on a rise at the 1.3-mile mark. Climb steeply up 0.3 mile to cairn #5, atop a 12-foot rock in a saddle *(GPS location 42.1619, -118.7351)*. Views here extend from Steens Mountain's snowy crest in the north to the Pine Forest Range in Nevada.

This is a possible turnaround point. If you're going strong, traverse 0.4 mile onward (and less steeply upward) to cairn #6, perched atop an overhanging cliff. In another 0.3 mile, cross a pass to the western side of the Pueblo Mountains' crest. Contour 0.4 mile to cairn #10 *(GPS location 42.1497, -118.7428)*. Continue contouring 0.2 mile to a shaley pass with cairn #11, and then follow the mountains' crest up 0.7 mile to the trail route's highest point, a bare viewpoint knoll just above cairn #14 *(GPS location 42.1385, -118.7372)*.

This viewpoint makes a satisfying turnaround point for day hikers after the trip's wearying elevation gain and cross-country scrambling. Determined backpackers can continue downhill past a pass, following the Desert Trail's rock cairns through alpine basins and cattle meadows along the western face of the Pueblo Mountains for 13 miles to Denio.

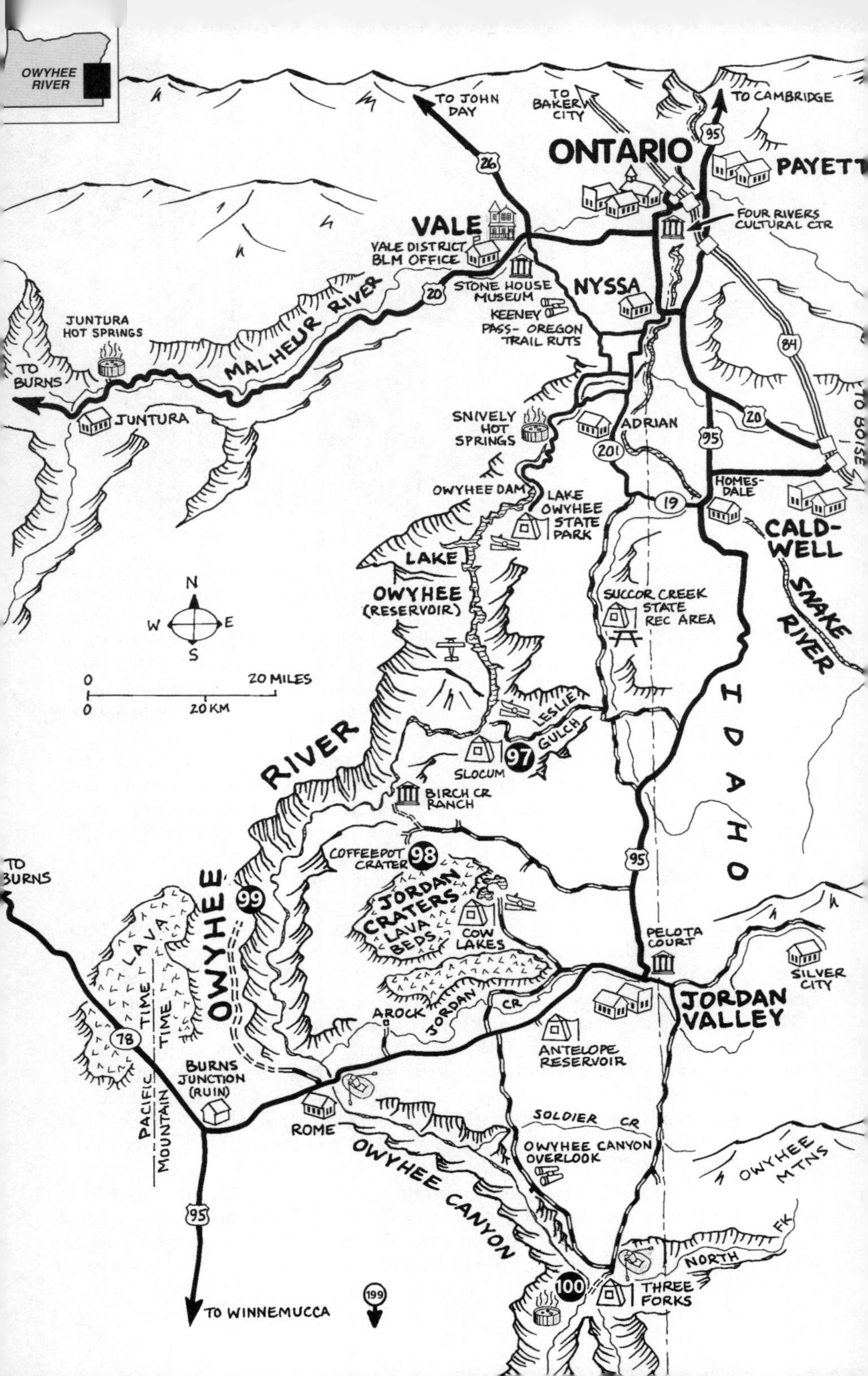
OWYHEE RIVER
TO JOHN DAY
TO BAKER CITY
TO CAMBRIDGE
ONTARIO
PAYETT
VALE
FOUR RIVERS CULTURAL CTR
VALE DISTRICT BLM OFFICE
STONE HOUSE MUSEUM
NYSSA
KEENEY PASS- OREGON TRAIL RUTS
JUNTURA HOT SPRINGS
MALHEUR RIVER
TO BURNS
JUNTURA
SNIVELY HOT SPRINGS
ADRIAN
TO BOISE
OWYHEE DAM
LAKE OWYHEE STATE PARK
HOMES-DALE
CALD-WELL
LAKE OWYHEE (RESERVOIR)
SUCCOR CREEK STATE REC AREA
SNAKE RIVER
N
W
E
S
0
20 MILES
0
20 KM
IDAHO
LESLIE GULCH
RIVER
SLOCUM
BIRCH CR RANCH
COFFEEPOT CRATER
TO BURNS
OWYHEE
JORDAN CRATERS LAVA BEDS
COW LAKES
PELOTA COURT
LAVA
SILVER CITY
JORDAN VALLEY
AROCK
JORDAN
CR
ANTELOPE RESERVOIR
PACIFIC TIME
MOUNTAIN TIME
BURNS JUNCTION (RUIN)
ROME
SOLDIER CR
OWYHEE CANYON OVERLOOK
OWYHEE MTNS
OWYHEE CANYON
NORTH FK
THREE FORKS
TO WINNEMUCCA

ONTARIO

The Owyhee and Malheur Rivers wind through spectacular desert canyons to the green farmlands surrounding Southeast Oregon's commercial center, Ontario. When in town, stop by the **Four Rivers Cultural Center & Museum,** a first-rate interpretive center describing the region's Native American, Basque, and other cultures. At 676 SW 5th Avenue, the museum is open 10am-5pm Monday-Friday and 10am-5pm Saturday. Admission runs $7 for adults and $5 for children and seniors.

Mural in downtown Vale.

Vale

Once an Oregon Trail campsite at a Malheur River ford, Vale now boasts a historic downtown decorated with more than two dozen murals. After strolling Main Street's shops, drive Glen Street south 6 miles toward Lake Owyhee to see the **Oregon Trail ruts at Keeney Pass.**

Lake Owyhee

The Owyhee River's reservoir twists 53 miles through colorful desert canyons. **Lake Owyhee State Park** (open March 1 to November 14) has 62 campsites, showers, 2 cabins, a boat ramp, and a nearby resort with boat rentals. For a free hot soak, drive the paved road 15 miles back from the campground toward Ontario to a sign for **Snively Hot Springs,** a natural riverside pool by a cottonwood grove on a spur road.

Succor Creek and Leslie Gulch

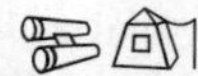

A 34-mile gravel road winds through a colorful rock canyon from Highway 201 (south of Ontario 34 miles) to Highway 95 (north of Jordan Valley 19 miles). The drive passes **Succor Creek State Natural Area,** a free, primitive camp (with 18 walk-in campsites and no drinking water) open year-round. Don't miss the 14-mile side trip down the spectacularly narrow canyon of **Leslie Gulch** (Hike #97).

Jordan Valley

Two-thirds of the residents are of Basque descent in this ranching town, where a restored 1915 stone **Pelota Court** is used for Basque handball games. From here, drive the 79-mile **Soldier Creek Watchable Wildlife Loop Road**, a mostly dirt route (impassable in wet weather) to a breathtaking overlook of the **Owyhee River Canyon** and the primitive riverside camping area at **Three Forks** (Hike #100). From Jordan Valley, drive Highway 95 west 16 miles, turn left on the dirt road toward Three Forks for 29 miles, and keep left for 33 miles back to Jordan Valley.

Owyhee River

Only experienced boaters should drift or kayak the **Owyhee River,** usually runnable from March through early June. The 39-mile section from Three Forks to Highway 95 at Rome includes half a dozen dangerous rapids, among them Widowmaker Rapids' 10-foot drop. The 55-mile stretch from Rome to Lake Owyhee includes three difficult rapids. The routes pass cliffs, caves, and hot springs.

Hike 97 Leslie Gulch

Most travelers view the slot-like canyons, rock pinnacles, and colorful badlands of Leslie Gulch through car windows.

Easy (Juniper Gulch)
1.6 miles round trip
400 feet elevation gain
Open except in wet weather

Easy (Dago Gulch)
1.6 miles round trip
190 feet elevation gain

Moderate (Timber Gulch)
1.2 miles round trip
350 feet elevation gain

Timber Gulch cliffs.

After you have driven all the way here, to Oregon's eastern border, why not explore this spectacular scenery by hiking a few of Leslie Gulch's five side canyons?

The rock formations date back 15 million years, when a volcano blasted out a 10-mile-wide caldera that filled with volcanic ash 1000 feet deep. Minerals colored the ash as it solidified to rock. When the land rose, flash floods carved narrow gulches lined with orange, yellow, purple, and red cliffs. Soft spots in the rock weathered into niches and small caves known as "honeycombs."

Leslie Gulch won its name when an 1882 lightning strike killed pioneer cattleman Hiram Leslie. Today the gulch is valued not only for its scenery, but also for several species of rare plants and a herd of bighorn sheep.

Getting There— From Ontario, take Interstate 84 east into Idaho 3 miles and turn south on Highway 95 through Parma and Homedale for 51 miles. Then turn right on gravel McBride Creek Road for 9 miles, keep right on Succor Creek Road another 1.8 miles, and turn left on the gravel Leslie Gulch road for 14.5 miles to road's end at the Owyhee Reservoir boat ramp.

If you're driving here from Jordan Valley (140 miles southeast of Burns), take Highway 95 north for 17 miles and turn left at a sign for Succor Creek for 8.4 gravel miles. At a T-shaped junction, turn left toward Succor Creek another 1.8 miles, and then turn left on the gravel Leslie Gulch road for 14.5 miles to road's end at the reservoir boat ramp.

Camping in Leslie Gulch is permitted only at Slocum Campground, a gravel flat 0.2 mile up the road from the boat ramp. This free camp has 12 picnic tables with shade shelters, but no water. Horses are not allowed anywhere in Leslie Gulch.

If you have time for only one hike, choose Juniper Gulch. From Slocum Campground, drive back up Leslie Gulch 3.6 miles to the marked Juniper Gulch parking pullout on the left. The trail hops across Leslie Creek and follows a narrow sandy wash up past gigantic, overhanging cliffs. After 0.6 mile keep right at a fork. Then follow the path up a ridge to its end at an orange cliff of "honeycomb" rock. Turn back here, because steep and slippery slopes lie ahead.

For another easy hike nearby, head for Dago Gulch. From Juniper Gulch, drive up the Leslie Gulch road 1 mile, turn right at a sign for Dago Gulch, and park in 0.2 mile at a turnaround just before a locked green gate. Then walk up the closed road 0.8 mile, past cliffs with columns and fluted green ash. Turn back at a cattle gate because the road ahead crosses patches of unmarked private land.

The prettiest gulch to explore, Timber Gulch, isn't marked with a sign. To find it, drive down the Leslie Gulch road exactly 1.25 miles from the Juniper Gulch sign (or 2.35 miles up from Slocum Campground) and park at a one-car pullout on the north beside some wild roses *(GPS location 43.3048, -117.2906)*. Walk up the (usually dry) bed of Leslie Creek about 100 feet and veer left up a dry sandy wash toward giant orange rock formations. There is no trail in this narrow, sagebrush-choked canyon, so you'll want to be wearing long pants. After 0.3 mile, where the canyon splits at a 200-foot-tall rock wall, turn left for 0.3 mile to the canyon's end at an amphitheater of sheer, pinnacled cliffs.

Leslie Gulch has two other explorable side canyons. From Slocum Campground, a faint trail goes up the left side of Slocum Gulch 0.5 mile before petering out; bushwhackers can continue another 0.8 mile before the canyon becomes too narrow and brushy. If you drive up Leslie Gulch's road from the campground 4.8 miles (past Dago Gulch 0.2 mile), you can park at an "Upper Leslie Gulch" sign and follow a trail 0.3 mile until it vanishes amid tall sagebrush.

Rock spires at Dago Gulch.

Hike 98 Coffeepot Crater

At the Jordan Craters lava beds, a row of spatter cones rises from one of Oregon's most remote sagebrush landscapes.

Easy
1.1-mile loop
140 feet elevation gain
Open except in wet weather

Bitterroot.

The easy hiking trail that circles Coffeepot Crater here is open all year, but you won't want to attempt this trip in just any weather. January temperatures may cower below freezing all day. The blazing August sun can bake the desert at 120°F. During rare rainstorms, the final miles of the dirt access road can become a quagmire of mud ruts and giant puddles. Perhaps the friendliest month is June, when the desert here greets visitors with giant pink bitterroot blooms.

The Jordan Craters lava beds are one result of North America's shearing collision with the North Pacific seafloor plate. That collision has stretched Oregon diagonally, allowing lava to leak up along a 200-mile swarm of fractures that extend

Spatter cone at Coffeepot Crater.

west to the Newberry National Volcanic Monument near Bend. Eruptions at Jordan Craters began less than 9000 years ago when lava spattered to the surface in a 300-yard-long row of cones. An explosion blasted Coffeepot Crater at the lower end of the string. Then vents unleashed a flow of soupy *pahoehoe* basalt lava that inundated 27 square miles of desert.

Locals have been known to boast that the Jordan Craters lava beds are so fresh you can find cowboy bootprints in them. An 18-acre portion of the lava field is less than 9000 years old, so native tribes may have witnessed the eruption.

Getting There— Start by filling your gas tank in the remote Highway 95 town of Jordan Valley, east of Burns 139 miles. Drive north on Highway 95 from Jordan Valley for 8.3 miles to a "Jordan Craters" pointer and turn left on a good gravel road for 24 miles. Stick to the larger road at junctions, avoiding a left-hand fork at the 11.4-mile mark and a right-hand fork at the 18.1-mile mark.

After 24 miles of gravel, fork left onto a rough dirt road, best suited for high-clearance vehicles. And after another 1.5 miles, fork left once again for 1.4 miles to a parking area at road's end *(GPS location 43.1462, -117.461).*

Hike a trail to the left around the black cinder rim of Coffeepot Crater for 0.2 mile. On the crater's far side, you'll pass a 4-foot rock trench that snakes down into the lava fields. This is one of the original sources of the lava flow. Detour down along the trench 300 feet to see where it becomes a lava tube and tunnels into two large pits, where the cave's roof collapsed. Next return to the crater rim trail to find a different detour—a slippery red cinder path that descends 0.1 mile to the bottom of Coffeepot Crater. Then complete the loop around the crater rim back to your car.

Before driving home, take a trail across the lava 300 feet to the first spatter cone, a 30-foot shell plastered with lava globs. Explore cross-country another 300 feet to see the other six spatter cones in this row. Then return to your car. But as you leave, pause where the road passes above the spatter cones. In May and June the barren desert gravel here erupts with the seemingly leafless, 2-inch-wide, creamy white blooms of *Lewisia rediviva*, the bitterroot flower.

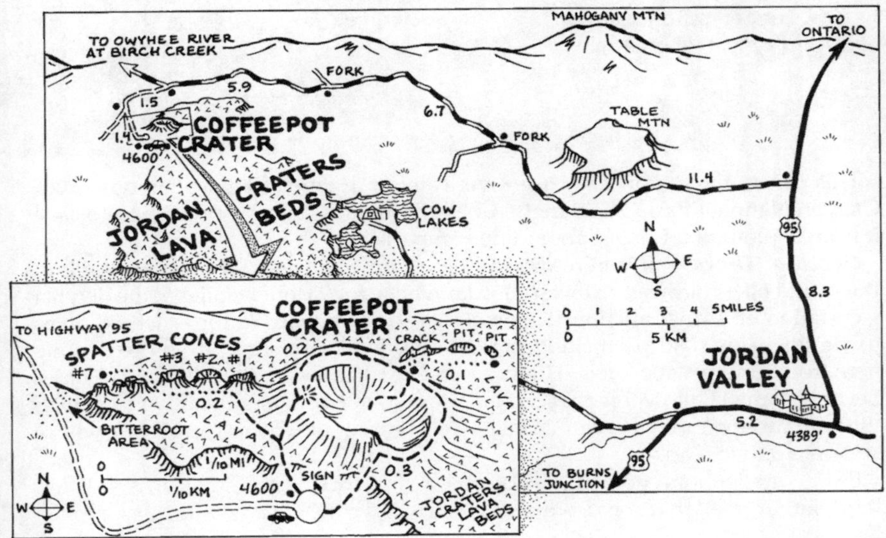

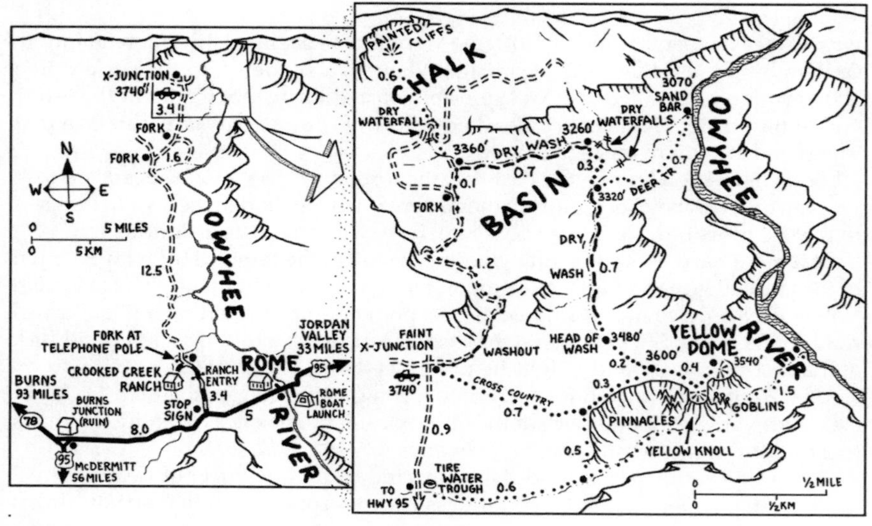

Hike

99 Chalk Basin

There are no trails in Chalk Basin's colorful badlands, but adventurers can discover dry waterfalls, pinnacles, and rock "goblins".

Moderate
5-mile loop
600 feet elevation gain
Open except when it rains

Pinnacles by the Owyhee River.

This part of the remote Owyhee River canyon resembles Utah's famous Bryce Canyon National Park. Shockingly, Chalk Basin lacks similar protection to save it from exploitation by foreign mining companies.

Getting There— If you're driving here from the west, fill your gas tank in Burns and take Highway 78 toward Jordan Valley for 93 lonely miles to the derelict gas station of Burns Junction. Then veer left on Highway 95 for exactly 8 miles to a gravel side road on the left marked only by a stop sign. (If you're driving here from Jordan Valley, take Highway 95 west 38 miles to the side road, 5 miles beyond Rome.) Follow this gravel road 3.4 miles north. Along the way you'll pass through an open ranch gate marked "No Hunting or Trespassing," but you're still on a public road.

Beside a telephone pole at the 3.4-mile mark, fork to the right on a smaller, bumpier dirt road that goes through a green metal gate. Then you'll cross Crooked

Chalk Basin's yellow dome.

Creek to a BLM sign, "Welcome to the Owyhee High Desert." This BLM road, traversing a treeless Martian landscape, is drivable by high-clearance cars unless there has been rain. In the event that the road becomes wet, your car will sink to its hubs in mud and you will camp for a day or two until the ground hardens.

Beyond the fork by the telephone pole 12.5 miles, you'll reach a second fork in the road. Veer to the right. In another 1.6 miles you'll reach a third fork. This time go left, although this branch of the road is fainter. Continue another 3.4 miles to a faint four-way X-shaped junction *(GPS location 43.0771, -117.7355)*. Park here! A washout makes the road ahead undrivable.

From the X-junction, hike to the right on an old roadbed that descends into Chalk Basin. May wildflowers amid the sagebrush include red paintbrush, yellow balsamroot, purple vetch, and purple sage. After 1.2 miles, veer right at a fork and follow the old road across a wash with some mining junk *(GPS location 43.0887, -117.7337)*. Here you'll see painted cliffs of banded chalk half a mile to the left. You can bushwhack up to these cliffs if you like, but for the loop hike, turn right down the dry wash—unless, of course, rain threatens to launch a flash flood.

Follow the creekbed 0.7 mile until a dry waterfall blocks the route *(GPS location 43.0898, -117.7235)*. Do not attempt to scramble down the 15-foot drop. Instead, backtrack 100 feet to a corner and go up a slope to the south. In 0.3 mile this detour leads to a side canyon with another big, hikable wash.

From here it is possible to follow a faint, very rough deer trail 0.7 mile east to the Owyhee River, but that's another side trip for adventurers. For the recommended loop, turn right (south) up the dry creekbed 0.7 mile, keeping left at junctions, until you reach the head of the wash. Bushwhack onward, heading uphill to the southeast, for 0.2 mile until you suddenly reach the edge of an amazing canyon rim.

Pinnacles and flutes and ridges and hoodoos of colored chalk stand like armies in a forgotten valley below you. Explore to the left 0.4 mile to a viewpoint atop a yellow knoll *(GPS location 43.0755, -117.7162)* and an even more spectacular yellow dome. To return to your car, head west along the canyon rim (to the right) for 0.3 mile up to a viewpoint that includes a distant glimpse of Steens Mountain. At this point you should also be able to see your car, on a tiny stripe of road to the west. Head directly there, cross country, for 0.7 mile to complete your tour.

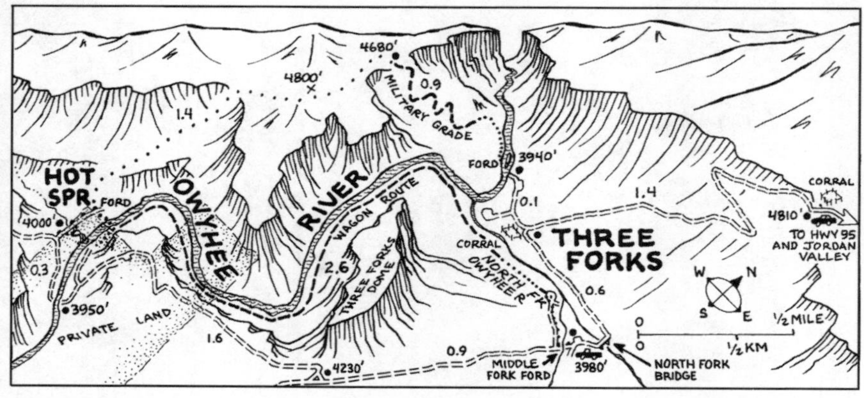

Hike 100 Three Forks

Warm springs pools perch between waterfalls on the bank of the Owyhee River, deep in a spectacular desert canyon of red rock cliffs. But be warned about the drive!

Moderate
5.4-mile loop
300 feet elevation gain
Open except after rains

The hot springs' waterfall.

At the oasis-like confluence of three river canyons, Three Forks is one of the most remote places in Oregon, wedged against the borders of Idaho and Nevada. The long dirt road here is awful, and if it's wet it becomes an undrivable morass.

Surprisingly, the area was more heavily trafficked in the 1800s. "Owyhee" was a common 19th-century spelling for Hawaii. The river won its name when two Hawaiians, hired by the Hudson's Bay Company as beaver trappers, disappeared here in 1819. In the late 1860s, thousands of gold miners and ore wagons passed through Three Forks on their way from Silver City, Idaho to the railroad in Winnemucca, Nevada. After the Bannock Indian War of 1878, the Army built an outpost at Three Forks to keep an eye on the local Paiutes. Today fragments of the area's 19th-century wagon roads help hikers make their way through the canyonlands, but it's still best to come prepared for cross-country routefinding and knee-deep river fords.

Getting There — From Burns, take Highway 78 east through Crane 93 miles to Burns Junction and turn left on Highway 95 for 30.5 miles. Near milepost 36 (west

The Owyhee River from the wagon road trail upstream from Three Forks.

of Jordan Valley 16 miles), follow a pointer for Three Forks south onto a dirt road that serves as part of the Soldier Creek Watchable Wildlife Loop. The long, lonely dirt road from Highway 95 to Three Forks turns to slick goo after rainstorms. Fortunately the area has just 11 inches of precipitation each year, Just don't run out of gas!

After 27.6 miles on the dirt road, you'll reach a signed junction. Ignore the loop route that heads left toward Jordan Valley, and instead turn right toward Three Forks. In 2.7 miles you'll reach a corral at the edge of the Owyhee canyon rim. If you're driving a passenger car, it's best to park here and add a total of 4 miles to your hike. If you're driving a high-clearance vehicle, continue down what suddenly becomes a very steep, rocky track. After 1.4 miles, turn left at a boater registration signboard for half a mile, cross the North Fork Owyhee River on a bridge, and 200 feet later park on the right, just before the road fords the Middle Fork.

Walk down the road 200 feet. cross the ford, and follow a spur road to the right 0.1 mile to its end at a turnaround. Then continue on a faint cattle trail, following the North Fork Owyhee downstream. Essentially you'll have to bushwhack through the sagebrush above the river plain for 0.2 mile. But then the path becomes a clear trail with stonework embankments from the historic wagon route, following the main stem of the Owyhee River upstream.

After 2.4 miles the tread peters out where cliffs pinch the trail against the river. Wade the river here (in summer, a pleasantly cool, knee-deep crossing) to a faint roadbed on the far shore. The largest hot springs pools, usually about 96° F, are to the left along this road 0.1 mile, just above the 10-foot waterfall of a side creek *(GPS location 42.5302, -117.1847)*. Note, however, that the hot springs and the entire riverbank for the next half mile upstream are on unmarked private land. Although hikers have been allowed to visit the hot springs for years, there is no guarantee this will always be so. If you proceed, carry out any litter you find and do not camp.

If you'd like to return on a loop, a rough dirt road on the far shore from the hot springs will take you back to your car in 2.8 miles. Just keep left at junctions.

Barrier-Free Trails of Eastern Oregon

People with limited physical abilities need not miss the fun of exploring new trails. Here are paved, graveled, or hard-packed paths accessible even to those with a stroller, walker, or wheelchair. All have accessible restrooms nearby.

COLUMBIA PLATEAU (map on page 38)

A. Columbia Gorge Discovery Center. Paved paths loop 0.2 mile behind this museum and extend 3 miles east along the Columbia River almost to The Dalles' downtown, passing ponds along the way. Drive Interstate 84 to exit 84 and follow museum signs.

B. Cottonwood Canyon State Park. Start at the picnic area of this park to tour the Murtha Ranch's restored barn, windmill, and corral. See Hike #1.

CENTRAL OREGON (map on page 58)

C. Lava Lands Visitor Center. Two paved, interpretive loops start from the back patio of this interpretive center, 8 miles south of Bend on Hwy 97. The Trail of the Molten Lands loops 0.8 mile across lava, steeply in places. The easier, 0.3-mile Trail of the Whispering Pines skirts a lava flow edge. Parking fee required.

D. Rim Rock Springs. This paved half-mile trail has interpretive signs and a birdviewing platform. The trailhead is beside Highway 26 southeast of Madras 10 miles (or northwest of Prineville 19 miles).

OCHOCO MOUNTAINS (map on page 74)

E. Story in Stone Trail. This 0.3-mile loop tours the colorful badlands of the John Day Fossil Beds Nat'l Monument. Half of the loop is paved. Drive to the Blue Basin area of Hike #23 and continue north on Hwy 19 about 3 miles. Near milepost 118, turn into a trailhead and picnic area.

F. Sugar Creek Trail. The Sugar Creek Campground (open May-Nov) has 17 mostly accessible campsites ($8 fee), a free all-accessible picnic area, and a 0.4-mile paved path that loops along the glassy stream beneath ponderosa pines, crossing two bridges. Drive 60 mi east of Prineville to Paulina, continue 3.7 mi, turn left on S Beaver Cr Rd, and follow signs toward Rager Ranger Station 9 miles.

STRAWBERRY MOUNTAIN (map on page 99)

G. Magone Lake. This fishing lake in the pines north of John Day was created by a landslide in the 1860s. Now a 2-mile packed dirt trail (usable by wheelchairs in dry weather) circles the lake from an all-accessible campground. From John Day take Hwy 26 east 9.5 miles, turn left up Bear Creek on Road 18 for 13 paved miles, turn left on Road 3620 for 1.2 miles, and turn right on Road 3618 for 1.5 miles.

H. Swick Creek Old Growth. Paved, all-accessible interpretive trail loops 0.7 mi through ponderosa pine woods. Drive Hwy 395 S of John Day 16 mi to signed parking area on left. (BM)

I. Stump Dodger Railroad. A nice rest stop on the drive east of John Day, this graveled 0.4-mile interpretive loop explores a woodsy portion of the abandoned narrow-gauge railroad that linked Prairie City with Baker City from 1910-1947. From Prairie City, drive Hwy 26 east 8 miles to milepost 184.

BLUE MOUNTAINS - SOUTH (map on page 112)

J. Oregon Trail Interpretive Center. At this world-class museum near Baker City (see page 111 and Hike #134), a 0-5 mile paved loop circles the building, and a more challenging 1.5-mile paved path descends to a bench by the Oregon Trail's actual route. Open all year.

K. Powder River. A mile below Phillips Lake's dam (16 miles south of Baker City on Highway 7), paved riverside trails visit an all-accessible picnic area and fishing dock. About half of the 1-mile path system is accessible.

L. Anthony Lake. High in the Elkhorn Range, a graveled path loops 1 mile around this alpine lake. See Hike #40.

Stump Dodger Railroad loop.

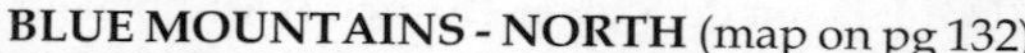

BLUE MOUNTAINS - NORTH (map on pg 132)

M. Jubilee Lake. Only half a mile is paved of the 2.5-mile path around this lake in the Blue Mountains, but adventurous wheelchair users can make it all the way around. See Hike #44.

N. Oregon Trail Interpretive Park. See Oregon Trail wagon ruts and excellent outdoor interpretive displays on a paved 0.5-mile loop in the Blue Mountain forest. Between La Grande and Pendleton, take I-84 exit 248, follow signs 3.3 miles. Open 9am-7pm daily (except Mondays) from Memorial Day to Labor Day.

HELLS CANYON (map on page 142)

O. Granny View Vista. Incredible views of the vast Imnaha River canyon open up at each turn on this 0.3-mile loop. Along the wide gravel path, expect dense alpine wildflowers in June and July, including paintbrush, penstemon, larkspur, and balsamroot. All-accessible restroom. Drive as to Hat Point (Hike #49), but only drive 17.4 miles up the steep gravel road from Imnaha.

P. Hat Point. Perched on the edge of Hells Canyon, a paved 0.3-mile path loops through a picnic area to a viewpoint. A separate 0.1-mile paved path spirals up to the base of the Hat Point fire lookout tower itself. See Hike #49.

WALLOWA MOUNTAINS (map on page 158)

Q. Mount Howard. The gondolas of the Wallowa Lake Tramway are wheelchair accessible, allowing everyone to ride up the mountain, although the broad dirt paths on top are not maintained expressly for wheelchairs. See Hike #56.

HIGH DESERT (map on page 206)

R. Klamath Falls railroad. The OC&E Woods Line State Trail is paved for 0.6 mile from Klamath Falls' East Main St to Washburn Way, and then for another 3.3 miles from Washburn Way in Klamath Falls to Highway 39. The route features a historic 1898 railroad bridge and nice trailheads. See Hike #83.

S. Link River in Klamath Falls. The Link River Trail is blocked by turnstiles at either end, but the gravel Wingwatchers' Trail is passable for wheelchairs from Main Street for 0.4 mile to the cattail slough. See Hike #84.

99 More Hikes in Eastern Oregon

Adventurous hikers can explore lots of additional paths in Eastern Oregon. Many of the trails listed below are rough or unmarked, and descriptions are brief, so be sure to bring appropriate maps. Unless noted, mileages given are one-way, not round-trip. Symbols after each entry identify trails suitable for children, winter use, backpackers, equestrians, and mountain bikers.

For more information, check with the trail's administrative agency, abbreviated as follows: (BE)-Bend-Fort Rock Ranger District, (BLM-L)-BLM Lakeview District, (BLM-P)-BLM Prineville District, (BLM-V)-BLM Vale District, (BL)-Bly Ranger District, (BM)-Blue Mountain Ranger District, (E)-Eagle Cap Ranger District, (HC)-Hells Canyon National Recreation Area, (HE)-Heppner Ranger District, (LA)-Lakeview Ranger District, (LG)-La Grande Ranger District, (LM)-Lookout Mountain Ranger District, (N)-North Fork John Day Ranger District, (O)-Oregon State Parks, (PA)-Paulina Ranger District, (PC)-Prairie City Ranger District, (PO)-Pomeroy Ranger District, (PY)-Paisley Ranger District, (WA)-Wallowa Valley Ranger District, (WH)-Whitman Ranger District, (WW)-Walla Walla Ranger District. Phone numbers for agencies are on page 37.

Easy | Moderate | Difficult

COLUMBIA PLATEAU
(map on page 38)

● **101. White River Falls.** This colossal 3-part waterfall in the desert is hidden at an unassuming state park wayside. Drive Hwy 197 between The Dalles and Maupin to milepost 34 in Tygh Valley and turn east onto Hwy 216 for 4 miles. A park path descends 200 feet in 0.2 miles to

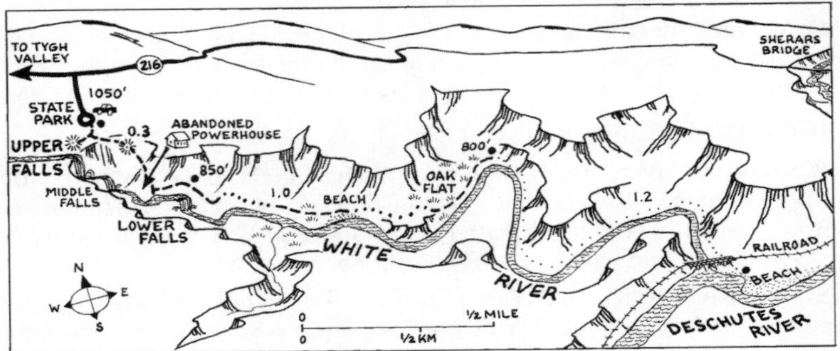

an abandoned powerhouse near the middle falls. A rougher route (with poison oak) continues a mile down the White River. Bushwhackers can scramble another 1.2 miles to the Deschutes River confluence. (O)

CENTRAL OREGON (map, p. 58)

102. Boyd Cave. Bring a flashlight and coat to explore this lava tube. Drive 2 miles south of Bend on Hwy 97 to Baker Rd/Knott Rd Exit #143, turn east on Knott Road for 1.2 miles, turn right on paved China Hat Road 18 for 9 miles, and turn left onto rough dirt Road 242 for 0.2 mile to the parking turnaround at road's end *(GPS location 43.942, -121.198)*. Descend a metal staircase and hike 0.2 mile to the cave's end. Two other nearby lava tubes, Skeleton Cave and Wind Cave, are permanently gated to protect bats and deter vandals. (BE)

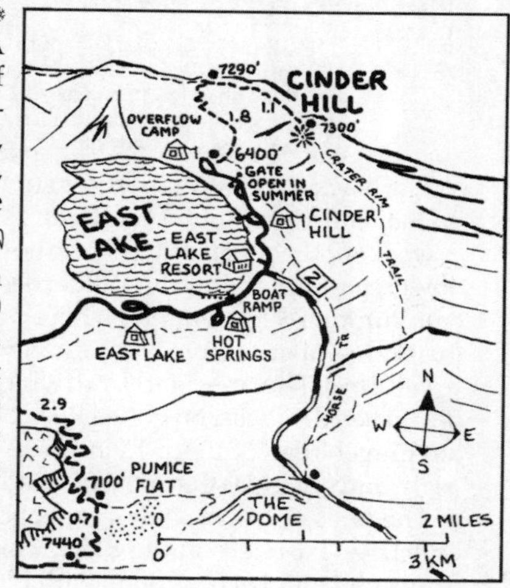

103. Newberry Caldera Rim. A 21-mile loop traces wooded rim of gigantic, collapsed volcano in Newberry National Volcanic Monument, passing views at North Paulina Peak, Cinder Hill, and Paulina Peak (Hike #14). (BE)

104. Cinder Hill. Climb to a view on Newberry Caldera's rim, gaining 1000 feet in 2.9 miles. Drive to Hike #14, continue 4.6 paved miles, and keep left through Cinder Hill Campground to the far end of the overflow loop. Hike 1.8 miles up to the rim and turn right 1.1 mile to the viewpoint. (BE)

OCHOCO MOUNTAINS
(map on page 74)

105. Owl Creek. A level trail amid junipers follows the shore 1.7 miles from Prineville Reservoir State Park's site B-14 to Jasper Point, and from the end of its parking loop another 0.6 mile. From Prineville, follow reservoir signs 16 miles south on Juniper Canyon Road.

106. Wildcat Trail via White Rock. This path traces the wooded rim of Mill Creek Wilderness 2.9 miles, where you can turn left on the Belknap Trail 2.8 miles down through a 1995 fire zone and turn left along Mill Creek 2.9 miles to Wildcat Campground (Hike #19). The 8.6-mile route loses 1630 feet. Drive Hwy 26 east of Prineville 24 miles, turn left at a sign for Wildcat Mountain for 6 miles on gravel Rd 3350, and turn right on Rd 300 for 2 miles to primitive White Rock Campground. (LM)

107. Wildcat Trail via Whistler Spring. Follow a wooded ridge into the Mill Cr Wilderness, losing 1000 feet and gaining 560 feet in 7.4 miles. Then either turn right on the Belknap Trail to Wildcat Campground (5.7 miles) or

Easy Moderate Difficult

go straight on the Wildcat Trail 2.9 miles to White Rock Campground (Hike #106). Drive past the upper Twin Pillar Trailhead (see Hike #19 map) and continue 3.2 miles on dirt Rd 27 to Whistler Spring Campground. (LM)

●● **108. Lookout Mountain via Ochoco Cabin.** This route to Lookout Mountain's summit is longer than Hike #20, gaining 2930 feet in 7.3 miles, but offers two other turnaround points—woodsy Duncan Butte (2.9 miles and 1600 feet up) and North Point's rimrock viewpoint (6.1 miles and 2600 feet up). Start at a highway pullout 0.1 mile east of the rentable Ochoco Cabin (see Hike #20). (LM)

● **109. Lookout Mountain's South Point.** A backdoor route to Lookout Mountain's prairie, the Line Butte Trail gains 1000 feet in 3.9 miles (keep right at junctions) to South Point's rimrock viewpoint. A side trail ambles 2.3 miles to Lookout Mountain's summit (Hike #20). Drive as to Hike #20 but continue straight on Rd 42 an extra 7 miles to Big Summit Prairie, turn right on Rd 4215 for 9 miles, turn right on Rd 4220 for 1 mile, and turn left on Rd 257 a mile to the Fawn Creek Trailhead. (LM)

110. Black Canyon

Moderate (to Black Canyon Creek)
5 miles round trip
1020 feet elevation **loss**
Open late May to mid-November
Use: hikers, horses

Difficult (to Second Crossing)
7.8 miles round trip
3240 feet elevation gain

The Black Canyon Wilderness stretches from the Ochoco Mountains' high forests to the South Fork John Day River's sagebrush canyonlands. There's room here for a weekend backpacking trek or horse trip, but hikers have trouble accessing the lower, eastern end of the Wilderness, where an iffy river ford is passable only in late summer's low water. So here's an easier, backdoor route to the high country. Just remember to save some energy for the return climb back out of the canyon.

Getting There— Start by driving to the Rock Creek Trailhead described in Hike #25. Then drive east on gravel Road 38 for 3.1 miles to a 4-way junction and turn right on gravel Road 5810 for 1.2 miles to a high meadow with a parking pullout on the right and a sign for the Boeing Field Trail on the left *(GPS location 44.3427, -119.7312).*

The path descends half a mile, hops across Owl Creek, and climbs briefly to a junction. Turn left on the Black Canyon Trail. In the next 2 miles you'll descend through Douglas fir woods with blue huckleberries (ripe in August), elderberry, lupine, and gooseberry. The path recrosses Owl Creek and then reaches the

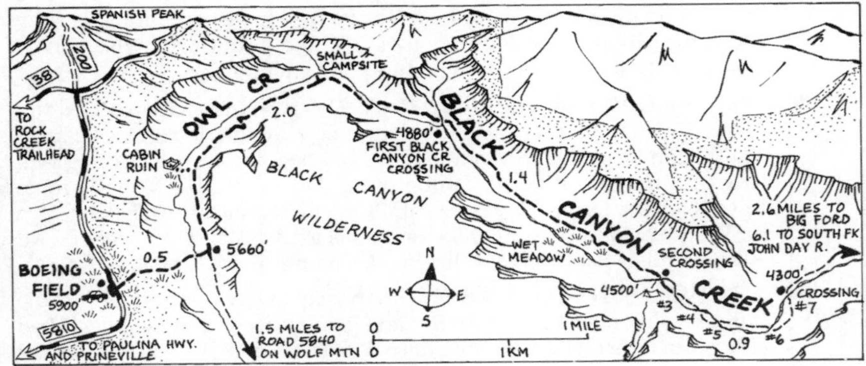

confluence of Owl Creek and Black Canyon Creek—a good turnaround point.

If you'd like a longer hike, hop across Black Canyon Creek and continue downstream 1.4 miles to the second of this creek's many bridgeless crossings. (PA)

111. Black Canyon via Wolf Mountain. A slightly longer route into the Black Canyon Wilderness than via Boeing Field (Hike #110), this trail starts near the historic 107-foot-tall Wolf Mountain lookout tower, built in 1947 and still staffed from June to October. Drive as to Hike #110, but continue 1.5 miles on Rd 5810, and turn left on rough Rd 5840 for 2.2 miles to a junction. The tower is left 0.3 mile; the trailhead is straight 0.2 mile. The trail loses 1450 feet in 3.5 miles to a crossing of Black Canyon Creek. (PA)

112. Black Canyon via South Prong. The South Prong Trail contours 3 miles through woods to Crowbar Spring, then dives down 1750 feet in 2.6 miles to Big Ford, a bridgeless crossing in the heart of the Black Canyon Wilderness. Drive 1 mile east of Prineville, turn right on the Paulina Hwy 59.5 miles, turn left to Rager Ranger Station 11 miles, continue on Rd 58 another 4.4 miles, turn left on Rd 5840 for 7 miles, and turn right on Rd 400 to the NE corner of Mud Spring Campground. (PA)

113. Cottonwood Creek. The east end of the 23.5-mile Ochoco Mountain Trail begins at the Payten Trailhead. Drive to the trailhead for Hike #25, continue straight on Rd 38 an extra 3.1 miles to a 4-way junction, and go straight on Rd 38 for 11.2 miles to the junction of Rd 700. The trail drops 1500 feet in 3 miles to the forks of Cottonwood Creek and then climbs west 7.6 miles to Rd 200 on Spanish Peak (Hike #25). (PA)

The summit of Fields Peak.

114. Fields Peak. A 2.2-mile trail (open to all-terrain vehicles) gains 1850 feet to this peak's panoramic view of the John Day Valley. Drive Hwy 26 east of Dayville 13 miles, turn south on paved Fields Creek Road 8.6 miles, turn left on gravel Road 115 for 0.4 mile, turn right on Road 2160 for 0.1 mile, and fork left on rough Road 041 for 1.2 miles to the McClellan Trailhead *(GPS location 44.3217, -119.266).* (BM)

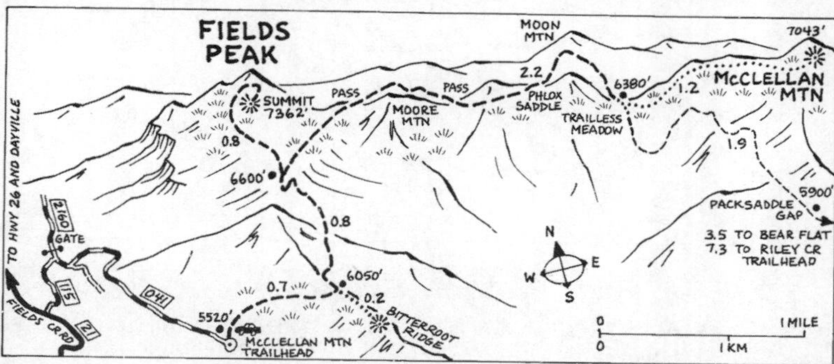

115. Aldrich Mountain Cedar Grove. Hike a 1-mile trail to a botanical oddity: 60 acres of Alaska cedars growing on an Eastern Oregon mountainside, 130 miles from other Alaska cedar stands. Drive Hwy 26 east of Dayville 13 miles (or west of John Day 18 miles), turn south on paved Fields Creek Rd 10 miles to a pass, and turn right on gravel Rd 2150 for 6 miles. (BM)

STRAWBERRY MOUNTAIN (map on page 99)

116. Nipple Butte. This unmaintained 3-mile ridgecrest trail to a craggy viewpoint north of John Day gains only about 500 feet, but is open to motorcycles. Drive Hwy 26 east of John Day 9.5 miles, turn left up Bear Creek on Rd 18 for 13 paved miles and 3 miles of gravel, and turn left on Rd 279 for 0.7 mile. (BM)

117. Magone Lake and Magone Slide. Circle this fishing lake on a 2-mile loop through pine woods from a campground, then cross a road and climb 0.7 mile to a landslide that created the lake in the 1860s. Drive Hwy 26 east of John Day 9.5 miles, turn left up Bear Creek on Rd 18 for 13 paved miles, turn left on gravel Rd 3620 for 1.2 miles, and turn right on Rd 3618 for 1.5 miles. (BM)

118. Arch Rock. Climb 0.3 mile to a natural arch in a cliff of welded ash. Drive Hwy 26 east of John Day 9.5 miles, turn left up Bear Creek on Rd 18 for 10 paved miles, turn right on gravel Rd 36 for 9 miles, and turn right on Rd 3650 for 0.7 miles. (BM)

119. Joaquin Miller Trail. A quiet 5.2-mile hike in the Strawberry Mtn Wilderness climbs through ponderosa pine woods that burned in a 2015 fire, but the route leads to a rocky knoll with a panoramic view, gaining 3250 feet. Drive Hwy 395 south from John Day 9.7 miles to a brown recreation pointer, turn left on County Rd 65 for 2.9 paved miles, turn left on gravel Rd 6510 at a sign for Alder Gulch, and keep left on Rd 6510 for 5 miles to its end, in an unbuned forest. The trail climbs 0.3 mile to a wire fence at a hilltop. Here the 2015 fire zone begins, with snowbrush and snags for the next 4 miles. (BM)

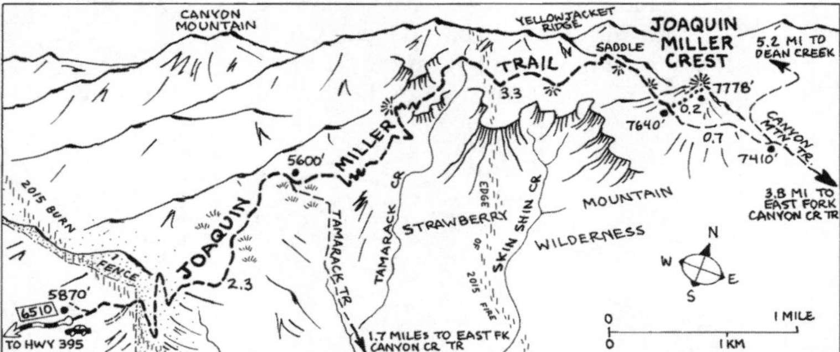

120. East Fork Canyon Creek

Easy (to Brookling Creek)
5.8 miles round trip
580 feet elevation gain
Open June through November
Use: hikers, horses

Difficult (Around Indian Cr Butte)
20.3-mile loop
3240 feet elevation gain
Open mid-July to early November

A 2015 wildfire burned the trailhead and the lower 3 miles of this trail, but the

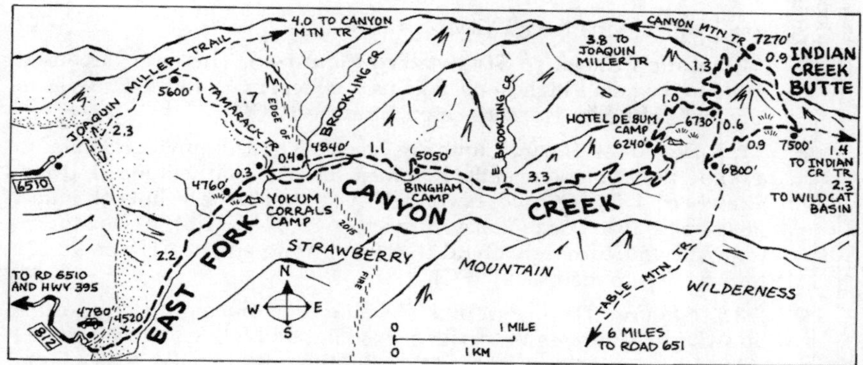

upper portion is still green and the views atop the Strawberry Range remain. In fall, dogwood and cottonwood trees fire the canyon with color.

Getting There — Take Highway 395 south from John Day toward Burns 10 miles to milepost 10C. At a brown recreation sign, turn left on paved, two-lane County Road 65 for 2.9 miles. Then turn left onto gravel Road 6510 at a sign for "Alder Gulch; Fawn Spring". Keep left on this road for 1.6 miles, and then turn right on Road 812 for 2.8 miles to a large gravel parking lot at road's end. Equestrians will find a loading ramp and hitching posts here.

The dusty trail sets off downhill through a shadeless slope of sagebrush and snags, crosses a rockslide, joins the creek, and heads upstream. After 2.2 miles a faint fork to the right leads across a grassy flat 300 feet to Yokum Corrals Camp, a possible campsite near the creek. In another 0.3 mile you'll cross Tamarack Creek (usually dry) and the junction with the Tamarack Creek Trail. Keep straight for another 0.4 mile and you'll reach 10-foot wide Brookling Creek, where the fire stopped. This shallow stream isn't an obstacle to serious hikers, but there is no bridge, so it's a possible turnaround point.

It's also possible to avoid bridgeless Brookling Creek by taking a detour path to the right at the Tamarack Trail junction. Another 4.4 miles up this greener portion of the canyon is Hotel De Bum Camp, a small campsite at the creek's headwaters. A subalpine marsh here offers a view of Indian Creek Butte. Yet another mile up the trail is a junction for the faint 3.7-mile loop around Indian Creek Butte. At the high point of that circuit, a 7500-foot saddle, adventurers can strike out cross-country up a rocky ridge 0.3 mile to the summit, with a view of the upper John Day Valley. (BM)

121. Table Mountain Trail. Climb a wooded ridgecrest into the Strawberry Mtn Wilderness. Gain 1500 feet in 3.7 miles to a viewpoint knoll, then continue level 2.3 miles to a junction with the 3.7-mile loop around Indian Creek Butte described in Hike #27. Drive south on Hwy 395 from John Day 9.7 miles, turn left on paved Rd 65 for 7.2 miles, and turn left on gravel Rd 651 for 3 miles. (BM)

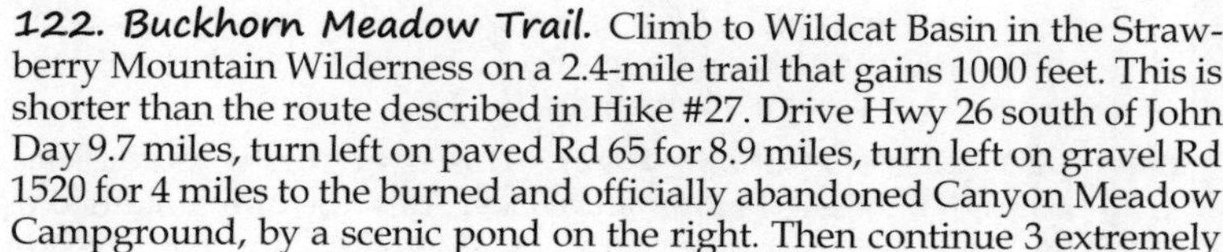

122. Buckhorn Meadow Trail. Climb to Wildcat Basin in the Strawberry Mountain Wilderness on a 2.4-mile trail that gains 1000 feet. This is shorter than the route described in Hike #27. Drive Hwy 26 south of John Day 9.7 miles, turn left on paved Rd 65 for 8.9 miles, turn left on gravel Rd 1520 for 4 miles to the burned and officially abandoned Canyon Meadow Campground, by a scenic pond on the right. Then continue 3 extremely

Easy Moderate Difficult

rough miles to road's end. (BM)

123. Onion Creek to Strawberry Mountain. This steep, less-used route to the area's highest peak gains 4000 feet in 4.9 miles. Drive as to Hike #29, but park 1.2 miles before Strawberry CG. (PC)

124. Big Riner Basin. Climb Big Creek's wooded canyon 5.8 miles to a Wilderness viewpoint at the head of a glacial cirque, gaining 2150 feet. Strawberry Lake is 4 miles beyond. Drive as to Hike #27, but continue 4 miles on Rd 16 to Logan Valley, turn left on Rd 924 for 2.5 miles to Murray Campground, turn right on Rd 1648 for 0.5 mile, and turn left on Rd 021 for 2.5 miles to road's end. (PC)

125. Skyline Trail. Part of a 37.1-mile route tracing the crest of the Strawberry Mountain Wilderness, this faint trail follows a dry, forested ridge 10 miles (gaining 2000 feet) to Big Riner Basin (Hike #124). From Prairie City drive 19.5 miles south on paved Rd 62 and turn right 1.4 miles on Rd 101. (PC)

126. Myrtle Creek. In a ponderosa pine canyon bordering the high desert, this trail ambles down along Myrtle Creek 2.1 miles to a junction. There you either climb right up West Myrtle Creek 2.7 miles to Rd 440, or continue down the main creek 6 miles to private land. Drive Hwy 395 north of Burns 18 miles and turn left on Rd 31 for 14 paved miles to a creek crossing. (Emigrant Creek Ranger District, 541-573-4300)

127. North Fork Malheur River. For a short hike, follow this river from its start as a mountain brook 2.8 miles down to the confluence of Crane Creek (Hike #128). Or continue 8.4 miles downriver through a canyon, losing 850 feet in all. From Prairie City, drive Rd 62 southeast for 8 miles, turn left on Rd 13 for 16.2 miles, turn right on paved Rd 16 for 2.2 miles, turn right on rough Rd 1675 for 3 miles to the North Fork Campground, and continue 1 mile to the trailhead. (PC)

128. Crane Creek. This 6.3-mile trail down Crane Creek's forested valley to the North Fork Malheur River (see Hike #127) begins as an abandoned road, and loses 1100 feet. From Prairie City, drive paved Rd 62 south 23 miles to Summit Prairie, keep left on paved Rd 16 for 4.5 miles, turn right on gravel Rd 1663 for 1 mile to Crane Creek, and fork left to a green metal gate at the start of the trail. (PC)

129. Little Baldy via Lookout Mountain. Stroll 3.6 miles along a panoramic ridge to a viewpoint of the John Day Valley. ATVs are allowed. From Prairie City, drive south on paved Rd 62 for 20.2 miles, turn left on gravel Rd 1665 for 4 miles, and turn left on very rough dirt Rd 548 past Sheep Mountain a total of 6 miles to a road closure at Lookout Mountain. Walk out the abandoned roadbed 2.5 miles and continue on a ridgecrest trail 1.1 mile to Little Baldy. Nearly level. (PC)

130. Lookout Mountainn via Sheep Creek. Gain 2400 feet in 5.2 miles through open woods along (often dry) Sheep Creek to Rd 548 at Lookout Mtn (Hike #129). From Prairie City, take Rd 62 southeast for 8 miles, and turn left on paved Rd 13 for 14.9 miles to a cattle guard and "Sheep Cr Tr" sign on the right. (PC)

131. Little Malheur River. This river begins as a creek tumbling through a forested mountain valley. Alas, the unmaintained trail along the creek is crisscrossed with blowdown logs and has seven bridgeless

Easy Moderate Difficult

crossings, so it's only for adventurers. From Hwy 26 in the middle of Prairie City turn south toward Depot Park 0.4 mile, turn left at a stop sign, keep straight on what becomes County Road 62 for 8 miles, turn left on paved Road 13 for 11.7 miles, turn left onto gravel Road 1370, and keep left 5 miles to the trailhead *(GPS location 44.3208, -118.3763)*. (PC)

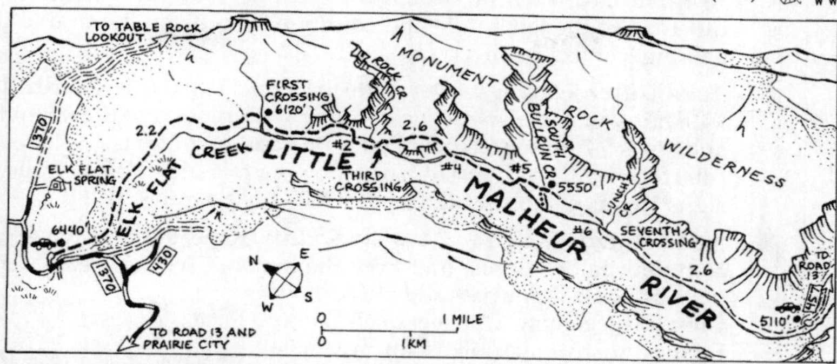

132. Bullrun Rock via Road 6010. If you're coming from Baker City or Ontario, try this route into the Monument Rock Wilderness instead of Hike #32. Take Hwy 26 to Unity, turn west on Rd 600 for 4.2 paved miles and another 3 miles on gravel, and turn left on Rd 6010 for 5.2 miles. Trail 1973 gains 1300 feet in 4.3 miles to a gate at Bullrun Rock. (WH)

133. Davis Creek Trail. This woodsy 7.8-mile path contours around Dixie Butte, crossing three creeks to Rd 2050. For a day hike, go 3.8 miles to Deerhorn Creek, gaining 400 feet. From Hwy 26 at Austin Junction, drive 0.2 mile toward John Day and turn right on gravel Rd 2614 for 2 miles to the trailhead on the left. (BM)

BLUE MOUNTAINS - SOUTH (map on page 112)

134. Oregon Trail Interpretive Center. This first-rate museum will reopen in 2023 after renovations. A hiking loop here visits a replica gold mine, a viewpoint, and a covered wagon on the Oregon Trail's ruts. The 2.9-mile loop gains 340 feet of elevation. See page 111. (541-523-1843)

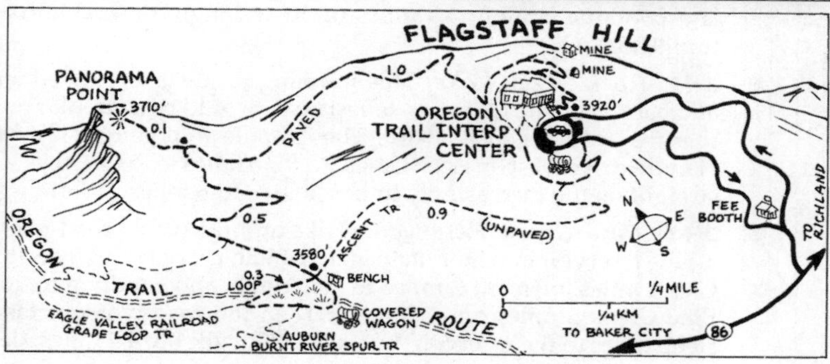

Easy Moderate Difficult

135. Van Patten Lake. Climb to a gorgeous alpine lake in a granite cirque. From I-84 at North Powder exit 285, follow Anthony Lake signs 18.4 miles, turn left on Rd 130 for 0.2 mile, and park. Walk up a steep dirt road to the left 1 mile and continue 0.5 mile on the trail to the lake, gaining 970 feet in all. (WH)

136. Dutch Flat. A shorter route to Dutch Flat Lake is described in Hike #40, but you can also ascend a valley with pines, meadows, old mines, and cows 5.7 miles to Dutch Flat. Continue 1.3 miles to the lake, gaining 2400 feet in all. From I-84 at North Powder exit 285, follow Anthony Lake signs 13 miles and turn left on Rd 7307 for 1.4 miles. (WH)

137. Peavy Trail to Cracker Saddle. Repeated fires have left snags along this faint 3.6-mile trail from the rentable, historic Peavy Cabin (see page 24) to an alpine pass and the Elkhorn Crest Trail, gaining 1700 feet of elevation. From Anthony Lake (Hike #40), drive 11.4 miles east on Rd 73 and turn left on gravel Rd 380 for 2.7 miles to the trailhead, 0.1 mile beyond the Peavy Cabin. (WH)

The rentable Peavy Cabin.

138. Cunningham Cove. A faint trail climbs steeply through woods to the Elkhorn Crest Trail, gaining 1930 feet in 2.8 miles. From Anthony Lake, drive Rd 73 east 11.4 miles, turn left on Rd 380 for 2.7 miles to road's end, 0.1 mile beyond the rentable 1934 Peavy Cabin (see page 24). (WH)

139. Summit Lake. This 22-acre subalpine lake (described in Hike #41) can also be accessed by a 1.2-mile trail that gains 1000 feet, but the access road is horrible. From Haines, drive 4 miles toward Anthony Lake, follow signs left through Muddy Creek and Bulger Flats 6 miles, and turn left on North Powder River Rd 7301 for 7 miles. (WH)

140. Red Mountain Lake. A steep trail gains 1100 feet in 1.3 miles to this alpine lake ringed by cliffs, but the road to the trailhead is horrible. Drive as to Hike #139 but go only 6 miles on Rd 7301. (WH)

141. Killamacue Lake. This trail follows Killamacue Creek to a lake basin high in the Elkhorn Range's crags, gaining 1800 feet in 3.2 miles. From Haines, drive west on Rock Creek Rd for 6 miles to Rock Creek and continue straight 4.5 miles on increasingly miserable road to the trailhead. (WH)

142. Rock Creek Lake. This stunning cirque lake, banked with snow and backed by the Elkhorns' tallest peak, would be a popular goal except that the access road is awful. The 3.5-mile trail gains 2400 feet. From Haines, drive west on Rock Creek Rd for 6 miles to Rock Creek. Continue straight on the increasingly impossible road 6 miles. (WH)

143. Pine Creek Reservoir. Hike an undrivable road past a scenic alpine reservoir into mountain goat habitat. Drive Hwy 30 north of Baker City 4 miles, turn left 2 miles to Wingville, and continue on Rd 646 up Pine Creek 5 miles on pavement. Then the road worsens fast. It's 5.4 steep miles to the reservoir, but expect to walk 1 to 4.4 miles, depending

Easy Moderate Difficult

on your car. (WH)

144. Phillips Reservoir. Paths through open pine woods along this reservoir's shore are best for mountain bikers or equestrians, and only then if the reservoir is full. From the popular Union Creek Campground (west of Baker City 19 miles on Hwy 7), take the North Shore Trail 4 miles west or 1.7 miles east. The South Shore Trail extends 6 miles from the south end of Mason Dam to Southwest Shore Campground. (WH)

145. Indian Rock Trail. Open to motorcycles, this 1.6-mile trail climbs 600 feet to a viewpoint of Phillips Reservoir. Start across Hwy 7 from the Union Creek Campground entrance. (WH)

146. South Fork Desolation Creek. Two trails now start at this quiet trailhead, making possible a 15-mile loop into the Greenhorn Range. First hike up the creek's forested valley 7 miles to the Portland Mine and continue 0.8 mile on an old road to Dupratt Spring Saddle (see Hike #34), gaining 2200 feet. Then keep left at junctions to return via Saddle Camp. Drive as to Hike #34, but continue past Olive Lake 6 miles on Rd 10 and turn left on Rd 45 for 1 mile. (N)

147. Indian Rock and Princess Trail. In woods regrowing from an old fire atop the Greenhorn Range, a 3.1-mile trail gains 800 feet to a junction near Head O'Boulder Camp. To the right, climb 0.8 mile to th eIndian Rock Lookout building on an ancient road, or venture straight on the unmaintained Princess Trail for 6 faint miles to Dupratt Spring Pass. Drive as to Hike #34, but continue 6 miles past Olive Lake on Rd 10 and turn left on Rd 45 for 4.5 miles to a pass. (N)

148. Lake Creek. From the Greenhorn Mountains at Saddle Camp (see Hike #34) hike 4.7 miles north down Saddle Ridge to a crossing of Rd 10 (east of Olive Lake 4.1 miles at pole fence gates). If you like, continue 7.5 miles to Granite Creek in the North Fork John Day Wilderness (see Hike #35). (N)

149. Lower North Fork John Day River. Ponderosa pines line the lower, western end of the 29.7-mile North Fork John Day River Trail (see also Hikes #35 and #36). Drive Hwy 395 south of Ukiah 14 miles (or north of Dale 1 mile), turn east on gravel Rd 55 for 5.5 miles, and then go straight on Rd 5506 for 6.5 miles of gravel and 3 miles of dirt road. The trail's first 3 miles are open to ATVs. (N)

150. Winom Creek. For a 10.2-mile loop in the North Fork John Day Wilderness canyonlands, start at Winom Campground, descend the Winom Creek Trail 4 miles, turn left up Big Creek Trail 4.5 miles, turn left on a tie trail 1.2 miles, and follow the campground road 0.5 mile left to your car. Cumulative elevation gain is 1700 feet. From Ukiah, drive the paved Blue Mountain Byway (Rd 52) southeast 23 miles and turn right on Rd 440 a mile. (N)

151. Tower Mountain. Start at Winom Campground (Hike #150), but take the Upper Winom Trail up 4.4 miles, turn right on the ridgecrest Cable Creek Trail 3 miles, and turn right on dirt Rd 5226 for 0.8 mile to the staffed Tower Mountain lookout, gaining 2400 feet. For a 16-mile loop, descend Trail 3156 to Big Creek Meadows and turn right on a tie trail. (N)

152. Silver Butte. From Ukiah, drive the paved Blue Mountain Byway (Rd 52) southeast for 25 miles, then turn right on Rd 5225 for 5 miles of

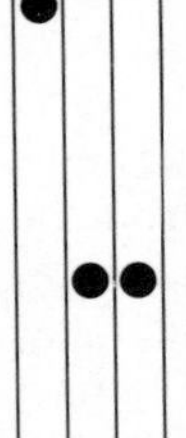

gravel and 4.5 miles of dirt. Hike the Silver Butte Trail along a ridge in the Wilderness 3.3 miles to a fork and a viewpoint of the river canyon. An optional 4.6-mile loop continues steeply down to the North Fork John Day River (see Granite Creek Hike #35). (N)

BLUE MOUNTAINS - NORTH (map on page 132)

153. Columbia River Railroad. Converted to a hiker/biker path, this abandoned, 4.8-mile gravel railroad grade along the scenic, windy Columbia River shore begins at McNary Beach Park, ends at Hat Rock State Park (picnic area, lake, historic rock). From I-82 in Umatilla, take Hwy 730 east 1.2 miles and follow McNary Beach signs left. (O)

154. Buck Creek and Buck Mountain. Two other Wilderness trails begin at the trailhead for Ninemile Ridge (Hike #155). The well-built Buck Creek Trail goes upstream 3 miles to a ford and climbs a ridge 3 miles to an upper trailhead. The faint, rough Buck Mountain Trail zooms up 2100 feet in 2.2 miles, contours along a rim 5.7 miles (crossing clearcuts and logging roads) to Buck Creek Trail's upper trailhead, making a 13.9-mile loop possible. (WW)

155. Ninemile Ridge

Difficult (to summit cairn)
7.2 miles round trip
2150 feet elevation gain
Open mid-July to early November
Use: hikers, horses

This trail climbs up, up, and up a grassy ridge to increasingly beautiful wildflower fields and viewpoints in the heart of the North Fork Umatilla Wilderness.

Getting There— Drive as for Hike #43 (North Fork Umatilla River), but when you reach the trailhead turnoff for the North Fork Umatilla Trail, cotinue straight on gravel Road 32 another 0.4 mile. A quarter mile beyond the Umatilla Forks Campground, veer left onto rocky Road 045 for 0.2 mile to a turnaround at road's end.

At the end of the parking turnaround, walk past several boulders on a broad path for 200 feet to a 4-way trail junction. Turn left, ignoring the Buck Creek Trail to the right. In another 0.1 mile you'll reach a T-shaped trail junction. Turn right past a Wilderness boundary sign on a steeper path that starts climbing up Ninemile Ridge in earnest. Almost immediately you leave the lush fir forest behind and climb through a drier band of big ponderosa pines. Then the trees give out altogether and you enter a steep grassland brightened with early summer wildflowers.

At the 2-mile mark the trail reaches a crest and turns east, marching up the back

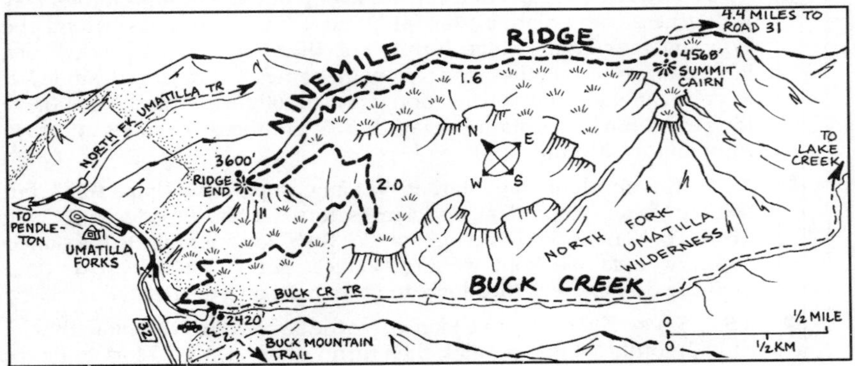

of Ninemile Ridge's spine. When the trail finally crosses the broad, grassy summit of Ninemile Ridge at the 3.6-mile mark, leave the path and walk 300 feet across a field to a 4-foot-tall rockpile, the summit cairn. Turn back here. Although the trail continues along Ninemile Ridge 3.6 miles, the tread becomes faint and the ridgecrest rollercoasters down and up. The final 0.7 mile traces an abandoned road (the Umatilla Rim Trail) to the Ninemile Ridge Trailhead on paved Road 31. (WW)

Ninemile Ridge.

156. Lookingglass Creek. The Eagle-Luger Trail crosses the forested canyon of this mountain stream. From Tollgate on Highway 204, drive east 4 miles to Woodland Campground and veer left on gravel Rd 3725 for 0.8 mile. The trail loses 1200 feet in 4.9 miles to a footbridge over Lookingglass Creek, then climbs 1.3 miles to a campsite at Luger Springs on a spur of Rd 63. (WW)

157. Upper Wenaha River

Moderate (to river ford)	**Difficult** (to Milk Creek ford)
4.6 miles round trip	**9 miles** round trip
850 feet elevation **loss**	**1300 feet** elevation **loss**
Open June through November	**Open** mid-July to early November
Use: hikers, horses	

The 31.4-mile Wenaha River Trail traces a gigantic canyon through the Wenaha-Tucannon Wilderness along the Oregon-Washington border. Here at the trail's upper end you can see the river begin at a high mountain spring in an old-growth larch forest. After just 2.3 miles the river has grown so large that hikers can't cross it with dry feet.

The old guard station at Timothy Springs.

Getting There— From Interstate 84 in Pendleton, take exit 210 and follow "Milton-Freewater" signs through Pendleton and onto Highway 11 for 20.5 miles. Between mileposts 20 and 21, turn right at a sign for Elgin, and in another 0.8 mile fork left to keep heading toward Elgin on Tollgate Road (Highway 204). After 19.9 miles (beyond the Tollgate Store 1.2 miles), turn left at a sign for Jubilee Lake onto Road 64. (If you're coming from La Grande, take Highway 82 north 20 miles to Elgin and turn left on Highway 204 for 22 miles to this junction.)

Follow gravel Road 64 north of Highway 204 for 13.5 miles. At a fork 2 miles past Jubilee Lake, veer left to stay on Road 64. In another 1.7 miles fork right to stay on Road 64. After 0.6 mile, turn right on gravel Road 6415 for 3 miles to a sign for the Timothy Springs Campground on the left. Take the middle road through a meadow, ignoring spurs to a historic guard station on the left and to the primitive campground's three picnic tables on the right. After 0.2 mile, park by posts marking the Wilderness boundary *(GPS location 45.866, -117.8922).*

The trail descends 2 miles through the woods, then hops on rocks across a 7-foot-wide creek, and continues 0.3 mile to a more serious crossing of the 20-foot-wide, foot-deep South Fork Wenaha River. Equestrians can simply splash across, but

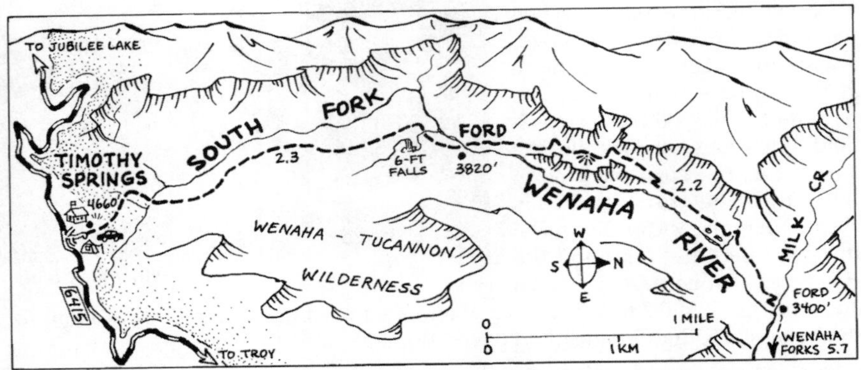

hikers will have to wade. Backpackers who continue can follow the Wenaha River Trail downstream for two or three days to Troy (Hike #45). (PO)

158. Wenaha River via Hoodoo Trail. This Wilderness trail switchbacks down 1400 feet in 3 miles to a thigh-deep river ford at the Wenaha River Trail (2.2 miles west of the Crooked Creek bridge site). From Troy, drive toward Elk Flats on gravel Rd 62 for 13 miles and turn right on Rd 6214 for 5 miles. (PO)

159. Wenaha River via Cross Canyon Trail. A Wilderness trail switchbacks down 1760 feet in 2.7 miles to a thigh-deep river ford and the Wenaha River Trail (7.9 miles west of the Crooked Creek bridge site). From Troy, drive toward Elk Flats on gravel Rd 62 for 17 miles and turn right on Rd 6217 for 3 miles. (PO)

160. Wenaha River via Elk Flats. This woodsy 4.6-mile Wilderness trail loses 2100 feet to a knee-deep ford at Wenaha Forks. From Troy, follow Elk Flats signs on Rd 62 for 21 miles, and turn right on Rd 290 for 0.7 mile. (PO)

161. Round Butte. Follow an open, relatively level ridgecrest from Indian Campground into the Wenaha-Tucannon Wilderness 3.1 miles to a saddle. Either bushwhack left 0.3 mile to Round Butte's viewpoint (gaining 300 feet) or continue 6 miles to Wenaha Forks, losing 2800 feet. From Walla Walla, drive east on a paved road up Mill Creek 12 miles to Kooskooskie, continue on what becomes gravel Rd 65 for 16 miles, and turn left on Rd 64 for 5.5 miles. (PO)

162. Bull Prairie Lake. Start at a 30-site campground with 3 fishing piers and hike 1.1 mile around a lake stocked with trout. From Heppner, drive Hwy 207 south toward Spray 44 miles and turn left on Rd 2039 for 3 miles. (HE)

HELLS CANYON (map on page 142)

163. Dug Bar

Easy (to Dug Bar viewpoint)
1.2 miles round trip
480 feet elevation gain
Open all year
Use: hikers, horses

Difficult (to Deep Creek)
8.6 miles round trip
1700 feet elevation gain

When the U.S. Army forced Chief Joseph to leave Oregon in 1877 he led his Nez

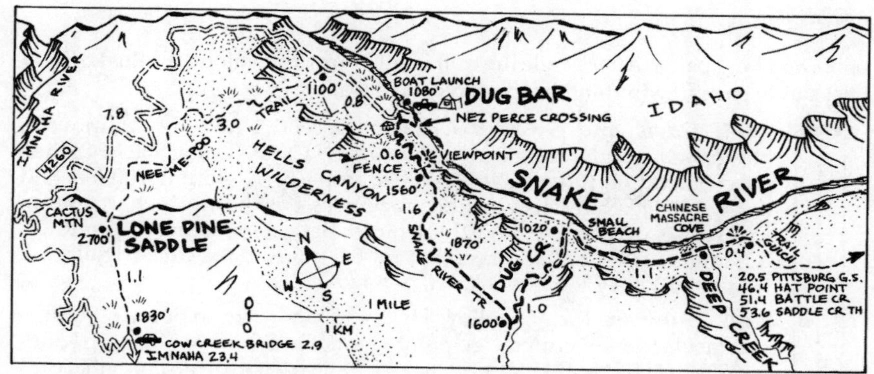

Perce band through Hells Canyon on a trail that crossed the raging Snake River at Dug Bar. Today that remote crossing site is still a trailhead amid colossal canyon scenery. It's also the only place where vehicles can drive to the Oregon shore of the Snake River in the heart of Hells Canyon—but the access road is so long and rough that you're apt to be reminded of Chief Joseph's travails. Passenger cars are not recommended.

Getting There— Begin by topping off your tank at the gas station in downtown Joseph. Then turn east beside the station at a "Hells Canyon Scenic Byway" sign and follow signs 29 paved miles to the village of Imnaha. One block past the Imnaha store, turn left on Lower Imnaha Road for 6.6 paved miles to Fence Creek.

At this point the Lower Imnaha Road suddenly becomes a rutted, steep one-lane dirt road strewn with rocks. Turn back if you don't like the first 200 feet, because this typifies the 25.4 miles ahead. The first 14 miles to the Cow Creek Bridge will take you a full hour. Beyond the bridge, the 11.4 miles to Dug Bar are slightly worse, requiring another full hour. If you're hauling a horse trailer, park at the Cow Creek Bridge and ride horseback to Dug Bar. In that case you'll need to follow the road only for another 2.8 miles. When you reach a rock cairn and a small trail sign, turn right on the Nee-Me-Poo Trail *(GPS location 45.7909, -116.7362)* over Lone Pine Saddle. If you're driving the final miles to Dug Bar you'll eventually reach a wire gate. Continue 0.5 mile across the grassy bar, turn left at a ranch house, and go through a metal gate to a fork. Park here beside a restroom *(45.8041, -116.6869).* The left-hand road leads to a boat ramp, while the right-hand fork peters out in a free, primitive camping area.

The Snake River at Dug Bar.

From the restroom, walk back up the road 150 feet and turn left on the Snake River Trail, skirting the ranch corral. Keep uphill to the right on the main trail for 0.6 mile to climb to a spectacular viewpoint of Dug Bar just before a wire gate marking the Hells Canyon Wilderness boundary.

If you continue past the viewpoint, you'll amble for 1.6 nearly level miles to a cairn with a trail signpost. Turn left down Dug Creek on a fainter path that repeatedly splashes across the creek and wades through patches of poison ivy. Wear good boots and long pants. After a mile the trail finally turns right along the Snake River past sandy coves, swimming holes, and campsites. (HC)

164. Davis and Swamp Creeks. Descend 1 mile through lovely, old-growth ponderosa pine woods to Davis Creek (losing 900 feet), then cross Starvation Ridge 2.3 miles to Swamp Creek (gaining 700 feet and losing 1250 feet). Intensive cattle grazing lessens the area's charm. From Enterprise, drive Hwy 3 north 21 miles. Between mileposts 23 and 22, turn right on Rd 174 and keep left for 0.3 miles to the Chico Trailhead. (Wallowa Valley Ranger District, 541-426-4978)

165. Summit Ridge. Follow Hells Canyon's rim to Somers Point, a spectacular, rarely visited viewpoint a vertical mile above Pittsburg Landing. From Hat Point (Hike #49) drive 1.5 miles back toward Imnaha, turn right on rough dirt Rd 315 for 4.5 miles, and park at Warnock Corrals. Hike a nearly level, ancient road along rim 9.2 miles, veer right on trail toward Pittsburg 2.5 miles, and turn left along a rim 1 mile to Somers Point. (HC)

166. Temperance Creek. From Hells Canyon's rim at Warnock Corrals (Hike #165), trace this creek 9.9 miles down through Wilderness to the Snake River Trail (losing 5250 feet!) and turn north through the scenic gorge for 9.2 nearly level miles to Pittsburg Guard Station. (HC)

167. High Trail. Traverse the Hells Canyon Wilderness on a zigzagging trail along a grassy benchland halfway between the Oregon rim and the Snake River. From the Saddle Creek Trailhead (Hike #50), hike 4.6 miles across Freezeout Saddle, and turn left on the High Trail. From there it's 10.1 miles to the Hat Creek cabin and 39.8 miles to the Pittsburg Guard Station. (HC)

WALLOWA MOUNTAINS (map on page 158)

168. Lick Creek. This backdoor route to Imnaha Falls (Hike #53) climbs 2.8 miles up Lick Creek to Imnaha Divide (gaining 800 feet) and then descends 2.2 miles to Imnaha River, losing 1660 feet in the Eagle Cap Wilderness. Drive as to Hike #53, but continue south on paved Rd 39 an extra 3 miles to the Lick Creek Campground, turn right on gravel Rd 3925 for 0.2 mile, and turn right on Rd 015 for 2.2 miles. (HC)

169. Wing Ridge. More popular in winter than summer, this 10.1-mile loop from a sno-park gains 1300 feet in 2.5 miles through burned woods to Wing Ridge, descends 2.5 miles to Big Sheep Creek (see Hike #54 map), and turns left to return on the Tenderfoot Wagon Road. The loop passes two Nordic ski camp bases that can be rented from Wing Ridge Ski Tours (*wallowahuts.com*, 541-398-1980). Drive as to Hike #54, but stop at Salt Cr Summit Sno-park. (WA, 541-426-4978)

170. Frances Lake. The well-graded, dead-end trail to this large, beautiful, rarely visited mountain lake has 8.9 miles of switchbacks, so the 17.8-mile round-trip gains 4235 feet of elevation. In the town of Lostine, where Hwy 82 turns sharply, drive south on Lostine River Road

Frances Lake.

Easy Moderate Difficult

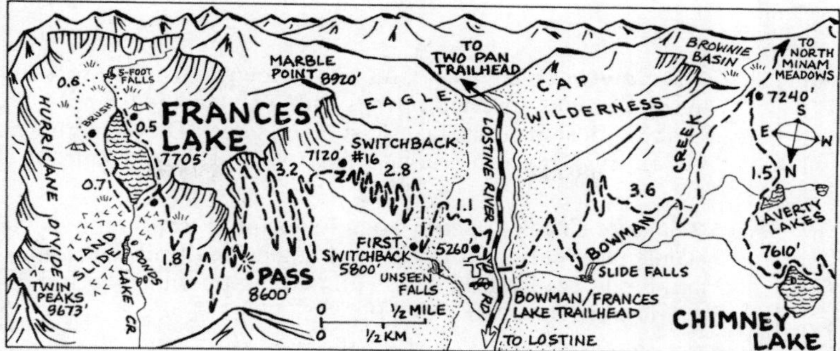

for 12.2 paved miles to the Lostine Guard Station. Continue on gravel another 2.9 miles to the Bowman/Frances Lake Trailhead. (E)

● **171. Huckleberry Mountain.** A panoramic view awaits at this former lookout site on an alpine ridge at the northern edge of the Eagle Cap Wilderness. The switchbacking 1.9-mi trail gains 1950 feet. Drive Hwy 82 to Wallowa, turn south on North Bear Creek Rd 8250 for 3.2 paved miles and another 5 miles of good gravel, then fork left on rougher gravel 7.4 miles, keeping uphill on the largest road at junctions to a parking area in Little Bear Saddle. Walk the gated road to the right half a mile to the old trailhead, just beyond Little Bear Creek *(GPS location 45.4302, -117.48).* (E)

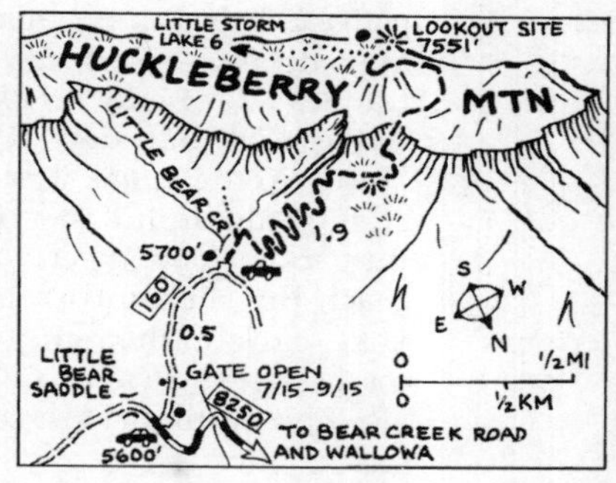

● **172. Cougar Ridge.** This faint, alternative 9.6-mile route to Standley Cabin (Hike #67) gradually gains 1600 feet along a dry, wooded ridge in Eagle Cap Wilderness. Drive as to Hike #67, but after 10.8 miles on Big Canyon Rd, keep right on Rd 8270 for 5.3 rough miles. (E)

● ● **173. Point Prominence and Mount Fanny.** Two peaks with classic views are accessible by rough dirt roads popular with ORVs. For Point Prominence, drive as to Hike #68, but just before the Rock Springs Trailhead follow "Pt. Prominence" sign to the right on Rd 6220 for 2 miles to Harris ORV camp and ride left up Rd 800 for 0.3 mile to a staffed lookout. For Mt. Fanny, park at Moss Spring Campground (Hike #69), follow Bellshears Trail signs 7 miles, and keep left 1 mile to summit. The 2 peaks can be connected with a 16.1-mile loop on roads, the Bellshears Trail, and Bell Trail. (LG)

● **174. Mule Peak Lookout.** Steep, faint trails make possible a grueling 11.4-mile loop to Mule Peak's abandoned lookout building (see Hike #71 map), gaining 3710 feet. From Union, drive Hwy 203 south 14.2 miles, turn left on gravel Rd 77 for 10 miles to a 5-way junction, and turn left on Rd 600 for 4 miles to South Fork Catherine Creek. Hike 3.1 miles, fork left 2.2 miles to Sand Pass, and keep right past Mule Peak to return on loop. (LG)

Easy Moderate Difficult

175. Sawtooth Crater. Climb to a viewpoint atop a rock knoll in the center of a giant, forested bowl, gaining 500 feet in 0.8 mile. From Hwy 203 at Medical Springs, take East Eagle Creek Drive 1.6 miles and fork right onto Collins Rd 70 for 5.6 miles to a trail sign on spur Rd 740 to left. (LG)

176. Fake Creek. A nearly abandoned 6-mile trail climbs 2000 feet over a scenic pass, connecting the West Eagle Trailhead (Hike #72) with the Main Eagle Trailhead (Hike #73), making possible a grand 3- or 4-day loop past Traverse Lake. (WH)

177. Crater Lake. Much smaller than Oregon's more famous Crater Lake, this pool's deep, circular basin is a dimple in an ancient glacier's bed. The demanding trail here gains 2970 feet in 5.9 miles of switchbacks. Park at the trailhead for Hidden Lake (Hike #75), but start at a "Little Kettle Creek Trail" sign on the uphill side of the parking loop. When you reach the shore of Crater Lake, circle to the right for the best views. Here you'll also find the tunnel that converted this lake to a reservoir. (WH)

Crater Lake in the Wallowas.

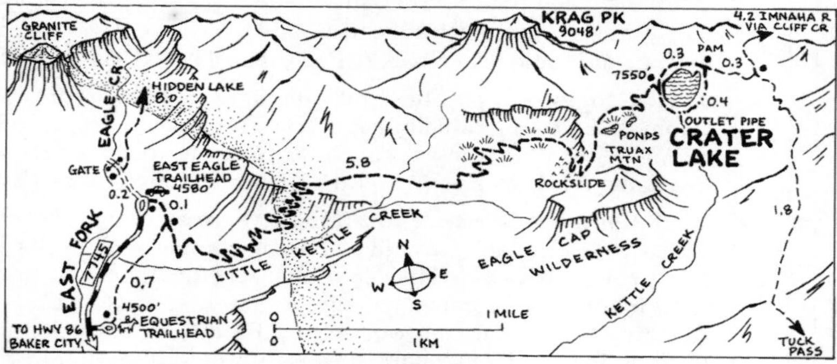

178. East Fork Falls. Park at the Cornucopia Trailhead (see Hike #77). Keep to the right at the pack station parking area and walk up an abandoned road 1.4 miles to East Fork Pine Creek's footbridge. Continue upstream 1.1 miles to 12-foot E Fk Falls, gaining 1200 feet in all. If you like, continue 4.6 miles to Blue Creek or 7.2 miles to the South Fork Imnaha River. (WH)

179. Deadman Canyon. Near Fish Lake Campground, climb 1.8 miles through open forest and high meadows heavily grazed by cattle to the Sugarloaf Trail. Jog left 0.3 mile, then continue right on the Deadman Canyon Trail 0.5 mile to a pass, gaining 650 feet in all. If you like, con-

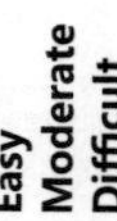

tinue down Deadman Canyon into the Eagle Cap Wilderness 3.5 miles to the South Fork Imnaha River near Imnaha Falls (Hike #53). Drive to downtown Halfway, continue straight on Main Street 0.6 mile, turn right and follow signs for Fish Lake 19.3 miles. Just beyond the Fish Lake Campground entrance, turn left on Rd 410 for 0.6 mile. (WH)

180. Twin Lakes. From a small lake with an 8-site campground, a faint 3.1-mile trail descends 1800 feet through burned woods to a South Fork Imnaha River ford at Blue Hole (see Hike #53). Drive as to Hike #179, but continue past Fish Lake 4.5 miles on Rd 66. (WH)

HIGH DESERT (map on page 206)

181. Silver Creek & Yamsay Mountain. Overswept by fire in about 2012, this northern portion of the Fremont Trail has become faint. Drive Hwy 31 west of the Silver Lake Ranger Station 0.3 mile, turn left on paved Rd 27 for 9.4 miles, turn right on gravel Rd 2804 for 2.6 miles, and fork left on Rd 7645 to a T-shaped junction. Turn left on Rd 036 and then keep right at junctions for 2.2 miles to the Antler Trailhead's 5-site campground. From there you can hike the Fremont Trail either downhill 8 miles along Silver Creek to Rd 27 or uphill 8.6 miles to Yamsay Mountain, gaining 2100 feet. (Silver Lake Ranger District 541-576-2107)

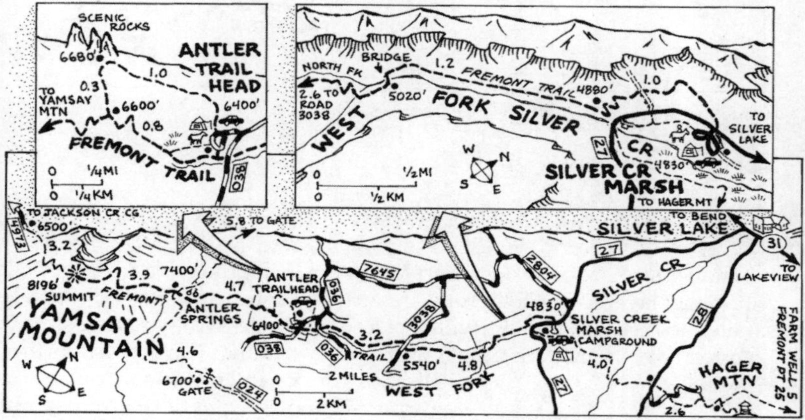

182. Hanan Trail. Follow the headwaters of the Sycan River through wildflower meadows to a viewpoint atop Winter Ridge's cliff, gaining 800 feet in 4.5 miles. The area has recovered well from a 2018 fire and was skipped by a 2021 fire, although the results of that blaze will close access roads until 2023. From Government Harvey Pass (see Hike #82 map), drive Rd 29 west 2 miles and turn left on Rd 28 for 4 miles. (Silver Lake Ranger District 541-576-2107)

183. Blue Lake. Perhaps the most popular hike in the Gearhart Mountain Wilderness gains 700 feet in 2.4 miles to Blue Lake, through woods that burned severely in 2021. Trails and roads in the area will remain closed until at least the summer of 2023. When they reopen, an 0.8-mile loop circles Blue Lake, and from there you can continue 4 miles to The Notch (see Hike #185). Drive paved Rd 28 as to Dead Horse Lake (Hike #186), but go 2.2 miles farther north on Rd 28, turn west on gravel Rd 3411 for 6 miles, turn left on Rd 3372 for 2 miles, and turn right on Rd 015 for 1.5

Easy Moderate Difficult

miles to the North Fork Trailhead. (BL)

184. Deming Creek to Boulder Spring. This backdoor route into the Gearhart Mountain Wilderness was closed by wildfire in 2021 but may reopen in the summer of 2023. The trail follows Deming Creek, gaining 2600 feet in 6 miles to the Gearhart Trail. Continue right 0.8 mile to a viewpoint at The Notch (see Hike #185). From Bly, drive Hwy 140 east 1.4 miles, turn left on Campbell Rd for 0.6 mile, turn right on paved Rd 34 for 4 miles, turn left on gravel Rd 335 for 1.5 miles, and turn right on Rd 018 up Deming Creek 3 miles to road's end. (BL)

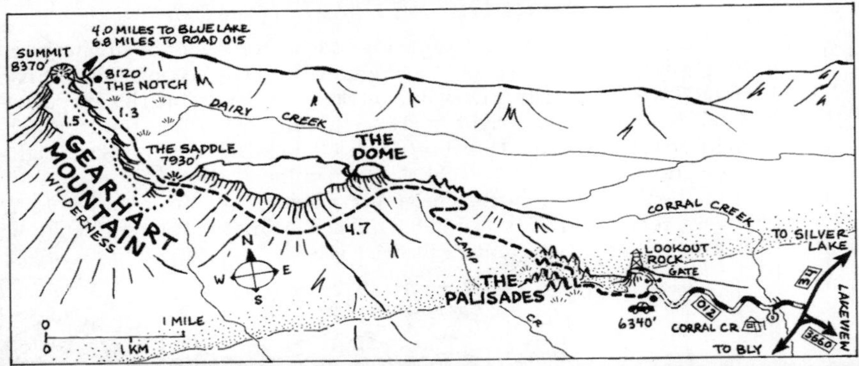

185. Gearhart Mountain

Difficult (to The Notch)
12 miles round trip
1920 feet elevation gain
Open mid-July through October
Use: hikers, horses

The centerpiece of the Gearhart Mountain Wilderness is a 8370-foot-tall ridge of strangely layered lava outcrops. Because the entire area burned severely in 2021, trails and access roads here will be closed until at least the summer of 2023. Patches of green trees remain in valleys and near timberline. The trail winds through The Palisades,a rock garden of 30-foot pillars arrayed like an army of gnomes. Later the path crosses two scenic passes snuggled below the mountain's summit cliffs. For the best view, bushwhack to the summit itself. Note that group size in the Wilderness is limited to ten "heartbeats," counting people and animals.

The Palisades.

Getting There— From Klamath Falls, drive east on Highway 140 toward Lakeview for 55 miles. Beyond the town of Bly 1.4 miles, turn left on Campbell Road for 0.5 mile, and then turn right onto narrow, pot-holed, paved Road 34 for 14.7 miles. At a sign for Corral Creek Campground, turn left on gravel Road 012 for 1.4 miles to the trailhead at road's end *(GPS location 42.4606, -120.801).* The final half mile is rough and steep.

If you're coming from Bend, drive Highway 97 south 29 miles and turn left on Highway 31 for 47 miles toward Silver Lake. Just beyond the Silver Lake Ranger Station, turn right toward East Bay Campground on paved Road 28 for 18 miles to

Gearhart Mountain.

a stop sign at a T-shaped junction. Then turn left to keep on Road 28 for another 40 miles (paved all the way), turn right on Road 34 for 10.4 miles to a pointer for the Corral Creek Campground, and turn right on gravel Road 012 for 1.5 miles to road's end. The final half mile is rough and steep.

At the trailhead, a road to the right with a locked green gate leads up 0.2 mile to Lookout Rock's fire tower, a possible side trip. The trail to Gearhart Mountain, however, starts on the left side of the trailhead turnaround. After 0.7 mile you'll enter The Palisades, where stratified andesite has weathered into pinnacles. At the 4.7-mile mark you'll reach a high saddle with wind-stunted whitebark pines *(GPS location 42.4823, -120.8657).* Ahead is a colossal view of Gearhart Mountain's summit and the alpine meadows at the head of Dairy Creek. This would make a satisfactory turnaround point for a day hike, except that the next 1.3 miles are the prettiest of all, crossing those alpine openings below the mountain's cliffs to an even better viewpoint at a pass called The Notch. Mosquitoes are a problem in July. (BL)

● **186. Campbell and Dead Horse Lakes.** The lodgepole pine forests here burned in 2012 and 2021, so trails and roads will be closed until at least the fall of 2023. From Campbell Lake, a 4.9-mile loop to a viewpoint atop Campbell Rim gains 810 feet of elevation. A 7.4-mile loop that adds Dead Horse Rim and Dead Horse Lake gains just 360 feet more. From Bend, drive Hwy 97 south 29

Campbell Lake before the 2021 wildfire.

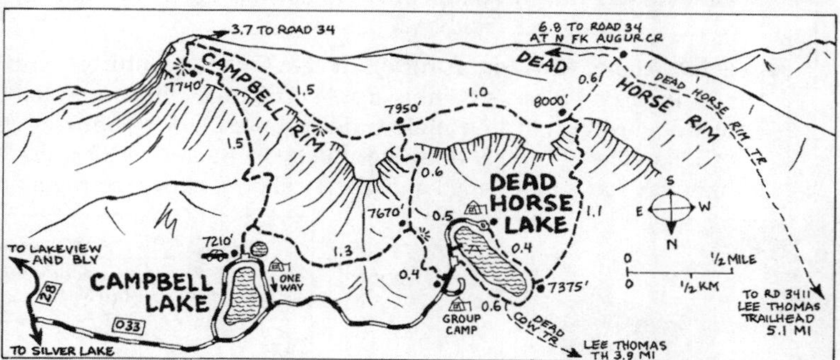

miles and turn left on Hwy 31 for 47 miles to Silver Lake. Near milepost 47 turn right on Road 28 for 18 miles to a stop sign, turn left to keep on Road 28 another 34 paved miles, turn right on gravel Road 033 1.7 miles, and turn left into the Campbell Lake Campground 0.4 mile. (PY)

●● **187. Dead Cow Trail to Dead Horse Lake.** Once popular with equestrians, a trail network here traverses lodgepole pine woods that burned in 2021. When trails reopen, perhaps in the fall of 2023, a 10.7-mile loop extends from Lee Thomas Trailhead to Dead Horse Lake (Hike #186). From Dead Horse Lake, return to paved Rd 28, follow it north 2.2 miles and turn left on gravel Rd 3411 for 4.4 miles to the trailhead. (PY)

188. *Chewaucan River to Moss Pass.* The 147-mile Fremont Trail atop the pine ridges of Lake County is faint and infrequently maintained. This 18-mile section burned in 2020, but still has great views, and is popular with equestrians or mountain bikers. From Highway 31 in Paisley, drive paved Road 33 west 9 miles to the Chewaucan Crossing Trailhead (elevation 4800′). The trail bridges the river, climbs 10 miles to a sweeping viewpoint atop 7234-foot Morgan Butte, and continues up and down for 8 miles to Road 3510 at Moss Pass (6400′). (PY)

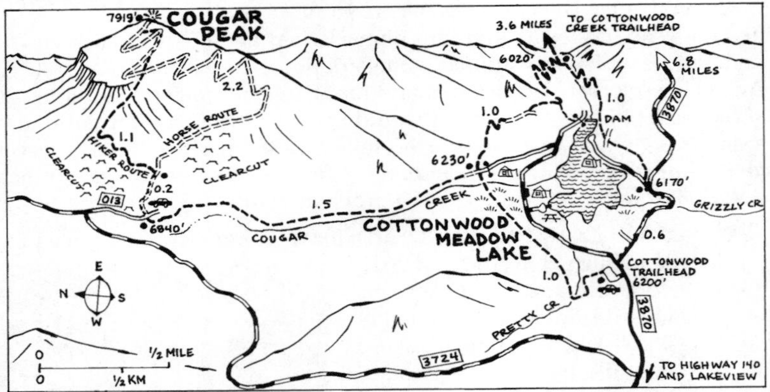

189. *Cougar Peak.* Narrowly missed by a 2021 wildfire, a 3.6-mile trail circles Cottonwood Meadow Lake, a pleasant little reservoir with campgrounds and picnic sites among the pines. An additional 6.6-mile loop climbs 1820 feet to Cougar Peak, with views from Mt. Shasta to Lakeview. Drive Hwy 140 east of Klamath Falls 74 miles (or west of Lakeview 22 miles). At milepost 74 turn north on Road 3870 for 5.8 miles to the Cottonwood Trailhead. (LA)

190. *Abert Rim via Juniper Creek.* Only adventurers with stamina and long pants can scramble up Abert Rim's cliffy face, gaining 2100 feet of elevation in 1.6 rough, trailless miles. Drive Highway 395 north of Lakeview 30 miles. Between mileposts 85 and 84 (2 miles after the highway starts following Lake Abert's shore), park in a gravel pullout on

Abert Lake from Abert Rim.

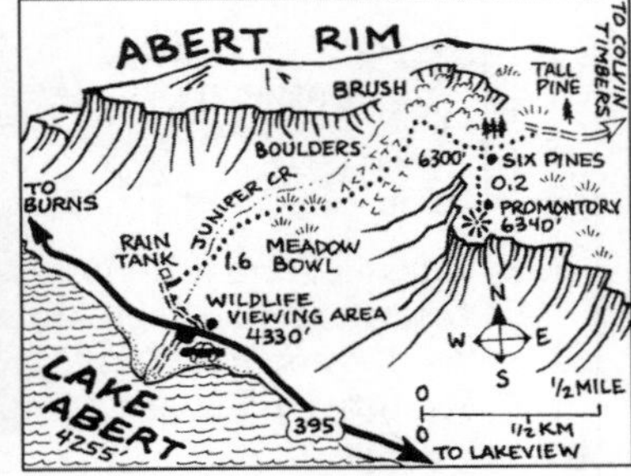

the left marked "Wildlife Viewing Area" *(42.5468, -120.2144)*. Cross the highway and bushwhack uphill through the canyon of (often dry) Juniper Creek to the rim's crest at a cluster of ponderosa pine trees *(42.5343, -120.2051)*. (L-BLM)

191. Crooked Creek

Moderate
6.9 miles one way
2100 feet elevation **loss**
Open early June to mid-November
Use: hikers, horses, bicycles

Completed segments of the Fremont Trail ramble 147 miles across south-central Oregon, through sagebrush desert, ponderosa pine forests, and high mountain meadows. Sample the trail's variety with a day trip along Crooked Creek, in the quiet Drake Peak area northeast of Lakeview. If you can arrange a car shuttle, the trip's all downhill. If you lack a shuttle, you can still explore either the upper or the lower end of Crooked Creek's canyon.

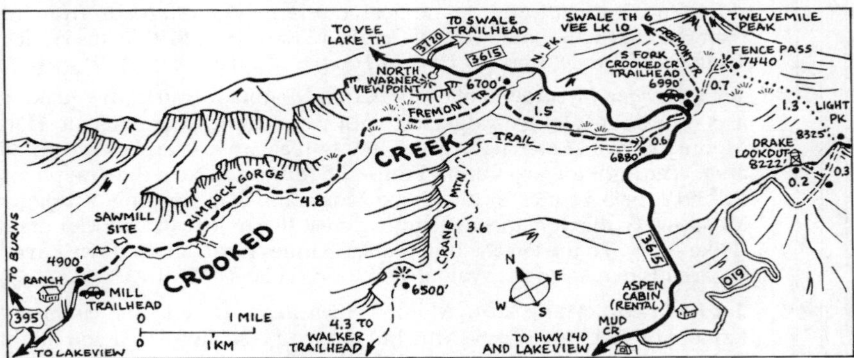

Getting There— Start with a visit to the lower trailhead. From Lakeview, drive Highway 395 north 11 miles. Just after milepost 132, where the highway curves left, veer right at a "Mill Trailhead" sign onto a gravel road. After 0.2 mile, continue straight across a yellow cattle guard, and then keep straight for another 1.3 miles to the trailhead at road's end, avoiding left-hand forks that lead to a private ranch.

Light Peak from Fence Pass.

Ponderosa pines surround the turnaround at this lower trailhead *(42.3372, -120.2714)*. The trail begins at a footbridge and follows the abandoned roadbed up through a scenic rimrock gorge.

If you plan to hike the trail downhill, leave a shuttle car at the Mill Trailhead and then drive a second car around to the South Fork Crooked Creek Trailhead. To find this upper trailhead, drive back on Highway 395 toward Lakeview 6 miles, turn left on Highway 140 toward Winnemucca 8.5 miles, and then turn left on narrow, paved North Warner Road 3615 for 10.6 miles to the South Fork

Crooked Creek Trailhead on the right *(42.3167, -120.1678).*

Walk across the paved road to find the faint start of the Fremont Trail opposite the parking lot entrance. The path ambles through a quaking aspen grove and soon enters a dense forest of lodgepole pine and white fir. After 0.6 mile the path crosses an abandoned road that serves as the Crane Mountain Trail. Continue straight on the Fremont Trail another 1.5 miles, hopping across first the South Fork and then the North Fork of Crooked Creek. Expect some cattle in July and August. For the next 2.4 miles the Fremont Trail descends across slopes with meadow openings where the tread can be a little faint. The final 2.4 miles of the path follow an old roadbed along the 15-foot-wide creek to a footbridge at the lower trailhead. (LA)

192. Walker Trailhead to Crooked Creek. Best on horseback or bicycle, this fairly level, 7.9-mile section of the Crane Mountain Trail skirts Bull Prairie through some clearcuts, largely on old roads, from the Fremont Trail at the South Fork of Crooked Creek (Hike #191) to the Walker Trailhead, 4.1 miles north of Hwy 140 on paved Rd 3615. (LA)

193. Rogger Meadow. Follow the Crane Mountain Trail from a quaking aspen meadow along a ridgecrest with views from Goose Lake to Hart Mountain. From Lakeview, drive Hwy 140 east up to Warner Canyon ski area, veer right toward Camas Prairie 2.5 miles, and turn right on paved Rd 3915 for 3.5 miles to the Crane Mountain Trail crossing at Rogger Meadow. To the right the trail climbs a crest 10.5 miles to Crane Mountain (Hike #194). To the left the trail ambles 3 miles north and follows paved backroads 6 miles to the Walker Trailhead (Hike #192). (LA)

194. Crane Mountain. Motor vehicles can drive to the collapsed lookout on 8347-foot Crane Mtn, but the road is so awful that you might rather walk, gaining 1400 feet in 2.7 miles. The trail that crosses the road just below the summit extends south 8.3 miles to California and north to Rogger Meadow (Hike #193). Drive as to Hike #193, continue on gravel Rd 3915 for 7 miles and turn right on Rd 4011 for 3 miles. (LA)

STEENS MOUNTAIN (map on page 228)

195. Shirk Ranch and Guano Creek. This abandoned ranch and its adjacent desert canyon are in one of Oregon's most remote spots, between the Hart Mountain preserve and the Nevada border. Start by driving Highway 140 east of Lakeview 54 miles toward Winnemucca. Halfway between nowhere and nowhere (technically, 25 miles east of Adel and 44 miles west of Denio Junction), turn north off the highway between mileposts 50 and 51 onto a dirt road marked only by a stop sign *(GPS location 42.067 -119.534)*. After 1.7 miles on this dirt road, ignore a fork to the right. Then continue straight 10 miles to a gate with the cutout iron letters, "SHIRK RANCH." Explore the derelict buildings cautiously on foot, but don't touch or take anything. To find Guano Creek, drive a mile past the ranch on a bad road crowded with sagebrush. Just beyond an exposed culvert pipe, park at a pullout on the left by an old diversion dike *(42.2532 -119.5186)*. Then bushwhack 2.5

The Shirk Ranch.

Easy Moderate Difficult

miles up the (often dry) creekbed through a slot canyon to the juniper oasis of Clover Swale. Return cross-country. (BLM-L)

196. Malheur Cave. This privately owned, half-mile long lava tube cave is used for Masonic ceremonies and is not open to the public. From Burns, drive Highway 78 east toward Jordan Valley 52 miles. Between mileposts 51 and 52, turn north on gravel Norman Ranch Rd for 3 miles. After a cattle guard turn left through a green metal gate for 0.4 mile on a dirt road.

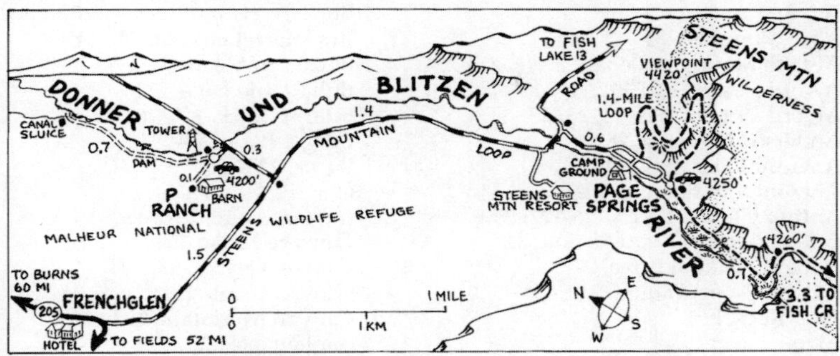

197. Donner und Blitzen River. Two trails begin at the far end of the Page Springs Campground, 3 miles east of Frenchglen on the Steens Mountain Loop Rd. The 1.4-mile Nature Trail climbs 200 feet to a rimrock viewpoint. Another path follows the Donner und Blitzen River upstream 4 miles to Fish Creek, but the last mile may be rough. (B-BLM)

198. Van Horn Creek. Bushwhack up a desert canyon to meadows high in the Pueblo Mtns, gaining 1500 feet in 3.6 miles. From the Nevada border near Denio, drive the paved road north toward Fields (and Burns) for 4 miles to the Van Horn Creek crossing. Park here and follow deer trails up the narrow canyon 2.3 miles to a cabin site amid cottonwoods. Continue scrambling upstream 1.3 miles to Van Horn Basin, a cattle meadow bordering the Oregon Desert Trail's route. (B-BLM)

OWYHEE RIVER (map on page 248)

199. West Little Owyhee. Only adventurers should venture into the cliff-lined canyon of this remote desert river. Drive Hwy 95 south of Burns Junction 39.8 miles (or north of McDermitt 15.1 miles). Between mileposts 106 and 107 at a sign, "To Antelope Flats" *(GPS location 42.2138, -117.7717),* turn east on a good gravel road 15.7 miles, and turn sharply right to stay on the main road 3.9 miles to a ford of Big Antelope Creek. Scout that your car has enough clearance to cross. Continue 15.6 miles to Anderson Crossing, a ford of the West Little Owyhee River usually 12 inches deep *(GPS location 42.1307, -117.3166).* If your vehicle crosses, turn left into a free camping area. Stroll 0.4 mile downriver to the canyon mouth. If you venture into the scenic chasm, be prepared for brush, rockfields, and deep wades. After 1.6 arduous miles *(GPS location 42.1397, -117.2992),* turn right up a slot canyon to return on a loop. (BLM-V)

The West Little Owyhee.

Index

Page numbers in **boldface** are featured hikes. Numbers in *italics* are locations on maps.

National Forest
WILDERNESS
Closed to motor vehicles
and motorized equipment